References for the Rest of Us ™

BESTSELLING BOOK SERIES

Do you find that traditional reference books are overloaded with technical details and advice you'll never use? Do you postpone important life decisions because you just don't want to deal with them? Then our *...For Dummies*® business and general reference book series is for you.

...For Dummies business and general reference books are written for those frustrated and hard-working souls who know they aren't dumb, but find that the myriad of personal and business issues and the accompanying horror stories make them feel helpless. *...For Dummies* books use a lighthearted approach, a down-to-earth style, and even cartoons and humorous icons to dispel fears and build confidence. Lighthearted but not lightweight, these books are perfect survival guides to solve your everyday personal and business problems.

> **"More than a publishing phenomenon, 'Dummies' is a sign of the times."**
> — *The New York Times*

> **"...you won't go wrong buying them."**
> — *Walter Mossberg, Wall Street Journal, on IDG Books' ...For Dummies books*

> **"A world of detailed and authoritative information is packed into them..."**
> — *U.S. News and World Report*

Already, millions of satisfied readers agree. They have made *...For Dummies* the #1 introductory level computer book series and a best-selling business book series. They have written asking for more. So, if you're looking for the best and easiest way to learn about business and other general reference topics, look to *...For Dummies* to give you a helping hand.

IDG BOOKS
WORLDWIDE

1/99

by Sinead O'Brien and David G. Allan

IDG Books Worldwide, Inc.
An International Data Group Company

Foster City, CA ✦ Chicago, IL ✦ Indianapolis, IN ✦ New York, NY

Ireland For Dummies?, 1st Edition

Published by
IDG Books Worldwide, Inc.
909 Third Avenue, 21st Floor
New York, NY 10022
www.idgbooks.com (IDG Books Worldwide Web site)
www.dummies.com (Dummies Press Web site)

Library of Congress Control Number: 00-107574

ISBN: 0-7645-6199-5

ISSN: 1531-152X

Printed in the United States of America

10 9 8 7 6 5 4 3 2 1

1B/QS/QR/QR/IN

Distributed in the United States by IDG Books Worldwide, Inc.

Distributed by CDG Books Canada Inc. for Canada; by Transworld Publishers Limited in the United Kingdom; by IDG Norge Books for Norway; by IDG Sweden Books for Sweden; by IDG Books Australia Publishing Corporation Pty. Ltd. for Australia and New Zealand; by TransQuest Publishers Pte Ltd. for Singapore, Malaysia, Thailand, Indonesia, and Hong Kong; by Gotop Information Inc. for Taiwan; by ICG Muse, Inc. for Japan; by Intersoft for South Africa; by Eyrolles for France; by International Thomson Publishing for Germany, Austria and Switzerland; by Distribuidora Cuspide for Argentina; by LR International for Brazil; by Galileo Libros for Chile; by Ediciones ZETA S.C.R. Ltda. for Peru; by WS Computer Publishing Corporation, Inc., for the Philippines; by Contemporanea de Ediciones for Venezuela; by Express Computer Distributors for the Caribbean and West Indies; by Micronesia Media Distributor, Inc. for Micronesia; by Chips Computadoras S.A. de C.V. for Mexico; by Editorial Norma de Panama S.A. for Panama; by American Bookshops for Finland.

For general information on IDG Books Worldwide's books in the U.S., please call our Consumer Customer Service department at 800-762-2974. For reseller information, including discounts and premium sales, please call our Reseller Customer Service department at 800-434-3422.

For information on where to purchase IDG Books Worldwide's books outside the U.S., please contact our International Sales department at 317-572-3993 or fax 317-572-4002.

For consumer information on foreign language translations, please contact our Customer Service department at 800-434-3422, fax 317-572-4002, or e-mail rights@idgbooks.com.

For information on licensing foreign or domestic rights, please phone 650-653-7098.

For sales inquiries and special prices for bulk quantities, please contact our Order Services department at 800-434-4322 or write to the address above.

For information on using IDG Books Worldwide's books in the classroom or for ordering examination copies, please contact our Educational Sales department at 800-434-2086 or fax 317-572-4005.

For press review copies, author interviews, or other publicity information, please contact our Public Relations department at 650-653-7000 or fax 650-653-7500.

For authorization to photocopy items for corporate, personal, or educational use, please contact Copyright Clearance Center, 222 Rosewood Drive, Danvers, MA 01923, or fax 978-750-4470.

is a registered trademark under exclusive license to IDG Books Worldwide, Inc., from International Data Group, Inc.

About the Authors

Sinead O'Brien is the editor of America Online's Digital City San Francisco.

David G. Allan is currently living in San Francisco and writing *Scotland For Dummies,* due out in 2001, as well as editing the news Web site WorkingForChange.org.

Authors' Acknowledgments

We would like to thank our friends and family who were so gung-ho about us writing this book. Particular thanks goes out to our Irish consigliori, cousin Clem McCloskey. Without him and the lovely Deirdre O'Riorden we would be living in a Dublin youth hostel to this very day. Thanks also to super siblings Dorothy and Patrick O'Brien, who let us turn their apartment into an office, hotel room, and Chinese food way station during the long writing of the manuscript. And to editor Matt Hannafin, who was daring enough to gamble on two eager young writers.

ABOUT IDG BOOKS WORLDWIDE

Welcome to the world of IDG Books Worldwide.

IDG Books Worldwide, Inc., is a subsidiary of International Data Group, the world's largest publisher of computer-related information and the leading global provider of information services on information technology. IDG was founded more than 30 years ago by Patrick J. McGovern and now employs more than 9,000 people worldwide. IDG publishes more than 290 computer publications in over 75 countries. More than 90 million people read one or more IDG publications each month.

Launched in 1990, IDG Books Worldwide is today the #1 publisher of best-selling computer books in the United States. We are proud to have received eight awards from the Computer Press Association in recognition of editorial excellence and three from Computer Currents' First Annual Readers' Choice Awards. Our best-selling ...*For Dummies*® series has more than 50 million copies in print with translations in 31 languages. IDG Books Worldwide, through a joint venture with IDG's Hi-Tech Beijing, became the first U.S. publisher to publish a computer book in the People's Republic of China. In record time, IDG Books Worldwide has become the first choice for millions of readers around the world who want to learn how to better manage their businesses.

Our mission is simple: Every one of our books is designed to bring extra value and skill-building instructions to the reader. Our books are written by experts who understand and care about our readers. The knowledge base of our editorial staff comes from years of experience in publishing, education, and journalism — experience we use to produce books to carry us into the new millennium. In short, we care about books, so we attract the best people. We devote special attention to details such as audience, interior design, use of icons, and illustrations. And because we use an efficient process of authoring, editing, and desktop publishing our books electronically, we can spend more time ensuring superior content and less time on the technicalities of making books.

You can count on our commitment to deliver high-quality books at competitive prices on topics you want to read about. At IDG Books Worldwide, we continue in the IDG tradition of delivering quality for more than 30 years. You'll find no better book on a subject than one from IDG Books Worldwide.

John Kilcullen
Chairman and CEO
IDG Books Worldwide, Inc.

Eighth Annual Computer Press Awards ≥1992

Ninth Annual Computer Press Awards ≥1993

Tenth Annual Computer Press Awards ≥1994

Eleventh Annual Computer Press Awards ≥1995

Publisher's Acknowledgments

We're proud of this book; please send us your comments through our IDG Books Worldwide Online Registration Form located at `http://my2cents.dummies.com`.

Some of the people who helped bring this book to market include the following:

Editorial

Editors: Alissa D. Schwipps, Matt Hannafin, Christine Ryan

Copy Editor: Robert Annis

Cartographer: John Decamillis

Editorial Manager: Jennifer Ehrlich

Editorial Assistants: Carol Strickland, Jennifer Young

Senior Photo Editor: Richard Fox

Assistant Photo Editor: Michael Ross

Cover photos: Richard Cummins

Production

Project Coordinator: Maridee V. Ennis

Layout and Graphics: Amy Adrian, Beth Brooks, Joe Bucki, LeAndra Johnson, Kristin Pickett, Brian Torwelle, Julie Trippetti, Jeremey Unger

Proofreaders: Laura Albert, Melissa D. Buddendeck, Susan Moritz

Indexer: Mary Mortensen

Special Help: Billie Williams

General and Administrative

IDG Books Worldwide, Inc.: John Kilcullen, CEO; Bill Barry, President and COO

IDG Books Consumer Reference Group

> **Business:** Kathleen A. Welton, Vice President and Publisher; Kevin Thornton, Acquisitions Manager
>
> **Cooking/Gardening:** Jennifer Feldman, Associate Vice President and Publisher
>
> **Education/Reference:** Diane Graves Steele, Vice President and Publisher; Greg Tubach, Publishing Director
>
> **Lifestyles:** Kathleen Nebenhaus, Vice President and Publisher; Tracy Boggier, Managing Editor
>
> **Pets:** Dominique DeVito, Associate Vice President and Publisher; Tracy Boggier, Managing Editor
>
> **Travel:** Michael Spring, Vice President and Publisher; Suzanne Jannetta, Editorial Director; Brice Gosnell, Managing Editor

IDG Books Consumer Editorial Services: Kathleen Nebenhaus, Vice President and Publisher; Kristin A. Cocks, Editorial Director; Cindy Kitchel, Editorial Director

IDG Books Consumer Production: Debbie Stailey, Production Director

IDG Books Packaging: Marc J. Mikulich, Vice President, Brand Strategy and Research

♦

The publisher would like to give special thanks to Patrick J. McGovern, without whom this book would not have been possible.

♦

Contents at a Glance

Cartoons at a Glance

By Rich Tennant

"OK—we got one cherry lager with bitters and a pineapple slice, and one honey malt ale with cinnamon and an orange twist. You want these in steins or parfait glasses?"

page 125

While on vacation in Ireland, Bill and Denise watch a local family working on the traditional thatched roof cottage, thatched roof satellite dish, and thatched roof Jeep Cherokee.

page 7

"This afternoon I want everyone to go online and find all you can about Native American culture, history of the old west, and discount airfares to Ireland for the two weeks I'll be on vacation."

page 81

"Let me ask you a question. Are you planning to kiss the Blarney Stone, or ask for its hand in marriage?"

page 239

"Douglas, I'd like to talk to you about the souvenirs you brought back from our trip to Ireland."

page 415

We've been through the thin and the thick of it
So lost that we're thoroughly sick of it
Our errors so far
Leave us in Erin go braugh
It's Limerick, the town that we're looking for.

page 299

Heck of a slide tackle! We should have you out in a few minutes.

page 371

Cartoon Information:
Fax: 978-546-7747
E-Mail: richtennant@the5thwavc.com
World Wide Web: www.the5thwavc.com

Maps at a Glance

Table of Contents

Introduction

● ●

*Y*ou've seen it in movies and on television: lush and green, with rolling hills and effervescent waters, and dotted with magnificent castles and cathedrals — and plenty of quaint little towns in between. That's Ireland, without question, but it's only part of the story. While that incredible backdrop really is the stuff the country is made of, there's so much more to Ireland that doesn't make it in the travel brochures. It's an island that's characterized by its lush scenery and remarkable natural phenomena, but it's also got its share of cosmopolitan cities and is an archeological gold mine, a cultural hotbed, and a land of myths, legends, beauty, history, and charm.

So which of these things are you looking to find? It could be one of these or all of them. Whatever the reason, the island is one of the fastest-growing tourist destinations in Europe — and rightly so.

Your Ireland vacation can capture all Ireland has to offer, but it takes some planning and the inside scoop on what is great and also what to look out for. Take it from us, putting forth a little extra effort in the planning stage will pay off big-time in the long run.

About This Book

In this book, we've tried to anticipate every question you might have about traveling to Ireland, and to provide the answers. If you've never been to the country before, we show you what to expect and how to plan for it. If you're an old Ireland hand, you've probably bought this book because you don't want to waste a lot of time sorting through a billion different hotels, restaurants, and attractions, trying to find the absolute best ones. You want a quick and easy, yet comprehensive, source of information, and that's exactly what we aim to give you here.

Of course you don't have to read the whole book. And you don't have to start at the beginning either. This is a reference book. Check out the Table of Contents, and then read the parts that answer your specific questions.

Besides just being practical, we've also written with the idea that the whole subject of travel should be just plain fun, so don't expect any dry lectures. That's just not our style.

Please be advised that travel information is subject to change at any time — and this is especially true of prices. Write or call ahead for confirmation when making your travel plans.

Conventions Used in This Book

In this book we've included write-ups on the best sights in Ireland; reviews of the best hotels, pubs, restaurants, pubs, shops, pubs, and more; and a quick-and-easy introduction to everything you'll experience in planning your trip and visiting the Emerald Isle.

Ireland For Dummies, 1st Edition employs a few conventions designed to convey critical information in a simple, straightforward manner.

In the hotel section, the listed price is a rack rate (the official rate published by the hotel, though the actual prices you'll pay are often discounted) and is good for one night only; additionally, parking charges are for one night only, unless otherwise noted.

In the restaurant section, the listed prices are the general range for the cost of a main course on the dinner menu, unless otherwise noted.

The listings for both restaurants and hotels are preceded by dollar sign symbols ($–$$$$), which give an indication of overall price range. For hotels, this again indicates the rack rate for one night's stay. For restaurants, this includes the price of a full meal for one person, including entree, drinks, and tip. Here's how the signs and the dollars actually match up:

Dining

$	£5 ($7.40), or less
$$	£6–10 ($8.90–$14.80)
$$$	£11–16 ($16.30–$23.70)
$$$$	£17 ($25.15), or more

Accommodations

$	£50 ($74) double, or less
$$	£50–100 double ($74–$148)
$$$	£100–200 double ($148–$296)
$$$$	£200 ($296) double, or more

In the attractions sections, we've provided an entry called "Time" at the end of each listing. This is our estimate of how much time you should budget to do and see most of what's available at each attraction. This is just a suggestion, and you may find you need more or less time depending on your interests.

The following is a list of the credit card abbreviations used in the listings in this book:

AE	American Express
CB	Carte Blanche

DC	Diners Club
DISC	Discover
ER	enRoute
EURO	Eurocard
JCB	Japan Credit Bank
MC	MasterCard
V	Visa

Foolish Assumptions

In this book, we make some assumptions about you and what your needs might be as a traveler. We assume you are one of the following:

✔ An inexperienced traveler looking for guidance when determining whether to travel to Ireland and how to plan for it.

✔ An experienced traveler who hasn't yet visited Ireland and wants expert advice when you finally do get a chance to go.

✔ Looking for a book that focuses on only the best and most essential Irish sights, tastes, and experiences — the places that'll give you big-time bragging rights for years to come.

If you fit any of these criteria, then *Ireland For Dummies, 1st Edition* gives you the information you're looking for!

How This Book Is Organized

This book is divided into seven parts. Parts I to III will get you ready to go, and Parts IV through VII deal with what you'll be seeing and doing once you're there. Each regional chapter begins with important and helpful information about how to get there and how to get around, and includes information like emergency contacts, Internet cafes, local genealogical resources, and tourism offices.

Part 1: Getting Started

This book starts exactly where it should: at the beginning. This is your guide to figuring out the best time of year to plan your vacation and when and how to divide your precious time once you're there. We introduce you to each of the regions in Ireland and give you the information you need to decide which parts you want to include in your trip. We give you a season-by-season description of what you can expect by way of temperature, crowds, costs, and the legendary precipitation. Then we introduce you to all of the top festivals and events around the island.

These chapters also answer all those nagging questions you've been asking yourself, such as how to get there, whether to book a package tour or not (with tips on finding the best deal if you do), and how much it's all going to cost (with lots of advice on how to make the most of your hard-earned dollars while you're traveling around Ireland). We also acquaint you with all of the different options for getting to Ireland so you can make educated decisions about what's right for you. We help you plan your own itinerary and give advice for those of you with special needs and requirements. You'll also find addresses, phone numbers, and Web sites where you can get more information on trip planing. We also give a concise history of Ireland and short list of films to get you psyched about your upcoming adventure.

Part II: Ironing Out the Details

Part II takes care of all the loose ends once you're ready to head off to the hills and valleys of ol' Ireland — such as how to get around the country once you're there, what kind of accommodation options you'll have, and what the best ways are for carrying money (and getting more, if you run out). We've created a good packing checklist (including important pointers on what not to bring, like your hair dryer), a glossary of fast facts all about the island, a rundown of various things you should know before you go (like how to protect your valuable documents and money while abroad and what to do if they're lost), and tips on how to keep in touch with your family and friends while you're on the road.

Part III: Dublin and the East Coast

Part III is dedicated to Dublin and the surrounding counties, heading north to the border of Northern Ireland and south to County Cork.

Dublin is Ireland's capital and its largest city. No other city surpasses it in terms of what to do and see, and we give you all the top picks to choose from. We preview it all, from the best cathedrals and most interesting landmarks to the top tours and which pubs have the best Irish music. Dublin is one city where you could get overwhelmed by everything going on, but with our help you're sure to see the best highlights. Chapter 11 is full of insider advice, money-saving tips, and easy-to-use maps.

Also covered in Part III are Counties Meath and Louth, just north of Dublin. These counties are the island's treasure trove of prehistoric sights, including the remarkable burial mounds at Knowth and Newgrange and the storied Hill of Tara, ancient seat of the Irish high kings. South of Dublin, the beautiful southeastern counties of Wexford, Waterford, Kilkenny, and Tipperary greet you with gardens, historic homes, horse farms and racetracks, and of course, the famous Waterford Crystal.

Part IV: The South

Part IV only covers two counties, Cork and Kerry, but together they attract the lion's share of visitors to Ireland, who come for popular attractions like the Blarney Stone and the Ring of Kerry and great towns like Cork City and Killarney. We give all the best places to eat, stay, and see as you make your way along the coast.

Part V: The West and Northwest

This part bundles the entire western side of Ireland into one neat package, from County Limerick all the way up to Donegal. You'll visit the amazing Cliffs of Moher and the otherworldly region known as The Burren in County Clare, a reproduction of John Wayne's cottage from *The Quiet Man* in County Mayo, the amazing Aran Islands off the coast of Galway, poet W. B. Yeats's grave in County Sligo, and much more.

Part VI: Northern Ireland

Part VI covers the separate country of Northern Ireland, which may be last in this book but is not least in terms of great and picturesque places to visit. Belfast is the largest city in Northern Ireland and, along with the walled town of Derry and the Antrim Coast, provides plenty of magnetism to attract your compass needle north. We give it the full treatment, and explain the differences you can expect while visiting this British region.

Part VII: The Part of Tens

The Part of Tens chapters include a synopsis of some of the most amazing elements of the Ireland experience. We also give you tips on getting bargains when shopping for Irish products like linen and fisherman's sweaters.

You'll also find two other elements near the back of this book. We've included an appendix — your "Quick Concierge" — containing lots of handy information you may need when planning your trip, and a bunch of worksheets to make your travel planning easier. Among other things, the worksheets help you determine your travel budget and keep a handy record of your flight arrangements. You can find these worksheets easily because they're printed on yellow paper.

Icons Used in This Book

Keep an eye peeled for these icons, which appear in the margins:

Find out useful advice on things to do and ways to schedule your time when you see the Tip icon.

Watch for the Heads Up icon to identify annoying or potentially danger-ous situations such as tourist traps, unsafe neighborhoods, budgetary rip-offs, and other things to beware.

 Look to the Kid Friendly icon for attractions, hotels, restaurants, and activities that are particularly hospitable to children or people travel-ing with kids.

 Keep an eye out for the Bargain Alert icon as you seek out money-saving tips and/or great deals.

 Check out the No Blarney icon for humorous, curious, or just plain bizarre facts about Ireland and the Irish.

Where to Go from Here

Now you're ready to go! Put a Chieftains CD on the stereo, pour your-self a glass of Guinness, and get ready to fling yourself headlong into the historic, friendly, beautiful, and ever-hip experience that is Ireland today.

Part I
Getting Started

The 5th Wave   By Rich Tennant

In this part . . .

*B*efore you can start planning your trip to Ireland, you have to do some legwork. When should you go? What parts of the country do you want to visit? How much will it cost? This section is where you'll find the answers to all these questions and more.

In Chapter 1 we introduce you to Ireland with a brief overview of Irish history and culture. We also clue you in to some of the basics of daily life in Ireland, such as dining, words and phrases that Americans might find confusing, and a primer on pub life. For those of you hoping to hunt down information on your ancestors while in Ireland, we tell you what you need to do before you go to make sure you have a successful search.

If you're not sure when to go to Ireland or what part of the country you want to visit, Chapter 2 will help you out. We describe each region of the country, discuss the impact the different seasons will have on your trip, and tell you about some great festivals and events throughout the country you might want to see. Once that's done, we help you start planning your itinerary in Chapter 3 and give you suggested itineraries to work from.

Wondering if you can really afford this trip? Turn to Chap-ter 4, where we help you figure out what this adventure realistically is going to cost you. We give you lots of money-saving tips as well as our opinions about what you *shouldn't* scrimp on.

We wrap up the first part of this book with Chapter 5, where we'll share traveling tips and resources for those of you with special needs, such as seniors, families, gays and lesbians, and travelers with disabilities.

Chapter 1

Discovering the Best of Ireland

● ●

In This Chapter
▶ Taking a short course in Irish history
▶ Talking, eating, and drinking like an Irishman
▶ Appreciating Guinness and Irish whiskey
▶ Getting the lowdown on golf, fishing, and other sports in Ireland

● ●

*I*reland is a mighty travel destination because of its riches — verdant beauty, ancient history, rich culture, and friendly people. And it doesn't hurt that millions of people around the world have Irish roots that they want to dig up, either.

In this chapter, we introduce you to the Irish and answer all the questions you didn't even know you had about Irish culture and history, so that when you get there and start reading historical markers, you'll be totally clued in to who's who and what's what. For readers more interested in their own history, we provide a section on tracing your Irish ancestry. By the time you finish this chapter, native Irish might be saying of you, "Well, if it walks like a duck and talks like a duck. . . ."

Don't Know Much about Ireland's History?

Ireland has one of the most storied and complex histories of any nation, and we're going to tell you about it. Don't worry, though! This is the CliffsNotes version.

Invaders welcome

From the beginning, Ireland wore a welcome sign to invaders, or so it seems. The first wave came around 500 B.C. with the Celts, who stayed and laid roots, splitting into tribes and even creating Ireland's four provinces — Munster, Leinster, Ulster, and Connaught. Well-intended Christians came in the fifth century A.D., and among them, brought as a slave by the Celts, was the future patron saint of Ireland, St. Patrick. Christianity took off like wildfire.

Centuries of peace were abruptly ended by the Viking invasions. They came to plunder, but they so fell in with the Irish way of life that they decided to make a home there. Vikings founded the first towns in Ireland: Dublin, Cork, Waterford, and Limerick. The Irish were none too happy about the unwelcome visitors, though, and the great Brian Boru, one of the High Kings, defeated the Viking armies and sent them sailing.

Ireland flourished for some time, until in the twelfth century, the Normans (also known as the British) attacked. They, too, loved the land, and despite Irish efforts to make them leave, the Normans set up permanent camp.

Beginning around the 1500s, Irish history turned bloody and ugly. The Irish had for years held the Normans at bay, keeping them in one spot around Dublin called "the Pale" (from which comes the phrase "beyond the Pale"), but then Henry VIII dubbed himself king of Ireland and set out claiming the whole island.

Rebel with a cause

If Ireland is a land that has seen its share of invasions, it's also certainly a place that has launched its share of rebellions. In 1600, the first of many rebellions was set in motion in defiance of Elizabeth I's ruling that forced Irish lords to hand over their land and increased her armies in Ireland. It was quickly quelled.

Irish Catholics were so persecuted and disenfranchised that by the end of the 1600s, Protestants — only 20 percent of the population — owned 86 percent of the land. Thanks to the cruelty of Oliver Cromwell, an agent of Britain, all opposition was swiftly and murderously stopped.

For a hundred years, Britain imposed harsh "Penal Laws," which completely crushed Catholics and the practice of their religion. When war between Britain and France gave Ireland a window of opportunity, Irishman Wolfe Tone conspired in 1798 with the French to invade his own country, with hopes of driving the British out, but his rebellion failed pitifully, and the great patriot Tone slit his own throat before facing execution by his enemies.

Ireland secured an edge when Daniel O'Connell, known as The Liberator, pushed the Catholic Emancipation Act through Parliament in 1828; but progress was stopped in its tracks when the Great Famine struck in 1845. For five years potato crops failed, and 2½ million people were lost to it, either from death or emigration to America.

The Irish kept fighting to regain their country, despite such crushing blows. The fight was hard, because many groups were working for the same thing — but not together. Charles Stewart Parnell, Ireland's representative to the British Parliament, united these groups in the late 1800s, laying the groundwork that would lead to independence.

Ireland

SCOTLAND

ATLANTIC OCEAN

NORTH CHANNEL

Campbeltown

Tory Island

Rathlin Island

Creeslough

Lough Foyle

Coleraine

Ballycastle

Letterkenny

Eglinton Airport

Garron Point

Aran Island

Gweebarra Bay

DONEGAL

Londonderry

SPERRIN MTNS.

ANTRIM

BLUE STACK MTNS.

Finn

Strabane

DERRY

Ballymena

Ardara

Donegal

Omagh

TYRONE

NORTHERN IRELAND (U.K.)

Larne

To Douglas

Donegal Bay

Ballyshannon

Lower Lough Erne

Dungannon

BELFAST

Bangor

Killala Bay

Sligo Bay

LEITRIM

FERMANAGH

Enniskillen

Upper Lough Erne

Portadown

Lough Neagh

Belfast Airport

Strangford Lough

DOWN

Ballina

Sligo

SLIGO

Sligo Airport

Lough Allen

ARMAGH

MONAGHAN

Newcastle

Blacksod Bay

MAYO

Nephin

Lough Conn

Annagh

Newry

Achill Island

CAVAN

Dundalk

Clare Island

Clew Bay

Westport

Knock Airport

ROSCOMMON

LONGFORD

Kells

LOUTH

Ardee

Dundalk Bay

Irish Sea

Inishturk

Lough Mask

Roscommon

Longford

MEATH

Drogheda

Inishbofin

Clifden

CONNEMARA

Tuam

GALWAY

Lough Ree

WESTMEATH

Mullingar

Trim

Boyne

Lough Corrib

Galway Airport

Athlone

Dublin Airport

To Holyhead & Douglas

Inishmore

Galway

REPUBLIC OF IRELAND

Liffey

DUBLIN

DUBLIN

Inishmaan

Galway Bay

Shannon

OFFALY

Kildare

Bray

ARAN ISLANDS

Inisheer

Ennistymon

Lough Derg

Port Laoise

KILDARE

WICKLOW

Wicklow Head

CLARE

Ennis

LAOISE

Lugnaquillia

WICKLOW MOUNTAINS

Wicklow

Shannon Airport

TIPPERARY

Carlow

CARLOW

Arklow

Loop Head

Limerick

Cashel

KILKENNY

Slaney

Mouth of the Shannon

Listowel

LIMERICK

Tipperary

Kilkenny

Barrow

Brandon Mtn.

Tralee

Clonmel

Carrick-on-Suir

Nore

WEXFORD

Dingle

KERRY

Killarney Airport

Galtymore

GALTY MTNS

Suir

Wexford

To Fishguard & Pembroke

Dingle Bay

Carrauntuohill

Killarney

Blackwater

WATERFORD

Rosslare

Valentia Island

MACGILLYCUDDY REEKS

Lough Leane

CORK

Waterford

Waterford Airport

Kenmare River

CAHA MTNS

Blarney

Lee

Dungarvan

Bandon

Cork

Youghal

Cork Airport

Cobh

Bantry

Kinsale

To Swansea

ST. GEORGE'S CHANNEL

Bantry Bay

Skibbereen

Mizen Head

To Le Havre, Roscoff, Cherbourg & St. Malo

0   50 Mi

0   50 Km

These recently united factions staged Ireland's most famous rebellion on Easter Monday, 1916. Fifteen hundred freedom fighters led by Patrick Pearse and James Connolly took Dublin's General Post Office (GPO), from the steps of which Pearse read the Proclamation of the Irish Republic. This rebellion naturally led to swift attack by the British, who sailed gunboats up the River Liffey and heavily shelled the town. After six days of desperate battling, the fighters in the GPO were overwhelmed. Connolly, Pearse, and 13 other leaders of the Rising (as the rebellion was called) were taken to Kilmainham Gaol (Jail), tried, and shot in the yard. The Irish were shocked and outraged at the savage executions, especially that of Connolly, who had been so badly injured from fighting that he couldn't stand and had to be tied to a chair to face the firing squad. The murdered patriots became martyrs in Ireland, and the Irish commitment to fight for freedom was secured.

In 1918, Sinn Fein (pronounced *shin fine*) won the General Election and began the first independent Parliament, essentially claiming independence from Britain. Britain retaliated, and the Irish responded by launching what's come to be called the War of Independence. Michael Collins led the Irish forces and induced the British to negotiate.

The Anglo-Irish Treaty of 1921 gave autonomy to 26 of Ireland's 32 counties. The remaining six counties stayed part of the United Kingdom and became known as Northern Ireland. Many Irish, eager to finally reach peace, accepted the accord for the Irish Free State, even though it kept Ireland in the British Commonwealth. Others, led by Eamon de Valera, disagreed. A civil war broke out, Collins and many others were killed, and de Valera's side won control. In 1937, he forced complete independence from England.

The question of British control of the North never ceased to be a catalyst for anger, though, and another war broke out in 1969. The IRA battled pro-British forces through nearly 30 years of guerilla warfare, mostly in the North. At this writing, leaders in the North and Republic are negotiating and a peace accord holds firm, with London having turned control of Northern Ireland's governance over to a representative body. Keep your fingers crossed.

Who's Who in Irish Mythology

As in myths everywhere, some of the folks we describe in this section lived more verifiably real lives than others, but all have entered the mythology to such an extent that you're almost sure to hear them mentioned at some point in your trip.

   ✔ **Cuchulainn:** The famous Celtic warrior of ancient myth (pronounced *coo-cul-*in). Many legendary stories are told of his feats (like "The Cattle Raid of Cooley") in which Cuchulainn grows to enormous sizes and strength (he can kill scores of men with one swing of a sword). A statue stands in Dublin's General Post Office (GPO) depicting Cuchulainn in bloody action.

History in the streets

Ireland's flag, three thick vertical strips of green, white, and orange, first flew publicly over Dublin's General Post Office during the Easter Rising of 1916. The green represents Ireland's Catholics, the orange represents Protestants (symbolic of William of Orange, a seventeenth-century king of Britain), and the white is the hoped-for peace between them. As for street names, you'll notice the same ones repeated in towns and cities, with many streets named for heroes of the Irish struggle for freedom. You'll invariably find an O'Connell Street. Parnell and Pearse are likely to have their streets, too.

✔ **Queen Maeve:** Cuchulainn's enemy, who legend credits with stealing the prize bull of Ulster and killing Cuchulainn, among other evil exploits (pronounced *mave*).

✔ **Finn MacCool:** Irish hero immortalized in poems by his son Ossian and in many ballads, called "Fenian" ballads after the *Fenians* (or *Fianna*), professional fighters whom Finn was said to have headed in the third century. Finn and his men defended the country from foreign aggressors and hunted for food, these two activities being the main subjects of the stories. He is often portrayed as a giant with supernatural powers, accompanied by his pet hound, Bran.

✔ **Ossian:** Finn MacCool's son, a great leader and warrior as well as one of the first poets of Ireland (pronounced *o*-sheen). The name means "fawn," and legend claims that his mother spent part of her life as a deer.

✔ **Turlough O'Carolan:** One of the best-known of the Irish harpers (sometimes called *Carolan*). After smallpox blinded him in his teens, he learned to play the harp and for the rest of his years traveled throughout Ireland as an itinerant musician. He wrote more than 200 compositions that are still played today, more than 300 years later.

✔ **Children of Lir:** This legendary story tells of how the wicked new wife of King Lir (pronounced *leer*) put a spell on his children to turn them into swans for 900 years. She later regretted her evil deed, but couldn't reverse the spell, so she gave the birds the gift of song instead. (Today it is illegal in Ireland to kill swans.) A beautiful sculpture depicting the Children of Lir is the centerpiece of Dublin's Garden of Remembrance.

✔ **Saint Brendan:** The "other" Irish saint. A wandering monk, he traveled all over the present-day U.K. during the sixth century before finding religious paradise in Ireland. His legend is an odyssey of difficulties. A mountain in County Kerry is named for him, and his feast day is May 16.

✔ **Saint Patrick:** The patron saint of Ireland. Brought to the country as a teenage slave, he later escaped, only to have a religious experience that called him back to Ireland as a missionary. His legendary feat of driving the snakes out of Ireland has been proven false by scholars, who say that snakes are simply not indigenous to the island. His feast day is well known and celebrated with great enthusiasm far beyond Ireland's borders.

Who's Who in Irish Literature

The Irish are fiercely proud of their rich literary tradition, and many great and honored standouts have places of honor around the country. You can't go to County Sligo without tripping over references to W. B. Yeats, whether it be in a museum or an area he adored. Repeated references to the novels of James Joyce fill Dublin, because the author paid such glorious tribute to the city in his work. The hallowed walls of Dublin theaters practically resonate with the plays of O'Casey, Shaw, and Beckett.

So that you don't find yourself scratching your head wondering who are some of these people you keep hearing about and why are they so important, here are some bite-sized bios of them.

✔ **James Joyce** (1882–1941): Controversial writer who set his famous pseudo-trilogy *Portrait of the Artist as a Young Man, Dubliners,* and *Ulysses* in Dublin. *Ulysses* was banned in Ireland as pornographic until the 1960s, and now Joyce's picture is on the ten-pound note — talk about ironic.

✔ **Samuel Beckett** (1906–89): Nobel prize-winning playwright and novelist, known for surreal writing. The best known and most performed of his plays is *Waiting for Godot.*

✔ **W. B. Yeats** (1865–1939): Poet and playwright who also won a Nobel prize and cofounded Dublin's Abbey Theatre. Many of his poems capture the horror and irony of Irish rebellion, like "Easter Rising, 1916."

✔ **Sean O'Casey** (1880–1964): Famed Abbey Theatre playwright who shocked theatergoers with the controversial plays based on his early, poverty-stricken days. Best known are *Juno and the Paycock* and *The Plough and the Stars.*

✔ **George Bernard Shaw** (1856–1950): Nobel prize-winning author of *Pygmalion, Major Barbara,* and *St. Joan.* A 15-year-old dropout, Shaw spent much time at the National Gallery in Dublin, later bequeathing it a third of his royalties.

✔ **John Millington Synge** (1871–1909): A noted Abbey Theatre playwright, Synge was born in Dublin but is best remembered for plays that explore the rural life of western Ireland, among them *Riders to the Sea, Shadow of the Glen,* and *Playboy of the Western World.*

Ireland for the Irish: Digging Up Your Roots

If there's one thing more popular these days than going to Ireland, it's being Irish. Those lucky enough to have an "O" or a "Mc" in front of their names (or a first name like Sinead) usually wear it like a badge of honor. It's inherently harder for people with names that smack of other national origins to gain Emerald Isle respect.

So are you sick of people saying, "You? Irish? With a name like Fornatale? Yeah, right"? There's only one thing to do: Prove it! You can easily trace your Irish roots thanks to endless resources created for the sole purpose of revealing your Irish ancestry. This kind of family-tree-tracing can enrich your whole trip to the homeland. Imagine visiting the places where your grandparents worked or your great-grandparents were born!

You do have to do a good amount of work before anyone delves into your family history. The most important thing is getting much of the legwork out of the way before you go to Ireland. Showing up empty-handed is not just a faux pax; in this case, it gets you nowhere. Genealogists need certain information before they can trace anything.

Doing your own research in advance

Your research should begin at home. The most immediate and valuable sources are living family members, whose own family papers and even traditions can give clues. Sometimes Irish-Americans named their homes after their old town or parish. Details like surnames, occupations, and religion are all important clues needed for a successful search.

Start the paper trail before you consult any agency. These won't be Irish documents, of course, but they can give information that connects people. Birth, marriage, and death certificates (civil and parochial), census returns, and immigration papers are all valuable. Don't carry originals overseas, though; make copies.

In the United States, the **National Archives,** 8601 Adelphi Rd., College Park, MD 20740-6001 (☎ **800-234-8861;** E-mail: inquire@nara.gov), has a great service for helping you trace your family back to the port of origin. In Canada, the bulk of research is being done at the Department of Irish Studies at **St. Mary's University** in Halifax, Nova Scotia, B3H 3C3 (☎ **902-420-5553;** E-mail: research@stmarys.ca). Australia has kept extensive records of the many Irish immigrants who went down under. Best sources there are the **National Library** in Canberra, ACT 2600 (☎ **61-2-6262-1111;** Internet: www.nla.gov.au), and the **Mitchell Library** in Sydney (☎ **61-2-9-273-1466;** Internet: www.slnsw.gov.au/ml/mitchell.htm).

Tapping into research agencies in Ireland

After you exhaust your home resources and have insight about where to start looking, you're ready to get real help from a research agency.

Costs range from small fees for copies of certificates to paying researchers by the hour. (You can ask the agency to give you a ball-park figure before it starts any major investigation.) Even though these

---

Common Irish names and where they come from

Here are just a few popular Irish surnames and the counties where they originated. Many of these families later spread throughout the island and beyond. Each name has plenty of variations; for instance, FitzGerald has derivations of Fitzpatrick, Flanagan, Flynn, Fogarty, Foley, and Gaffney!

Ahearne: Clare, Limerick

Butler: Kilkenny

Donoghue: Cork, Kerry

FitzGerald: Kildare, Kerry, Cork

MacCarthy: Munster

Maguire: Ulster

Martin: Connaught

Murphy: Tyrone, Sligo, Wexford

O'Brien: Clare, Limerick

O'Donnell: Donegal

O'Keeffe: Cork

O'Kelly: Galway

O'Neill: Ulster

O'Sullivan: Tipperary

Power: Wicklow, Waterford

Regan: Meath, Dublin

Ryan: Tipperary, Limerick

Walsh: Dublin, Kilkenny, Leitrim, Waterford, Wicklow

What's in a name? Ages ago, the prefixes of Irish last names signified a great deal. "Mc" or "Fitz" meant "son of," and "O" before a name meant "grandson of" or "from the family of." So the name O'Brien means "ancestors of the Brien family" (in this case, the ancestors of Brian Boru, the most famous of the High Kings of Ireland). You'll also occasionally see a name with an "Ní" prefix (such as Ní Dhomhnaill), but this configuration is, for the most part, archaic these days. Literally it means "formerly of," as in Triona Briain Ní Dhomhnaill, the name Triona might go by if she were a proud Dhomnaill who married a Briain.

Now, about "Mc" versus "Mac": These days, people generally associate the prefix "Mac" with Scottish names (MacHugh, for example) and "Mc" with Irish (McCourt, McGuinness, and so on), but that's not necessarily so — especially when talking about history. In fact, the MacNamaras built up Clare even before Brian Boru and later inaugurated him as High King.

services cost you some cash, they save a lot of time and hassle. They're probably also able to get information that someone off the street could never find.

The leader of the pack is the **Hibernian Research Company**, P.O. Box 3097, Dublin 6 (☎ **01-496-6522**), the oldest and largest genealogical agency in Ireland. Its staff is trained under the Chief Herald of the Genealogical Office.

In Northern Ireland, the two best-known companies are the **Irish Heritage Association,** Queens Rd., Belfast (☎ **028-9045-5325**), and **the Ulster Historical Foundation,** Balmoral Buildings, 12 College Square East, Belfast BT1 6DD (☎ **90-33-2288;** Fax: 90-23-9885; E-mail: enquiry@uhf.org.uk; Internet: www.uhf.org.uk).

Finding sources in Ireland for doing the work on your own

In addition to the following organizations, counties throughout Ireland have local genealogical sources that we list in the different chapters of this book. These sources function more as record storage facilities or archives than as full-service research services.

- ✔ **Irish Genealogy Ltd.,** 5th Floor, 25-28 Adelaide Rd., Dublin 2. (☎ **01-6617-334;** Fax: 01-6617-332; E-mail pbrinkley@igl.ie) Cost per inquiry: £5. A good starting point for narrowing your search.

- ✔ **Births, Deaths, and Marriages** (records office), General Registrar House, Joyce House, 8/11 Lombard St. East, Dublin 2. (☎ **01-671-1000**) Cost: varies for type of research and certificate obtained.

- ✔ **The Genealogical Office** of the National Library of Ireland, 2 Kildare St., Dublin 2. (☎ **01-603-0200**) Cost: advisory service for genealogy is free. The Library houses pre-1880 records, newspapers, trade directories, and more.

- ✔ **National Archives,** 8 Bishop St., Dublin 8. (☎ **01-407-2300**) Cost: varies for type of certificate obtained. The largest variety of sources, including health and school records, parish registers, land titles, wills, and grants or public and private sources.

- ✔ **The Public Records Office of Northern Ireland,** 66 Balmoral Ave., Belfast BT9 6NY. (☎ **028-9025-1318;** Fax: 028-9025-5999) Cost: just the price of photocopying. The office has baptism, marriage, and burial records for the North on microfilm.

Talking to the Irish

Sure, they speak English in Ireland, but between occasional odd words and the accent, it might sound like a foreign language at times. So that you don't have to keep one of those polite but puzzled smiles on your face while talking with locals, read our handy glossary. You'll be one step ahead and won't miss a beat if you're asked to put "some tins in the press" (cans in the cabinet).

Learning the lingo

Some of the following terms are slang or just Irish usage, and some are bonafide Gaelic. We've marked the Gaelic ones, so you'll know:

An Lar	city center
bonnet	car hood
boot	car trunk
Bord Fa'ilte	Irish Tourist Board (Gaelic)
cheers	thanks
crack, craic	good times, fun (pronounced *crack*)
creche	day care
deadly, brilliant	great, excellent
fa'ilte	welcome (Gaelic)
fir	men (Gaelic)
footpath	sidewalk
garda	policeman
lift	elevator
mna	women (Gaelic)
off-license	liquor store
petrol	gas
press	cabinet
quay	waterfront (pronounced *key*)
quid, or bob	pounds, or money
sla'inte	cheers or goodbye (Gaelic — pronounced *schlancha*)
take-away	fast food, to go
till	cash register
tins	canned goods
windscreen	windshield

Translating Gaelic place names

Picture this: You're passing through a quaint town with an even quainter name. Wonder what it means? Use the following list to mix and match parts of names to get their Gaelic meaning. For example, Tullamore translates into Great Small Hill (tul + mor). Sounds better their way, huh?

ard	height, hill
aw, ow	river
bal, bally	town
bawn	white
beg	small
carrick, carrig	rock
cloch	stone
derg	red
doo, du	black
dun	fort
drom, drum	ridge
innis, ennis, inch	island
glen, glas	valley
kil, kill	church
knock	hill
lis, liss	fort
lough	lake
mone, mona	bog
mor	great, large
owen, avon	river
rinn, reen	a point
ross	peninsula
shan, shane	old
tra, traw	beach
tul, tulagh	small hill

Guarding against miscommunication

In the same way that sayings and gestures vary in meaning all across the United States, so are there different meanings for certain things in Ireland. The last thing you want to do is offend someone by inadvertently saying something vulgar! For instance, when looking for someone to drive you someplace, ask for a *lift,* not a *ride.* Asking for a ride is the equivalent of asking for a roll in the hay. Along the same lines, holding two fingers up in a V with your palm faced inward is the same as raising your middle finger to someone. Careful when ordering two pints!

Look at this issue the other way, too. The Irish have some sayings that may sound quite rude to your ears but actually are acceptable and mean no offense. Some examples:

- ✔ "Piss take" or "Take the piss out of you" just means, essentially, "pulling your leg" or messing with you.

- ✔ "Feck" and "shite" are not what you think. Both words are a bit worse than "shoot," but fall more into the "crap" or "suck" category — little kids shouldn't say them, but they're not profanity and are used widely as a (marginally) acceptable way of cussing.

- ✔ "Slagging you" means "teasing you."

And don't recoil too quickly if someone asks if you have a "fag." It means cigarette.

Understanding the different regional accents

Just like people from the American South and New England sound remarkably different in their accents, the Irish brogue varies all across the island.

The typical accent that you hear most often in the American media (the Lucky Charms leprechaun comes to mind) is really a brogue from the Southwest of Ireland.

It's generally in the smaller, more remote towns that people really tend to hang on to a brogue that is beautiful but not friendly to the untrained ear. You'll be hard-pressed to understand someone in Dingle or Connemara on the first recitation. Don't give up too fast; ask people to repeat themselves. They'll be happy to, and you'll be happy they did.

Ireland Dining and Irish Cuisine

Yes, there is such a thing as Irish cuisine, and it's *good,* so if you think food in Ireland is all potatoes, all the time, you're just plain wrong.

For years, the boundaries of cooking in Ireland stretched to no great limits. Food consisted mainly of overcooked and oversalted meats, accompanied by butter-laden vegetables and potatoes. Often even the green stuff was omitted, making Ireland the true home of "meat and potatoes."

But all that has changed, drastically and for the better. The country appears well aware of its cooking renaissance, too, and takes great pride in wowing restaurant patrons with succulent sauces and masterful preparation of worldwide cuisine.

Even traditional Irish food, while still solidly established in the average diet, has had a makeover. Hearty stews and soups are still everywhere, but their quality has been jacked up a few notches, and the selection is vast. Specialty dishes like *boxty* (a potato pancake stuffed with various meats) and *colcannon* (potato, scallions, and kale) abound, but unlike their older counterparts, these meals now have flavor and variation and don't rely so heavily on salt for taste.

Some foods have always been served in Ireland, and from the looks of things, they always will. They're often fatty and probably don't show up in your normal daily diet, but they are so delicious that they're worth the extra hours you'll have to put in on the treadmill. The famous all-pork sausages may be the best you've ever had. No questionable meat is put in this pure sausage, and the fine texture proves it. Bacon in Ireland is another treat: It's virtually a thick slice of ham.

The Irish are particularly proud of their delicious farmhouse cheeses, and opting for a cheeseboard after dinner rather than a dessert isn't exactly making a sacrifice.

Homemade bread, baked daily, is everywhere, and although considered a quite humble food, it's one of the country's most delicious (and addictive) offerings. Visitors rave about the classic, hearty brown bread and slightly sweet soda bread long after they return home.

Eating out: What to expect

If you're looking for a real traditional Irish meal, you can find it in a hotel restaurant, where tradition holds court and where quality and succulence reign. Aside from the hotels, you won't find many traditional Irish restaurants that aren't geared toward tourists, like **Gallagher's Boxty House** in Dublin (see the section on dining in Chapter 11).

Loads of small cafes and lunch counters offer hearty Irish lunches, like soups and sandwiches. Even more plentiful are *chippers* and *takeaways,* fast food places where you can get, among other things, traditional fish and chips.

What you may be surprised to notice is the number of ethnic restaurants in Ireland. You can get a fine Italian meal here that rivals some in the boroughs of New York City. And while the Irish have always had a taste for Chinese food — from fast food to classy — Indian Tandoori and other Eastern cuisines are making a major breakthrough. And don't laugh, but American food is big, from gargantuan hamburgers to pizza, and usually served up at American theme restaurants. Even vegetarian food has carved out a niche for itself.

Larger cities, of course, are where you find the widest selection of restaurants. Smaller villages often adhere pretty strongly to old ways, and menus from town to town don't differ much. But again, you're likely to find delicious food in any one of them.

Checking out meal prices

One good thing about meal costs in Ireland is that you probably don't have to factor in the cost of breakfast, which usually comes standard with your room. Lunch typically sets you back around £10 ($14.80) if you eat in a restaurant or as little as £5 ($7.40) if you have fast food or carry-out, like the ubiquitous fish and chips.

Dinner is more expensive, with entrees ranging from £8 ($11.85) to £10 ($14.80) on the low end to more than £16 ($23.70) on the high end. After you factor in wine and service, the tab can get rather high. We include a few dining-related money-saving tips in Chapter 3 — like going to a fancy restaurant for lunch rather than dinner (same food, better price).

Restaurants in the "Dining" sections of this book are categorized by the following scale:

$ £5 ($7.40) or less

$$ £6–10 ($8.90–$14.80)

$$$ £11–16 ($16.30–$23.70)

$$$$ £17 ($25.15) or more

It's Emily Post time! Irish meal times and dining customs

Rules of dining are similar to those in the States, with just a few exceptions. One, which you may notice right away, is the manner of eating. The Irish, like many Europeans, keep the knife in their right hand and lift food on the fork with the left hand. Table settings are the same, except that often a large soup spoon lays across the top of your place setting.

Meal times mirror those in the States, with breakfast beginning around 7:00 a.m. and finishing at 10:00 or 11:00 a.m. Lunch goes from noon to about 3:00 p.m. Having lunch between 1:00 and 2:00 p.m. is difficult in major towns and cities; that's generally the hour that businesses close for lunch, and most places are a madhouse. Dinner is served beginning at 5:00 p.m. and goes as late as 11ish, but expect to order by around 9:00 p.m.

Choice restaurants often have set lunch menus that are reasonably priced and offer the same good food as at dinnertime. Some restaurants also have early-bird menus, which are similar to those at lunch: three to four courses, good food, and low prices. Also, if you find yourself in a pub and hunger creeps in, you don't have to worry because pubs serve some of the best and most traditional Irish food you'll find anywhere. They're a popular place for lunch, too. Pub grub is fully covered later in this chapter.

Deciphering the menu

Here are a few food terms you may run up against. Some are Irish, some derived from the Brits, and some just vaguely European.

aubergines	eggplants
boxty	potato pancakes filled with meats and vegetables
chassuers	mushrooms
chipper	traditional fast food
chips	french fries
courgettes	zucchini
crisps	potato chips
mange tout	snap peas
minerals	sodas
rasher	bacon
shepherd's pie	ground beef and vegetables topped with mashed potatoes
sultanas	similar to raisins but with a slightly different taste

Livin' the Pub Life

Irish pubs are much more than places to have a drink. They have a culture of their own, providing people a place to meet, laugh, eat, hear music, and relax. Great care is taken to preserve the mood of the rare auld times, with even the newest pubs filled with antiques and tons of old-looking woodwork. Music and good food enhance the magic, all combining to create what the Irish call *craic,* or good times.

If you're drinking among a group, think rounds. Everyone takes turns buying each person a drink, so don't think you're hanging out with the friendliest and most generous people in Ireland when a pint is bought for you; you're expected to reciprocate.

Absorbing a little pub history

Going back to the Middle Ages, Irish pubs began as places for merchants and travelers to replenish themselves with a drink. Later, when the strong arm of Britain was upon Ireland, these watering holes flourished even though they'd been declared illegal, serving as a wonderful escape from the colonial tyranny. Later, in Victorian times, pubs went from being drab and dark to being beautifully decorated, and many of the older establishments still bear their original counters and elaborate windows.

The word *pub* has an interesting story. "Pub" is short for "public house," which was the opposite of a "private house," where only members could go. The people who frequented public houses often were the hard-working lower classes. Someone who ran a pub was called a "publican."

In small towns, the local pub in olden days doubled as the corner grocery store. Even today, many rural pubs carry on the tradition, providing milk and eggs to the locals along with a refreshing nip.

Pubs also have a grand place in Ireland's history, as they're the places where many revolutionaries secretly met and planned for the country's freedom fights. Irish literary figures graced many Dublin pubs with their presence. (See the section on organized tours in Dublin in Chapter 11.)

Snug-gling Up

You'll notice many small partitioned areas in a lot of pubs, called *snugs*. These are great places for quiet conversation or to get away from the crowd. But that's not what they were for originally. Until the late 1960s, it was impolite for women to drink in public, so they were confined to the snugs. The barman would pass drinks (only half pints, of course!) through a small opening.

Savoring the black stuff: Guinness

You may have had one or two pints of Guinness beer in the States. But the pint of Guinness you have in Ireland will taste like nothing you've had before. Call it the home-court advantage or credit the fact that the stuff is as fresh as all-get-out in Ireland, shipped right from the St. James's Gate brewery to the nation's pubs, but it's a fact that the Guinness you'll have in Ireland is a high cut above the Guinness you'll have anywhere else.

When Arthur Guinness took over a small brewery in Dublin, he had fantastic foresight. He may not have known then that his brew would account for one of every two pints sold in Ireland or would be sold in 150 countries, but he definitely was going for longevity — in 1759 he signed a 9,000 year lease on the brewery's site!

We're here to clear up a few misconceptions about Guinness. One misconception is that it has a huge number of calories. Actually, a pint of Guinness has about as many calories as a pint of skim milk — around 100. Another misconception is that Guinness is a particularly heavy drink, an idea that probably comes from the look of it. Really, Guinness is very easy to drink and refreshing — don't let the thick head scare you. An extra bonus is that the famous ad campaign "Guinness is good for you" is pretty much on the mark. With only four all-natural ingredients — barley, hops, yeast, and pure Irish water — and no preservatives, Guinness is almost guaranteed not to give you a hangover. (But note: We can't be responsible if you start downing shots of whiskey with it!)

Finally, five words to live by: A good pint takes time. Barkeeps draw the pint halfway and let it sit for about two minutes. Then, by pushing the tap forward so the stout comes out even slower than the first draw, they fill the glass the rest of the way (some fill the glass in a three-step process). This slowness isn't cruel taunting; it's how a real pint is pulled. Even when you finally get the pint in your hands, don't drink just yet. Wait until it has settled completely and has turned a deep ruby, almost black. A good test is to take a pound coin and tap it against the glass, working upward. When the coin makes a heavy thud throughout the glass, rather than a tinny tap, your brew is ready!

Sampling other Irish brews

You may not believe it, but there are other Irish beers. Just because we tend to forget that doesn't mean you should, too. Some of the more popular are Harp, a light lager that's good for people who aren't into dark beers; Caffreys, an ale that settles like a stout; Smithwicks, a dark ale; Kilkenny, an ale very popular across Europe; Murphy's Amber, a thick-tasting ale; Murphy's Stout, which is a bit sweeter than Guinness; and Bulmer's Cider, a sweet, entirely too drinkable hard cider.

Now that you have the rundown, you may be wondering what the real difference is between Guinness and Murphy's Stout. Well, employees at St. James's Gate, where Guinness is brewed, have an idea. According to rumor, a drawing inside the brewery shows a donkey drinking from a trough labeled "Guinness." Behind the donkey is another trough, in which the animal is urinating. This trough, of course, is labeled "Murphy's." We assume Murphy's has its own ideas about its rival.

Sipping some Irish whiskey

Monks did a lot for Ireland. They painstakingly crafted the Book of Kells and protected Irish antiquities in their round towers during invasions. But ask your average man on an Irish street, and you can bet he'll say the best thing monks did for Ireland was invent whiskey.

Whiskey! That's right. In the sixth century, missionary monks brought the secret of distillation home from the Middle East, forever changing the face of Ireland. Irish whiskey is known all over the world for its smoothness and quality, and it has done more than brighten the lives of many Irish; it has brought Ireland huge revenues over the centuries. The original Gaelic term for whiskey, *Uisce Beatha* (pronounced *ish*-ka ba-ha) means "Water of Life." Even today, every European country that distills a native spirit refers to theirs as the Water of Life: *Eau de Vie* in France, *Akvavit* in Scandinavia, *Lebenswasser* in Germany, *Agua de la Vida* in Spain, and *Aqua della Vita* in Italy.

Poteen

You may have heard of a potent potable called Poteen and are wondering just what it is. Well, poteen (or *potcheen*) is unlawfully distilled clear whiskey, banned since 1661. Basically it's the Irish equivalent of moonshine. Not too long ago, though, the government gave a license to **Bunratty Mead and Liqueur,** Bunratty, County Clare (☎ 061/36-2222), to make poteen, so you can now legally get a bottle of Ireland's original spirit. (But you can't bring it into the States; it's too potent.) We triple-dog dare you to try some.

Scotch versus whiskey

Irish whiskey and Scotch whisky have always been in healthy competition, but it was the Irish who taught the Scottish how to make the spirit. Distillation of Scotch began around the thirteenth century, making Irish whiskey nearly twice as old. You'll notice that Scotch whisky is spelled without the letter "e."

Whiskey became more than just a home brew in 1608, when the world's first distillery license was given to Old Bushmills Distillery. Next came John Jameson & Son in 1780 and John Powers & Son in 1791. These licenses blew open the whiskey export trade in Ireland, and the world's love affair with Irish whiskey began. By the end of the nineteenth century, more than 400 brands of it were available in America alone!

The money stopped rolling in when Prohibition was introduced in America in 1919. Bootleggers began distributing lousy liquor under the respected name of Irish whiskey, which destroyed its good reputation. Meanwhile, Ireland and England were recoiling from Irish insurrection and engaged in an economic war. They stopped buying each other's products completely. With Irish whiskey out of the picture, Scotch jumped in to fill the void.

Even Prohibition's end in 1934 didn't really help. Irish whiskey takes seven years to distill, so the Irish didn't have any product to sell! (Under Irish law, whiskey must mature in oak casks for no less than 3 years; but premier distilleries mature whiskey from 5 to 12 years.) Even worse, American GI's got a taste for Scotch during World War II and were content with drinking that. Irish whiskey has regained a foothold in American markets now and is rebuilding its international lead.

Irish whiskey has a distinctive smoothness, and that's no accident. Unlike any other whiskey, the Irish distill theirs three times before it's ready to drink. (By way of comparison, American whisky is distilled only once and Scotch twice.)

If you're interested in the distillation of Irish whiskey (or just love the stuff), go on the Irish Whiskey Trail. You can tour the country's three historic and popular distilleries: **The Old Bushmills Distillery,** County Antrim (☎ 080-12657-31521), **The Old Jameson Distillery,** Dublin (☎ 01-872-5566), and **The Old Midleton Distillery,** Cork (☎ 021-61-3594). They're pretty spread out over Ireland from north to south, but they're worth the trek. Each hosts tours daily.

Noshing on pub grub

Pub food in Ireland is much more than your average bag of peanuts or basket of pretzels. On the whole, pub grub is hearty, wholesome food that makes for a great meal. You can find beef and lamb stews, creamy potato and leek soup, meaty sandwiches on thick-sliced brown bread, salads, and, of course chips (which are like steak fries).

One thing to keep in mind is that many pubs serve food only during lunch time, from noon to 3:00 p.m. You can't even get a crust of bread after that in some places. On the other hand, plenty of pubs do serve all day.

Many pubs advertise a *carvery* — really just a buffet, and hot food's heaped onto your plate by the chef. Just pick and choose the items you want. As a general rule, carverys are served during lunch time.

If you just want a little something to keep the wolf from the door, a nosh offered in many Irish pubs could change your attitude toward junk food forever. Hot Nuts are spicy cracker-coated peanuts. Look for the lighted little roasters on the bar. At around 90p ($1.30) for a tiny cupful, they're no great bargain, but one taste and you won't be able to stop.

Examining pub hours and drink prices

Most pubs open at 10:30 a.m., for you go-getters. In the winter, pubs close at 11:00 p.m. and in the summer at 11:30. These times are likely to be extended by a half-hour, thanks to a proposed law that's quickly gaining popularity.

A pretty strict rule in Ireland says pubs can't open before noon on Sundays; Sunday is considered a holy day, and the rule keeps people out of the pubs before they go to Mass with their families. Another part of the rule says that late-night bars are supposed to close up at midnight on Saturdays — because at midnight it's actually Sunday — but this part of the law is rarely enforced.

Quite possibly one of the most fun evenings you can have in Ireland is when the doors of the pub close with you inside. This wink-and-nod arrangement usually happens only in small-town places and shouldn't be expected. But there's a chance that the publican will allow a small gathering to stay, a situation that often ends up in music, conversation, and getting to know the locals. It's then that you're liable to make life-long friends.

Wondering what a night in a pub will run you? Well, you can be sure the price of a pint varies from pubs in big cities to small towns. Ballpark figures, though, are about £1.80 ($2.65) for a pint in a small town to as much as £2.45 ($3.65) in the city. The price for a glass of liquor (called a "short") ranges from £1.85 ($2.75) on the low end to £2.35 ($3.50) for the more expensive areas. For you nondrinkers, keep in mind that a small bottle of soda costs nearly the same as a pint of Guinness!

Also, if you order a mixed drink (a vodka tonic, for instance) don't be surprised when the barkeep hands you a glass with ice and liquor and a bottle of tonic. It's not out of laziness; that's just how it's done.

Tipping like a local

Thanks to the proliferation of American tourists, many barkeeps know of the Yankee tendency to tip when given a drink, so they're not surprised when some money is left after the round is paid for. It's not really customary, though. More common is buying the bartender the odd drink for his labor. After leaving some silver on the bar, we watched a bartender pick it up, look at it quizzically, and then toss it atop a shelf. Even this reaction was odd; many will run after you with your change, even if it's just a few pence!

Appreciating Irish Music

This should say something about the importance of music in Ireland: It's the only nation in the world with a musical instrument as a national symbol. The Tara Harp appears on all official documents of the Irish government. You can see the oldest Tara Harp in Ireland on display in the Old Library of Trinity College in Dublin. (See Chapter 11.)

Thankfully, traditional Irish music enjoyed a huge revival in the folk music days of the 1960s, with credit due to such popular groups as The Dubliners and the Wolfe Tones. And now those unique Celtic sounds are even aspects of Irish bands like Solas, Clannad, and The Corrs.

The real place to hear Irish music is in a pub. Music is such a huge part of Irish culture, whether it be a pick-up session of jigs and reels or a heartfelt set of ballads, that it's as vital to the pub experience as having a pint. Irish songs tell the story of Irish history and can alternate from the raunchy and hilarious to the moving poignancy of a hero's last moments.

You can find scheduled music in many pubs, especially during the high season. Another type of music, which isn't necessarily scheduled, is a "session." This is a group of people informally playing traditional instruments — the tin whistle, uillean pipes (the Irish version of bagpipes; pronounced *ill*-un), the bodhrán (a hand-held drum, pronounced *bow*-ron), and fiddle. This lively, raucous music, including jigs and reels, is likely to entice you to drum your fingers or tap your feet.

Enjoying Sports and the Great Outdoors

All that green Irish grass gets used for more than feeding sheep, and whether you want participatory sports like golf or fishing, spectator sports like soccer or rugby, or traditionally Irish sports like hurling or Gaelic football, you'll find it in Ireland — and in this section, so read on.

Golf

Ireland, it's said, is one large golf course with a few towns and hills scattered around it, the whole thing surrounded by a huge water hazard. More than 250 courses are spread around a country that's only about the size of Maine. That's remarkable but not surprising, given that the country likes to take credit for starting the sport.

Irish courses compare favorably with the perfectly groomed courses in the United States. In fact, they set the standard. While the grass is not as chemically enhanced as in the States and many clubhouses are not as decked out, the lush Irish countryside makes for excellent natural courses and hazards. While courses in Ireland can be challenges, don't let the rough put you off. If you're a golfer, you know what a rite of passage it is to hit at least one round in Ireland.

Golf package tours

Golf enthusiasts may want to consider a golf package tour where you book your play and your stay all together. Here are a few of the best tour companies that merge the links and the land for an unforgettable golf vacation:

- ✔ **Jerry Quinlan's Celtic Golf:** 1129 Rte. 9 South, Cape May Court House, NJ 08210. (☎ **800-535-6148;** Fax: 609-65-0670; E-mail: Celticgolf@aol.com; Internet: www.jqcelticgolf.com) This place will customize your vacation package and personally host golf tours.

- ✔ **Irish Links Tours & Travel:** 400 Main St. Suite 315, Stamford, CT 06901. (☎ **800-824-6538** or 203-363-0970) Tee times are on the best courses with this package, and you stay in choice accommodations, from B&Bs to luxury hotels (seven-day packages begin at $995 per person).

- ✔ **AtlanticGolf:** 237 Post Rd. West, Westport, CT 06880. (☎ **800-542-6224** or 203-454-1086) These golf tours are all-inclusive, including the top courses, airfare, accommodations, and more.

- ✔ **The Tower Hotel Group:** 44-45 Middle Abbey St., Dublin 1. (☎ **01-677-3333**) With excellent accommodation in Dublin, Waterford, Killarney, and Sligo, the Tower Group has golf and accommodation packages at fantastic courses. Contact them for their brochure, "Tee Time in Ireland."

Some hotels have deals with local golf courses in which they give greens fees discounts to guests. See individual hotel reviews throughout the book for info on nearby courses.

More golf info

For further information about good courses near the areas you plan to visit, stop by the local tourism center in the area. Many regional publications for golfing are available.

Golfing Ireland, a booking service and good source of contact information on courses around the Republic, can be reached at 18 Parnell Square, Dublin 1 (☎ **01-872-6711;** Fax: 01-872-6632; E-mail: golf@iol.ie; Internet: www.golfing-ireland.com.). Its Northern Ireland counterpart is **Golfers Abroad,** 6 Park St., Wombwell, Barnsley, S. Yorks, England (☎ **01226-75-1704).**

The **Golfing Union of Ireland,** 81 Eglinton Rd., Donnybrook, Dublin 4 (☎ **01-269-4111),** publishes a calendar of golf events. Contact them for a copy.

For a rundown of some of the best Irish courses, see the perfect Irish itinerary for golfers we've outlined in Chapter 3.

Fishing

With its many lakes (called *loughs*) and coastal villages, Ireland is an excellent country for serious anglers as well as for those who like to just cast a reel and then kick back and relax.

You can fish year-round, but the popular salmon season begins in February, and the sea trout season begins in March; both run until the end of September. Angling licenses are required and are available at most tackle dealers. A temporary holiday angling license, good for 21 days in all districts, costs £10 ($14.80), and a one-day license costs £3 ($4.45).

The **Irish Federation of Sea Anglers** (☎ **01-280-6873**) has information on fishing areas in the Republic, and the **Kingfisher Angling Centre** (☎ **028-2582-1301**) has the same for Northern Ireland. For more informal advice, **Rory's Fishing Tackle,** 17a Temple Bar, Dublin 2 (☎ **01-677-2351**), is the most popular and well-stocked fishing store in Ireland.

The best resource for a fishing vacation is *The Anglers Guide to Ireland,* printed by Guinness and the Tourism Board. It's 80 pages of places to go, accommodations near fishing locales, and tips and insider advice on different types of fishing in Ireland. Pick one up at the Dublin Tourism Centre.

Running, cycling, walking, and more

You're bound to do quite a bit of trekking while you're in Ireland, but for the more serious or more competitive among you, here are a few options you may want to explore:

 ✔ **The Golden Pages Dublin Marathon:** More than 3,000 runners participate in this popular and circuitous route through the capital on the last Monday in October. Runners are welcome from all over the world, and the race gets bigger every year. For information and entry forms, contact the Dublin Marathon Office, 2 Clare St., Dublin 2 (☎ **01-676-4647;** Fax: 01-676-1383).

 ✔ **The Co-operation North Maracycle Event:** Thousands of cyclists race between Dublin and Belfast on this 206-mile round-trip. It starts in Dublin on June 21 and ends in Belfast on the 22nd. Contact Alison McCrum, organizer, 37 Upper Fitzwilliam St., Dublin 2 (☎ **01-661-0588;** Fax: 01-661-8456).

✔ **The Wicklow Mountains May Walking Festival:** This festival organizes walks of between 9 and 16 miles in West County Wicklow in the first week of May. For more information contact the **Wicklow County Tourism Office** in Kilmantin Hill, Wicklow (☎ **0404/66-058**). The Wicklow Way trek goes through the Wicklow and Dublin mountains, exploring 82 miles of paths.

✔ **Kenmare Walking Festival:** The town of Kenmare in County Kerry holds a walking festival in April, with guided walks during the day and entertainment venues in the evening. Contact the **tourism office in Killarney** (☎ **064-31-633**) for more information.

Walking Ireland — The Waymarked Ways is a really complete guide to walking trails in the country. It can be picked up at the Dublin Tourism Centre and other tourism offices for routes to the Wicklow Way, Royal Canal Way, Grand Canal Way, and 22 other trails throughout the country. In addition, the **National Sports Council** (☎ **01-873-4700**) has information on long-distance walking routes in the Republic, and the **Sports Council of Northern Ireland** (☎ **028-9038-1222**) puts out Ulster Way leaflets detailing walking routes in the North.

Sailing

Ireland's clear waters and Gulf Stream winds rival the Caribbean, so if you want to do some sailing, contact the **Irish Sailing Association,** 3 Park Rd., Dun Laoire, County Dublin (☎ **01-280-0239**). It has a list of approved teaching schools that rent boats.

The charming fishing village of Kinvarra, County Galway, is host to **Cruinniu' na mBad** (literally, "Gathering of the Boats") at the end of August, featuring all kinds of sailing. Contact the **Galway Tourist Office** for information (☎ **091-56-3081**).

Horseback riding

Seeing Ireland from atop a beautiful steed is a remarkable way to tour some of the island's rural areas. For more information about places that offer horseback riding, contact the **Association of Irish Riding Establishments,** 11 Moore Park, Newbridge, County Kildare (☎ **045-43-1584**), in the Republic or the **British Horse Society,** House of Sport, Upper Malone Rd., Belfast (☎ **028-9038-3816**), in Northern Ireland. To plan a horse-riding vacation, contact **Equestrian Holidays Ireland,** 1 Sandyford Office Park, Foxrock, Dublin 18 (☎ **01-295-8928**).

Spectator sports

Spectator sports are hugely popular in Ireland. Many pubs, especially in larger cities, have the local game on — whether it's football (soccer),

Gaelic football, hurling, or horse racing. You'll also have plenty of opportunities to see live sports — provided you can get tickets.

Horse racing

Steeplechases are year-round. The flat season (races without hurdles) is from mid-March to early November. The Irish Tourist Board draws up an Irish Racing Calendar every year. Here are some of the highlights:

- ✔ **The Kerrygold Dublin Horse Show:** Held during the first two weeks in August at the Royal Dublin Society (RDS) Showgrounds, Ballsbridge, Dublin 4. Contact Niamh (pronounced Neeve) Kelly at ☎ **01-668-0866;** Fax: 01-660-4014. One of the biggest social and sporting events in the country, this show has the best in Irish horses, fancy balls, and the awarding of the Nation's Cup and the Aga Khan Trophy.

- ✔ **Christmas Horse Racing Festival:** Three days of thoroughbred racing at Leopardstown Racetrack, in Dublin, in late December. Call ☎ **01-289-3607** for information.

- ✔ **Irish Grand National:** Takes place at Fairyhouse in County Meath. For information, call ☎ **042-825-6167.**

- ✔ **The Budweiser Irish Derby:** Held in the Curragh, County Kildare, on the last Sunday in June or the first weekend in July. For info, contact the **Curragh Racecourse Office** at ☎ **045-441-205.**

- ✔ **The Ulster Harp National Steeplechase.** Takes place in Downpatrick, County Down, in mid-February. Call ☎ **0396-61-2054** for information.

Off-track betting is prevalent in many towns in Ireland, especially the larger ones. They're all listed in the Golden Pages and work just like any betting window, with results posted on screens. Pay-off is immediate.

Greyhound racing

Greyhound racing takes place around the country, usually Monday through Saturday at 8:00 p.m. and 10:00 p.m. The largest racetracks are the **Shelbourne Park Stadium** in Dublin and **Kingdom Greyhound Stadium** in Tralee. For more information, contact the **Irish Greyhound Board** (☎ **061-31-6788;** Fax: 061-31-6739).

Rugby, soccer, hurling, and Gaelic football

These four sports are played throughout the country. Gaelic football is a rough-and-tumble sport that combines that best aspects of American football, soccer, and rugby. Hurling is a fast-paced and thrilling game akin to field hockey or lacrosse and is played with a stick called a *hurley stick*. The game is traced to the pre-Christian folk hero Cuchulainn (see "Who's Who is Irish Mythology" earlier in this chapter). Big matches are played in Croke Park in Dublin City (north of O'Connell Street). Schedule information can be obtained from the **Gaelic Athletic Association (G.A.A.)** at ☎ **01-836-3222.** The **Football Association of Ireland** is located at 80 Merrion Square, Dublin 2 (☎ **01-676-6864**).

Chapter 2

Planning Your Trip to Ireland

- -

In This Chapter

▶ Discovering the Emerald Isle, region by region

▶ Visiting Ireland: Anytime is a good time

▶ Experiencing Ireland's best festivals and events

▶ Planning your trip: A few quick tips

- -

*Y*ou don't want to spend a lot of time and energy planning your trip to Ireland just to end up going at the wrong time. Worse, you don't want to plan poorly, giving yourself too long in one area and not enough time in another. Bad weather, too many tourists, being stuck in a small town for too long, not having enough time to see the big attractions — these factors can detract from a great trip. This chapter provides insight to help you decide the best time and right places to spend your vacation.

Everywhere You Want to Be: What This Book Covers and Why

Should you fly into Limerick or Dublin? Do you want to see the Ring of Kerry or Donegal? Is Northern Ireland worth the time? If you've never been to Ireland you're not yet prepared to make these big decisions. Here's your quick primer to the various regions of the island so you can make informed choices about where to spend your precious vacation time.

Experiencing the beauty of Dublin

Sometimes people fly into Dublin airport and set off to the western, more scenic, part of the country before their plane even comes to a complete stop. Unless you know there's a honest-to-goodness pot o' gold waiting for you out west (and we'll bet there's not), there's no reason to rush away. **Dublin,** with its big-time hotels, restaurants, clubs, and museums, is a place whose imprint will last in your memory. South of the city, Wicklow and Kildare contain some of the best of Irish outdoors. And just north of Dublin are Meath and Louth, which contain magnificent ancient ruins. Prepare to be amazed.

Touring the Southeastern Counties

If you pass through all the southeastern counties of **Wexford, Waterford, Kilkenny,** and **Tipperary,** you'll take in a city, a vivid harbor town, verdant farmland, and an impressive archeological site. Sound good? It is, but you'll have to read Chapter 14 to find out more.

One thing that brings endless tourists to this region is the world-famous Waterford Crystal Factory. The tour's great, and if you're even the slightest fan of the pristine crystal, you'll be hard-pressed to pass up the well-stocked shop that you visit when the tour's over.

Swinging by the Southern Counties

Cork City and its surrounding towns aren't just pretty and bustling, they have plenty of historical importance as well. If shopping for great Irish souvenirs is your passion, you'll love the wide array of trinkets and baubles you'll find here. All of this comes second, though, to County Cork's leading attraction: the **Blarney Stone.**

If the southern region of Ireland were a high school, County Kerry would be the prom queen. It's long been Ireland's hottest tourist spot, and it doesn't look as if that's going to change anytime soon. Beginning with the **Ring of Kerry** and **Killarney National Park,** the area is a natural wonder. And when you throw the quaint and timeless towns of Killarney, Tralee, and Kenmare into the mix, you have tourist heaven.

Wandering the Western Counties

Immortalized in some of the most unforgettable Irish ballads and rebel songs, the west of Ireland seems to typify the country. The visual evidence is striking: the **Cliffs of Moher,** the stark **Aran Islands,** the lush land of **Sligo** that prompted poet W. B. Yeats to adopt it as his home. It's also where you'll find many of the amazing, storied Irish sights you've been told not to miss: **the Burren, Bunratty Castle,** and John Wayne's cottage from the movie *The Quiet Man.*

In this region, Irish hospitality reigns. Whether you're in a bustling restaurant on one of Galway's busy streets, in a roadside tavern you found while hunting down the Cliffs of Moher, or up in Donegal, splurging on some of the county's famous seafood, you'll find a level of friendliness and welcoming that's never breached. You're sure to hear "You're very welcome" quite often — and they really *mean* it!

Rambling through Northern Ireland

When you cross that invisible border between the Republic and Northern Ireland, the first thing you might notice is that you don't notice anything. The landscape is as green, the people are as friendly, and the history is the same as the Republic. There's no immediate

Ireland's Regions

difference between the two areas, and if you blink, you could miss the noneventful border crossing altogether. Not much really separates the two countries, except for their governments. (Though, as on the rest of the island, the accents change from region to region, too.)

The Secrets of the Seasons

Whether you're lucky enough to have the luxury of traveling exactly when you want to or whether you're happy to simply get some time — *any* time — off for a vacation, here's a list of the highlights and drawbacks of the four seasons (see Table 2-1 for the average temperature of each month).

Summer

Let's start with the obvious. The most popular and arguably the best time to tour Ireland is the summer. For the unsure traveler, this is your time to go; you'll have lots of touristy company and plenty of leads to follow.

Summer is great because

- ✓ First, and most importantly, is the weather. Ireland is just plain gorgeous during this time of year, so just think of the extra pounds you're paying for your hotel because of the high season as a cover charge for the great weather. Temperatures stay comfortably warm and breezy during the day, and drop to that perfect "light sweater temperature" at night. Don't hold us to this forecast — you'll still get caught in the rain, but it will be a bearable, if not pleasant and refreshing experience.

- ✓ Summer is the busiest tourist season by far, which can be a good thing. Empty pubs don't make for lively fun. Shops, streets, and attractions that are teeming with people may only enhance your trip. Ireland is such a friendly place in general that throwing a ton of people into the mix makes for a spirited atmosphere.

But keep in mind

- ✓ As we said, summer is the high season, so during the months between May and August, every major attraction, hotel, and restaurant is jam-packed. So if you're craving a break from people, this is not the time to go.

- ✓ The tourism industry in Ireland primarily exists for summer travelers, so you can count on being welcomed with open arms or to put it more bluntly, open palms. Most of the people who operate visitor services make their entire year's income in one season, so they take full advantage of flush American wallets and increase their prices for the summer.

Fall

Fall is probably the most underrated time to visit Ireland, but, at the risk of making our Irish friends and family mad (because it's such a well-kept secret), we're here to tell you that we're huge advocates of going in the fall. Days are mild with not too much rain, and daylight that lasts until nearly 9:00 p.m. is great for marathon sightseeing.

Fall is great because

- ✔ Beginning around October, the high season ends and prices drop. Even the summertime price increase isn't outrageous, but for most of us, any money saved is good. Some tours also cost less, and even restaurants offer new menus (translation: same food, lower price).

- ✔ Plenty of people still travel the country during the fall. In fact, many Europeans take vacations in autumn, so Ireland certainly isn't a desolate place and you'll still get that feeling of being among a group. However — and this is especially true in larger cities — after the bulk of tireless travelers have headed back to their homes, the Irish come back out to play. In fact, many Irish have just done the same as many of you and gone on holiday during the summer months. So in the fall, you're likely to find pubs filled with the Irish natives rather than tourists.

But keep in mind

Honestly, we really can't think of any downside to traveling to Ireland in the fall.

Winter

Okay, if we didn't love Ireland so much we'd probably tell you to high-tail it down to the warm and sunny Caribbean for your winter vacation. But we are such unabashed Celtophiles that, although winter is not the ideal time to travel to Ireland, we'll still point out the benefits of going in this harsh season.

Winter is great because

- ✔ Winter is an ideal time for money-minded people to go. Because it's the least popular time to go, prices are at their lowest all across the country, and you're likely to find the cheapest fares of the year to get there.

- ✔ If you hate crowds of any kind, this too is the time for you. From November to March, you're liable to have the run of the country! And the landscape is still beautiful — winter doesn't take as hard a toll on Ireland's plants and trees as it does in many U.S. states.

But keep in mind

- ✔ Ireland is spared snow for the most part, and the temperature doesn't dip to extreme lows, but the elements are, well, miserable: It's cold and rainy and windy.

- ✔ Lots of things close for the season, including many attractions and some small hotels and B&Bs. Other places have shorter hours during this time, too. This is all because tourism slows to a crawl. You can still find plenty of things to see, but you'll get an abbreviated tour offering fewer highlights that you'd see during the other seasons.

Spring

Many argue that spring is the perfect time to travel in Ireland.

Spring is great because

- ✔ The warmer temperatures, the lush, verdant scenery, and longer days combine to make wonderful circumstances for touring the country.

- ✔ The locals are fresh from their own break from tourists and are ready to start playing host. On the whole, it's quite a nice time to go.

But keep in mind

- ✔ Almost all of the factors involved in going during the summer apply here. This is the beginning of the high season, so prices go up. Tourists start flooding in (though it's not as crowded as in the summer).

- ✔ The weather's pretty rainy in the spring, but often the rain showers last only part of the day, opening up the sky to sun and yes, even rainbows.

Walking on Sunshine and Singing in the Rain: Ireland's Climate

If there's one stereotype about Ireland that actually rings true, it's about the rain. Yes, folks, no matter what time of the year you go, chances are slim that you'll make it back without having had the rain drops falling on your head. But that's all part of the ambiance! You'd be cheated out of the experience if it didn't happen!

Rain falls heavier and more often during certain times of the year — winter especially. Also, certain places on the island see more rain, too. The southwest of the country (Counties Limerick, Clare, and Kerry) tends to get more rain all year round. See Table 2-1 for the average monthly temperature in Ireland.

Table 2-1	Average Monthly Temperature in Ireland	
Month	*Temp (F)*	*Temp (C)*
January	34–46	1–8
February	35–47	2–8
March	37–51	3–10
April	39–55	4–13
May	43–60	6–15
June	48–65	9–18
July	52–67	11–20
August	51–67	11–19
September	48–63	9–17
October	43–57	6–14
November	39–51	4–10
December	37–47	3–8

One phenomenon that's sure to surprise you is the palm trees in Ireland! The country has a fairly high latitude, but is spared very cold weather thanks to the curved path of the Gulf Stream, which roars out of the Gulf of Mexico, through the straits of Florida, across the Atlantic, and along Ireland's west coast. So, surprisingly, you really can see palm trees throughout the country. (You can bet it still won't feel tropical, though.)

Weather and temperatures aren't the only factors involved in deciding when to go. The amount of daylight varies greatly from season to season. Ireland is situated at such a high latitude that summer days are really long (sunset as late as 10:30 p.m.), while winter days are tragically short (sunset as early as 4:30 p.m.). So the more daylight there is, the more sights you'll get to see.

The best site on the Web for Ireland's weather forecasts is `http://cnn.com/WEATHER/cities/world.html`. It gives the four-day forecasts for seven Irish cities as well as the sunset and sunrise times.

Calendar of Festivals and Events

No matter when you visit Ireland, some sort of event or festival is sure to be going on. The Irish take these things seriously, so it's bound to be a big deal. About a zillion events are held each year, of all sorts and kinds, but we've sorted through and picked only the best.

Some of these dates can fluctuate each year by a day or two, depending on when weekends fall and so on. Call ahead to confirm dates.

Attention sports fans: Check out Chapter 1 for the sections on golf, horse racing, hiking, and fishing for events that may be of particular interest to you.

March

✔ **St. Patrick's Day** (March 17): The feast day of the patron saint of Ireland. It's a religious day for most of the country but there are parades and festivities and lots of drinking everywhere, especially in Dublin, Cork, Limerick, Armagh, and Downpatrick (where the ol' saint is buried). The biggest parade is in Dublin, down O'Connell Street. Call for information: ☎ **01-676-3205** or 1550-22-4324; E-mail: info@paddyfest.ie.

April

✔ **International Pan-Celtic Festival** (April 17–22): Festival of Celtic music and dancing that includes street entertainment, poetry readings, and a Celtic Pub Trail in Tralee, County Kerry. Contact the festival coordinator at ☎ **066-80-050**; E-mail: panceltic@tinet.ie; Internet: www.panceltic.com.

✔ **Dublin Film Festival** (April 6–16): The best of Irish and world cinema, as well as seminars and lectures on film-making, all centered around the Irish Film Centre of Temple Bar and other theaters. It's one of the best-attended film festivals in Europe. Contact the **DFF** at UCG Cinemas, Parnell St., Dublin 1, for schedules and ticket information at ☎ **01-679-2937**; Fax: 01-679-2939; E-mail: dff@iol.ie; Internet: www.iol.ie/dff.

May

✔ **Belfast City Summer Fest** (May 22–June 6): Festival, parades and floats, exhibitions, bands, concerts, and tours for two weeks throughout the city. Contact the **City Events Office** at ☎ **028-9027-0345**.

June

✔ **The Music Festival in Great Irish Houses** (June 10–19): Classical music by internationally renowned musicians combined with some of Ireland's best architecture. Homes are in Dublin and neighboring counties Wicklow and Kildare. Contact **Crawford Tipping** of the Blackrock Post Office at ☎ **01-278-1528**; Fax: 01-278-1528.

✔ **Bloomsday** (June 16): This festival commemorates Leopold Bloom, the main character in James Joyce's 900-plus page novel *Ulysses,* which takes place in Dublin on this date in 1904. Restaurants and pubs do everything to look the part, pretending to be part of the book or just celebrating its homage to Dublin. You can take guided tours and attend ceremonies in areas associated with the story. Contact the **James Joyce Cultural Centre** at 35 North Great George's St., Dublin 1 by calling ☎ 01-878-8547.

✔ **The Budweiser Irish Derby** (last Sunday in June or first Sunday in July): Held in the Curragh, County Kildare, this is Ireland's version of the Kentucky Derby. For info, contact the **Curragh Racecourse Office** at ☎ 045-441-205.

July

✔ **Irish Open** (first week of the month): This golf championship attracts the best of the best, and each year one of the country's top courses plays host. Because the venue changes from year to year, contact the organizers for more information so you can stand rough-side to the world's most famous matchup of the masters. (☎ 01-662-2433; E-mail: info@murphysirishopen.ie; Internet: www.murphysirishopen.ie)

✔ **Galway Arts Festival** (July 19–30): Two weeks of concerts, street theater, and children's shows that ceremoniously end with the famous Galway horse races at the end of the month. Contact the **Galway Arts Festival Office** at ☎ 091-509-700; Fax: 091-562-655; E-mail: info@gaf.iol.ie; Internet: www.galwayartsfestival.ie.

✔ **Lughnasa Fair** (last Saturday of the month): Medieval harvest-time fair with crafts, entertainment, and costumes, all set inside and on the grounds of the twelfth-century **Carrickfergus Castle,** in County Antrim. Call the castle for more information at ☎ 028-9335-1273.

✔ **Galway Arts Fest** (last two weeks of the month): Located in the old part of town, the medieval city shines with varying entertainment these two weeks. Concerts, parades, street theater, and more showcase the town and serve as an exciting kickoff to five days of Galway horse racing at the town racecourse. Call for more information at ☎ 091-56-1516.

August

✔ **Rose of Tralee Festival** (August 20–25): Five days of concerts, entertainment, horse races, and a beauty pageant in this County Kerry town to pick the new "Rose of Tralee." Contact ☎ 066-712-1322.

September

- **All-Ireland Hurling and Football Finals** (first two weeks of the month): Tickets to the live matches (held at Croke Park in Drumcondra, outside Dublin) are impossible to get, but they're televised and the excitement shouldn't be missed. Contact the **Gaelic Athletic Association** for more information by calling ☎ 01-836-3222.

- **Galway Oyster Festival** (end of the month): Besides eating, other events at Galway's major mollusk fest (or should we say feast?) include dancing, an oyster-shucking competition, a golf tournament, and a yacht race. Call ☎ 091-52-7282 for information.

October

- **Wexford Opera Festival** (October 15–November 1): The biggest event in Southeast Ireland, attracting the best and most prestigious in the business. The featured artists change annually. Contact **Theatre Royal**, Wexford at ☎ 051-87-4402.

- **Halloween (Shamhana)** (October 31): Celebrated a bit differently than in the United States, with fireworks and bonfires and the eating of "monkey nuts" (peanuts in the shell). If you're in the country at the end of October and want to find out where the party's going to be, just look for the field or lot where kids are stacking up wood scraps.

November

- **Belfast Festival at Queens** (first week of the month): All-out arts festival hosted by Queen's University featuring ballet, dance, film, opera, jazz, and traditional and classical music. Call ☎ 028-9066-7687 for more information.

December

- **St. Stephen's Day** (December 26): Boys dress up as Wren boys (chimney sweeps) and sing carols for charity all over the country.

Chapter 3

Deciding on an Itinerary

• •

In This Chapter

▶ Tips for touring Ireland

▶ Determining what itinerary is right for you

▶ Hitting the highlights on a one-week trip

▶ Traveling with family

▶ Planning a trip for golfers

▶ Stepping off the beaten path (on purpose!)

• •

$\mathcal{S}$ome people like to travel with absolutely no direction — they just get off the plane and go wherever the wind takes them. While this approach may sound daring and adventurous, you're probably looking for a little more structure in your tour of Ireland. This chapter is for those of you who don't want to be locked into a tour group's itinerary, but who would prefer to have some sort of game plan before crossing the Atlantic. We'll offer suggestions and give you tips for custom-designing your own itinerary. Go anywhere, do whatever you want; it's your trip!

For a great film tour of the country, see the "Emerald green on the silver screen" sidebar later in this chapter.

Itinerary Planning for Do-It-Yourselfers

There are plenty of ways to put together your own custom trip, but the two easiest ways to see Ireland on your own are the base camp approach and the nomadic approach.

The base camp approach

This approach is the one we recommend. Pick two or three cities and make day trips out from them. Base yourself in lovely towns like **Cork** or **Killarney** (to explore the South), **Galway** (for the West), or **Dublin** (for, well, Dublin). If you have only one week, you will have to pick and choose what you see. Planting yourself in Dublin for a couple days, and then staying in a West Coast city like Killarney for a few more is a good idea because many sights are an easy drive from these two points. By staying a couple nights in the same place, you also save the time and hassle of switching hotels every day and worrying about check-in times.

Self-catering is one cost-efficient option that families and groups choosing the base camp approach may want to consider. Self-catering means you rent a home with kitchen facilities for a week or two and head off on your sightseeing excursions from there. You can save money on both accommodations and dining, and some of the cottages and apartments available are just beautiful. (For more information, check out Chapter 8.)

The nomadic approach

The nomadic approach may take more planning and require you to waste time checking in and out of hotels as you move from city to city, but the advantage is that you won't ever see the same thing twice. We've laid out this guidebook to introduce areas in a counterclockwise direction from Dublin to the Southern coast, the West, and finally **Northern Ireland.** If you take the nomadic approach, go in that direction and decide what to see and what to skip based on your interests and the amount of time you have. But don't spread yourself too thin: The longer the distance between each day's destinations, the less time you'll have to stop and really savor the attractions before you run out of daylight.

The most important thing is to have fun. Sit down with this guidebook (and maybe a pint of Guinness, if you like) and pick out some places you really want to see. Be realistic, though. You can spend a full (and tiring) day seeing only a few big sights while driving just the distance between Cork and Waterford. If you're staying in **Dingle** and the next night in Dublin, you won't have time to see much along the way. **The Ring of Kerry, Dingle Peninsula,** and the **Antrim Coast** all deserve a full day. And one day in either **Dublin** or **Belfast** may not be enough to soak up all that city has to offer.

Day tours: The Gilligan's Island option

Like, you know, a three-hour tour. (A three-hour tour?)

City walking tours, bus tours, and tours through museums and castles are excellent ways to discover history and highlights you may otherwise miss.

In general, tours are informative, interesting, and worth the time and expense, but they aren't for everybody. If you're the kind of person who likes to make your own discoveries and do your own homework, you may feel that such a spoon-fed tour is a waste of time. Before you sign on, really get the lowdown on what the tour covers and how much time you have to devote to it. Make sure the things you really want to see are covered on the tour and find out if you can leave the group to explore on your own. (Some places require you to stick with the group.) Throughout this book we've listed tours that we can vouch for, but asking questions first — like how long the tour takes, how much it costs, and what it includes — is still smart.

Dealing with the Daily Tourist Grind

Two things that can really frustrate travelers when it comes to making and fulfilling a custom-made itinerary are

- ✔ Trying to pack too much into one day
- ✔ Burnout

Be realistic about the amount of time you'll spend in the car or bus, burning up precious daylight hours. We suggest getting up and out early to see the sights — that means having breakfast by 9:00 a.m. instead of rolling out of bed at 11:00. And, when it's time to move on to your next destination, hit the road late in the day rather than making the trip early and wasting daytime; as an added benefit, you'll have the whole night to rest up before your next round of sightseeing. And remember that you don't always have to act like an army on a campaign, marching, fortifying yourself somewhere, and then attacking. What we mean is, don't think you always have to go to the hotel first, and then hit the sightseeing trail. Going from Waterford to Cork and you want to see the Blarney Stone? See it on your way to the hotel — you'll save yourself daylight and also assure that you'll get it in (Blarney Castle closes after dark).

You should make an A-list of places you most want to see and a B-list of things to look for only if you have extra time (like our top-ten picks and alternates in Chapter 1). Make your A-list items a priority when mapping out your itinerary and fill in the gaps with secondary sights. (And remember, some places that look small and quick on a map — like the Ring of Kerry — can surprise you and take all day.) Just don't try to cram too much into one day. If you're constantly rushing from one place to the next, you'll enjoy none of them. Relax and enjoy yourself — you're on vacation. See the helpful worksheets printed on yellow paper at the back of this book. The "Places to Go, People to See, Things to Do" and "Going My Way" worksheets help you efficiently plan your trip.

Money-Saving Tips for Your Trip

If you do plan your trip on your own, turn to the following sections of the book for money-saving advice.

- ✔ Turn to Chapter 4 for tips on how to get the best deals on airfares and other money-saving tips.
- ✔ If you're 50-plus, check out Chapter 5 for tips on cost-cutting deals for mature travelers.
- ✔ Chapter 7 can help you get the best deals on wheels.

Finding the Itinerary That's Right for You

A whole country's worth of attractions to choose from — how do you decide what to do? Here's a good start. We've put together three tours that cover the best of what Ireland has to offer. Depending on your interests, you can choose the highlight trip, the family itinerary, or if you're a duffer you can choose a nine-day golf tour that covers much of the country. Or, on the other hand, you can always make up your own tour — it's a free country, after all.

You can find details on all the individual attractions listed in the various destination chapters. See the index for easy reference.

Hitting the highlights: Ireland in one week

If you have only one week you'll have to make some sacrifices, but we've mapped out a thorough one-week "see the highlights" tour. Follow our itinerary, and you won't go home dissatisfied. Tired maybe, but not dissatisfied.

Day 1: Dublin

Fly into **Dublin** (most flights arrive in the morning). Take a taxi or a bus into city centre. Head to your hotel or B&B if you have it booked in advance, or go straight to the **Dublin Tourism Centre** and have people there find you accommodations in the city. (The Tourism Centre is a good place to start if you arrive with any questions or want to scope out some free literature.) After you're settled, get over to **Trinity College** and take the historical walking tour. Grab a quick lunch at a chipper (fish and chips) and catch the bus or walk out to the **Guinness Brewery.** On your way back to the city centre, stop and see **St. Patrick's Cathedral, St. Stephen's Green,** and the shopping area of **Grafton Street** and **Nassau Street.** Have a nice sit-down dinner before heading to **Duke's Bar** for the **Literary Pub Crawl** or to **Oliver St. John Gogarty's** for the **Musical Pub Crawl.**

Day 2: Dublin to Waterford

Walk off your traditional Irish breakfast by visiting (and photographing) some of Dublin's landmarks like the **Ha'Penny Bridge** and the **General Post Office** building. Pick up your rental car in town or take the bus out to the airport to get it. Head south. Skip the less-than-stunning southeast coastline and head toward **Waterford.** Stop in **Kilkenny** on the way to stretch your legs and take a picture. By the time you get to Waterford you'll have time for dinner, a walk along the water, and maybe a pint or two.

Day 3: Waterford to Cork

Walk along the river Suir and climb **Reginald's Tower** early, and then head to the **Waterford Crystal Factory** before noon. After the tour, pick up a $100 crystal paperweight in the factory store (or don't), have lunch back in town, and head southwest to Cork. You'll have enough time to visit **Blarney Castle** before checking into your hotel. Go out for dinner and have a pub-crawl afterward on **Oliver Plunkett Street.**

Day 4: Cork to Killarney

Do a little souvenir shopping around **Cork,** maybe ring the bells in **St. Anne's Shandon Church,** and then make a beeline for **Killarney National Park.** You'll see the **Lakes of Killarney, the Torc Waterfall,** and **Muckross House,** and end up in **Kenmare,** where you can have a late lunch. Keep your camera handy as you wind along the park's famous mountainy drive. By the time you get back to **Killarney,** where you'll stay the night, you'll be ready for a good meal and a slow stout by the fire. We recommend the restaurant **Teo's** and a raucous good time in **Laurels,** the self-proclaimed "Singing Pub."

Day 5: Killarney to Galway City

Get on the road early because lunch and a visit to **Limerick's Hunt Museum** and **King John's Castle** are your only stops on the way to the majestic **Cliffs of Moher** — a long drive from Killarney, but worth it. The cliffs are one of those sights to which the postcards just can't do justice. Don't stand near the edge and don't wear a hat — the wind gods have been known to take sacrifices. From the cliffs, take the scenic route up to the oft-sung-about **Galway Bay,** snap a picture of the **Aran Islands** off in the distance, and stop on the way to **Galway** to see the **Poulnabrone Dolmen** and **Aillwee Cave** in **The Burren.** You'll get into Galway City early enough for dinner.

Day 6: Galway City to Dublin

Galway is a great town, compact enough for walking around and shopping — but you're flying back out of Dublin tomorrow morning, and you have a 180-mile drive ahead of you, so get up and hit the road early. Even though the midlands can be a bit of a yawn, your adventure doesn't have to end. If you still have the stamina, drive north of the city first to see the ancient burial site of **Newgrange** and the **Hill of Tara,** old seat of the Irish kings, and then head back to Dublin. When you get there, you may be tempted to get a good night's sleep for your early flight the next morning. Nonsense. Tradition requires a pub-crawl through trendy **Temple Bar.** You can sleep on the plane.

Bringing the kids: A one-week itinerary for families

Ireland is a family-friendly place, so with a little planning there's no reason you can't have a great family vacation here. In this itinerary we've pulled together some of the most kid-friendly sights, hotels, and restaurants to help you map out a trip that the whole family can enjoy.

How do I find a place when there's no #&@*$! address!?

Welcome to one of the facts of life you'll discover as you plan your trip around Ireland: Outside of the major cities, American-style street names and addresses simply aren't used. If you leaf through this book you often see the address of a B&B listed with just the town name after it. This is just the way it works. In fact, if you were to write a letter to the place, you'd address it the very same way: with just its name and the town.

We know what you're thinking: "How the #&*@! am I supposed to find any of these places?!" Fear not: It's not as hard as it seems. Often these places are right on the town's main thoroughfare (such as R236 or the Dublin-Waterford road), and in these cases if you drive into the town you can't miss them. You can find many exceptions to this generalization — for instance, in some cases a place is on a small side street, and that little street doesn't necessarily have a name. In such cases we list more specific directions.

Day 1: Dublin

Fly into **Dublin** (most flights arrive in the morning). Take a taxi or your rental car into city centre and head to your hotel or B&B if you have it booked in advance. Your best option for a hotel is **Jury's Christchurch Inn,** which has family-friendly rates and is in walking distance to most sites and restaurants. Kids will love **Dvblinia,** a hands-on museum on the history of the city, connected to **Christ Church Cathedral**. For lunch, **Eddie Rockets** is a good choice with its menu and diner-style fun. On your way back to the city centre, stop and see **St. Patrick's Cathedral.** A fun dinner pick is **Gallagher's Boxty House,** which has traditional Irish food and group-style dining tables.

Day 2: Dublin to Waterford

The little ones won't be so restless in the car if you take a good walk around Dublin visiting (and photographing) some of the city's landmarks like the **Ha'Penny Bridge** and the **General Post Office** building. Because it's easier to get there by car, on your way out of town stop at **Phoenix Park and Zoo** to take in the animals and maybe have a picnic in the park. As you make your way to **Waterford,** play some good car games like, "Count the Sheep!" Get your bearings in Waterford with a short walk before dinner. The novelty of eating on a boat at the **Galley Cruising Restaurant** should keep the kids from getting bored.

Day 3: Waterford to Cork

Take the time to see **Reginald's Tower** by the water before you leave Waterford; it's a fun climb. Then head to the **Waterford Crystal Factory.** Depending on the age of your kids, you may want to skip this. Young kids may actually like the noise and all the sites but older kids may be easily bored. Next stop: **Cork.** You'll have plenty of time to visit **Blarney Castle** on the way, which the young ones will love — not just for the precarious climb to the top of the ruins but also for the trail-heavy grounds. In Cork, **Ristoranti Rossini** is a safe dining bet with its traditional Italian fare and **Jury's Hotel** is a great place for the family to stay.

Day 4: Cork to Killarney

Cork doesn't have much by way of kid-friendly attractions, but about 15 minutes away is the town of **Cobh,** home to the **Fota Wildlife Park.** The park has some great exotic animals like ostriches and kangaroos. Also in Cobh is the **Queenstown Story,** which gives an interesting history of the area. You should also head out to **Killarney National Park** for lakes, waterfalls, and plenty of scenery to keep young tourists occupied while driving through the park. In the town of Killarney, **Allegro Restaurant** has some great pizza — a staple of many a family meal. A good place to stay is **Murphys Guesthouse,** which has a kid-friendly food menu and a baby-sitting service if you have little ones. (*Note:* the Irish call a baby-sitting area a creche.)

Day 5: Killarney to Galway City

Get on the road early because you have a long jump to the **Cliffs of Moher.** Have lunch in **Limerick** at **Nestor's** with its quasi-American menu and visit **King John's Castle** before you make the long-but-worth-it drive out to the majestic cliffs. Keep a close eye on the kids while at the cliffs because strong winds can make getting near the cliff edge very dangerous and there are no barriers. On the way to Galway stop and see the **Poulnabrone Dolmen** and Aillwee Cave in Burren. You'll get into Galway City early enough for dinner at **Maxwell McNamaras,** a nice family restaurant with a extensive kids' menu. Your best bet for a hotel is the **Galway Great Southern Hotel** — children will love the heated pool and you'll love the special kids' rates.

Day 6: Galway City to Dublin

You have to hit the road early to get back to Dublin, but try to take a walk around Galway before you go and make a fun stop in the resort and amusement park town of **Salthill.** It's a long drive through the midlands from there but with any luck the rugrats will be too tired to still be fighting in the backseat. If you still have the stamina once you reach Dublin, drive a little north of the city to see the ancient burial sites of **Newgrange** and the **Hill of Tara** — which the kids can explore a la Indiana Jones. By the time you get back to Dublin, the whole family will be tuckered out.

The nine-day, all-golf Ireland tour

While you can't walk too far in any direction in Ireland without stumbling upon a golf course, and while almost every hotel and B&B boasts proximity to three or four courses, why play at lesser courses when we can direct you to the very best?

Emerald green on the silver screen

If you're a diehard movie buff, you can plan your itinerary around locations from some of your favorite films. Here are several areas and the movies that were filmed there:

Dublin: *Michael Collins, The General, Angela's Ashes, Into the West, In the Name of the Father* (Kilmainham jail), *Educating Rita* (Trinity College), *An Awfully Big Adventure* (Olympia Theatre)

County Wicklow: *Zardoz* (with Sean Connery)

County Wexford: *Saving Private Ryan*

Counties Kildare and Meath: *Braveheart*

Cahir, County Tipperary: *Excalibur* (Cahir Castle)

Cork City: *Angela's Ashes*

Dingle: *Far and Away*

County Galway: *Lion in Winter*

Aran Islands: *Man of Aran*

Limerick: *Angela's Ashes*

Cong, County Mayo: *The Quiet Man*

Donegal: *Dancing at Lughnasa*

Belfast: *The Boxer*

First hole: St. Margaret's

One of the hosts of the Irish Open, St. Margaret's is a new, challenging, and exciting course of the highest standard, with an infamously difficult finishing hole. Located in Stephubble, St. Margaret's, County Dublin. (☎ **01-864-0400;** E-mail: Stmarggc@indigo.ie) Par: 73. Fees: ₤40 ($59.20) for 18 holes in the summer, ₤25 ($37) in the winter.

Second hole: Portmarnock

This course was the home of the first Irish Open in 1889 and was renovated and reopened in the early 1990s. It's a natural golf course, incorporating the rugged landscape of the region rather than being predesigned. Located 25 minutes from Dublin city centre, Portmarnock, County Dublin. (☎ **01-846-2968;** E-mail: secretary@portmarnockgolfclub.ie) Par: 72. Fees: ₤65 ($96.20) midweek, ₤80 ($118.40) weekends.

Third hole: Mount Juliet

This Jack Nicklaus "Signature" course was host of the Irish Open from 1993 to 1995. The lakes and waterfalls make a picturesque backdrop to this course, called the "Augusta of Europe" and voted the best inland course in Ireland. Located on the N9 Waterford-Dublin Rd., Thomastown, County Kilkenny. (☎056-73-000) Par: 72. Fees: £70 ($103.60) midweek, £75 ($111) weekends.

Fourth hole: Old Head Golf Links

A new course located on a stunning outcrop of land and surrounded by the Atlantic, the Old Head Links was a cooperative project, built by the top golfers of the country. It can be challenging. Located in Kinsale, County Cork. (☎ 021-77-8444; E-mail: info@oldheadgolf.ie; Internet: www.oldheadgolflinks.com) Par: 72. Fees: £50 ($74) summer, £45 ($66.60) winter.

Fifth hole: Killarney Golf and Fishing Club

Home of the 1991 and 1992 Irish Open Championship, this course is nestled among the beautiful lakes of Killarney and below the majestic MacGillycuddy's Reeks Mountains. Located at Mahony's Point, Killarney, County Kerry. (☎ 064-31-034; E-mail: kgc@iol.ie; Internet: www.killarney-golf.com) Par: 72. Fees: £38 ($56.25).

Sixth hole: Ballybunion

A seaside club with two fine 18-hole courses, the old course is the more challenging of the two; the newer course was fashioned by the legendary Robert Trent Jones. Located on Sandhill Rd., Ballybunion, County Kerry. (☎ 068-27-146; E-mail: bbgolfc@iol.ie) Par: 71. Fees: £55 ($81.40).

Seventh hole: Lahinch Golf Club

Now you're golfing in Ireland! High elevations provide amazing views of sea and valley, and local goats are known to cross the fairway. The club has two 18-hole courses; one is a championship course. Located in Lahinch, County Clare. (☎ 065-81003; E-mail: lgc@iol.ie) Par: 72. Fees: £25 ($37) midweek, £30 ($44.40) weekends.

Eighth hole: County Sligo Golf Club

This difficult course challenges top players, but dabblers have fun playing it, too. The course is set between striking Atlantic beaches and the hill of Benbulben. Located in Rosses Point, County Sligo. (☎ 071-77-186; E-mail: cosligo@iol.ie) Par: 71. Fees: £27 ($39.96) midweek, £35 ($51.80) weekends.

Ninth hole: Royal Portrush

Three excellent 18-hole courses all offer amazing seaside views of the northern Antrim Coast. Located on Dunluce Rd., Portrush, County Antrim. (☎ 028-7082-2311) Par: 72. Fees: £55 ($90.75) midweek, £65 ($107.30) weekends.

Here's one more course, to round out your golf trip with a little stargazing: The **Waterville Golf Links,** Newrath, Waterville, County Kerry (☎ 066-74-102). Waterville is scenic, overlooking the Atlantic, but more importantly, it's where Bob Hope and Sean Connery play when they're in Ireland. Par: 71. Fees: £50 ($74).

Getting off the Beaten Path

We're pretty sure that between these itineraries and our top-ten list in The Part of Tens, we've covered the most worthwhile destinations for you to see in Ireland, but much has still gone unmentioned. Ireland has a thousand small towns with friendly pubs, and maybe a castle that bears your last name, or a church honoring your favorite saint. How do you find those places, the ones that are ready to fill you with warm memories and are story fodder for when you get back home? You get off the beaten path, that's how. You stay in a small town you like instead of worrying about getting to the next landmark by sundown. You talk to the locals (that's how we found some great stuff that made it into this guide). Believe us, the lasting memories you have of Ireland can be those from the out-of-the-way village you stumbled upon and the gregarious locals you met, as much as they may be of the Cliffs of Moher and the Blarney Stone.

Chapter 4

Planning Your Budget

● ●

In This Chapter

▶ Controlling your total trip costs

▶ Understanding the pricing shorthand in this book

▶ Figuring out a skeleton budget

▶ Discovering tips for saving big bucks

● ●

As far as destinations go, Ireland is neither the cheapest nor the most expensive place you can choose. While this guide gives you lots of money-saving insider tips and offers accommodation and dining selections that won't tap your wallet like a keg of Guinness on St. Patrick's Day, you should have a realistic view of what your vacation will cost you.

Can you do Ireland on $5 a day? Maybe in 1965, but not now. $50 a day? Sure, if you don't mind hostel bunk beds and convenience store dinners. Being realistic, you can bet on a figure more like $100 to $150 per person per day — and that doesn't include a rental car and airfare. When the credit card statement greets you a month after you've returned home, you'll know it was worth every penny; but it's best to know what you're getting into before you leave, so read on.

Getting a Handle on Your Total Trip Costs

So how much is this trip going to cost? It depends how smart a traveler you are. One week in Ireland can cost you hundreds or even thousands of dollars if you let it. You have this guide in your hand, and that's a huge step in the right money-saving direction, but — and this is a big but — keeping to a tight budget does not mean you have to sacrifice a memorable vacation.

Finding out what things cost

To cut out the hassle of closely reading to find out the exact prices of hotels and restaurants, we've denoted the relative cost of things with dollar signs. The actual prices are listed, too, but the dollar signs will allow you to get an idea of a place's price with just a quick glance. Here's how the signs and the dollars actually match up:

Dining

$ £5 ($7.40), or less

$$ £6–10 ($8.90–$14.80)

$$$ £11–16 ($16.30–$23.70)

$$$$ £17 ($25.15), or more

Accommodations

$ £50 ($74) double, or less

$$ £50–100 double ($74–$148)

$$$ £100–200 double ($148–$296)

$$$$ £200 ($296) double, or more

Sketching a skeleton budget

We've listed specific money-saving tips later in this chapter, but just to give you an idea, let's try to create a skeleton budget based on the level of luxury you expect and the number of days you'll be visiting Ireland. Look over the sections of this guide that cover the cities and regions you want to see to get an idea of how much a hotel or dinner will cost you. These greatly depend on your particular tastes. Do you want only the best rooms in the best hotels in the best locations? That will cost you a little more. Do you plan to play golf every day? Factor in greens fees and the price of renting clubs (assuming you're not lugging your own along). Horseback riding and fishing also mean added costs.

Generally speaking, your costs will be in these ranges:

- ✔ **Airfare:** Airfare to and from Ireland will vary depending on where you're flying from, the time of year, and the totally arbitrary whims of the airline gods. As a vague example, airfare from New York to Ireland and back can run you about $700 — but don't hold us to that! See Chapter 6 for tips on getting the best deals.

- ✔ **Ground transportation:** Transportation costs vary depending on whether you're busing it or renting a car. Driving — the transportation choice for most tourists — costs around $50 a day, plus an additional $15 in gas.

- ✔ **Lodging:** A double room runs about $80; those on the low end go for about $50 and those on the high end about $130 to $170.

- ✔ **Meals:** A good per-person allowance for lunch is $10, and for dinner between $15 and $30. Breakfast is included with most accommodations, so you don't have to figure that in your daily costs.

- ✔ **Attractions:** Even if you see two or three attractions each day, a fair amount to budget for sights is $15 per day.

- ✔ **Shopping:** Are you planning to buy clothes, jewelry, Waterford Crystal, and antiques, or just a few postcards, a snow globe, and a couple other inexpensive souvenirs? A modest piece of Waterford Crystal can set you back $80; a nice Guinness sweatshirt about $50. So gauge your impulse-buying tendencies and factor that in as well.

This is a skeleton budget. Make sure you have access to emergency money, too.

Examining a low-end, one-week tour budget

Use the one-week tour budget in Table 4-1 to estimate your per-person costs. When figuring for a second person you should deduct the cost of the rental car and gas from the total, and if you're traveling with a child and planning to share a hotel room, you might be able to lower the hotel figure as well by about $10 or $15 (an average rate for a third guest in a room). Keep in mind, though, that a lot of places in Ireland charge by the head for accommodations.

Table 4-1	One-Week Tour Budget
Expense	**Cost**
Airfare (round trip NY-Dublin)	$700
Rental car	$350
Two tanks of gas	$60
Seven nights in hotels ($40 per person average)	$280
Seven lunches (at $10 each average)	$70
Seven dinners (at $22 each average)	$154
Sightseeing admissions ($15 per day)	$105
Souvenirs and miscellaneous ($10 per day)	$70
TOTAL FOR ONE WEEK	**$1,789**

Money-Saving Tips

Worried you can't afford your trip? Well, you can rent *Far and Away*, read *Angela's Ashes*, listen to a Chieftains CD, and just pretend you're in Ireland; but what fun is that?

Relax, you probably can afford to go. There are lots of corners you can cut if necessary that will make your vacation actually quite a bargain. It just takes a little traveling know-how.

For example, stay at smaller lodges and guesthouses and avoid big hotels. And, even if you simply stick to the many free attractions scattered around the country, you'll still see a lot. There are plenty of ways, some little and some big, to cut down on costs. We've scattered various money-saving tips throughout this book, which offer hints on places to trim your budget, but here's a list of 20 general ones all in one place.

✔ **Go in the off-season:** Traveling between November and April will save you a lot off your airfare and the cost of accommodations. Christmas week is the exception — airfare will break you, as it's the main time of year many Irish in other countries come home to visit, and the airlines cash in. (See Chapter 6 for more info on airfares.)

✔ **Travel on off days of the week:** Airfares vary depending on the day of the week. If you can travel on a Tuesday, Wednesday, or Thursday, you might find cheaper flights. Also remember that staying over a Saturday night can occasionally cut your airfare by more than half.

✔ **Reserve your flight well in advance by taking advantage of APEX (advance-purchase excursion) fares:** You can also book your ticket through a consolidator (also known as a "bucket shop," for reasons no one in the whole world can explain) — which is basically a wholesaler who buys airline tickets in bulk and resells them at a discount. (See Chapter 6 for more information on booking your flight.)

✔ **Try a package deal or group deal:** A single phone call to a package tour operator can cover your flight, accommodations, transportation within Ireland, and sightseeing. Packages may not only save time but money as well. Even if you don't want to go with a complete package you can book directly through some hotels for room-car deals (where they throw in the rental car for free) or other special packages. Most people believe that by planning out the trip entirely on their own they will save a lot of money, but this is not necessarily true. (See Chapter 6 for more on package deals.)

Group rates: Whether for packages or for admission to individual attractions, group rates are a fantastic way to save money, and you don't necessarily have to travel with a busload of other people to get them. Sometimes a "group" is as few as three people, so always ask. And sometimes you and the folks behind you can be a makeshift "group" to get the discounted price.

✔ **Always ask about discounts:** Membership in AAA, frequent-flier plans, trade unions, AARP, the military, or other groups might qualify you for discounted rates on plane tickets, hotel rooms, and car rentals (these apply mainly to U.S. companies). Some car rental companies give discounts to employees of companies that have corporate accounts. With valid identification, students, teachers, youths, and seniors can be entitled to discounts. Many attractions have discounted family prices. Ask about everything — you could be pleasantly surprised.

✔ **Book your rental car at weekly rates when possible:** This will save you money for sure over the steeper daily rates.

✔ **Walk:** All cities in Ireland and Northern Ireland can be easily walked, even Dublin and Belfast. So save the bus and cab fare (or worse, the rental car fees) and hoof it to save a few extra pounds.

✔ **Never make a phone call from a hotel:** The marked-up fees they charge are scandalous. Walk to the nearest coin or card phone for calls in and out of the country.

✔ **Skimp on souvenirs:** As a general rule, souvenirs (and we're talking especially about those created for the tourist market) are poorly made and often kitschy. Take pictures, keep a journal, and let your memories suffice. Also, wait to develop your film till you get back home — it'll be cheaper.

✔ **Use American Express to exchange money:** AmEx offers the best rate, and will exchange American Express Travelers Cheques for free. (Do this instead of using the checks as cash at a hotel or restaurant.) It charges a £3 commission to exchange dollars to pounds or pounds to dollars, but that beats the competition, which invariably charges a percentage. (See Chapter 9.)

✔ **Pick up those free, coupon-packed visitor pamphlets and magazines:** Detailed maps, feature articles, dining and shopping directories, and discount and freebie coupons give these pocket-sized giveaways a good wallop. Especially popular and reliable are _Visitor, Discover Ireland, Ireland,_ and _Southeast Holiday Guidebook._

✔ **Skip the fantabulous views:** Rooms with great views are the most expensive rooms in any hotel, and because you probably won't be hanging out in your room all day, why pay the price?

✔ **Get out of town:** In many places, hotels just outside the popular tourist areas may be a great bargain that will only require you to do a little more driving — and they may even offer free parking. The rooms may not be as fancy, but just as comfortable and a whole lot cheaper.

✔ **Ask if your kids can stay in your room with you:** Although many accommodations in Ireland charge by the head, some might allow your pint-sized ones to stay for free. Even if you have to pay $10 or $15 for a rollaway bed, in the long run you'll save hundreds by not booking two rooms.

✔ **Take rooms that aren't "en suite":** Rooms without a bathroom are cheaper. Sharing a bathroom is a small sacrifice when it comes down to saving money. And it's not going to detract from your trip. Group hostel rooms are even cheaper. (See Chapter 8.)

✔ **Check out self-catering accommodations:** By renting these apartments or houses for a week or more you can save money overall on accommodations (especially if you're traveling with a group) and on food, because you'll be able to prepare your own meals in the kitchen. (See Chapter 8.)

✔ **Take advantage of free breakfasts:** Most accommodations include a free Irish breakfast, so don't oversleep. If you have a big breakfast and then wait to have a late lunch or early dinner, you'll save the cost of a meal a day. If the meal is buffet-style, stash away a piece of fruit for an afternoon snack.

✔ **Have the same meal for less money:** If you have a late lunch at a nice restaurant and have a small dinner later, your wallet and stomach will thank you. Lunch menus often offer the same food as on the dinner menu, but the prices are much less expensive — for the same food.

✔ **Look before you tip:** Many restaurants already add a service fee (gratuity) onto the bill. Always look first. Otherwise you may pay a double tip by mistake.

Three Corners You Should NOT Cut

Now that you know how to save a lot of money on your vacation, here's how we think you should spend it. These are the three most important things you can invest your hard-earned cash in to ensure you have a great trip.

- ✔ **Don't skip sightseeing:** The sights are what you came for. If £3 seems like a lot for the Blarney Castle and Stone, remember that this is something you'll wish you had done when you're back home and everyone keeps asking you, "Did you see this? Did you do that?"

- ✔ **Don't trade money for time:** Maximizing time is essential, so don't wait hours for a cheaper bus when the more expensive one is leaving now. For example, if it costs a little more to fly from England rather than come by ferry, you need to weigh that against the fact that the ferry can take all day and the plane takes an hour. It just might not be worth saving a few bucks when you're losing a few hours.

- ✔ **Invest in good shoes:** Whether you like to walk or not, you'll be doing a good bit of it once you're there. So don't bring a pair of cheap sneaks or straight-from-the-box dress shoes and just figure you'll brave the blisters. Go for comfortable and sturdy. And watch out for sandals — they may seem comfy at first, but after ten hours you'll have strap sores that kill!

Chapter 5

Tips for Travelers with Special Needs

* *

In This Chapter

▶ Sightseeing with your family

▶ Discovering senior and student discounts

▶ Navigating Ireland for gay and lesbian travelers

▶ Finding vegetarian restaurants and meals

* *

*W*hile every traveler has different needs, some special cases — families with kids, vegetarians, people with disabilities, senior citizens, and gay and lesbian travelers, for instance — are common enough that special travel services around the world have been set up just for them. Additionally, each country holds special challenges for some people. In this chapter we run through some services, give some tips, and note some challenges of travel in Ireland.

Family Planning: Tips on Traveling with Kids

Ah, the Family Vacation. A rite of passage for many households, but one that holds the lurking possibility of becoming a National Lampoon movie. Fear not, adventurous parents: Taking the family to Ireland can be as pleasant a trip as if it were your honeymoon. But you have to lay the groundwork.

The first thing you may notice while traveling in Ireland with children in tow is that you're not alone. Plenty of people make Ireland a family vacation destination each year. Ireland is a kid-friendly place, as it has to be — you know what they say about Irish Catholics and big families.

Throughout this book, we point out the places where kids are not only welcome, but also where they enjoy themselves most. We let you know restaurants that are kid-friendly, and point you to the attractions that keep them *oohing* and *ahhing* all day. (Moms and Dads: It's okay if you like this stuff, too.)

Identifying hints and special services for families

Before liftoff, you should take care of a few preliminaries that help ensure a peaceful trip. First, even if your children are old enough to pack for themselves, check what they've packed anyway. If they've never been to Ireland, they can't know the clothes necessary for the weather (see the section on climate in Chapter 2). Also, make sure they don't overdo the packing. Even if they're the ones who presumably will carry their bags, you know they can guilt you into lugging those bags for them. Think of it as lower-back self-preservation.

Bring a few toys for younger children, but nothing that you can't replace upon return. Also, you don't want them paying more attention to an action figure than to the sights you've traveled so far to see, so don't go overboard.

Puzzles and car games are great for when the scenery from the back window isn't sufficiently engaging. These, as well as a deck of cards, also work well when children are waiting for the food to come at a restaurant. When the place isn't too fancy, we also bide the time waiting for dinner with a small travel chessboard. (Guess you don't actually have to have kids to appreciate this section!)

 Keep in mind that most attractions offer reduced fares for children and occasionally so does public transportation. And most have family group prices (usually for two adults and two or three children), even for attractions that don't seem to be family-oriented. Be sure to ask. (See more money-saving tips in Chapter 4.)

When you book your flight, let the ticket agent know the age of your children. Some airlines offer child-companion fares and have a special kids' menu upon request. Flight attendants are usually happy to warm up baby food and milk if you ask.

Car rental companies provide necessary car seats, and all vehicles have rear seatbelts. The law requires that children are buckled in the front and back seats.

 If your kids will be bunking in a room with you along the way, you may be able to add an extra cot for a child at a small additional cost. Check with the concierge or manager at your hotel, guesthouse, or B&B.

Parents who want to see the sights alone or have a night on the town will be in search of a *creche* (pronounced *cresh*). This is the Irish term for day care. (And you thought it was some kind of arts and crafts project.) You can find them in some hotels, for when you need a break. (You do have to pay for the service.) Also, hotels, guesthouses, and some B&Bs have a babysitter list at their fingertips, so parents have every reason to head out and kick up their heels for an evening.

Publications for family travelers

For more specific information and advice on traveling with families, contact **Travel With Your Children (TWCH)**, (☎ 212-206-0688) for an info packet. Six times a year, TWCH also publishes *Family Travel Times*. Subscriptions ($39 a year) include a weekly Wednesday call-in service where you can talk to an expert who has traveled the world with her kids. A free publication list and a sample issue are available by calling ☎ 888-822-4388 or visiting the Web site at www.familytraveltimes.com.

A few books geared specifically toward traveling with little ones are also available. Most concentrate on the United States, but two, *Family Travel* (Lanier Publishing International) and *How to Take Great Trips with Your Kids* (The Harvard Common Press), are full of good general advice that applies to traveling anywhere. Another reliable tome with a worldwide focus is *Adventuring with Children* (Foghorn Press).

A World of Possibility: Travel Advice for Savvy Seniors

The worldwide travel market has never been more open to senior citizens. With fantastic discounts available for seniors on almost every aspect of travel, you can hardly find a reason not to pack up and get out there. Whether you always wanted to go to Ireland or you picked your destination on a lark, there's no time like the present.

Discovering how to get travel discounts

When booking your flight and rental car, remember to ask about senior discounts. In addition, some hotel chains and rental car companies offer discounts for being a member of **AARP (American Association of Retired Persons)**. Call the AARP (☎ 800-424-3410) for information on Ireland in particular.

Seniors will find many discounts after they actually get to Ireland as well, typically 10 percent at attractions and theaters, unless otherwise posted.

Publications for senior travelers

The **Irish Tourist Board** (☎ 800-223-6470 in the United States; Internet: www.ireland.travel.ie) publishes a list of reduced-rate hotel packages, usually restricted to off-peak months in the fall and spring, and also puts out a smaller version of its *Discover Ireland* magazine called *Golden Holidays,* which lists premier accommodations across Ireland that offer special, inclusive price breaks for seniors. You can get this list at any Irish Tourist Board office.

American tour operators that specialize in senior travel programs include **CIE Tours** (☎ 800-CIE-TOUR), which gives discounts on select tours for persons over 55; **SAGA Tours** (☎ 800-343-0273); **Grand Circle Travel** (☎ 800-221-2610); and **Road Scholar Tours** (☎ 800- 621-2151). **Elder Hostel** (☎ 877-426-8056; Internet: www.elderhostel.org) has two- and three-week comprehensive educational programs for anyone over 55, and will send you a free catalog of its tours.

Simple Suggestions for Travelers with Disabilities

These days, sensitivity to persons with disabilities extends to most of the world's best-loved travel destinations. So, generally speaking, a physical impairment shouldn't stop anyone from traipsing the globe. Specifically, getting around Ireland and having a great time won't be too difficult.

Ireland has accessibility regulations for public areas, though they're not as comprehensive as in the United States. Most sidewalks have ramps, and many accommodations are wheelchair accessible. Getting around in cities and towns won't be hard, but Ireland is an old country, and many of its more popular attractions prove it. Not every museum has closed captions for video presentations, and not every castle has an entrance ramp. The fitness center we belonged to in Dublin, for example, has a handicapped toilet in the lobby — but you have to go up several stairs to get there! Calling ahead for attractions (and for B&Bs, many of which aren't disability friendly) is always a good idea, but you can feel fairly confident that most restaurants and newer hotels are entirely accessible.

Discovering tips and services for travelers with disabilities

Wheelchairs for travelers in Ireland are available from the **Irish Wheelchair Association** (☎ 01-833-8241) at the cost of £20 ($29.60) a week. It has offices in Dublin, Kilkenny, Cork, Limerick, and Galway.

Ireland tours and vacation planning geared specifically toward the disabled are available through **Grimes Travel** (☎ 800-937-9767; Internet: www.grimestravel.com). You can also point your Internet browser to www.access-able.com if you're looking for a travel agent who offers tours or can plan trips for travelers with disabilities. Hands down, it's the best source for disabled travelers. This user-friendly site also provides relay and voice numbers for hotels, airlines, and car-rental companies, as well as links to accessible accommodations, attractions, transportation, and tours; local medical resources and equipment repairers; and much more.

Directions Unlimited (☎ 800-533-5343) and **The Guided Tour, Inc.**
(☎ 215-782-1370), both conduct annual trips to Ireland for mentally
challenged travelers.

Publications for travelers with disabilities

For further information, the Access Department of the **National
Rehabilitation Board,** 24/25 Clyde Rd., Dublin 4 (☎ 01-68-4181; Fax:
01-60-9935), has free, comprehensive guides for accommodations,
restaurants, attractions, and even pubs with wheelchair accessibility in
the Republic. In the North, the **Disability Action's** information center
(☎ 028-9032-2504) offers advice over the phone.

The **American Foundation for the Blind** (☎ 800-232-5463) offers specific travel advice for the seeing-impaired, including information on
bringing a seeing-eye dog into Ireland. And you can obtain a copy of
its publication *Air Transportation of Handicapped Persons* by writing to
Free Advisory Circular No. AC12032, Distribution Unit, U.S. Department
of Transportation, Publications Division, M-4332, Washington, DC
20590.

Making a Shoestring Budget Work: Help for Students

Having been starving college students ourselves once, we thoroughly
understand your situation. Also, we're inclined to congratulate you on
not shying away from what we think is a rite of passage — traveling
when you're young!

The biggest mistake potential travelers make is assuming that globe-
trotting is too expensive. Obviously, for some young people this is true,
but luckily for you we're not the only people to respect the plight of fis-
cally challenged students. An entire market out there is devoted to
making travel accessible to you.

Council Travel, under **CIEE (Council on International Educational
Exchange),** is a great source for cheap flights, reasonably priced traveler's insurance, and international student and youth identification
cards that get you discounts at many attractions in Ireland. You don't
need to bring photos of yourself; they take them at the office. And you
don't even have to be a student to use CIEE — it has the same fares
available for anyone 25 years and younger, as well as for teachers,
as long as you have an ID card to prove it. Call ☎ 800-2-COUNCIL or
access www.ciee.org for information, flight bookings, and the nearest
location to you. The Canadian version of CIEE is **Travel CUTS**
(☎ 416- 979-2406).

While you're in Ireland, you can look up Council Travel's partner organization, called **usit NOW**, with offices open year-round in Dublin (☎ 01-602-1600), Cork (☎ 021-27-0900), Galway (☎ 091-56-5244), Limerick (☎ 061-41-5064), Waterford (☎ 051-87-2601), and Belfast (☎ 028-9032-4073). If you lose your ticket or need to change your departure date, these offices can and will happily help you. The CIEE toll-free number for Traveler's Assistance is ☎ 877-370-ISIC. Outside the United States, you can call ☎ 715-342-4104 collect.

The Web site www.collegetravelers.com is another great online resource for young travelers.

A travel save stamp from usit NOW gives members a 50 percent discount on Irish Rail and Irish Ferries, as well as discounts on Bus Eireann in the South and Ulsterbus in the North. Other discounts include restaurants, accommodations, and theater. Pop into one of the offices previously mentioned for the free stamp.

Getting an international student, teacher, or youth ID is worth the money. Even if you don't see a sign advertising student discounts, always ask. In some cases the savings cover more than half of the ordinary admission!

Recommendations for Gay and Lesbian Travelers

While not necessarily the Miami Beach or San Francisco of Europe, Ireland is a place where gays and lesbians feel welcomed. This attitude stems mainly from how tolerant the people are in general, rather than because Ireland is exceptionally progressive when it comes to homosexuality. Actually, homosexuality was illegal in Ireland until 1993! (And in Northern Ireland until 1982.) If that attitude seems dated, just remember: Divorce was also against the law until the early 1990s.

Today, Dublin has a pretty thriving gay scene. From bars to hotels to magazines, the city offers a niche for the homosexual market. Dublin is where you can find the most gay-friendly places and where the gay nightlife is most active.

As for the rest of the country, again, it's not a place renowned for progressively fostering the homosexual life. Smaller towns and villages won't have a gay club — you can count on that. But then again, you're probably not going to Ireland for the happening nightlife, either.

Sharing tips and travel services for gay and lesbian travelers

The International Gay & Lesbian Travel Association (IGLTA), (☎ 800-448-8550 or 954-776-2626; Fax: 954-776-3303; Internet: www.iglta.org), links up travelers with the appropriate gay-friendly service organization or tour specialist. With around 1,200 members, IGLTA offers quarterly newsletters, marketing mailings, and a membership directory that's updated quarterly. Membership often includes gay or lesbian businesses but is also open to individuals for $150 yearly, plus a $100 initial fee for new members. Members are informed of gay and gay-friendly hoteliers, tour operators, and airline and cruise line representatives. Contact the IGLTA for a list of its member agencies, which are tied into IGLTA's information resources.

Travel agencies geared to both gay men and lesbians include **Family Abroad** (☎ 800-999-5500 or 212-459-1800) and **Yellowbrick Road** (☎ 800-476-5466). **Above and Beyond Tours** (☎ 800-397-2681) is primarily geared toward gay men.

The following organizations (all located in Dublin) offer advice and progressive locations:

- ✔ **Gay Switchboard** (☎ 01-872-1055): Open Sunday through Friday 8:00 p.m. to 10:00 p.m., Saturday 3:30 p.m. to 6:00 p.m.

- ✔ **LEA:** A lesbian organization located at 5 Capel St., Dublin 1. Access the organization's Web site at http://indigo.ie/~leanow. You can also call (☎ 01-872-0460) or E-mail leanow@indigo.ie.

- ✔ **Outhouse** (6 South William St., Dublin 2. ☎ 01-670-6377; E-mail: outhouse@indigo.ie; Internet: http://indigo.ie/~outhouse): A good lesbian and gay community resource center in the city. It also has a cafe.

Publications for gay and lesbian travelers

We know of two good, biannual English-language gay guidebooks, both focused on gay men but including information for lesbians as well. You can get the *Odysseus* or *Spartacus International Gay Guide* from most gay and lesbian bookstores and often in the large chain stores as well. Or you can order them from **Giovanni's Room** (☎ 215-923-2960), or **A Different Light Bookstore** (☎ 800-343-4002 or 212-989-4850). Both lesbians and gay men may want to pick up a copy of *Gay Travel A to Z* ($16). The **Ferrari Guides** (Internet: www.q-net.com) is yet another comprehensive series of gay and lesbian guidebooks.

Out and About, 8 W. 19th St. #401, New York, NY 10011 (☎ 800-929-2268 or 212-645-6922), offers guidebooks and a monthly newsletter packed with good information on the global gay and lesbian scene. A year's subscription to the newsletter costs $49. **Our World,** 1104 North Nova Rd., Suite 251, Daytona Beach, FL 32117 (☎ 904-441-5367), is a slicker monthly magazine promoting and highlighting travel bargains and opportunities. Annual subscription rates are $35 in the United States, $45 outside the United States.

For more information while you're in Ireland, the *Gay Community Newspaper* is a free monthly publication mostly found in Dublin and geared toward both gays and lesbians. The stylish glossy magazine

In Dublin has a section devoted to gay community news and events. It is published twice a month and is available on most magazine racks throughout the country.

Knowing where to find lesbian/gay bed-and-breakfasts

In Cork, **Roman House,** 3 St. John's Terrace, Upper John St., Cork City (☎ **021-50-3606**), caters to lesbians and gay men and is centrally located in the city. Double rooms run £36 ($53.28).

Dublin has several good gay- and/or lesbian-friendly lodgings. **Horse & Carriage Guest Hotel,** 15 Aungier St., Dublin 2 (☎ **01-478-3537;** Fax: 01-478-4010), caters to lesbians and gay men and is located five minutes from Grafton Street and Saint Stephen's Green. A room costs run £55 ($81.40) for a double; Sunday through Thursday £40 ($59.20); £70 ($103.60) for an extra large room; and £90 ($134.10) on weekends. **Inn on the Liffey,** 21 Upper Ormond Quay, Dublin 7 (☎ **01-677-0828** or 01-872-4172; Fax: 872-4165; E-mail: plat@clubi.ie), caters to lesbians and gay men. A double rooms cost £45 ($66.60) midweek and £55 ($81.40) on the weekends.

In Galway, **The Centurion,** 20 Lower Abbeygate St. (☎ **091-561-957**), is located in the heart of Galway and caters to gay men. Rooms go for £35 ($51.80) per double.

Advice for Minorities

Racism isn't a major problem in Ireland, but the country is just beginning to get minority immigration. Some minority tourists may get unfriendly looks if the natives perceive them to be refugees, which is a growing source of tension in Ireland. Racial slurs are not common. Just remember that the ignorance of a few does not represent the sentiments of the whole. Currently no national statistics on race- or gender-related crime are available.

Cautions for Women Traveling Alone

In general, Ireland is a safer place than most for women traveling alone, but be careful not to be lulled into a false sense of security. To read more, we recommend the book *Safety and Security for Women Who Travel,* by Sheila Swan Laufer and Peter Laufer (Travelers' Tales Guides), which caters to the concerns of the female traveler. It's well worth the $12.95 cover price.

Ideas for Vegetarians

Any place that loves blood pudding and rashers as much as Ireland does is enough to frighten a vegetarian, but you will not go hungry on your trip, we promise. Surprisingly, a huge variety of meatless meals are to be had. We've included some good vegetarian restaurants in this guide (yes, Ireland has some!), and you can rest assured that most restaurants in general have at least a couple of veggie selections.

A traditional Irish breakfast is a pretty meaty event, and it's nearly always included in the cost of a room. You can still partake in this element of true Irish culture by asking your host to hold the meat and lavish you with eggs, beans, toast, fried tomatoes, potatoes, and homemade breads and goodies. You can count on a selection of cereals and fruit, too.

Foods in stores carry labels marked by a green leaf icon and the phrase "suitable for vegetarians." And something that may really shock you is the amount of vegetarian fast food! McDonald's and Burger King have a veggie burger, and the King has a delicious spicy bean burger. **Abrakebabra,** the country's own kebab chain, has *falafels* (a spicy mixture of ground vegetables formed into balls or patties and then fried) and other vegetarian options. *Chippers* (take-outs) usually offer veggie burgers too, plus things like *salad burgers* (a hamburger without the meat). Strict vegetarians may want to pass on chips — they're fried in the same oil as everything else.

Chapter 6

Getting to Ireland

● ●

In This Chapter

▶ Booking your flight through a travel agent

▶ Finding a package tour or traveling with a group tour

▶ Locating your flight through a consolidator or over the Internet

▶ Connecting through the U.K. or taking a ferry to Ireland

● ●

Sightseeing, souvenir shopping, and stuffing yourself silly are the easy parts of traveling. Tougher, though, is making all the plans to get you there and get around. Lucky for you there are several resources to get you through the rigmarole of travel planning. This chapter outlines the advantages and disadvantages of bargain airfares, travel agents, and package tours.

If you're traveling with children, let your travel agent know their ages when you're booking your flight. Some airlines offer child-companion fares and have a special kids' menu upon request.

Travel Agent: Friend or Foe?

A good travel agent is like a good mechanic or a good plumber: hard to find, but invaluable when you have the right one. And the best way to find a good travel agent is the same way you found that good plumber or mechanic — word of mouth. The best travel agents can tell you how much time you should budget for each destination; find a cheap flight that doesn't require you to change planes three times on your way to Ireland; get you a hotel room with a view for the same price as a lesser room; arrange for a competitively priced rental car; and even give recommendations on local restaurants. Travel agents work on commission. The good news is that you don't pay the commission — the airlines, hotels, and tour companies do. The bad news is that unscrupulous travel agents often try to persuade you to book the vacations that land them the most money in commissions.

In the past two years, some airlines and resorts have begun limiting or eliminating travel agent commissions altogether. The immediate result has been that travel agents don't bother booking these services unless the customer specifically requests them. But some travel industry analysts predict that if other airlines and accommodations follow suit, travel agents will have to start charging customers for their services.

Finding a travel agent you can trust

Here are a few hints for tracking down the travel agent of your dreams:

✔ **Ask among friends.** Your best bet, of course, is a personal referral. Not only is this agent already a relatively proven commodity,
but he or she's extra-likely to treat you well, knowing that he or
she may lose two customers — not just one — if your vacation
gets screwed up.

✔ **Go with what you know.** If you're pleased with the service you
get from the agency that books business travel at your workplace,
ask if it books personal travel, too. Again, this option is another
relatively proven commodity — one that has a vested interest in
not screwing up (even if you are just one pea in a really big corporate pod). Also, because business travel tends to be booked in
volume, many of the agencies that specialize in this kind of business have access to discounts that they can extend to you for
your personal travel, too.

✔ **Go to the travel agent source.** If you can't get a good personal or
business referral, contact the **American Society of Travel Agents**
(Internet: www.astanet.com), the world's largest association of
travel professionals, which can refer you to one of its local member
agents. ASTA asks all its member agents to uphold a code of ethics,
and has its own consumer affairs department to handle complaints
and help travelers mediate disputes with ASTA member agencies —
which doesn't guarantee anything, but does offer you a measure of
consumer protection in case something goes wrong.

More tips for choosing a travel agent

Once you decide to seek the services of a travel agent, keep the following tips in mind:

✔ Look for an agent who specializes in planning vacations to your
destination.

✔ Choose an agent who has been in business for a while and who
has an established client base.

✔ Consider everything about the agent, from the appearance of
his or her office to the agent's willingness to listen and answer
questions.

Remember: The best agents want to establish a long-term relationship
with a client, not make just one sale.

Making your travel agent work for you

To make sure you get the most out of your travel agent, do a little
homework. Read about your destination (you've already made a sound
decision by buying this book) and pick some accommodations and

attractions that you think you'll like. If you have access to the Internet, check airfare and package prices on the Web to get an idea of what things cost.

After you've made some basic decisions and feel appropriately armed with information, take your book and Web information to the travel agent and ask him or her to make the arrangements for you. Because they have access to more resources than even the most complete Web site, travel agents should be able to get you a better price than you can get by yourself. And they can issue your tickets and vouchers immediately. If they can't get you into the hotel or resort of your choice, they can recommend an alternative, and you can look for an objective review in your book right then and there.

 If you don't feel that you're getting what you need from a particular travel agent — or you don't think he or she knows enough about Ireland to plan your trip appropriately — move on to one who makes you feel more comfortable.

The Ins and Outs of Package Tours

Package tours are a way to buy your airfare, accommodations, and other elements of your trip (such as car rentals and airport transfers) at the same time — kind of like one-stop vacation shopping.

For popular destinations like Ireland, packages can be a smart way to go because they save you a ton of money. In many cases, a package that includes airfare, hotel, and transportation to and from the airport costs you less than just the hotel alone if you booked it yourself. Packages are sold in bulk to tour operators, who resell them to the public. Package tours are kind of like purchasing your vacation at a buy-in-bulk store, except that the tour operator buys the 1,000-count box of garbage bags and resells them ten at a time at a cost that undercuts what you'd pay at your average neighborhood supermarket.

Understanding the limitations

Packages vary as much as garbage bags, too. You almost always save money, but packages do have limitations, such as a small selection of hotels or a fixed itinerary. Some packages offer a better class of hotels than others. Some offer flights on scheduled airlines, while others book charters. In some packages, your choices of travel days may be limited. Some packages let you choose between escorted vacations and independent vacations; others allow you to add on a few guided excursions or escorted day trips (also at prices lower than if you booked them yourself) without booking an entirely escorted tour.

Every destination — including Ireland — usually has one or two packagers that tend to be better than the rest because they buy in even bigger bulk than the others. Not only can that mean better prices, but also more choices — a packager that just dabbles in Ireland may have only a half-dozen hotels or so for you to choose from, while a packager that focuses much (or all) of its energy on Irish vacations may have dozens of hotels for you to choose from, with a good selection in every price range.

Telling the deals from the duds

When you start delving into packages, you will find that you have plenty to choose from; in fact, the choices may even overwhelm you — but you don't have to let them. Here are a few tips to help you tell one from the other and figure out which package is right for you.

- ✔ **Read this book.** Do a little homework; read up on Ireland. Decide what cities, towns, and attractions you want to visit, and pick some accommodations that you think you may like. Compare the *rack rates* (the published "sticker prices") that we list to the discounted rates being offered by the packagers to see what kinds of deals they're offering — verify if you're actually being offered a substantial savings. And remember: Don't just compare packagers to one another; compare the prices that packagers offer on similar deals. The amount you save depends on the deal; most packagers can offer bigger savings on some deals than others.

- ✔ **Read the fine print.** When you compare packages, make sure you know exactly what's included in the price you're being quoted, and what's not. Some packagers include extra discounts on restaurants and activities, while others don't even include airfare.

- ✔ **Know what you're getting yourself into — and if you can get yourself out of it.** Before you commit to a package, make sure you know how much flexibility you have. Some packagers require iron-clad commitments, while others charge minimal fees for changes or cancellations. Ask a lot of questions: What's the cancellation policy if my kid gets sick at the last minute, and we can't go? What if we have to adjust our vacation schedule — can we do that?

- ✔ **Use your best judgment.** If a package appears to be too good to be true, it probably is. Go with a reputable firm with a proven track record. This is where your travel agent can come in handy; he or she should be knowledgeable about different packagers, the deals they offer, and the general rate of satisfaction among their customers. If the agent doesn't seem savvy, take your business elsewhere.

Picking a peck of pickled packagers

The best place to start looking for packagers is the travel section of your local Sunday newspaper. Also check the ads in the back of national travel magazines like *Travel + Leisure, National Geographic Traveler, Travel Holiday,* and *Condé Nast Traveler.* Then call a few package-tour companies and ask them to send you their brochures.

For one-stop shopping on the Web, go to www.vacationpackager.com, an incredibly extensive Web search engine where you can link up with hundreds of different package tour operators and custom design your very own package.

The following operators offer the best package tours in the business, with the most options and comprehensive tours. Among them, we believe Moore and CIE to be the best.

- **CIE Tours International** (☎ **800-CIE-TOUR;** Internet: www. cietours. com): CIE does tours of Ireland and the U.K., and has 14 Irish-only escorted tours and many more that combine Ireland with Britain or Scotland. Its Web site has a helpful tour index, and each package link clicks to price range, description, itinerary, discounts for seniors, or early booking, and so on. It has all varieties of tours: rail and bus, escorted, self-drive, B&Bs, and more.

- **Grimes Travel** (☎ **800-937-9767** or 914-375-3068; Fax: 914-375-3901; Internet: www.grimestravel.com): Grimes organizes airlines, car, hotels, and all the rest, and offers very well-priced specials. It mostly handles Ireland but also has links to other destinations.

- **Brendan Tours** (☎ **800-421-8446;** Internet: www.brendantours. com): Based out of Dublin, Brendan Tours offers packages all over the world but is most proud of its Irish tours. It has three categories: Escorted, Self-Drive, and Rent an Irish Home.

- **Brian Moore International Tours** (☎ **800-982-2299**): Brian Moore Tours has about a dozen escorted tours in different geographic areas, as well as self-drive tours and independent customized travel. It's based out of Boston and specializes in Scotland and Ireland.

- **Sceptre Tours** (☎ **800-221-0924;** E-mail: infosales@ sceptretours.com; Internet: www.sceptretours.com): Sceptre custom tailors its inclusive Irish tours for different interests, and has a specific one for golfers. It requires you to specify lengths of stay and other info to find the tour that is right for you, and it also finds weekly specials.

Buying packages through the airlines

Another good resource is the airlines themselves, which often package their flights together with accommodations. Disreputable packagers are uncommon, but they do exist, so buying your package through an airline is a safer bet — you can be pretty sure that the company will still be in business when your departure date arrives. Prices are usually comparable to what you get from other packagers.

The newest of the tours offered by **Aer Lingus "Discover Ireland" Vacations** (☎ **800-223-6537;** Internet: www.aerlingus.ie) is the "Go-As-You-Please" package, which allows you to pick and choose your destinations.

Although you can book most airline packages directly with the airline itself, your local travel agent can also do it for you. No matter who does the booking, be sure to give the airline your frequent-flier account number. Most airline packages reward you with miles not only based on the flight, but on all the dollars you're spending — which can really add up and earn you credit toward your next vacation.

When escorted-tour brochures say "double occupancy," they almost always mean a room with twin beds rather than a queen- or king-size bed. If you're committed to cuddling with your honey under the covers, be sure you're familiar with your operator's policy before you commit to a tour.

Touring by Bus: Escorted Tours

Some people love escorted tours. They free travelers from spending a great deal of time behind the wheel; they take care of all the details; and they tell you what to expect at each attraction. You know your costs up front, and you can get to the maximum number of sights in the minimum amount of time with the least amount of hassle.

You have plenty of reasons to take an escorted tour: If your mobility is limited, if you like the ease and security of an escorted tour, or if you're just the sociable type who likes to travel in a group, an escorted tour may be for you.

Asking the escorts: Important questions to keep in mind

If you do choose an escorted tour, ask a few simple questions before you buy:

- ✔ **What's the cancellation policy?** Do you have to put a deposit down? Can they cancel the trip if they don't get enough people? How late can you cancel if you are unable to go? When do you pay? Do you get a refund if you cancel? If they cancel?

- ✔ **How jam-packed is the schedule?** Do they try to fit 25 hours into a 24-hour day, or is there ample time for relaxing, shopping, or hitting the pubs? Will you have to get up at 7:00 a.m. every day to catch the bus?

- ✔ **How big is the group?** The smaller the group, the more flexible the tour and the less time you spend waiting for people to get on and off the bus. Tour operators may not know the exact size of the group until everybody has made their reservations, but they should be able to give you a rough estimate. Some tour companies have a minimum group size and cancel the tour if they don't book enough people.

- ✔ **What's included?** Don't assume anything. You may have to pay to get yourself to and from the airport. Or a box lunch may be included in an excursion but drinks may cost extra. Can you opt out of certain activities, or does the bus leave once a day, with no exceptions? Are all your meals planned in advance? Can you choose your entree at dinner, or does everybody get the same chicken cutlet?

If you choose an escorted tour, think strongly about purchasing travel insurance, especially if the tour operator asks to you pay up front. But don't buy insurance from the tour operator! If they don't fulfill their obligation to provide you with the vacation you've paid for, you have no reason to think they'll fulfill their insurance obligations either. Buy travel insurance through an independent agency. (See Chapter 10 for recommended agencies and other insurance tips.)

Hopping on the magic bus

If you do decide to join an escorted tour, there are lots to choose from. Most of them are priced all-inclusively, which means you pay one price and don't have to worry about paying your hotel bill or tipping your bus driver when you get there. When you're considering prices, however, always remember to check whether your airfare is included — some tour operators include it with their quoted prices, and some don't.

For details on the first three companies listed in this section, see "Picking a peck of pickled packagers," earlier in this chapter.

- ✔ **CIE Tours International** (☎ **800-CIE-TOUR;** Internet: www. cietours.com).

- ✔ **Brian Moore International Tours** (☎ **800-982-2299**).

- ✔ **Sceptre Tours** (☎ **800-221-0924;** E-mail: infosales@ sceptretours.com, Internet: www.sceptretours.com).

- ✔ **Globus** (☎ **800-221-0090;** Internet: www.globusandcosmos.com). A first-class worldwide tour company, Globus has four or five tours of Ireland, each of which is rather comprehensive. You can book a whole package (including airfare, meals, hotels, and so on) or find your own cheap plane ticket (good for people racking up frequent-flier miles) and just book the bus-tour part. The lengths of trips run from 8 to 14 days. You have to book these tours through a travel agent, and because the tours all visit different sites, you should be specific with your agent about what you want to see. Price ranges from $950 to $1,400.

- ✔ **Cosmos** (☎ **800-221-0090;** Internet: www.globusandcosmos.com). The budget arm of Globus offers downscale versions of the Globus trips (though there isn't so great a price difference), with a tour guide and motorcoach on hand at all times.

You can book any of these guided tours directly through your travel agent. The companies themselves can refer you to a local agent if they can't book your tour directly.

The Independent Traveler: Making Your Own Arrangements

Okay, so you're a John Wayne type. You want to get out in front of that wagon train, whip your hat in the air, and hit the trail. In modern terms, that attitude means foregoing both package tours and escorted tours and traveling with total independence. The first step is booking your flight over, so in this section we give you a short course in flying to Ireland.

Knowing who flies where

There was a time when Aer Lingus only flew from New York to Shannon. But growing demand for flights to the Emerald Isle has increased the competition and options. (By the way, "Aer Lingus" is Gaelic for — guess what? — "airline.") Today, four U.S. airlines fly to Shannon and Dublin airports and many more fly to England, where you can catch a connecting flight to Ireland (see "Finding Other Ways to Get There," later in this chapter). Calling more than one airline to compare prices is a good idea.

Here's a list of the major airlines that fly to Ireland from the United States.

- **Aer Lingus** (☎ 800-223-6537; Internet: www.aerlingus.ie/): Out of Boston to Shannon, Dublin, and Belfast; out of Chicago to Shannon, and Dublin; and out of New York to Shannon, Dublin, and Belfast.

- **Delta Air Lines** (☎ 800-241-4141; Internet: www.delta-air.com/home/index.jsp): Out of Atlanta to Shannon and Dublin; out of New York to Shannon and Dublin.

- **Continental** (☎ 800-231-0856; Internet: http://cooltravelassistant.com): Out of Newark, NJ (just outside New York) to Shannon and Dublin.

- **American Airlines** (☎ 800-433-7300; Internet: www.americanairlines.com/): Out of New York to Shannon.

Unfortunately, no airlines fly directly from Canada, Australia, or New Zealand to Ireland. Canadian travelers can connect through Boston, New York, or Chicago or England (see "Connecting through Britain"). All flights on international airlines from Australia and New Zealand go through England, requiring a connecting flight to Dublin, Shannon, or Belfast.

Picking an arrival airport

Your options for international airports in the Republic of Ireland are **Dublin Airport** (☎ 01-844-4900), located 9 miles outside Dublin on the East Coast of Ireland (via the N1), and **Shannon Airport** (☎ 061-47-1444), located 15 miles west of Limerick, on the West Coast (via the N18).

If you plan to stay in Northern Ireland, **Belfast** also has an international airport, located 19 miles west of the city (☎ 028-9448-4848).

In general, they're all perfectly fine airports, and no option outweighs the other in terms of niceness or proximity to a city. For more pointers on planning your itinerary, which is the main factor in deciding which airport to choose, see Chapter 3.

Getting the best airfare

Airfares represent capitalism in its purest form. Passengers sitting right next to each other on an airplane rarely pay the same fare. Rather, they pay what the market bears on the day they book their flight.

Passengers who can book their ticket long in advance, who don't mind staying over Saturday night, and who are willing to travel on a Tuesday, Wednesday, or Thursday pay the lowest fares, usually a fraction of the full fare — what's known in industry lingo as an *APEX* (Advance-Purchase Excursion) fare.

The general rule of thumb about APEX fares is this: As the ticket gets cheaper, the restrictions get tighter. If you luck into a sale fare at the height of the high season, don't be surprised if the schedule isn't changeable. Period.

So when you're quoted a fare, make sure you know exactly what the restrictions are before you commit. And if the restrictions are tight, don't buy until you're sure the schedule you've booked works for you. Otherwise, if your boss doesn't approve your vacation schedule, or your kid comes down with the flu at exactly the wrong moment, you may be stuck with some expensive scrap paper you used to call an airline ticket.

The airlines also periodically hold sales in which they lower the prices on their most popular routes. These fares have advance-purchase requirements and date-of-travel restrictions, but you can't beat the price. So keep your eyes peeled for a sale as you plan your vacation, and pounce if you get wind of one. But don't hold your breath if you travel in the high season; you almost never see a sale around the peak vacation months of July and August, and forget Christmas altogether.

Booking through bucket shops

Consolidators (also known as *bucket shops,* for reasons no one can figure out) buy tickets directly from the airlines and resell them at lower prices. You see their ads in the small boxes at the bottom of the page in your Sunday newspaper's travel section. There's nothing shady about the reliable ones — basically, they get discounts for buying in bulk and pass some of the savings on to you. But be careful and make sure you know what you're getting before you give anybody your credit card number; if a fare sounds too good to be true, it probably is.

We know what you're thinking: If a consolidator can save me 200 bucks on the same flight my travel agent can get me, why haven't consolidators taken over the travel world? Here's the catch: Using a consolidator can be very time-consuming. When you finally get past the busy signal, plan to be on hold for a good while before you get to an agent — and then they may just write down your name and number and take their sweet time getting back to you. And if you want to comparison shop, you have to go through this process a few times. When you finally get through, some consolidators may not even have flights going your way at the moment. That's the price you pay for the great deal you may end up with. Still, using a consolidator is often worth the aggravation; just don't tell your faithful travel agent you're going to the dark side!

Our favorite consolidators are **Cheap Tickets** (☎ **800-377-1000;** Internet: www.cheaptickets.com) and ☎ **1-800-FLY-4-LESS.** We've gotten great deals on a number of occasions from both of these reliable companies. **Council Travel** (☎ **800-226-8624;** Fax: 617-528-2091; Internet: www. ciee.org/) is relatively easy to get through to and has also quoted us very competitive fares. Part of the Council on International Educational Exchange, it has especially good deals for travelers under age 26.

TFI Tours International (☎ **800-745-8000**) also has good fares, though we've found their operators to be less than polite on more than one occasion.

Reserving your tickets online

Another way to find the cheapest fare is by using the Internet. The number of virtual travel agents on the Internet has increased exponentially in recent years. There are too many companies now to mention them all, but a few of the better-respected ones are:

- ✔ **Travelocity** (www.travelocity.com), which includes maps, flights, rooms, cars, packages, a currency converter, weather forecasts, and destination guides featuring updated information on some 260 destinations worldwide.

- ✔ **Microsoft Expedia** (www.expedia.com), which has maps, flights, rooms, cars, and packages.

- ✔ **Yahoo!** (http://travel.yahoo.com/travel). Just enter the dates you want to fly and the cities you want to visit, and the computer looks for the lowest fares.

American Express (http://travel.americanexpress.com/travel/) may be the most comprehensive Internet airline information source and reservations service to date. Some of the site's features are: links to virtually every airline in the world; Internet-only airfare deals posted on one easy-to-scan page; and the best fare-finder on the Web. You can call **American Express** (☎ **800-253-9822** or 650-494-1557) before or after you make your reservation if you have any questions or concerns about what you see on-screen.

Finding Other Ways to Get There

If you're driving from the American West or Midwest, just start heading east on any major freeway, start picking up speed when you hit Ohio, and when you see the ocean, pull back on the steering wheel *hard* and hope for liftoff.

But seriously, folks, you have a couple other ways of getting to Ireland besides flying direct — the most practical of which we discuss in the following sections.

Connecting through Britain

Instead of flying directly into Ireland, you can fly into England and pick up a short connecting flight from there. Many more airlines fly from the United States to England than from the United States to Ireland, so you may be able to find a lower fare. If you plan just right, this flight arrangement can also give you a chance to fit a little trip to England into your travel.

The major airlines that fly from the United States and Canada to England are

- **Air Canada** (☎ 800-776-3000), from Canada only
- **American Airlines** (☎ 800-223-7776)
- **British Airways** (☎ 800-247-9297)
- **Canadian Airlines** (☎ 800-426-7000), from Canada only
- **Continental Airlines** (☎ 800-231-0856)
- **Delta Airlines** (☎ 800-241-4141)
- **Northwest Airlines** (☎ 800-447-4747)
- **TWA** (☎ 800-892-4141)
- **United Airlines** (☎ 800-241-6522)
- **Virgin Atlantic** (☎ 800-862-8621)

Major airlines that fly between England and Ireland are

- **Aer Lingus** (☎ 800-223-6537), from Heathrow and Stanstead
- **British Midland** (☎ 800-788-0555), from Heathrow

Taking ferry service between England and Ireland

Ferries are not the fastest or cheapest way to come to Ireland or Northern Ireland but are still popular because they're a more interesting and relaxing way to travel than by air — getting there becomes part of the adventure. Ferry service to Ireland leaves from the U.K. and France and brings you within striking distance of Cork, Dublin, or Belfast. Length of trip varies from a few hours to overnight. After you arrive, public transportation is readily available from the ferry terminals to Belfast, Dublin, and Cork City.

✔ **Irish Ferries:** Sails from Holyhead (Wales) to Dublin or Pembroke (Wales) to Rosslare. For advance reservations in the United States and Canada, contact the **Scots-American Travel Advisors** (☎ **561-563-2856;** Fax: 561-563-2087; E-mail: info@scotsamerican.com; Internet: www.scotsamerican.com).

✔ **Stena Sealink:** Sails from Holyhead (Wales) to Dun Laoghaire, Fishguard (Wales) to Rosslare, or Stranraer (Scotland) to Belfast. For advance reservations in the United States and Canada, contact the **Britrail Travel International** (☎ **800-677-8585**). HighSpeed Sea Service (HSS) is also available on all three routes.

✔ **Swansea Cork Ferries:** Sails from Swansea (Wales) to Cork. For advance reservations, contact the **Swansea** offices in Cork (☎ **21-27-6000;** Fax: 21-27-5814).

✔ **SeaCat Scotland:** Sails from Stranraer (Scotland) to Belfast. For advance reservations, contact **SeaCat** in Belfast (☎ **01208-81-2508**).

Part II
Ironing Out the Details

The 5th Wave   By Rich Tennant

"This afternoon I want everyone to go online and find all you can about Native American culture, history of the old west, and discount airfares to Ireland for the two weeks I'll be on vacation."

In this part . . .

Now that you have an idea about which parts of Ireland you want to concentrate on, when you want to visit, and how you're going to get there, it's time to take care of the details. For example, you need to figure out how you're going to get around after you arrive, where you're going to stay, what's your best option for carrying money, and so on.

This section gives you all the information you need to plan a successful trip. In Chapter 6 we discuss your options for getting yourself to the Emerald Isle — from travel agents to package tours. In Chapter 7, we give you the pros and cons of all your options for getting around Ireland once you arrive — cars and buses and trains (oh, my!). You also need to figure out where to rest your tired head (and feet) after long days of sightseeing. You can find information on all your options, from hostels to luxury hotels, in Chapter 8. In Chapter 9 we explain the ins and outs of money in the Republic and Northern Ireland, including where to get the best exchange rates. And, in Chapter 10 we cover loose ends that you may want to know about before you go — including how to get a passport, what you should pack, and options for keeping in touch with the folks back home after you're in Ireland.

And rest assured — we show you how to get the most for your money every step of the way.

Chapter 7

Getting around Ireland

● ●

In This Chapter
▶ Renting a car in Ireland
▶ Getting to know Ireland's road signs and driving rules
▶ Traveling through Ireland by bus and train

● ●

Meeny, miney, mo. Once you get to Ireland you have three choices when it comes to getting around: cars, buses, and trains. We recommend renting a car — it's the best way to see the country — but your budget, length of stay, and destination choices could make buses or trains preferable. In this chapter we'll help you make an informed decision.

Seeing Ireland by Car

We think the best way to see Ireland is by car. No timetables, plenty of leg room, and control over the music — what more could you want? Besides, we can guarantee you'll want to pull over at random moments to take in the scenery and snap a few thousand pictures for bragging rights. So, if this sounds like your cuppa' tea, let's move on and focus on how exactly to get those wheels of freedom.

Booking a rental car

In the off-season (between October and March) you should have little difficulty getting a car on short (or no) notice. Booking anything during the summer, however, is a different story. To stay on the safe side, it's a good idea to book anytime from a few weeks to a month in advance. Because prices are bound to increase based on demand, the earlier you book your car, the better your chance of beating the rush.

If you fly into Dublin and plan to stay in the city for two or more days, wait to get a car until you're just about to head out to the countryside. With the public transportation in the city you don't need a car — and with the lack of parking you don't want one either! However, if you're planning to leave town straightaway, or if you fly into Shannon airport, getting the car upon arrival is a good idea. You could even stay in Dublin for a couple days, take a bus to Limerick, and get a car at

Shannon Airport. The biggest thing you want to avoid is paying for a car you're not using.

Cars are due back at the same time you picked them up — if, for example, you get the car at 9:00 a.m., it's due back at 9:00 a.m. If you return the car late you will have to pay for an extra day (or pay an extra charge). With this in mind, figure out ahead of time how long it will take you to get back to the rental agency on the day your car is due. Early afternoon is a good time to pick up a rental car, because pretty much everyplace is drivable in half a day.

A few companies allow you to drop off cars in places other than where you picked them up, and of course there are other pick-up locations than the airports, like Cork, Killarney, and Belfast. Ask about your options and if there are drop-off fees.

If you think you might end up changing your plans, it's better to book your rental car for a shorter amount of time and then extend it from the road with a simple phone call. If you do the opposite — booking the car for a week but bringing it back after only four days, for example — you'll still get your credit card refund, but not anytime soon. We found this out the hard way.

Knowing what kind of car to expect

There are three levels of rental cars: economy (small), compact (medium), and intermediate (large). You might think you want a larger vehicle, but keep in mind that most roads are nail-bitingly narrow, and while winding down a street lined with cars and oncoming traffic you'll appreciate driving a mini-mobile. So, try to get the smallest car you think you'll be comfortable in. Another thought: Smaller is cheaper.

Always expect a stick shift. Unlike the States, where it's standard for rental cars to have an automatic transmission, the standard in Ireland is a manual transmission. You can get an automatic — but it will cost you. Prices vary widely, so if you're going to get an automatic, shop around for the best deal.

Because the driver's side is on the right-hand side of cars in Ireland, the stick shift is controlled by your left hand, not your right. Sounds wacky and hard to do, but we promise you'll get the hang of it in no time.

Air conditioning and unlimited mileage are standard, but a radio isn't, necessarily. To be on the safe side, ask if the car has one. The charge isn't any higher for one with, and you probably don't want to rely on your coriders' musical ability for entertainment between sightseeing stops.

Paying for a rental car

Some companies require a deposit when you make your reservation, generally on a credit card. If you book by phone they might ask for it then; otherwise your credit card will be run through at the rental desk. Don't be shocked if they charge you a gas deposit on your card, too.

Just be sure to fill the tank before drop-off and the deposit will be taken off (good thing, because the deposit is always way higher than a tankful actually costs). And always ask about discounts when you book. Besides obvious big-time groups like AARP and AAA, many companies, both large and small, have corporate accounts with rental companies, and employees can take advantage of this to get a discounted rate. Often you need some sort of proof of affiliation like a business card or pay stub.

Gas, called *petrol* In Ireland, is very costly. You'll notice that the signs at petrol stations advertise prices that seem comparable to home, but those are the prices per litre, not gallon. So in essence you're paying more than four times what you would in the States. Consider this as another reason to get a smaller car: better gas mileage.

Dealing with rental car companies in Ireland

In the following list, we give the biggest, most reputable companies with pick-up and drop-off locations throughout the country.

- ✔ **Murrays Europcar/AutoEurope** (☎ **800-223-5555** in the United States, 800-12-6409 in Australia, 800-44-0722 in New Zealand, or 800-55-8892 or 01-668-1777 in Ireland; Internet: www.europecar.ie). Locations: Dublin City and Airport, Shannon, Belfast Airport, Galway, Waterford, Sligo Airport, Cork Airport, and others.

- ✔ **Budget** (☎ **800-527-0700** from the United States or 01-844-5150 in Ireland; E-mail: reservations@budgetcarrental.ie). Locations: Dublin City and Airport, Shannon, Galway City and Airport, Cork City and Airport, Killarney, Belfast, and more.

- ✔ **Alamo** (☎ **800-522-9696** from the United States or 800-343-536 or 01-844-4086 in Ireland; Fax: 01-844-5297). Locations: Dublin, Cork, and Shannon Airports.

- ✔ **National** (☎ **800-227-3876** from the United States or 800-301-401 in Ireland; Fax: 800-844-4991). Locations: Dublin Airport, Cork City and Airport, Galway Airport, Kerry Airport, and Shannon Airport.

- ✔ **Argus** (☎ **01-490-9999**; Fax: 01-490-6328 or toll-free fax in the United States 888-249-8877; E-mail: info@argus-rentacar.com; Internet: www.argus-rentacar.com). Locations: Dublin City and Airport, Cork Airport, Shannon, Galway and Rosslare.

- ✔ **Avis** (☎ **800-331-1084** from the United States or 01-605-7555 in Ireland). Locations: Dublin City and Airport, Cork City and Airport, Galway City and Airport, Shannon, Killarney, Kerry Airport, Sligo Airport, and others.

- ✔ **Hertz** (☎ **800-654-3131** from the United States or 01-813-3550 in Ireland; Fax: 01-668-1961). Locations: Dublin City and Airport, Cork Airport, Shannon, Galway Airport, Killarney, Sligo Airport, Waterford City and Airport, and Wexford.

Figuring out the rules of the road

For some of you, just the idea of driving in a foreign country is overwhelming. Different cars, different roads, and different laws don't make for a welcome invitation. Don't let that deter you, though — driving a car around Ireland is a great experience, one that shouldn't be missed just because you think it's going to be hard.

These are some important traffic rules and laws that will help you get around safely and legally.

- ✔ **The general speed limit is 60 mph (96 km/h) unless otherwise posted.** Standard 60 mph signs are indicated only by a black circle with a slash mark through it. When the speed limit is other than 60 mph, there'll be a sign with a red circle and the limit written inside in black. You'll see this often when entering small towns where you should reduce speed to 30 mph. On motorways (highways), the speed limit is generally 70 mph.

- ✔ **A sign that is a red circle with a red "X" through the middle means no stopping or parking during posted hours.**

- ✔ **A flashing yellow light means yield to pedestrian traffic but proceed with caution if it's clear.**

- ✔ **Yield to traffic coming from your right.**

- ✔ **Seat belts must be worn by drivers and front seat passengers.** If your car has back seat belts, they must be worn as well.

- ✔ **Drinking and driving is a serious offense and is dealt with harshly.** Do not drink and drive under any circumstances.

- ✔ **Jane, get me off this crazy thing!** There's an arcane law in Northern Ireland that prohibits a driver from going around a roundabout more than three times. So, no getting yourself dizzy just for kicks when you're up North.

If you have any further questions about traffic laws you can call the **National Safety Council** in Dublin at ☎ **01-496-3422.**

Funny, there aren't any road signs

One of the biggest complaints that tourists have about traveling around Ireland is the lack of road signs. There you are, driving along, looking out for a sign that leads you to your destination, but there don't seem to be any!

Here's the reason some roads are lacking signs: They get stolen! Pub owners and, yes, tourists, steal signs as decoration and souvenirs, especially if they have a family name or ancestral town name on them. You know the kind: white, arrow-shaped signs that you've undoubtedly seen in Irish bars in the United States. And you thought they were reproductions. . . .

Boots, bonnets, and other brouhaha: An Irish driving glossary

To save you confusion about the odd words and phrases the Irish have for car-related things, here's a list of the most commonly used (and most commonly confused):

- ✓ **Roundabout:** Circles (or "rotaries" to you New Englanders). These are common, especially entering and leaving cities. Make sure you go left and yield to the right!
- ✓ **Boot:** Trunk
- ✓ **Bonnet:** Hood
- ✓ **Gear stick:** Stick shift
- ✓ **Footpath:** Sidewalk
- ✓ **Motorways:** Highways
- ✓ **Petrol:** Gasoline

When planning your car trips, you can check out the handy mileage chart we've provided on the tear-out card in the front of this book.

The scoop on driver's licenses and insurance

To drive a car in Ireland, all that is required is a valid U.S. driver's license. This is not to say it'll be as easy to drive. The newness of it all takes a little getting used to.

Your personal insurance does not extend to rental cars in Ireland. You must get a Collision Damage Waiver (CDW), which is included in the price of the rental. If you have one, use a Diner's Club Card to pay for the rental (which pays for the CDW at no cost to you). American Express and Visa no longer cover CDW in Ireland, and MasterCard's coverage is only accepted by some companies.

If you plan on taking the car into Northern Ireland, be sure to inform the rental company and ask if additional insurance is required.

Driving on the wrong side of the road

To get an idea of what it's like to drive in Ireland, simply imagine driving here, and then turn that image upside down. The steering wheel is on the right-hand side and the gearshift is on the left (the position of the gas, clutch, and brake are the same). This causes most people an initial shock. Thankfully, it's a temporary feeling and soon you'll comfortably drive from town to town. (Not our guarantee — just our experience!) It helps to have a good navigator along to watch for road signs so you can focus completely on the road.

In highway traffic, you merge to the right while slower traffic stays on the left. Roundabouts are tricky and you'll probably pop a few curbs while making sharp lefts, but don't get discouraged. Driving in Ireland just takes practice, practice, practice.

Parking rules and regulations

A couple points on parking. First, there's no law, as in the United States, that prohibits you from parking a car facing into traffic. You will often see cars on one side of the road parked in both directions, which makes it tough to tell if you're going the wrong way on a one-way street.

In larger towns, there are some, but not many, parking garages. Street parking is fine, but don't think that parking is free just because there are no meters. In Ireland you have to buy "parking disks" that indicate how long you've been in the spot. Disks can be bought at machines marked "P" that you may mistake for small phone boxes. Purchase a ticket and stick it to your window. Residential neighborhoods and some towns also require disks but have no parking disk machines. In those cases, local corner shops usually sell them.

Doing the Bus Thing

Despite their not-so-great reputation, buses are a pretty great way to see Ireland. First, Irish buses are downright posh — they're coaches, really. They make many more stops than the trains (see later on in this chapter), you get a great view of the countryside from the huge windows, and the cost is soooo much cheaper. But, the usual downsides apply. You're not free to stop wherever and whenever you want. You're stuck with the same people for hours at a time. And not all buses have toilets. Regardless, the seating is comfortable, and buses in general are a good way to meet people.

Bus Eireann is the country's principal public coach line, and it has a vast network of routes that webs through all the principal towns of Ireland and into Northern Ireland. However, it's pretty much a tool of transportation rather than tourism — it doesn't always stop at or even pass near all of the tourist sights along the way. But once you get to a major town, local transportation can usually get you where you want to go.

Investigating bus routes and prices

The following list includes current fares between major cities.

- **Dublin–Waterford:** £15 ($22.20) round trip, £7 ($10.35) one way or midweek return

- **Dublin–Cork:** £32 ($47.35) round trip, £13 ($19.25) one way or midweek return

- **Cork–Killarney:** £8.80 ($13.00) round trip, £13.50 ($20.00) one way

- **Killarney–Limerick:** £17 ($25.15) round trip, £15 ($22.20) one way

- **Limerick–Galway:** £25-27 ($37.00-$39.95) round trip, £15-21 ($22.20-$31.10) one way

- **Galway–Sligo:** £18 ($26.65) round trip, £13.50 ($20.00) one way

- **Dublin–Belfast:** £26 ($38.50) round trip, £11.50 ($17.00) one way or midweek return

Irish Bus Routes

Under 25? You can rent a car in Ireland

Unlike the States, Ireland is a place where most people under the age of 25 (but over 21) can rent a car without a problem. Some places will charge an "underage driver fee," so be sure to ask before you make a reservation. Members of Hostelling International not only get discounts on car rentals, they're directed to companies that rent to underage drivers. Here's the scoop on your prospects:

- **Murrays Europcar:** Must be at least 21; £10.15 ($15) a day up to age 23.

- **Budget:** Must be at least 23; no extra fee.

- **Alamo:** Must be at least 21; £4.50 ($6.65) a day up to age 25.

- **National:** Must be at least 23; no extra fee.

- **Argus:** Must be at least 23; no extra fee.

- **Avis:** Must be at least 23; no extra fee.

- **Hertz:** Must be at least 21; £11.50 ($17) a day up to age 25.

Buses between major cities run as many as a dozen times daily (usually hourly, year-round) and are very reliable. Tickets can only be purchased at the station just before you board.

Information, prices, times, and routes can be found at **Bus Eireann** on Store St., Dublin 1 (☎ **01-836-6111**). The number in Limerick is ☎ **061-31-3333.**

In Northern Ireland, **Ulsterbus** is the area's bus service and it does have routes that pass sights of interest to tourists. The two stations in Belfast are at Europa Bus Station on Glengall Street, and Oxford Street Bus Station. Call ☎ **028-9033-7004** for more information or call the timetable hot line at ☎ **028-9033-3000.**

Enlisting bus packages and tours

Bus Eireann also has guided sightseeing tours that cover a number of favorite tourist sights, and may even pick you up at your hotel (if you're staying at one of its designated pickup points). Routes become more limited in the off-season, so it's best to call ahead to find out which tours will be offered on the dates you're going to be there. The major day trips out of Dublin are

- Glendalough and Wicklow (for information, see Chapter 13)
- Newgrange and Boyne Valley (see Chapter 12)
- Kilkenny City (see Chapter 14)

✔ Jerpoint Abbey and Nore Valley Drive (see Chapter 14)

✔ Ballykissangel and Wicklow Mountains (see Chapter 13)

✔ Russborough House and Powerscourt Garden (see Chapter 13)

✔ Waterford (see Chapter 14)

✔ The Mountains of Mourne (see Chapter 23)

There are also seasonal trips out to Cork, Galway, Sligo, and Donegal, and a tour of Bunratty Castle, the Cliffs of Moher, and the Burren. For more information call ☎ **1850-36-6222.**

Riding the Rails

Ireland has an excellent rail system that connects the major cities of the Republic and Northern Ireland. The advantages of train travel are that it's fast and very comfortable. On the down side, trains are more expensive and travel to fewer destinations than the buses. So, train travel is a comfortable way to get from one part of the country to another but doesn't offer service that's comprehensive enough to allow you to see all the sights.

Looking into train routes and prices

Below are current fares between major cities. You'll notice there are no routes between major cities like Waterford and Cork or Galway and Sligo. You have to go all the way back to Dublin to connect those towns.

✔ **Dublin–Waterford:** £8 ($11.85) round trip, £6 ($8.90) one way

✔ **Dublin–Cork:** £17 ($25.15) round trip, £12 ($17.75) one way

✔ **Cork–Killarney:** £12.50 ($18.50) round trip, £8.80 ($13.00) one way

✔ **Killarney–Limerick:** £13 ($19.25) round trip, £9.30 ($13.75) one way

✔ **Limerick–Galway:** £12.50 ($18.50) round trip, £9 ($13.30) one way

✔ **Galway–Sligo:** £11.50 ($17.00) round trip, £10.50 ($15.55) one way

✔ **Dublin–Belfast:** £14 ($20.70) round trip, £10.50 ($15.55) one way

Trains between major cities run three to five times daily and are reliable. Year-round, you should have no problem buying tickets a half-hour before departure, but during the high season it's advisable to call the day before to confirm availability. For information about destinations, times, and fares call **Iarnro'd E'ireann** (Irish Rail) at ☎ **01-836-6222.** In Northern Ireland, **NI Railways** information is ☎ **028-9066-8258.**

Irish Rail Routes

Utilizing train packages and tours

There are packages for train travel that connect to bus tours of more popular destinations like the Burren, Connemara, and the Ring of Kerry and include hotel accommodations. **Railtours Ireland** at 58 Lower Gardiner St., Dublin 1 (☎ **01-856-0045**) is one private tour operator. Other bus-rail packages are listed in the following sections.

Iarnro'd E'ireann (Irish Rail) has Rail Breaks packages that include accommodations as well as family-oriented "InterCity KID +" tickets that go to places like Bunratty Castle or explore the lakes of Killarney by waterbus and specialize in commentary and special destinations. Contact the **Travel Centre** at 35 Lower Abbey St., Dublin 1 (☎ **01-836-6222**) for more information.

Combining Bus and Rail Packages

The following bus and rail deals are available through **CIE Tours International** (☎ **800-243-7687**). For a flat price, you'll get a pass allowing you unlimited use of trains and buses. Pick one package that suits your needs.

- ✔ **Irish Explorer:** Five-day rail only (includes Intercity, DART, and Suburban Rail), $100 adult, $50 under 12. Eight-day combined rail and bus (includes Intercity, DART, and Suburban Rail, Bus Eireann Expressway, Provincial Bus, and city buses in Cork, Limerick, Galway and Waterford), $150 adult, $75 under 12.

- ✔ **Irish Rover:** Five-day all-Ireland rail only (includes Intercity, DART, Suburban Rail, and Northern Ireland Railways), $124 adult, $62 under 12.

- ✔ **Emerald Card:** Eight-day combined rail and bus (covers Intercity, DART, Suburban Rail, Northern Ireland Railways, Bus Eireann Expressway, Provincial Bus, Ulsterbus Provincial Services, and city buses in Belfast, Cork, Limerick, Galway, and Waterford), $174 adult, $87 under 12. Fifteen-day costs $300 adult, $150 under 12.

Getting Out to the Islands

The only way you're getting out to those celebrated islands off the coast of Ireland — the **Arans, Skelligs, Rathlin,** and so on — is by ferry. You can take your car on some, but not all. The famed Aran Islands, for instance, are vehicle free, and want to stay that way. Check out the chapters for each area you want to visit for more information (Chapter 18 for the Arans, 16 for the Skelligs, and 22 for Rathlin). Remember to call the day before you hope to go out, as bad weather can severely limit ferry travel.

Chapter 8

Booking Your Accommodations

● ●

In This Chapter

▶ Figuring out what your accommodations will cost you

▶ Getting the scoop on hotels

▶ Exploring the B&B, guesthouse, hostel, and self-catering options

● ●

So where do you want to stay, castle or cottage? Although there are more than 3,000 castles in Ireland (in varying degrees of ruin and renovation) and more cottages than you can shake a stick at, you probably won't be sleeping in one — although you can if you want to, and we'll tell you how. Instead, you'll probably be staying in a hotel or guesthouse.

Hotels in Ireland are rated by the tourist board and range from five to one stars for quality. They're comparable in variety to those you'll find back home. The other option is a guesthouse, which is essentially a Bed & Breakfast. We've included more hotels than B&Bs in our guide because hotels are more often right on the tourist trail, but B&Bs are peppered throughout the country and easy to find.

There are other options as well, from self-catering to hostels, and the following sections will tell you more about each, help you find the type of accommodation that's best for you, and fill you in on how to make all your reservations before you even leave home. The accommodations listed in this book are places where you should definitely enjoy your stay. And if you choose to color outside the lines and stay someplace not in the book, chances are you probably won't be disappointed. Why? Because the Irish really are masters at the art of hospitality. Accommodating people in a friendly and warm way is something they all seem to take quite seriously.

Figuring Out the Costs

You can expect a really wide range of prices for accommodations. To make it easy for you to quickly gauge whether one of our options is affordable to you, we've listed the cost of a *double room* — what it will cost for two of you to stay in one room together. The range typically indicates the price for the room during the off-season (the lower price) to the high-season (the highest cost). So, where we list a price of, say, £40–65 ($59.20–$88.80), this means the cost of a room for two people will be any price between those two numbers. However, this also refers to the differences in cost of a room with a sea view, extra-large beds, and so on. If you're traveling alone, most accommodations charge a single supplement (in other words, an extra cost) of about £10 ($14.80). This charge is compensation for the hotelier, who'll only be getting half what he could get for the room you're in if he rented it to a couple.

Almost every place we've listed in the book includes a full Irish breakfast.

Use the following scale for quick reference:

$ £50 double ($74) or less

$$ £50–100 double ($74–$148)

$$$ £100–200 double ($148–$296)

$$$$ £200 double ($296) or more

Dublin Central Reservations has a fantastic (and free!) **Accommodation Booking Service** (☎ 01-820-0394; Fax: 01-822-0493; E-mail: bookings@ dublinreservations.com; Internet: www.dublinreservations.com) for Ireland and Northern Ireland. It will search out and reserve all levels of accommodations, from five-star hotels to B&Bs, hostels, and self-catering houses. Another organization, **Res Ireland** (☎ 800- 668-6866 in the United States; E-mail: reservations@gulliver.ie), is good, too.

Lodging in Luxury

The hotel experience in Ireland is similar to what you expect back home, with a few minor differences. Many places have tea- and coffee-making facilities in the rooms. Bellhops aren't as common. And smaller hotels sometimes lock up the doors at a certain (late) hour, so you're faced with the situation of having to ring or knock to be let in after hours. (But don't worry; they're used to it.)

Even among hotels, the range of accommodations is wide — from castles on down to small, family-run lodges. Hotels are used to catering to tourists and have a deserved reputation of helpfulness and friendliness. You can expect the furnishings to be comfortable and many of the larger and chain hotels to have fitness equipment, room service, and in-house pubs and restaurants.

Phoning overseas

Before you can book your room, you need to know how to call Ireland. To call Ireland from anywhere in the world, dial the international access code (011 from the United States), then the country code (Ireland is 353; Northern Ireland is 44), then the city code (for example, Dublin is 1), and then the number.

So, let's say you wanted to call Guinness Customer Service in Dublin to make sure they'll have enough Guinness waiting for you. You would dial:

Int'l		Country		City		Number
011	+	353	+	1	+	454-3911

Remember, Ireland is five hours ahead of Eastern Standard Time, so if you're trying to call a business, call between 9:00 and 5:00 their time.

The following chains have top-quality hotels in major cities throughout the country. We've ranked them beginning with the most posh at the top:

- ✓ **Great Southern:** ☎ **01-214-4800;** Fax: 01-214-4805; Internet: www. gsh.ie; E-mail: res@sales.gsh.ie (Dublin, Rosslare, Killarney, Galway, County Clare)

- ✓ **Tower:** ☎ **071-44-000;** Fax: 071-46-888; Internet: www. towerhotelgroup.ie; E-mail: towersl@iol.ie (Dublin, Waterford, Killarney, Sligo)

- ✓ **Jury's:** ☎ **01-660-5000;** Fax: 01-660-5540 (Dublin, Waterford, Cork, Galway, Limerick, Belfast)

- ✓ **Ryan Hotels:** ☎ **01-878-7966;** E-mail: ryan@indigo.ie; Internet: www.ryan-hotels.com (Dublin, Killarney, Limerick, Galway)

- ✓ **Travelodge:** ☎ **800-70-9709** (Dublin, Waterford, Cork)

Weekends are often the cheapest time to stay at hotels in major cities. These hotels often thrive on business travelers, who tend to go home on the weekends. Hotels are eager to keep the house full, so some offer great deals to tourists like yourself. If it means saving a few pounds, it's worth asking.

Staying in Casual Comfort: Bed-and-Breakfasts and Guesthouses

It's said that Irish B&Bs are the best in Europe, and it's easy to see why. Unlike in a big hotel, you'll get to know the owners of the B&B, because they'll probably be the same folks who check you in, cook and serve your breakfast, clean your room, and lug your bags upstairs. You'll probably go away from your B&B experience feeling you've made a new friend.

A *guesthouse* is for the most part the same thing as a B&B, though possibly a little larger.

A big advantage of choosing a B&B over a huge hotel is the price. The cost of a double room averages between £30 ($44.40) and £45 ($66.60). You won't get some of the amenities of a hotel (pool, gym, room service), but really, how often do you take advantage of those anyway?

Also, keep in mind that many B&Bs don't accept credit cards, so have enough cash on hand.

B&Bs aren't vast — most have between four and ten rooms only. The better B&Bs tend to fill up quickly during the high season. You should book at least a week in advance of your trip; even sooner if possible. However, some places only accept guests on a first-come, first-serve basis, so in those situations it's the luck of the draw.

Some B&B rooms are not *en suite,* meaning they don't have a private bathroom. So if you're completely against sharing facilities with the folks down the hall, make sure you ask for a room with its own bathroom. It might cost you a little bit more, but for some people, it's worth it.

The Family Homes of Ireland, the largest guide to B&Bs, can be found on the Web at www.family-homes.ie, by phone at ☎ **091- 55-2000,** or by E-mail at info@family-homes.ie. **Town and Country Homes Association** has information on B&Bs in the Republic (☎ **072- 51-377**). And Northern Ireland B&Bs are covered by **Town and Seaside House Association** (☎ **028-7082-3823;** Fax: 028-7082-2741).

Enjoying Self-Catering Cottages: The Choice for Families

Self-catering cottages are the Irish equivalent of that condo you rented for a week at the beach last year. They're a place for you to drop your bags, settle in, and do things family style, cooking your own meals and making your own beds. For those of you making the trip with children, this might be a perfect option, both convenience- and money-wise.

With self-catering, you pay one price, generally for the week. (Some rent by the weekend, for two to three days.) When you take into account the amount of money you would pay for hotels and B&Bs on a nightly basis, this can cut down on costs considerably. Food costs decrease when you're buying your own and cooking it, too.

The drawback is location. While some self-catering cottages and apartments are in *great* locations — right on the seashore, in perfect little villages, or in the heart of Dublin or Cork — the trouble is that they don't move: Rent one and you're in one place, all week, and to see the sights around the country you've got to drive to them, and then drive "home." Of course, this is a plus if you intend to spend all your time in one area — there's no better way to really get the feel of a place, and is especially worthwhile if a big goal of your trip is to learn about your family's history. However, trying to make day trips to sights in far-flung parts of the country may be seriously tough.

The variety of self-catering options is as diverse as types of hotels. You can stay in actual thatched-roof cottages or completely modernized units. All of these accommodations are registered with the tourism authorities and are rated from one star to four (four being the best).

As with any place to stay, all you have to do is call the tourist board in the area you wish to visit and the staff there will help you with bookings. To get you started, though, here are some organizations that deal solely with self-catering cottages:

- ✔ **Self-Catering Ireland** (☎ **053-33-999**; Fax: 053-33-808; Internet: `www.selfcatering-ireland.com`) is the most comprehensive reservation service, offering three- and four-star self-catering apartments throughout Ireland and Northern Ireland, with up to four bedrooms.

- ✔ **Rent an Irish Cottage,** 85 O'Connell St., Limerick (☎ **061-41-1109**), organizes self-catering in traditional whitewashed cottages. In Northern Ireland, contact rural **Cottage Holidays** (☎ **01232-23-1221;** Fax: 01232-24-0960).

- ✔ **Irish Farmhouse Holidays** (☎ **01-825-0240**) has lists of rural farmhouses in the Republic that take paying guests.

- ✔ **Home from Home Holidays,** 26/27 Rossa St. Clonkilty, West Cork (☎ **023-33-110;** Fax: 023-33-131), also offers a good selection.

Exploring Inexpensive Hostels

Hostels have a reputation of being the accommodation of choice for the micro-budgeted, and if you've got the image in your head of hostels being full of young, tireless travelers who don't mind going long stretches without showers or food, you're partly right — though only partly. The more accurate byword is, hostels are for independent travelers who cherish flexibility.

Hostels located across Ireland vary in quality and services. Some offer community kitchens, and the majority sleep people dorm-style, with anywhere from four to dozens of people per room (some, though, have private rooms with bathrooms). Families can even stay in hostels, renting a room with four bunks. You won't get to cuddle with your honey, unless you can both squeeze into a sagging bunk bed, but even that won't work sometimes, because many hostels have separate dorm rooms for women and men.

Hostels provide a blanket and pillow, and some beds have sheets, but to be safe bring your own sleep-sack — basically two sheets sewn together.

Many people wonder how safe their luggage will be in hostels, because your personal belongings will most likely be sitting at the foot of the bed, asking to be rifled through. It's certainly not a major problem, but is something to consider. Many hostels provide security lockers, but if not, take some precautions: Make your luggage as difficult to get into as possible by, for instance, stacking bags atop each other, with the most valuable at the bottom. Also, bring your wallet, passport, purse, and other important personal belongings to bed with you for safekeeping.

As for bathrooms: Think of high school gym restrooms — cold tiles, a row of small sinks and toilet and shower stalls. You might not love it, but it will get the job done.

We can't vouch for every hostel in Ireland, but if there's one undeniable fact, it's that they're cheap. You can get a warm bed for as little as £6 ($8.90) and never pay more than £20 ($29.60). And, you'll meet people from all over the world doing the same thing as you. Sure, you'll run into your share of hostels that don't exactly disinfect the toilet daily, but on the whole they're clean places: In fact, Irish hostels are the cleanest we've seen anywhere.

Some hostels take reservations, but only a day ahead. Others are first come, first sleep. So call ahead. If you're planning to do the hostel tour of Ireland, you'll really benefit from contacting **Hostelling International** (☎ **202-783-6161**) before you leave the United States. In fact, some places only accept card-carrying members. Fees are $25 a year; $10 if you're under 18; and $15 if you're over 54. With the card you'll get discounts at places affiliated with the group and even save on car rentals.

A resource to check out for yourself is on the Web at www.hostels. com. It's a complete site, offering everything a hostel seeker may need: a worldwide hostel database, Q&A about staying in hostels, postings from readers, and maps. The section on finding a hostel in Ireland (Internet: www.hostels.com/ie.html) digs deep.

Discover Ireland Holiday Breaks magazine lists accredited hostels across the country. Pick one up at any tourist board office. For more info, contact **An Óige Irish Youth Hostel Association** (☎ **01-830-4555;** Fax: 01-830-5808; E-mail: anoige@iol.ie; Internet: www.irelandyha. org) and the **Youth Hostel Association of Northern Ireland** (☎ **028-9032-4733;** Fax: 028-9043-9699).

Considering Other Accommodation Options

Here are a few other options for accommodations in Ireland.

> ✔ **University housing:** Check with local tourist boards or directly with universities to find out if they have unused dorm space in campus housing to rent. This is a cheap, fun option for younger people, putting you right in the heart of a college setting. Cities

with large universities include Dublin, Galway, Cork, and Limerick. Don't count on this being available, though. Currently housing for students is in high demand all over the country, so it's usually only available during the summer and Christmas holidays.

✔ **Castles and Manors:** A company called **Elegant Ireland** (☎ **01-475-1665**) rents castles and country houses that are furnished to the nines with antiques and period furniture.

✔ **Camping and Caravans:** This is a popular option with Irish vacationers. Check out **Irish Caravan and Camping,** P.O. Box 4443, Dublin 2, Ireland (no phone; Fax: 098-28-237; E-mail: `info@ camping-ireland.ie`), an organization that lists camping destinations.

Chapter 9

Money Matters

● ●

In This Chapter

▶ Spending and exchanging money in Ireland

▶ Finding ATMs: The traveler's best friend

▶ Utilizing your credit card and traveler's check options

▶ Dealing with a lost wallet

● ●

Money, money, money makes the world go 'round. The rise of the mighty ATM has made money matters a cinch for modern travelers, but you still need to keep a few things in mind. In this chapter we sort out the punts and the pounds and set you up with information about other currency matters in Ireland — what to bring, how to get more, and what to do if you lose your money.

Cash in Hand: Making Sense of the Irish Currency

The currency in the Republic of Ireland, the Irish *punt* (often called the *pound*), is not too different from American currency, with denominations that are the same except that Ireland has a coin for two *pence* and the single pound is a coin rather than a bill. In Northern Ireland, the currency is the British pound (often called *Sterling*), and the coins and bills are very similar to their Irish counterparts — although if you go to Northern Ireland you can't use Irish money and have to switch to British currency.

Understanding the exchange rates

Generally speaking, things are more expensive in Ireland than in the States. We found that many items in Ireland cost the same amount as they do in America in numerical amounts — for instance, if a soda is a dollar in America, it's often a pound in Ireland. That means that, because you get about 68 pence for every dollar you exchange, things cost about 48 percent more in Ireland. This disparity isn't true of all items, but it gives you a general idea of how far your new cash and weighty coins can go.

The exchange rate fluctuates daily (by small amounts), but the average rates are similar to those listed in Tables 9-1 and 9-2.

Table 9-1	Republic of Ireland
Home Currency	*Irish Punt*
$1 U.S.	£0.68 (£1 = $1.48 U.S.)
$1 Canadian	£0.45 (£1 = $2.21 Canadian)
£1 British	£1.23 (£1 = £.86 Sterling)
$1 Australian	£0.43 (£1 = $2.31 Australian)
$1 New Zealand	£0.37 (£1 = $2.71 New Zealand)

Table 9-2	Northern Ireland
Home Currency	*British Pound*
$1 U.S.	£0.61 (£1 = $1.65 U.S.)
$1 Canadian	£0.41 (£1 = $2.45 Canadian)
$1 Australian	£0.39 (£1 = $2.57 Australian)
$1 New Zealand	£0.32 (£1 = $3.03 New Zealand)
£1 Irish	£0.86 (£1 = £1.23 Irish)

The best sources for current currency exchange information are on the Internet, at www.cnn.com/TRAVEL/CURRENCY and www.xe.net/ict.

Making way for the Euro: A matter of common currency

Don't sweat it, at least not yet. The new European common currency, the *Euro,* won't be in circulation in Ireland until 2002. You may see Euro equivalents calculated on some money transactions, but that's only to get the population familiar with the new money.

Finding out where to exchange money

You can exchange money anywhere you see the Bureau de Change sign, but generally, you'll get the best rates at banks. The following numbers are for the major banks in Ireland, so call if you have any questions or need to find the nearest location while you're there.

✔ **Allied Irish Bank** (☎ **800-24-2000,** or 800-AIB-1234 from the United States)

✔ **Bank of Ireland** (☎ **01-670-0600;** Internet: `www.international.boi.ie`)

✔ **National Irish Bank** (☎ **800-60-0600**)

✔ **Ulster Bank** (☎ **01-677-7623;** has branches in both the Republic of Ireland and Northern Ireland)

Accessing ATMs, Just Like at Home

As long as your ATM card is hooked to one of the major networks, you can use your ATM card in Ireland. The machines work just like at home, but they're called *service tills* in Ireland. Most ATMs can give cash advances for major credit cards as well, but you need a PIN number (Personal Identification Number). If you don't know it, contact your bank before you leave home and have it mailed to you.

Before you leave, be sure to check the daily withdrawal limit with your bank. Also, if your card covers both your checking and savings accounts, be sure to stow any cash you may need in checking, because that's the only account some overseas ATMs can access (and many won't allow you the option of switching money between the two).

ATMs are linked to networks that most likely include your bank at home. **Cirrus** (☎ **800-424-7787;** Internet: `www.mastercard.com/atm/`) and **Plus** (☎ **800-843-7587;** Internet: `www.visa.com/atms`) are the two most popular networks; check the back of your ATM card to see which network your bank belongs to. You can call the toll-free numbers to locate ATMs in your destination, if you can't find one.

If you lose your ATM card (or if it's stolen), contact your bank at home and report it. This long-distance call will be expensive, but it's cheaper than if your card (and, in a worst-case scenario, PIN number) falls in the wrong hands. Don't expect the bank to send you an emergency replacement card, either. Sometimes this procedure can take up to a month.

Using Credit Cards on the Road

Credit cards are invaluable when traveling. They're a safe way to carry money, provide a convenient record of all your expenses, and allow you to take cash advances at any bank or most ATMs, as discussed earlier in this chapter. However, you should know that you'll start paying hefty interest on the advance the moment you receive it.

Visa, MasterCard, American Express, and Diners Club are all widely used in Ireland, but Discover is not accepted.

If you lose your credit cards (or if they're stolen), every minute counts. Call your credit card companies immediately and have the cards deactivated. Most Irish merchants are careful about checking the signatures on receipts against the cards, but a smart thief can quickly master the fine art of forging your signature. By getting to your credit card company before any illegal purchases are made, you save the hassle of getting those purchases exempted and help the *garda* (the Irish police) find the thief. Do a thorough search and make sure your cards really are lost before going through the hassle of canceling and reporting them.

Almost every credit card company has an emergency toll-free number that you can call to report a loss or theft. The company may be able to wire you a cash advance from your credit card immediately, and in many places it can deliver an emergency credit card in a day or two.

The issuing bank's toll-free number is usually on the back of the credit card — but that doesn't help you much if the card was stolen. Write it down somewhere.

The phone numbers to report stolen credit cards while in Ireland are

- ✔ **Visa** (☎ **800-55-8002**)
- ✔ **MasterCard** (☎ **800-55-7378**)
- ✔ **American Express** (☎ **800-62-6000**)
- ✔ **Diners Club** (☎ **702-797-5532**; members can call collect)

Odds are that if your wallet is gone, the police won't be able to recover it for you. However, after you cancel your credit cards, informing the authorities is still important. Your credit card company or insurer may require you to give a police report number.

If you're an American Express card member, bring a single blank personal check and keep it in a safe place away from your card. If your card is lost or stolen, you can use that check to draw a cash advance against your account. Just bring it, unsigned, into an AmEx office and they can cash it on the spot. The only American Express offices in Ireland are in Dublin (41 Nassau St.; ☎ **01-617-5597**) and Galway (c/o International Hotel, East Avenue Road; ☎ **64-35722**).

Considering Traveler's Checks: Old-Fashioned or Useful?

Traveler's checks, while providing a measure of security for people away from home (you can get them replaced if they're stolen) are something of an anachronism from the days before ATMs made cash accessible at any time. So what's the plus side of traveler's checks? Many banks impose a fee every time you use an ATM in a different city or bank, which can add up if you withdraw money every day. Traveler's checks eliminate that problem, but they can be a bit of a hassle, because you need to show identification every time you want to cash a check.

Don't use traveler's checks to pay for a meal or a room. The exchange rate is worse than at a bank or exchange bureau. If you're carrying American Express checks, try to cash them at an American Express office to avoid commission costs and get a good rate.

You can get traveler's checks at almost any bank. Here are some of the big guns in the field:

- ✔ **American Express** Traveler's Cheques are available over the phone by calling ☎ 800-221-7282; by using this number, AmEx gold and platinum cardholders are exempt from service fees, which range from 1 to 4 percent. Members of AAA can obtain checks without a fee at most AAA offices.

- ✔ **Visa** offers traveler's checks at Citibank locations across the United States and at several other banks. The service charge ranges between 1.5 and 2 percent. You can get Visa checks at most banks.

- ✔ **MasterCard** also offers traveler's checks. Call ☎ 800-223-9920 for a location near you.

If you opt to carry traveler's checks, be sure to keep a record of their serial numbers in a location separate from the checks themselves so you can get a refund if your checks are lost or stolen. Call **American Express** toll free (☎ 800-62-6000 in the Republic, 0800-521-313 in Northern Ireland) to have the lost checks replaced. The company needs to know exactly which checks were unused. The best way to keep track of this is by creating a list of the check numbers and crossing them off as you use them. If your **Visa** checks are lost or stolen, call ☎ 44-207-937-8091.

If you're traveling as a couple, note that dual checks are available that allow either person to sign for them.

Dealing with Stolen Cash and Credit Cards

Don't panic. If you don't have any money or traveler's checks and you have reported all your credit cards and bank cards stolen, you may be in bad shape, but (hopefully!) you still have your return ticket, and you still have a couple of ways left to get emergency cash. (Look at it this way: You're sure to stay within your budget.)

First, contact your bank (some larger ones accept collect calls). You may be able to have cash from your checking account wired via money-gram and sent to a travel agent or perhaps to your hotel in Ireland. Fees will apply, but at least you won't starve.

The other option is to have someone back home wire you money through a **Western Union money transfer.** You can do this at more than 400 locations throughout Ireland. Completing the transaction and getting your money takes only minutes. Call the toll-free number (☎ 800-39-5395) for the nearest location and information.

Chapter 10

Tying Up Loose Ends: Last-Minute Details to Keep in Mind

● ●

In This Chapter

▶ Getting a passport or a visa

▶ Dealing with customs

▶ Insuring yourself (if you need to, or want to)

▶ Falling ill in a foreign land

▶ Keeping in touch with the home front

▶ Packing your bags

▶ Making your flight more comfortable

● ●

Deciding to go on a trip is easy; the tough part is preparing for it. In this chapter we go through some things you need to do before boarding the plane, from getting your passport to packing and figuring out how you can keep in touch with the people back home. (Assuming you want to, of course.)

Papers, Please!: Getting Your Passport

Who needs a passport? You, that's who! A valid passport is the only legal form of identification that every nation recognizes.

For U.S. citizens

Getting a passport is easy, but completing the process takes some time. If you're applying for a first-time passport, you can do it in person at one of 13 passport offices throughout the United States, at many federal, state, or probate courts, or at a major post office (call the number listed later in this section to find the ones that accept applications). You need to bring a completed (but not signed) application, which you can get at the post office, and proof of citizenship — a certified birth certificate. It's wise to bring along your driver's license or other identifying documents as well. You'll also need two identical 2 x 2 photos taken within the last six months. You can get these taken at just about any corner photo shop. You cannot use the strip photos from photo vending machines.

When you get your passport photos taken, have them make up six or eight total. You'll need them to apply for an International Driving Permit (and for getting things like student or teacher IDs). Take the extras with you on your trip. If you lose your passport, you can use one of the extras as a replacement photo.

For people age 16 and over, a passport is valid for 10 years and costs $60 ($45 plus a $15 handling fee); for those age 15 and under, the passport is valid for 5 years and costs $40 total.

If you're over 15 and have a valid passport issued less than 12 years ago, you can renew it by mail by filling out the application, available at the places described earlier in this chapter or at the State Department Web site, http://travel.state.gov. By mail, you bypass the $15 handling fee, and it costs just $45.

Apply for your passport at least two months before your trip — preferably earlier. The processing takes four weeks on average, but can run longer in busy periods (especially spring). It helps speed things along if you write on the application a departure date within the next three weeks. To expedite your passport — in which case you'll get it in five business days — visit an agency directly (or go through the court or post office and have them overnight it), and pay an additional $35 fee.

At certain times of the year, travelers literally flood the agencies with applications. Passport agencies are busiest during January, and are generally jumping constantly from then until fall. To get your passport quickly (and that's a relative word), the best time to apply is between September and December.

For more information, and to find your regional passport office, consult the State Department Web site at http://travel.state.gov or call the **National Passport Information Center** (☎ **900-225-7778**; 35 cents a minute for automated service; $1.05 a minute to speak with an operator).

For non-U.S. citizens

Procedures for getting a passport vary from country to country. Here are some for the English-speaking world:

✔ **For British citizens:** You can get applications at British post offices. You'll need proof of citizenship (such as a birth certificate) and two identical photographs. See the application for specific instructions. You can also find more information online at www.ukpa.gov.uk.

✔ **For Canadian citizens:** To find the nearest passport location call ☎ 819-994-3500 within Canada. In addition to the application, you must have a birth or citizenship certificate and two matching photos.

✔ **For Australian citizens:** Contact the Department of Foreign Affairs and Trade at ☎ 131-232 within the country or go to www.dfat.gov.au/passports (or e-mail passports.australia@dfat.gov.au) for all questions about how to obtain a passport.

✔ **For New Zealand citizens:** Contact the Department of Internal Affairs, Documents of National Identity, Passport Division toll free at ☎ 0800-22-5050 within the country or online at www.passports.govt.nz/. In addition to the application you must have a birth or citizenship certificate and two matching photos.

Keeping your passport safe

Not having your vital documents in a foreign country can be dangerous and scary, so don't leave it to chance. If they are lost or stolen, being able to prove who you are is important. Before you go on your trip, photocopy your passport (and your driver's license, Social Security card, and any other pertinent information, too). Make a few copies, and pass them on to friends and family, keeping one set for your luggage, stored separately from the originals.

When you're on the road, always keep your passport with you. Never let it out of your sight. In the terrible event that you do lose your passport while you're in the Republic of Ireland, the first thing you need to do is contact your country's embassy or consulate. People there need to know that someone else may be posing as you, and they can help you get a replacement passport. (You cannot return home without a passport, so getting another one is a top priority.) Bring any identification you have, plus the photocopy of your passport. In the Irish Republic, embassy locations are as follows:

✔ **United States:** 42 Elgin Rd., Ballsbridge, Dublin 4 (☎ 01-668-8777).

✔ **Canada:** 65/68 St. Stephen's Green, Dublin 2 (☎ 01-478-1988).

✔ **New Zealand:** The New Zealand Consulate is no longer in operation, so for emergencies contact the High Commission New Zealand House, The Haymarket, London SW1Y42Q UK (☎ 171-930-8422).

✔ **Australia:** Fitzwilton House, Wilton Terrace, Dublin 2 (☎ 01-676-1517).

✔ **United Kingdom:** 29 Merrion Rd., Dublin 4 (☎ 01-205-3700).

The United States is the only one of these countries with a diplomatic presence in Northern Ireland (at 14 Queen St., Belfast, BT1 SEQ; ☎ 028-9032-8239). Embassies for other countries are all located in London.

Getting an Irish passport

Were your parents or grandparents born in Ireland? If so, you may be eligible for an Irish passport. Why would you want one? Shorter immigration lines for one thing. Having an Irish passport also allows you to legally work anywhere in Europe. Contact the Irish embassy in your home country for full details about how to get a passport. The embassy in the United States is at 2234 Massachusetts Ave. NW, Washington DC, 20008. ☎ **202-462-3939;** Fax: 202-232-5993.

And no, you don't need a visa

When people hear the word visa, they think it's a formal document they must get before entering a foreign country. For some countries, it is; but not Ireland. There, the word reverts to its less intimidating incarnation: a stamp in your passport, which is a country's OK for you to stay within its borders for a certain amount of time. In Ireland, that means 90 days. If you want to stay longer than that, you have to submit an "aliens registration form" after you arrive. For more information, contact the **Embassy of Ireland,** 2234 Massachusetts Ave. NW, Washington, DC, 20008 (☎ **202-462-3939**). You can also find more information on the embassy's Web site at www.irelandemb.org.

Getting more info on passports

For more information on passports, contact the **Irish Embassy,** 2234 Massachusetts Ave. NW, Washington DC, 20008 (☎ **202-462-3939;** Fax: 202-232-5993). For most questions, the embassy will direct you to Irish consulates in New York (☎ **212-319-2555**), Boston (☎ **617-267-9330**), San Francisco (☎ **415-392-4214**), or Chicago (☎ **312-337-1868**). The Irish Embassy in Canada is at 130 Albert St. Suite 1105, Ottawa, Ontario, K1P 5G4 (☎ **613-233-6281**).

Well, I Do Declare: Understanding the Customs of Customs

If you come to Ireland bearing gifts, you may not necessarily be that well received. You have a limit on what and how much you can bring into the country. These guidelines are strict and can result in a mess if you try to get around them.

What you can't bring in

You cannot bring any of the following: firearms, ammunition, or explosives; narcotics; poultry, plants and their immediate byproducts; domestic animals; and snakes (St. Pat worked so hard to get them all out). Also, you can bring in no more than 200 cigarettes, one liter of liquor, and two liters of wine.

If you're flying out of or back to the United States, information about what goods you can bring in and out is available on the U.S. State Department's Web site: http://travel.state.gov.

Customs channels: Red, green, or blue?

After you arrive in Ireland and gather your luggage, you'll have to confront one last obstacle. Ireland and Northern Ireland have three Customs channels: Red, green, and blue.

- ✔ **Red:** To make a declaration if you're bringing in more goods than the rules allow.

- ✔ **Green and blue:** If you have nothing to declare — blue if you're traveling from another country in the European Union, green if you're traveling from anywhere else.

    So, if you're not entering Ireland through Britain, you should go through the green channel. You won't be asked any questions or, under most circumstances, have to open your suitcases.

When you go back home you'll be given a simple customs form to fill out that you'll present to immigration officials when you arrive stateside. Provided you follow customs guidelines, you should have no hassles.

Buying Travel and Medical Insurance

The differences between travel assistance and travel insurance are often blurred, but in general the former offers on-the-spot assistance and 24-hour hot lines (mostly oriented toward medical problems), while the latter reimburses you for travel problems (medical, travel, or otherwise) after you have filed the paperwork. The three different kinds of travel coverage are trip cancellation, lost luggage, and medical insurance. Trip cancellation insurance is sensible for many travelers, but most people can do without the other two types. Your homeowner's insurance should cover stolen luggage. If you're carrying anything really valuable, you should keep it in your carry-on luggage rather than checking it. Rule number one: Check your existing policies before you buy any additional coverage.

Trip cancellation insurance is a good idea if you have paid a large portion of your vacation expenses up front — you'll be covered if, for whatever reason, your trip gets cancelled. Trip cancellation insurance costs approximately 6 to 8 percent of the total value of your vacation.

If you do require additional insurance, try one of the following companies.

- ✔ **Access America,** 6600 W. Broad St., Richmond, VA 23230 (☎ **800-284-8300**)

- ✔ **Travel Guard International,** 1145 Clark St., Stevens Point, WI 54481 (☎ **800-826-1300**)

- ✔ **Travel Insured International, Inc.,** P.O. Box 280568, East Hartford, CT 06128 (☎ **800-243-3174**)

- ✔ **Columbus Travel Insurance,** 17 Devonshire Square London EC2M 4SQ (☎ **0171-375-0011;** Internet: www.columbusdirect.com)

- ✔ **Travelex Insurance Services,** P.O. Box 9408, Garden City, NY 11530-9408 (☎ **800-228-9792**)

Your existing health insurance should cover you if you get sick while on vacation (though if you belong to an HMO, you should check to see whether you are fully covered when away from home). If you need hospital treatment, most health insurance plans and HMOs will cover out-of-country hospital visits and procedures, at least to some extent. However, most make you pay the bills up front at the time of care, and you'll get a refund after you've returned and filed all the paperwork. **Medicare** covers only U.S. citizens traveling in Mexico and Canada. Members of **Blue Cross/Blue Shield** can now use their cards at select hospitals in most major cities worldwide (☎ **800-810-BLUE**). For independent travel health insurance providers, find them later in this chapter.

Before buying any additional insurance, check your existing health insurance or other policies to see if they cover you while you're traveling. Some credit card companies may insure you against travel accidents if you buy plane, train, or bus tickets with their cards, and some (American Express and certain gold and platinum Visa and MasterCards, for example) offer automatic death or dismemberment insurance in case of an airplane crash.

Companies specializing in accident and medical care include

- ✔ **MEDEX International,** P.O. Box 5375, Timonium, MD 21094-5375 (☎ **888-MEDEX-00** or 410-453-6300; Fax: 410-453-6301; Internet: www.medexassist.com)

- ✔ **Travel Assistance International** (Worldwide Assistance Services, Inc.), 1133 15th St. NW, Suite 400, Washington, DC 20005 (☎ **800-821-2828** or 202-828-5894; Fax: 202-828-5896)

Additionally, you can check out **International SOS Assistance,** P.O. Box 11568, Philadelphia PA 11916 (☎ **800-523-8930** or 215-244-1500), a medical evacuation assistance program. If you get sick abroad it will get you home and to the proper medical people. This coverage is more useful for travelers going to countries with less-modern medical facilities than you find in Ireland, but the program is still a good idea if you have a difficult medical condition that may pose problems while you're in Ireland.

Dealing with Getting Sick Away from Home

Finding a doctor you can trust when you're in an unfamiliar place can be hard. If you suffer from a chronic illness, consult your doctor before your departure. For conditions like epilepsy, diabetes, or heart problems, contact **Medic Alert** (☎ 800-825-3785; Internet: www.medicalert. org) to get an identification tag that will immediately alert doctors to your condition and give them access to your records through Medic Alert's 24-hour hot line. Membership is $35, plus a $15 annual fee.

Pack prescription medications in your carry-on luggage. Carry written prescriptions in generic form rather than under a brand name and carry all prescription medications in their original labeled vials. Also bring along copies of your prescriptions in case you lose your pills or run out.

Contact the **International Association for Medical Assistance to Travelers** (IAMAT) (☎ 716-754-4883; Internet: www.sentex.net/ ~iamat). This organization offers tips on travel and health concerns in the countries you're visiting. The **United States Centers for Disease Control and Prevention** (☎ 404-332-4559; Internet: www.cdc.gov/ travel) provides up-to-date information on necessary vaccines and health hazards by region or country. (By mail, its booklet is $20; on the Internet, it's free.)

When you're abroad, any local consulate can provide a list of area doctors. If you do get sick, you may want to ask the concierge at your hotel to recommend a local doctor — even his or her own. Doing so will probably yield a better recommendation than any toll-free number can. You can also try the emergency room at the local hospital. Many emergency rooms have walk-in clinics for emergency cases that are not life threatening.

Communicating with the Folks Back Home

You've just landed in Ireland. So much to do, so much to see. Yet what's the first thing you want to do? Phone home to make sure your plants will be watered and the dog walked twice a day. That's fine. Calling America from Ireland is pretty easy, after you know the basics.

Using the phones

You can find two types of pay phones in Ireland, coin phones and card phones. Both kinds of phones are spread throughout the country, and you may often see them side by side.

If you use a coin phone, read the directions before you start feeding in coins. Some phones require putting the coins in before you dial, while others have you put in the coins after the other party answers.

Coin phones in the Republic and Northern Ireland cost either 20p or 30p, and the amount of time you get depends on how far you're calling. Have change in hand — the phone gives an extremely short warning before disconnecting.

Got no calling card? Got no change? Got no problem. The Irish have phone cards that work the same as those in the United States, like a debit card, and you can get one in any shop or post office. They come in varying denominations. What's different about the Irish version is that it's used in its own phone booth, designated by the sign *Cardphone*. When you enter the booth, slide the card in the slot like you would a credit card. There's a screen on the phone that says how many units the card has left. The units decrease while you're on the phone, so you know how much time is left before you're hung up on. No more "Thephone'sgoingtohangupI'lltalktoyoulatergoodb–"

If possible, never make a call from your hotel room. You may have to foot surcharges, pay astronomical fees, and incur charges to get your calling card company on the line.

Numbers beginning with 800 within Ireland are called *Freephone numbers* and are toll free, but calling a toll-free number in the United States from Ireland is not free. In fact, doing so costs the same as a regular overseas call.

Making calls before or after Irish business hours (8:00 a.m. to 6:00 p.m.) is much cheaper. This is sometimes tough to finesse when calling home because of the time difference, but will save you some bucks if you can swing it. (Ireland is five time zones ahead of the United States, so when it's noon in New York it's 5:00 p.m. in Ireland, and when it's noon in Los Angeles, it's 8:00 p.m. in Ireland.)

Making calls from and within Ireland

Here you go: One-stop shopping for all your telephone needs.

- ✔ **To make international calls to places outside the United Kingdom:** You first dial 00 and then the country code (United States and Canada 1, Australia 61, New Zealand 64). Next you dial the area code and number. For example, if you wanted to call the Irish Embassy in Washington, D.C., you would dial 00-1-202-462-3939.

- ✔ **To call Northern Ireland from the Republic:** Dial 08 and then the area code and number.

- ✔ **To call the Republic from Northern Ireland:** Dial 00-353 and then the area code and number.

- ✔ **To call the U.K.:** From the Republic, dial 00-44 and then the area code and number. When calling the U.K. from Northern Ireland, just dial the area code and number.

✔ **For directory assistance from the Republic:** Dial ☎ **1190** if you need a number in the Republic and Northern Ireland, ☎ **1197** if you need a number in Great Britain, and ☎ **1198** for a number in all other countries.

✔ **For directory assistance from Northern Ireland:** Dial ☎ **192** if you want numbers in the U.K. and Republic, and dial ☎ **153** for numbers to all other countries.

✔ **Operator assistance:** If you need operator assistance in making a call, dial ☎ **114** if you need to make an international call and ☎ **10** if you want to call a number in Ireland or Britain.

Throughout this guide phone numbers are preceded by their city codes (Dublin numbers are preceded by the city code 01, for example), but you can drop the city codes if you call within the same city.

Using your U.S. calling card

AT&T, MCI, and Sprint calling cards all operate worldwide, so using any of them in Ireland is no problem. Each has a local access number, which saves you the cost of dialing directly to the United States. When you want to use your card, just call ☎ **800-55-0000** for **AT&T,** ☎ **800-55-5381** for **MCI,** and ☎ **800-55-2001** for **Sprint.** The operator will then explain how to make the call.

If you have a calling card with a company other than one of the three we named, you must call before you go on the trip to see if the calling card company has a local access number in Ireland. After you've arrived, it's too late; directory assistance deals only with those three companies. Whatever card you have, call the company before you go on your trip to see if it has a discount plan for calling overseas.

Using Internet Cafes

If you're going global, go all the way! By using one of Ireland's many Internet cafes you can send quick e-mail postcards to your friends and retrieve your most pressing (or entertaining) incoming messages as you go. You can find *cybercafes* sprinkled throughout the country; we've listed some of them in the "Fast Facts" sections at the end of each area chapter. Most cafes are part of the **Irish Internet Cafe Association.** You can get addresses and phone numbers of cafes from that group's Web site, www.iica.net.

If your Internet provider isn't worldwide, set up a free Hotmail account before you go on your trip. Doing so is easy. Just go to www.hotmail.com and follow the directions. You can have your free account in minutes. Give your new address to friends before you go and you can send and receive messages from any cybercafe in the world, just by going to the Hotmail Web site and entering your name and password.

America Online (AOL) is available at many Internet cafes, and if you already have an AOL account, you just have to sign on as a guest. This way, you don't need to get a Hotmail account. Best of all, you don't have to pay to access your AOL account abroad.

The cost of Internet cafes is generally between £4 and £5 ($5.90 to $7.00) an hour, but if you just need to pop in for a quick fix, most cafes allow you to pay by the quarter hour.

Sending and Receiving Snail Mail in the Republic and Northern Ireland

You do know you'll be hard-pressed to get someone to pick you up at the airport if you don't send home any postcards, right? Post offices in the Republic are called *An Post* and are easy to spot: Look for a bright green storefront with the name across it. Ireland's main postal branch, the **General Post Office,** on O'Connell St., Dublin 1 (☎ **01-872-6666**), is in the heart of Dublin and is the hub of all mail activity. Its hours are 8:00 a.m. to 8:00 p.m., Monday through Saturday; 10:00 a.m. to 6:00 p.m., Sunday. Major branches, found in the bigger towns and cities, are open 9:00 a.m. to 6:00 p.m., Monday through Saturday. Minor branches, which are in every small town, are open 9:00 a.m. to 1:00 p.m. and 2:15 p.m. to 5:30 p.m., Monday through Friday and 9:00 a.m. to 1:00 p.m., Saturday. Irish post offices are more than just places to mail postcards; you can buy phone cards and lottery tickets there, too, and even change money at main branches.

It costs you the same to send a postcard to the United States as it does to send a pretty hefty letter (45p), and it usually takes mail about a week to get to the States. If you plan to mail packages, you can save money by sending them economy, or surface mail. This idea comes in handy when mailing things to yourself. (See "Packing It Up" later in this chapter.)

An Post has a Web site for general information and a tracking system for packages (www.letterpost.ie). **UPS** (☎ **800-575-757**) and **Federal Express** (☎ **800-535-800**) offer overnight service to Canada and the United States for about £32, and they have free pickup.

Sending mail from Northern Ireland is just as easy, though a couple of things make it different. Up North, they're called Post Offices, like in the States. They're also identifiable by color, but here the offices and post boxes are bright red. The general hours are the same as An Post, too. The cost to send a letter outside Europe is 67p Sterling.

If you need mail sent to you while on your trip in Ireland, no problem. Just have the sender address the mail with your name, care of the General Post Office, Restante Office, and the town name (for instance, Joe Smith, c/o General Post Office, Restante Office, Galway, Ireland).

Your mail will be held there for you to pick up. Larger post office branches (all those we list in the "Fast Facts" sections of this book) provide this service, but smaller post offices won't.

American Express cardholders can also have mail sent to them at the AmEx office in Dublin (see the AmEx listing in the appendix in the back of this book).

Packing It Up

Know what's much more important than what you bring on your trip? What you leave at home. So many hapless travelers make the easily avoidable mistake of simply bringing too much with them. Believe us, though: You'll not only not need your bathtub headrest or fur-lined, self-warming slippers, you'll forget all about them.

Consult our packing checklist (later in this chapter). Seem skimpy? It's not. If you want to bring an item not on our checklist, ask yourself if you will really need it. If not, you have one fewer thing to drag around the country. Remember, you're not going to a fashion show and you're almost certain not to run into anyone you know. Who cares if you wear the same pants every day and a sweater four times?

Also, keep in mind that there won't be anyone to carry his or her load and take care of yours, too. There's nothing worse than being slow and miserable with too much luggage to handle. So fill 'em up and lug those bags around while you're still at home. If getting your luggage from the door to the driveway is any struggle, you can be sure you'll never make it through the airport, let alone down a crowded street.

Weighing your luggage options: Carry-on or checked bags

Why waste time (and sanity) watching the luggage carousel go 'round and 'round, as you wait for your bags? If you pack sparingly, everything you really need most likely fits snugly into bags that fit into the over-head compartments of your plane. (Just don't tell the airlines we said that!) So instead of looking at carry-on baggage as a place to stow all those distractions you bring for the plane ride but never get to, con-sider it your ticket out of the airport, fast!

If you do manage to fit everything into carry-on luggage, remember you do have some restrictions. Each airline is different (so be sure you know what the rules are for yours), but allowing passengers one larger bag (generally 10x14x36) and one smaller one, like a purse, is pretty standard for overseas flights. If at all possible, try to board quickly, as the overhead compartments fill quickly (and often with the bags of someone six rows behind). You don't want to be stuck with two-week's baggage at your feet for the whole flight.

For those of you packing on the other extreme, you also have to know about certain restrictions. When it comes to checked baggage you are allowed two bags, each weighing up to 70 pounds (again, this number is general; you need to check with your particular airline for its rules). Don't worry: 140 pounds may not sound like much considering how much you may need to bring, but it's really a lot to work with. If you're worried, place your packed bags on the bathroom scale. That should be a close indicator.

Wear your bulkiest clothes on the plane. This way, you can have more packing room. Also, wearing layers makes it easier to adjust to the ever-varying temperatures onboard the plane.

Deciding what to bring and what to leave at home

The biggest mistakes you can make when packing are bringing too much clothing and bringing the wrong kind. First, *forget about anything that wrinkles easily.* Unless you'll be staying in upscale hotels, you'll be hard-pressed to find an iron. Bringing your own is a dead weight and besides, it won't work in Ireland (see "Ireland unplugged: Leaving that electric nosehair trimmer at home" later in this chapter). Whites are also a no-no, for travel in general and Ireland in particular: With so much rain, a white outfit wouldn't make it to the curb before becoming a piece of abstract art, with mud as the medium.

For the most part, Ireland is a casual country, and even if it weren't, what you'll be doing as a tourist pretty much requires warm, loose-fitting clothes. You'll spend a lot of time outside or in drafty castles and abbeys, and you'll want to be comfortable.

Layering is the best way to ensure your comfort no matter what the temperature. The clothes you bring depend on what time of year you'll be visiting, but even if you go in summer, don't bother with shorts and tank tops — the weather is never really warm enough for that. Another reminder: From September to April Ireland is cold enough for sweaters and jackets. (See Chapter 2.)

It does rain a good deal in Ireland, but a raincoat isn't really necessary. A compact umbrella is light and small and will do just fine for the light, yet almost constant, drizzle characteristic of the country.

One exception to the Irish casual dress code is Dublin. As in most European capitals, people there dress stylishly to just go down the street. Bring one nice outfit if you plan to spend time there.

Remember, you don't need 14 outfits for a 2-week trip. Nearly every town has a laundry service — for a few pounds you can get your clothes washed and dried, and you'll be lugging around so much less.

Bringing the essentials: A checklist

Here's what we consider the must-have items for a two-week trip:

Clothes

✔ **Two pairs of pants.** One pair of jeans for running around and one pair of slacks for going out.

✔ **A casual dress/a buttoned-down shirt.** For a nice dinner, Mass, and so forth.

✔ **Underwear, socks, and T-shirts.** Underclothes keep outer clothes cleaner longer.

✔ **Two long-sleeved shirts.**

✔ **One dark sweater.** Warm, and potentially dressy.

✔ **One pair of good walking shoes.** Much of your time will be spent walking, and you'll want to be comfortable. Be warned, though: a few restaurants and clubs in Dublin won't allow tennis shoes, so you may think about bringing a second, dressier pair if the city is on your itinerary. A pair of solid walking shoes would do the trick nicely.

Toiletries

✔ **Toothbrush and toothpaste.**

✔ **Brush or comb.** A comb takes up less space.

✔ **Soap and shampoo.** Travel sizes should be enough for the trip, as you'll get some from hotels — though not from B&Bs and hostels.

✔ **Razor and shaving cream.** A light, small, travel-size shaving cream and three razors will last weeks. You may be tempted to bring an electric razor, but it could be useless due to voltage differences. We explain later in this chapter.

✔ **Deodorant.** Never leave home without it.

✔ **Medicine.** Be sure to bring an extra week of your prescription, just in case. Bringing common ailment relievers like aspirin, antacids, cold medicine, and Dramamine is a good idea, rather than taking chances with equivalents or nothing at all.

✔ **Glasses, contacts, and ample saline solution.**

✔ **Feminine hygiene products.**

✔ **Laundry bag.** A pillowcase will do just fine.

✔ **Towel.** A must if you stay at hostels, and you may prefer your own to those at some B&Bs.

✔ **Condoms.** Yes, you can get them in Ireland, but U.S. brands are safer.

✔ **Pocket-size tissue packs.** Aside from the obvious rescue from a runny nose, they make great napkins in a pinch.

✔ **Odds and ends.** Lotion, makeup, nail file, and so on.

The rest

✔ **This book.** Don't leave us behind!

✔ **A travel log.** Even if it's just a cheap spiral notebook, use it to keep track of every day of your trip. No matter how memorable your trip seems, you'll probably never remember every detail otherwise.

✔ **Camera.** Unless you have the disposal kind, bring extra batteries; also, all a camera bag is really good for is letting potential thieves know what an expensive camera you have. Use a small daypack instead.

✔ **Film.** Bring plenty of extra rolls, because film is much more expensive in Ireland; also, be aware that your film (especially the high-speed variety) really can be damaged in airport X-ray machines. They can make your pictures look cloudy. To avoid putting the film through the machine with the rest of your carry-on bags, put the rolls in a clear bag and hand them to the security officer for inspection.

✔ **Travel alarm clock.** They're standard in hotels, but you'll need one in B&Bs and hostels.

✔ **Address list.** Leave behind the whole address book, and instead jot down those people you want to send postcards to — you can use on of the "Notes" pages in the back of this book if you like.

✔ **Small umbrella.**

✔ **Paperback novel(s).**

✔ **Gum.** For ear popping during take-off and landing.

✔ **Passport.**

✔ **Money.** Travelers checks, some cash, credit cards, calling card, and ATM card.

✔ **Driver's license.** It doesn't hold as much power in terms of identification as it does at home, but you definitely need it to rent a car.

✔ **Student or youth ID.** Great for discounts and backup identification.

✔ **Airline tickets.**

If you have any room left, that's where you can put souvenirs. No matter how much room you leave, though, you will never have enough. If you can't cram everything into your luggage for the return trip, either buy an inexpensive bag or mail yourself your dirty laundry. Doing so is safer than risking your souvenirs to the care of the postal service.

Ireland unplugged: Leaving that electric nosehair trimmer at home

Basically, don't bother bringing anything that must be plugged in or recharged. The plugs in Ireland are different. You can buy a cheap adapter, but then you have the problem of different voltages.

In the States the current is 110 volts. In Ireland it's 220 to 240 volts. So if you plug in your hair dryer, and the voltage is different, even with an adapter the machine may light up like a Roman candle or blow a fuse. You can buy a voltage transformer, but they're expensive and not worth the cost for a short stay. If you bring electronic items (such as an alarm clock or personal cassette or CD player), make sure they're battery-powered, and bring extra batteries.

Some travel appliances like shavers and irons have a nice feature called *dual voltage* that will adapt to the change, but unless your appliance gives a voltage range (such as 110v to 220v), don't chance it. Most laptop computers have this feature, but always check with the manufacturer as a precaution. Plug adapters are not hard to find; your local hardware store or even the airport should have what you need. For more information, call the **Franzus Corporation** (☎ **203-723-6664**) for its pamphlet on foreign electricity and a converter order form.

If you plan on bringing a video camera (something we don't encourage — better to look at and remember the country than devote all your attention to the camera), bring enough battery packs but also enough videotape. Blank cassette tapes in Ireland look identical to the ones from home, but they won't work in your camera!

Making Your Plane Ride More Comfortable

Whoever said, "Getting there is half the fun" was wrong. Plane rides, especially bad ones, can be particularly uncomfortable. Cramped legs, infamously bad cuisine, and a movie you can barely see can put a big damper on the first leg of your trip. But again, your airplane experience comes down to packing. Bringing just a few essential items in your carry-on bag can make the trip great.

- ✔ **Water:** Pressurized cabins are notorious for leaving you dehydrated, so bring a large bottle of water to drink throughout the trip. Alcohol can be pretty free-flowing on flights, but beware: The added dehydration will not only knock you for a loop, it will add to jet lag.

- ✔ **Diversions:** The in-flight magazine will soon wear thin, and you can't guarantee the movie will be one you haven't seen already, so plenty of diversions are a must. A novel, favorite magazine, and crossword puzzles are all good time-passers.

- ✔ **Snacks:** It could take eons for the dinner cart to make it to your row, and even then you may hate the meal, so be prepared! There's nothing worse than starving your way through a long flight. Pack some snacks that are filling but not too salty, like dried fruit or bagels.

These things may not make you feel like you're in first class, but they can at least take your mind off the man snoring in your ear.

These days, airlines are gracious and willing to accommodate passenger food restrictions and limitations. So if you're a vegetarian, are restricting your salt or fat intake, are allergic to fish, keep kosher or hallal, or have some other special dietary regime, call the airline two days before you leave and request a special meal. You'd be surprised at how many options they have.

My Luggage Is WHERE!?!?

There is, of course, the slim chance that your luggage will be lost or delayed. You can prepare yourself for this, though. Simply pack your carry-on bag with a light change of clothes and necessary toiletries. This way, even if you are high and dry for a day or so, you won't frighten the natives.

Part III
Dublin and the East Coast

The 5th Wave   By Rich Tennant

"OK—we got one cherry lager with bitters and a pineapple slice, and one honey malt ale with cinnamon and an orange twist. You want these in steins or parfait glasses?"

In this part . . .

Sometimes people fly into Dublin airport and immediately whisk themselves off to the western part of the
country in a "see ya, wouldn't wanna be ya" sort of way.
These people are missing out. Dublin and the counties
that surround it — Wickow, Kildare, Meath, and Louth —
are all spectacular places.

Dublin City, with its big-time hotels, restaurants, clubs,
and museums, is a place whose imprint will last in your
memory. In fact, there's so much to do and see in Dublin
that we've devoted all of Chapter 11 to it. Dublin also
makes a great base camp for exploring the region's many
attractions. Just north of the city are Meath and Louth,
which contain Ireland's most magnificent ancient ruins
(which we tell you about in Chapter 12), while to the
south there are Wicklow and Kildare, two counties that
contain some of the very best of Irish outdoors (covered
in Chapter 13). Prepare to be amazed.

And let's not forget the southeastern counties of Ireland —
Wexford, Waterford, Kilkenny, and Tipperary — which we
cover in Chapter 14. You'll find a little bit of everything
here: a few castles, beautiful sunny countryside bordered
by the sea, the famous Rock of Cashel, and the even more
famous Waterford Crystal Factory.

Chapter 11

Dublin

● ●

In This Chapter

▶ Arriving in Dublin and getting around once you're there

▶ Getting your bearings in the city's major neighborhoods

▶ Deciding where to stay and where to eat

▶ Learning more about Dublin's best sites, landmarks, museums, and cathedrals

▶ Shopping for distinctly Irish items

▶ Finding all the top pubs

● ●

Consider a place that combines history, architecture, and rich culture, couples cosmopolitan flair with old-time tradition, and unites the diversity of an entire country. Sounds like a great place to visit, huh? Well, that's just what you're doing, because Dublin provides all of this and more. Along its cobbled streets you'll find buildings that date back to a time before America was a twinkle in England's eye, and everywhere you look are reminders of the Irish patriots who fought and died for their country.

On top of all this, Dublin has come into her own in recent years. Once barely passable as a European capital, Dublin is on the fast track these days, quickly becoming a hub of computer software development and booming with the roar of Ireland's "Celtic Tiger" economy. And with such prominence comes the key components to any major city: money, young people, and flair. Dublin is now a hip, young place with excellent international cuisine, five-star hotels, and posh nightclubs.

Fear not: The city retains its original charm and history in the middle of all this modernizing. In fact, it's the booming economy that has allowed Dublin to clean up its act and drop money into restoring public buildings and historical exhibits. There really never was a better time to visit the city.

County Dublin and the East Coast

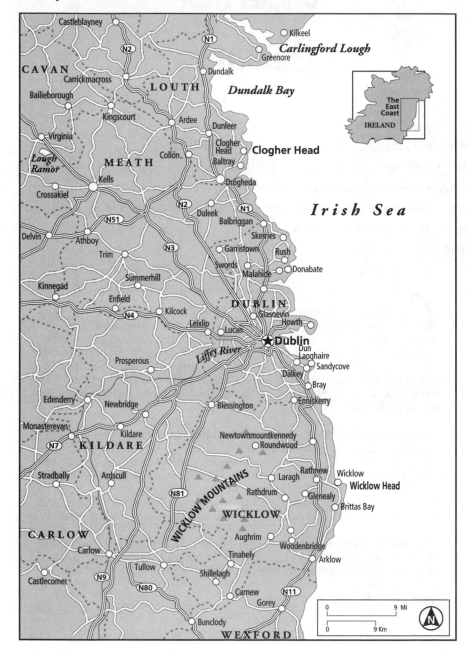

Getting to Dublin

Dublin is one of Ireland's two international gateways, so if you're flying to the country there's a good chance it's where you'll be touching down.

By plane

Dublin International Airport (☎ 01-844-4900) is seven miles north of the city, about a 25-minute drive from City Centre (*An Lar* in Gaelic). Aer Lingus, Continental, Delta, and American fly directly into Dublin from the States. British Midlands, Aer Lingus, and Ryanair have regular flights from England.

All the major car rental companies listed in Chapter 4 have desks in the Arrivals Hall of the terminal. Taxis are available outside the terminal's main entrance; just look for the signs. The fare to downtown Dublin is about £12–16 ($17.75–$23.70), depending on traffic. There are two buses that will take you to Dublin City Centre (near O'Connell Street). The number 41 Dublin bus only takes passengers with little or no luggage and the fare is £1.20 ($1.80). You'll need change to pay the fare, as the drivers don't carry any. The other option, the AirLink cargo bus (the number 747 or 748), is a cheap way to get to the city from the airport; it costs £3 ($4.45) per person, and the buses have room for luggage. You'll be dropped near a taxi rank and can take a cab from there to your hotel — much cheaper than taking one from the airport. The buses generally run from 7:00 a.m. to 11:00 p.m. daily. Lastly, if you're booked in one of the larger hotels in the city, you could make arrangements to use its airport pick-up service.

By ferry

Passenger and car transportation from Britain's town of Holyhead are run by two companies. **Irish Ferries** (☎ 01-855-2222; E-mail: info@ irishferries.ie; Internet: www.irishferries.ie) arrive at Dublin Ferryport (on the Eastern tip of the North Docks). **Stena Sealink Line** ferries (☎ 01-204-7777) arrive at the Ferryport in Dun Laoghaire, a southern suburb of Dublin. Public transportation into the City Centre is available from both ports.

Whether arriving from other parts of Ireland or by ferry, major roads (N1, N2, N3 from the north; N4, N7 from the west; N11 from the south) all lead directly into the City Centre. The M50 Westlink (80p toll) is Dublin's beltway, linking all the major routes (for example N1, N2) out of town.

By train

Irish Rail (Iarnro'd E'irrann) InterCity service (☎ 1850-36-6222; Internet: www.irishrail.ie) links Dublin to the major towns of Ireland and to Belfast. Trains arrive at one of three stations: Connolly Station,

Amiens Street (serving trains from the North, including Northern Ireland); Heuston Station, Kingsbridge, off St. John's Road (serving trains from the South and West); and Pearse Station, Westland Row, Tara Street (serving trains from the Southeast). The **DART** (Dublin Area Rapid Transit) is a commuter train that connects the city to the coastal towns north (as far as Howth) and south (as far as Greystones); call the same number previously given in this paragraph for more information.

By bus

The city's bus terminal is on Store Street (☎ **1850-36-6222;** Internet: www.buseireann.ie), three blocks east of O'Connell Street, north of the river behind the Trading House building. The bus system, **Bus Eireann,** connects Dublin to most cities and towns all over the country.

Orienting Yourself in Dublin

One of the first things you'll notice when you start thinking about what to see in Dublin is that the addresses all have a number after their address, such as the General Post Office, O'Connell Street, Dublin 1. These numbers indicate what part of the city the area is in, in the same way that American addresses use zip codes. Most of central Dublin is located within postal codes 1, 2, and 8. Odd numbers are north of the River Liffey and even numbers are south of it.

A few words on street names: They're not what you call logical, at least not all the time. For instance, you'll be walking along, when all of a sudden the street name changes! One minute you're on Aungiers Street, next you're on South Great George's Street. Did you make a turn without knowing it? No, that's just how the streets go in Irish cities. Names sometimes change from block to block, so pay careful attention as you go.

Here's how the different neighborhoods break down:

- ✔ **O'Connell Street (north side):** Although this area once thrived as a fashionable and historical part of the city, it's now something of an aging starlet, largely ignored and left to seed. Between stately buildings like the **General Post Office** and **Gresham Hotel** are fast-food joints, movie theaters, and amusements. O'Connell Street's center median is dotted with impressive statues of noted Irishmen. Just north of the street is the serene **Garden of Remembrance** and the **Dublin Writers Museum,** and only a few blocks away is the famous **Abbey Theatre.** This area stands out for its shopping, with Henry and Mary streets providing the city's largest selection of stores.

- ✔ **Trinity College Area (south side):** Just across O'Connell Bridge on the south side of the River Liffey stands Trinity College. This sprawling and well-kept campus sits in the heart of the city, and is surrounded by classy bookstores and shops.

✔ **Temple Bar (south side):** Tucked into a spot between Trinity and Dublin Castle is the ever-fashionable Temple Bar. Here you'll find funky shops and hip bars along cobbled alleys. This is the cultural and entertainment hub of the city. There's no shortage of lively pubs, late-night bars, unique shops, and interesting people.

✔ **Old City-Historical Area (south side):** For a taste of history, step into this area of narrow streets and ancient buildings. Some date as far back as Viking and Medieval times. Some highlights are **Dublin Castle, Christ Church Cathedral** and **St. Patrick's Cathedral,** and the **old city walls.** A bit further on, in the area known as the Liberties, you'll find the **Guinness Hop Store.**

✔ **St. Stephen's Green and Grafton Street (south side):** This area begins at the bottom of the pedestrian Grafton Street and finishes up in St. Stephen's Green, the city's park. This pretty part of town has plenty of upscale shopping and cafes, and is always teeming with people. The green is an enclosed park at the head of the street, and nice weather brings out plenty of Dubliners.

✔ **Merrion and Fitzwilliam Squares (south side):** These two square parks are surrounded by fashionable townhomes, some the very best examples of Georgian architecture, and each with a distinctive, brightly colored door. Some were once the homes of Dublin's most famous citizens, but today many of them house professional offices.

For visitor information, go to the **Dublin Tourism Centre** on Suffolk Street (☎ **1850-23-0330** from inside the country, call ☎ 066-979-2083 from outside the Republic, open year-round.) It also provides reservation services. For telephone directory assistance, dial ☎ **1190.** A good online source of Dublin information is www.visit.ie/countries/ ie/dublin/index.html.

Getting around Dublin

The best way to get around Dublin and really see it is by lacing up a good pair of walking shoes and start hoofing. Dublin is entirely accessible by foot, and walking can actually save you a lot of hassles. Driving a car in the city is like going to war, and if you opt for mass transit you can waste precious sightseeing time figuring out local bus routes and then waiting for them — often you could walk there in half the time.

Just remember before stepping into the street that the cars are going in a different direction! Coming from a "driving on the right" country, your tendency will be to look to the left first when stepping onto the street, when the cars will really be coming from the right. At crosswalks in Dublin and other bigger cities you'll hear a beeping or chirping sound. These are for the seeing-impaired, signaling when it's safe to cross.

The **DART** connects the city to the suburbs and coastal towns north (as far as Howth) and south (as far as Greystones). Call ☎ **1850-36-6222** (www.irishrail.ie) for information. There are only three stops in Dublin: Connolly Station, Pearse Street Station, and Tara Street Station (the closest to City Centre, next to the River Liffey just east of the O'Connell Street Bridge). The DART runs from 6:00 a.m. to 11:45 p.m. Monday through Saturday and 9:00 a.m. to 11:45 p.m. on Sundays. Trains run every 5 to 15 minutes, depending on time of day. (See the Cheat Sheet in the front of this book for a DART map.)

Dublin Bus, 59 Upper O'Connell St., Dublin 1 (☎ 01-872-0000), operates local bus service throughout Dublin city and county, with fares ranging from 55p to £1.20 (80 cent to $1.80). Try to have exact change because the newer buses don't give change back. The double-decker buses are still in use (although they're no longer all green) but there is also a fleet of small, red and yellow, short-distance buses called City Imps. Buses run from 6:00 a.m. to 11:30 p.m. (Sunday service begins at 10:00 a.m.) and there's a late-night route Thursday through Sunday nights until 3:00 a.m. There are discounted one-day to four-day passes available with some restrictions. Call for more details.

The way to get a taxi in Dublin is by going to a taxi rank, where cabs line up along the street. You can hail a cab, but it's not common and the cab is liable not to stop. There are taxi ranks at larger hotels, train stations, the bus station, the O'Connell Street median near the General Post Office, opposite St. Stephen's Green shopping center, near Trinity College in front of the Bank of Ireland, and at other locations throughout the city. Getting a taxi during the day is usually not a problem, but you can end up waiting up to an hour for one on weekend late nights. There are no meters, but the initial rate is £1.80 ($2.65) plus £1.20 ($1.80) per mile. As a rule, only get in a cab that's marked (with a rooftop sign or lettering on the doors); unmarked cars might not be sanctioned by the city and therefore have no fixed prices. **Blue Cabs** (☎ 01-676-1111) operates a 24-hour service.

Unlike cab etiquette in the States, it's protocol for passengers to sit up front with the driver rather than in the back seat, chauffeur-style. And hold on to your hats: Dublin cabbies are notorious for their crazy — yet strangely capable — driving.

If you can avoid renting a car while staying in Dublin, do it. If you do drive into the city, blue-and-white signs marked "P" direct you to car parks and blue computerized signs list the number of spaces available in each. Street parking is on a "disk" system. You can buy disks from black-box vending machines in the city and from newsstands in outer neighborhoods. Check signs to make sure you don't park illegally, because the *garda* (police) will clamp your car, making it impossible for you to drive it away. The only large 24-hour car park in Dublin is Usher's Quay on the south of the River Liffey near O'Connell Street.

Where to Stay in Dublin

Dublin is home to what seems like a zillion hotels, ranging from luxurious to simple. We've picked out some of the best, and we cover all the bases that'll help you find the kind of place that says "you."

If you're at all concerned about the quality of a hotel you choose, just find out how many stars it's been given by the Irish Tourist Board. This system ranks hotels from one to five stars. Of course, more stars usually means more pounds! The **Dublin Tourism Centre** on Suffolk Street will help you find accommodation based on price, location, and other factors. You can reserve a room (from within Ireland) by whipping out your credit card and calling ☎ **1800-66-8668** or e-mailing reservations@dublintourism.ie.

Dublin Central Reservation also has a free booking service that will book you into anything from a five-star hotel to a hostel. Contact them at ☎ **01-820-0394;** Fax: 01-822-0493; E-mail: bookings@dublin reservations.com; or Internet: www.dublinreservations.com.

The **Self-Catering Accommodation Association** for weekly rentals can be reached at ☎ **01-668-6641.**

Unlike the rest of the country, Dublin hotels don't really lower prices during the off-season (October through April). Some rates go down, but don't expect a deal at one of the city's finest hotels just because it's the dead of winter. However, city hotels often offer great weekend packages, so be sure to ask about those.

Unless otherwise noted, accommodations have parking available. The price for parking isn't generally included in the rate, but if it's in a garage, often the price is discounted for guests.

The Clarence

$$$$ Temple Bar, Dublin 2

This high-class, five-star hotel has everything: location, elegance, a modern look, and superior service. It's even touched by fame: The hotel is partly owned by Bono and the Edge of the Irish rock band U2. Its decor is simple and chic, and it lies in the heart of the ever-popular Temple Bar area. It also boasts the classy Octagon bar, raved-about Tea Room restaurant, and one of Dublin's poshest night clubs, The Kitchen. This place is strictly for those looking for some lavish pampering.

6–8 Wellington Quay, Temple Bar, Dublin 2. ☎ *01-407-0800. Fax: 01-407-0820. E-mail:* clarence@indigo.ie. *DART: Tara St. Station. Bus: 51, 51B, 68, 68A, 69X, 78A, 79, 90, 210. Valet parking. Rack Rates: £190–216 ($281.20–$319.70) double. Breakfast not included. AE, DC, MC, V.*

College House B&B

$ Dublin 9

The main road between City Centre and the airport is lined with B&Bs, but the quaint and quiet Victorian residence of Lord Boyce Molloy, across the street from St. Patrick's College, stands out. The rooms are comfortable and the location is convenient to the city, airport, and ferries.

50 Upper Drumcondra Rd., Dublin 9. ☎ *01-836-7070. Bus: 3, 11, 16, 41. Rack Rates: £15–30 double ($22.20–$44.40). No credit cards.*

Hotel Isaacs
$$ O'Connell St. Area, Dublin 1

This moderately priced hotel is close to Dublin's main shopping area and is a mere five-minute walk to the City Centre. Isaacs is a restored wine warehouse, and much of the original brickwork is still visible, giving it a lot of character. Rooms are furnished with a modern and tasteful flair. The hotel is right across the street from the bus station, making it a perfect place for those coming into the city by bus. There's an Italian restaurant, Il Vignardo, downstairs.

Store St., Dublin 1. ☎ *01-855-0067. Fax: 01-836-5390. E-mail:* hotel@isaacs.ie. *Internet:* www.ibi.ie/isaacs. *DART: Connolly St. Station. Bus: 90. Rack Rates: £40 ($59.20) double. AE, MC, V.*

Hotel St. George
$ O'Connell St. Area, Dublin 1

Situated within a row of classic Georgian townhomes, the Hotel St. George stands out for its great location at the top of O'Connell Street on the north side of the city. From here, you're close to the Abbey and Gate theaters, the Writers Museum, the James Joyce Centre, and shopping galore. Rooms are reasonable, too.

7 Parnell Sq., Dublin 1. ☎ *01-874-5611. Fax: 01-874-5582. E-mail:* hotels@ indigo.ie. *Internet:* www.indigo.ie/hotels. *DART: Connolly St. Station. Bus: 1. Rack Rates: £40–45 ($59.20–$66.60) double. MC, V.*

Jury's Christchurch Inn
$$ Old City (near Temple Bar), Dublin 2

You can't beat Jury's for value if you're traveling as a family: This hotel group is one of the few in Ireland that offers a flat rate per room, rather than per person. The rooms here are large and modern, and the hotel offers baby-sitting services. There's live traditional music in the bar on weekend nights. Christchurch Inn is situated conveniently at the top of Dame Street, in the heart of the city.

Christ Church Place, Dublin 8. ☎ *800-843-3311, toll free from the United States; 01-454-0000. Fax: 01-454-0012. E-mail:* info@jurys.com. *DART: Tara St. Station. Bus: 21A, 50, 50A, 78, 78A, 78B. Rack Rates: £70 ($103.60) for up to three adults or two adults and two children. AE, DC, MC, V.*

Jury's Custom House Inn
$$ O'Connell St. Area, Dublin 1

Apart from having a few less rooms than its counterpart across the River Liffey (see previous), the Custom House Inn has all the perks Jury's Christchurch offers, down to the rates. This hotel is on the north side of the river near the Custom House, and comparably as convenient as its sister hotel to Dublin attractions.

Custom House Quay, Dublin 1. ☎ ***800-843-3311,** toll free from the United States;*
01-607-5000. Fax: 01-829-0400. E-mail: info@jurys.com. *DART: Tara St. Station.*
Bus: 27B, 42, 43, 53, 53A. Rack Rates: £70 ($103.60) for up to three adults or two
adults and two children. AE, DC, MC, V.

Leeson Court Hotel

$$ St. Stephen's Green Area, Dublin 2

This small hotel is just five minutes' walk from St. Stephen's Green, in
one of the classier parts of town. The Leeson is a restored Georgian
building and seems to exude relaxation. Darby O'Gill's is the hotel bar,
which is quaint looking and really picks up at night.

26–27 Lower Leeson St., Dublin 2. ☎ ***01-676-3380.** Fax: 01-661-8273. DART: Tara St.*
Station. Bus: 11, 11A, 11B, 13B, 46A, 46B, 84X. Rack Rates: £70–78 ($103.60–$115.45)
double. DC, MC, V.

North Star

$$ O'Connell St. Area, Dublin 1

This family-owned hotel is just a stone's throw from the Connolly rail
and DART station on the north side of the River Liffey. It underwent
major renovations last year, boosting the number of rooms and
transforming it into a plush hotel. The restaurant is grand and the pub
is comfortable. Mentioned in Joyce's *Ulysses,* the hotel is a good starting
point for sightseeing.

Amien St., Dublin 1. ☎ ***01-836-3561.** Fax: 01-836-3561. E-mail:* north@
regencyhotels.com. *Internet:* www.regencyhotels.com. *DART: Connolly*
St. Station. Bus: 90. Rack Rates: £70–120 ($103.60–$177.60) double. AE, MC, V.

Phoenix Park House

$ Phoenix Park Area, Dublin 8

This family-run guest house is a perfect choice for people entering town
from Heuston Station. It's next to the beautiful and serene Phoenix Park
and is walking distance to the Guinness Brewery and National Museum.
The City Centre is very accessible by bus, and besides, it's pretty cheap.

38–39 Parkgate, Dublin 8. ☎ ***01-677-2870.** Fax: 01-679-9769. E-mail:*
phoenixparkhouse@tinet.ie. *Internet:* www.dublinguesthouse.com.
DART: Heuston St. Station. Bus: 25, 26, 51, 66, 67, 68, 69. Rack Rates: £20–50
($29.60–$74) double. AE, MC, V.

Shelbourne

$$$$ St. Steven's Green, Dublin 2

Since it was opened in 1824, this luxurious hotel has seen its share of
history. It was one of the first buildings in Dublin to have electric lights.
The door numbered 112 opens to the Constitution Room, where Michael
Collins and others drafted the constitution of the Irish Free State in 1922.

JFK and Jackie stayed during a visit in 1957. Even if staying here's too much of a splurge, you can have a cup of tea in the Lord Mayor's Lounge and gaze at the grand chandelier in the lobby. No two rooms are the same in this historical tribute to old-world tradition. If you do decide to spend the dough here, get a room overlooking St. Stephen's Green, not one with a bland view from the back of the hotel.

27 St. Stephen's Green, Dublin 2. ☎ *800-848-8415, from the United States; 01-676-6471. Fax: 01-661-6006. E-mail:* shelbourneinfo@forte-hotels.com. *Internet:* www.shelbourne.ie. *DART: Tara St. Station. Bus: 32X, 39X, 41X, 66X, 67X. Rack Rates: £208–263 ($307.85–$389.25) double. Breakfast not included. AE, DC, MC, V.*

Temple Bar Hotel

$$$ **Temple Bar, Dublin 2**

As the saying goes, "Location, location, location." This hotel has that, and a lot more. Starting with the courteous staff that's eager to help, and carrying on to the immaculate and comfortable rooms, this is what a hotel should be. They do all they can to make you feel welcome, from the bottled water in your room to the towel warmers in the bathroom. The Terrace Restaurant has good food and it's a pleasure to relax in its atriumlike dining room.

Fleet St., Temple Bar, Dublin 2. ☎ *01-677-3333. Fax: 01-677-3088. E-mail:* templeb@iol.ie. *DART: Tara St. Station. Bus to Fleet St.: 51, 51B, 68, 68A, 69X, 78A, 79, 90, 210. Rack Rates: £140 ($207.30) double. AE, DC, MC, V.*

Trinity Arch

$$ **Temple Bar, Dublin 2**

Nestled in an eighteenth-century building, this relatively small hotel is on the edge of Temple Bar and smack-dab between Trinity College and Dublin Castle. Oliver Goldsmith's Bar, in the downstairs, is a multileveled and elegant place that serves fabulous nibble food at low prices. This is a fine place to stay, especially for its location, right on Dame Street. For the health-conscious, price of a room includes use of the nearby Riverside Gym.

46 Dame St., Dublin 2. ☎ *01-679-4455. Fax: 01-679-4511. DART: Tara St. Station. Bus: 51, 51B, 68, 68A, 69X, 78A, 79, 90, 210. Rack Rates: £85–110 ($125.80–$162.80) double. AE, DC, MC, V.*

Where to Dine in Dublin

Dublin is chock-full of great places to eat. It may come as a surprise, but Ireland's capital is not the place to find traditional Celtic food. Just the opposite; in fact, Dublin is home to a wide variety of international foods and places ranging from casual to formal. You truly can find whatever it is you're craving. Looking for Indian or Mediterranean? You've got it. Or is it French haute cuisine, Tex-Mex, or creole that's tempting your taste buds? No problem. Finding a place to eat in Dublin is easier than finding a politician in Washington.

If you're dining with children, the best chain restaurant for kids is **Eddie Rockets.** This chain of diner-style restaurants features burgers and super-good shakes at family-friendly prices. The service is good and the breakfasts are yummy. Locations include 77 Dame St., 33 Upper Baggot St., 52 Upper O'Connell St., 17 Anne St., and 19 Wexford St.

A lovely spot for tea

If there's one thing you just have to do in Dublin, it's partake in the age-old practice of relaxing with a cuppa' at **Bewley's Oriental Cafe.** You'll see Bewley's signs at little mom-and-pop cafes all over Ireland to show they serve the finest tea and coffee, but the Bewley's branch you want to visit is at 78–79 Grafton St., Dublin 2 (☎ **01-677-6761**). It's open Monday to Wednesday 7:30 a.m. to 1:00 a.m., Thursday to Saturday 8:00 a.m. to 2:00 a.m., Sunday 9:30 a.m. to 10:00 p.m.

Pub grub

Hungry, but don't feel like leaving the bar for some good food? Fear not. You'd be surprised at the quality of meals available at some pubs. The following pubs have great grub:

- ✔ **Oliver St. John Gogarty,** 57–58 Fleet St., Temple Bar, Dublin 2 (☎ **01-671-1822**)
- ✔ **Oliver Goldsmith's,** Trinity Arch Hotel, 46 Dame St., Dublin 2 (☎ **01-679-4074**)
- ✔ **Foggy Dew,** 1 Upper Fownes St., Temple Bar, Dublin 2 (☎ **01- 677-9328**)
- ✔ **Stag's Head,** 1 Dame Ct., Dublin 2 (☎ **01-679-3701**)

Dublin's top restaurants

Of course, "top" doesn't mean just fancy places. We've also included a few great little "cheap eats" places where you can pick up fast (but good!) food. Being hungry is the easy part. Choosing a place to eat is what's hard. Good thing for you we've done the legwork and found the prime spots so you don't have to waste time, money, or good taste.

Apache Pizza

$ Temple Bar, Dublin 2 PIZZA

Located in the very heart of the city, Apache is a perfect stop for some quick chow. You can get pizza by the pie or slice, or try a famous Totem Roll — all kinds of pizza ingredients stuffed into a hoagie bun and baked. Plenty of places to sit, from the counter upstairs to the tables downstairs, and there's a fabulous jukebox to sort through while waiting for your order. Great for post-bar food, too.

58 Dame St., Temple Bar, Dublin 2. ☎ *01-677-8888. DART: Tara St. Station. Bus to Fleet St.: 46, 46A, 46B, 63, 150. Main courses: £1.80–3.95 ($2.65–$5.85). Open: Mon–Thur 11:30 a.m.–11:00 p.m., Fri–Sat 11:00 a.m.–3:00 a.m.*

Bad Ass Cafe

$$ Temple Bar, Dublin 2   PIZZA-AMERICAN

No, you don't have to be tough to go there (the name actually refers to a donkey), but you do have to be hungry! It's an open place, with different levels and tons of windows looking out to the teeming cobbled streets of Temple Bar. The Bad Ass is an institution, serving up some of the city's best pizza. Plenty of other quasi-American dishes round out the menu, and for the health conscious, the salads are good and fresh. It's a place kids will enjoy — not only is it lively (and sometimes noisy), but they'll also get food that will remind them of home. For the parents, there's a great wine list, too.

9 Crown Alley, Temple Bar, Dublin 2. ☎ *01-671-2596. DART: Tara St. Station. Bus to Fleet St.: 46, 46A, 46B, 63, 150. Main courses: £5.50–10.50 ($8.15–$15.55). AE, MC, V. Open: Mon–Sun 11:30 a.m.–midnight.*

Beshoff's

$ Trinity Area, Dublin 2   FISH AND CHIPS

Although opened the same year as Leo Burdocks (see later in this section), Beshoff's doesn't claim to be the original fish and chips shop — it claims to be the best! And it might well be. The fish, and there's quite a variety, is as fresh as can be, and the chips are crisp and done just right. Unlike its counterpart, Beshoff's has seating, giving it a restauranty feel rather that just take-out.

14 Westmoreland St., Dublin 2. ☎ *01-677-8026. DART: Tara St. Station. Bus: 7A, 8, 15A, 15B, 15C, 46, 55, 62, 63, 83, 84. Main courses: £1.90–4.95 ($2.80–$7.35). Open: Mon–Thur 11:30 a.m.–11:00 p.m., Fri and Sat 11:00 a.m.–3:00 a.m.*

Botticelli's

$$$$ Temple Bar, Dublin 2   ITALIAN

This is food for people who know and love their Italian cuisine. Run by Italians, it's a place oft-frequented by Dubs, making it a hot spot that's nearly impossible to get into on weekends. But the *gnocchi* (dumplings) or *tiramisu* (an Italian dessert) alone make it worth the wait you're likely to encounter. The Wellington Quay entrance by the River Liffey well represents the crisp, clean decor, while the Temple Bar entrance makes the place look like an upscale take-out joint. Don't be fooled, though; nothing about Botticelli's is like a pizza place (though they do have great pizza!).

3 Temple Bar Rd., Temple Bar, Dublin 2. ☎ *01-672-7289. DART: Tara St. Station. Bus to Fleet St.: 46, 46A, 46B, 63, 150. Main courses: £21–29 ($31.10–$42.90). AE, DC, MC, V. Open: Daily 10:00 a.m.–midnight.*

Eastern Tandoori

$$$ Trinity Area, Dublin 2   INDIAN

Indian tandoori cuisine enjoys a huge following in Dublin, and this place well represents the best of it. Offering a menu that's sure to please everyone, Eastern Tandoori features a variety of foods that even the pickiest of eaters can choose from and enjoy. Everything inside is authentic, from the food to the comfortable surroundings. It's such a popular restaurant that the owners have branched out across the city and into the South. We recommend the barbecued beef.

34–35 S. William St., Dublin 2. ☎ 01-671-0506. DART: Tara St. Station. Bus to Fleet St.: 10, 16, 22, 46, 46A. Main courses: £13.95–18.50 ($20.65–$27.40). AE, DC, MC, V. Open: Mon–Sat 12:00 p.m.–2:30 p.m. and 6:00 p.m.–midnight, Sun 6:00 p.m.–11:30 p.m.

Elephant & Castle

$$$ Temple Bar, Dublin 2   AMERICAN

What you might notice first about this place is that it's always bustling. So if you won't take our word for how good the place is, take everyone else's! This wide-open restaurant offers interesting twists on American favorites, turning old standbys into sumptuous meals. Hamburgers and nachos will never be the same! And brunches are hugely popular, partly for the great omelettes and *huevos rancheros* (fried eggs with a creole sauce) and partly for the relaxed atmosphere and reasonable prices. Hey parents, take note: Kids love this place!

18 Temple Bar St., Temple Bar, Dublin 2. ☎ 01-679-3121. DART: Tara St. Station. Bus to Fleet St.: 46, 46A, 46B, 63, 150. Main courses: £5.50–13.95 ($8.15–$20.65). AE, DC, MC, V. Open: Mon–Thur 8:00 a.m.–11:30 p.m., Fri 8:00 a.m.–midnight, Sat 10:30 a.m.–midnight, Sun 12:00 p.m.–11:30 p.m.

Fitzer's

$$$ St. Stephen's Green Area, Dublin 2   CAFE

Owned by the Fitzpatricks of Dublin, a family that began as fruit and vegetable merchants in the city, Fitzer's cafes are a testament to how fresh, quality produce can enhance a meal. From creative and filling salads to innovative pasta dishes, Fitzer's incorporates a worldwide theme in its menu while staying true to the basics of an upscale cafe. The selection is varied without becoming complicated, and the atmosphere is classy without being unapproachable. The staff is smart and friendly, too. You'd never guess, but Fitzer's is a chain. There are four locations in the city, each with different menus and prices. The one located on Dawson Street, just blocks from Grafton Street, is the one we recommend. Just for the record, though, the other locations are in RDS Ballsbridge, Dublin 4 (☎ 01-667-1301); National Gallery, 42 Fownes St., Temple Bar, Dublin 2 (☎ 01-679-0440); and Merrion Sq., Dublin 2 (☎ 01-661-4496).

Dublin Accommodations and Dining

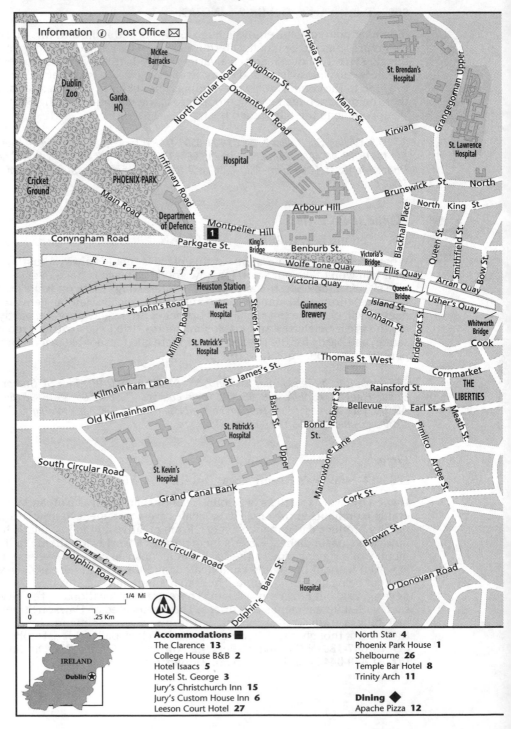

Accommodations ■
The Clarence **13**
College House B&B **2**
Hotel Isaacs **5**
Hotel St. George **3**
Jury's Christchurch Inn **15**
Jury's Custom House Inn **6**
Leeson Court Hotel **27**

North Star **4**
Phoenix Park House **1**
Shelbourne **26**
Temple Bar Hotel **8**
Trinity Arch **11**

Dining ◆
Apache Pizza **12**

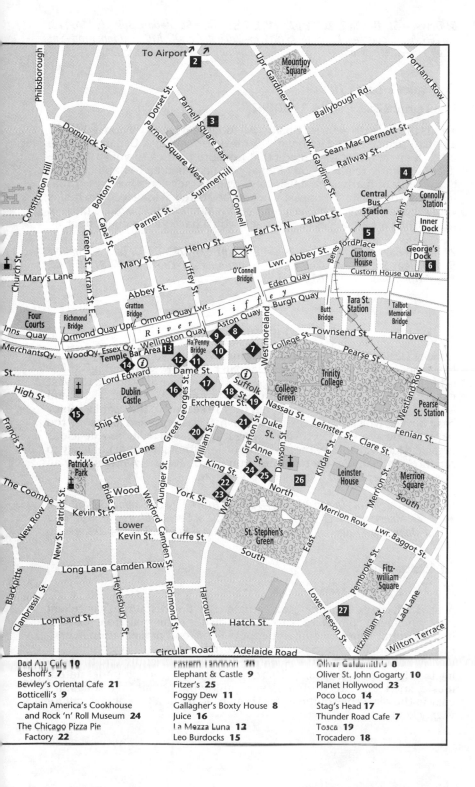

51 Dawson St., Dublin 2. ☎ *01-677-1155. DART: Tara St. Station. Bus: 10, 11A, 11B, 13, 20B. Main courses: £7.95-13.95 ($11.75–$20.65). AE, DC, MC, V. Open: Mon–Sat 12:00 p.m.–4:00 p.m. and 5:30 p.m.–11:30 p.m., Sun 11:00 a.m.–11:00 p.m.*

Gallagher's Boxty House
$$ Temple Bar, Dublin 2   IRISH

This is the place to get traditional Irish food! Featuring (obviously) *boxty*, a potato pancake filled with various meats or cabbage, Gallagher's also offers a menu full of Irish foods that are sure to stick to your ribs. The decor instantly reminds you of what you imagined an Irish place to be like: plenty of hardwood, music, and friendly service. One aspect that instantly adds to its hominess: You may be seated at long wooden tables with other diners, much like a family-style dinner. And because most of the patrons are travelers like yourself, you'll have lots to chat about.

20 Temple Bar Rd., Temple Bar, Dublin 2. ☎ *01-677-2762. DART: Tara St. Station. Bus to Fleet St.: 46, 46A, 46B, 63, 150. Main courses: £5–12 ($7.40–$17.75). AE, MC, V. Open: Mon–Sun 12:00 p.m.–11:30 p.m.*

Juice
$$ Old City, Dublin 2   CALIFORNIA CUISINE

A slice of California in the heart of Ireland! Whether you're simply looking to veg out or want excellent, filling food in cool, stark surroundings, Juice is the place for you. Its high ceilings and funky decor only add to the vast menu, which spans all kinds of ethnic foods. Items like *tofu miso soup* and *falafels* in a tangy sauce are great, but they're second to the heaping, spicy bean burger, which is a challenge to finish. If fresh-pressed juices are too tame for you, there's a pretty good wine list that even includes a delicious organic wine available by the glass or bottle. Although you're not likely to run into too many fellow travelers, you'll probably be waited on by an American eager to find out where you're from.

South St. George's St., Dublin 2. ☎ *01-475-7856. DART: Tara St. Station. Bus: 50, 50A, 54, 56, 77. Main courses: £6–12 ($8.90–$17.75). MC, V. Service Charge of 10 percent added. Open: Sun–Thur 11:00 a.m.–10:00 p.m., Fri and Sat 11:00 a.m.–4:00 a.m.*

La Mezza Luna
$$ Temple Bar   ITALIAN

A pleasant, cozy atmosphere accentuates this tiny restaurant's excellent food. The menu comprises basic Italian dishes done well, from *tortellini* in red pepper sauce to stuffed peppers. The food presentation is first-rate, too. The daily specials venture more into the creative realm: The night we ate there, ostrich was featured. Service is friendly, and the lighting is bright and welcoming. There's usually live (though understated) music, such as an accordion player quietly piping out love songs. It's cozy in the real sense of the word, though, so we don't recommend it for wiggly kids.

1 Temple Lane, Temple Bar, Dublin 2. ☎ *01-671-2840. DART: Tara St. Station. Bus: 46, 46A, 46B, 63, 150. Main courses: £6.50–11.95 ($9.60–$17.70). AE, DC, MC, V. Open: Mon–Thur 12:00 p.m.–11:00 p.m., Fri and Sat 12:00 p.m.–11:30 p.m., Sun 12:00 p.m.– 10:30 p.m.*

Leo Burdocks

$ Near Temple Bar, Dublin 8 · FISH AND CHIPS

Burdocks, which calls itself the original fish and chips shop, is a Dublin landmark. The smell of frying fish wafts up the street to Christ Church, where you're likely to be when tempted to the "chipper." Don't be surprised if the line (or "queue") snakes out the door, but don't pass it up, either!

2 Werburgh St., Dublin 8. ☎ *01-454-0306. Across from Christ Church Cathedral. DART: Tara St. Station. Bus: 50A, 78, 78A. Main courses: £2.50–4.95 ($3.70–$7.35). No credit cards. Open: Mon–Fri 12:30 p.m.–midnight, Sat 2:00 p.m.–11:00 p.m., Sun 4:00 p.m.–midnight.*

Poco Loco

$$ Dublin 2   TEX-MEX

If you're looking for some filling, authentic-tasting Tex-Mex food, this is the place — and all at a cheap price. Some things belie the fact that you're not in a cantina in Austin, like a lack of jalapenós, and refried beans that lack the saltiness you're used to. But when it comes to burritos and enchiladas smothered in cheese, tacos stuffed with spicy beef, and fab nachos, Poco Loco is on the mark. It's small and dim with painted wooden tables and you might hear Elvis crooning in the background. Best of all, it has a full liquor license.

32 Parliament St., Dublin 2. ☎ *01-679-1950. DART: Tara St. Station. Bus to Fleet St.: 46, 46A, 46B, 63, 150. Main courses: £3.95–8.50 ($5.85–$12.58). AE, DC, MC, V. Open: Mon–Thur 5:00 p.m.–11:00 p.m., Fri and Sat 5:00 p.m.–2:00 a.m., Sun 5:00 p.m.– 10:30 p.m.*

Tosca

$$$ Trinity Area, Dublin 2   ITALIAN

If you've just spent a long day traipsing in and out of shops on Grafton Street, you're ready for a hearty meal in one of the city's best Italian restaurants. Delicious pasta dishes are the cornerstone of this lively place, owned by Norman Hewson, brother of U2's Bono. The fettuccine alfredo is marvelous, especially with chicken. Check out the bargain early-bird specials. And don't pass up the gourmet sandwiches — the focaccia bread is delicious.

20 Suffolk St., Dublin 2. ☎ *01-679-6744. DART: Tara St. Station. Bus: 5, 7A, 8, 15A, 15B, 15C, 46, 55, 62, 63, 83, 84. Main courses: £11.50–18.25 ($17–$27). AE, DC, MC, V. Open: Sun–Wed 12:30 p.m.–2:30 p.m. and 5:30 p.m.–11:00 p.m., Thur–Sat 12:00 p.m.– 2:30 p.m. and 5:30 p.m.–1:00 a.m.*

Trocadero

$$$ Trinity College Area   INTERNATIONAL

One foot into this sunken, red-walled restaurant and you'll get the feeling you're among important people. And it could be true. Trocadero is the place Dublin's literati, actors, and "in" people go for a meal and a bottle of wine while tucking themselves into an oversized half-moon booth. The food is delicious and quite reasonably priced given the chichi atmosphere. It's the kind of place that you'll feel somewhat lucky to have gotten a table in, and dinner here offers a real taste of Dublin. Word has it the "Troc" comes to life around 1:00 a.m., when upper-echelon Dubliners settle in. But fear not: You're fine as long as you're out before the theaters. We got a table one Monday night only by promising to vacate by a certain time!

3 St. Andrew St., Dublin 2. ☎ *01-677-5545. DART: Tara St. Station. Bus to Fleet St.: 16A, 19A, 22A, 55, 83. Main courses: £7.50–13.95 ($11.10–$20.65). AE, DC, MC, V. Open: Mon–Sat 6:00 p.m.–12:15 a.m., Sun 6:00 p.m.–11:15 p.m.*

Exploring Dublin

What's your pleasure? Do you want to spend the day in museums? Duck in and out of historical pubs? Relax in a park? Hunt out exemplary architecture? Dublin's got it all — and everything's conveniently within a stone's throw of everything else. There's so much to see and do here, you'll have to take a few minutes to figure out first what things you really want to see — it's easy to get sidetracked!

Money- and time-saving touring tips

Here's a time-saving tip: **The Guinness Hop Store, Kilmainham Gaol, the Modern Art Museum, Phoenix Park,** and **Dublin Zoo** are all in the same general vicinity — west of the City Centre. It is a good walk to the park, but you can hit these other sites on the way and make it worth the time, or take a bus to the **Guinness Hop Store** and walk a little further to the **Gaol.**

And, there's no need to bankrupt yourself sightseeing. The following attractions in Dublin are free: **Phoenix Park, St. Steven's Green, the Glasnevin Cemetery tours, St. Ann's Church, the National Museum, the National Gallery, the Irish Museum of Modern Art,** and **the National Botanic Gardens.** You can also get combined tickets to some attractions, which could save a few pounds (see reviews for further information).

Also, the Dublin Tourism Centre on Suffolk Street sells a **SuperSaver Card** that gives discounts for the **Viking Adventure, Malahide Castle, Fry Model Railway, Dublin Writers Museum, Newbridge House,** and **James Joyce Museum.** It's worth purchasing if you visit at least three of them.

Seeing the top sights

St. Stephen's Green and Newman House
Dublin 2

This beautiful park in the heart of the city provides a welcome rest from the bustle of Dublin. One step through Fusilier's Arch — the entrance at the top of Grafton Street — and you may feel like you've magically left the city and entered an enchanted forest. The park is fully enclosed by trees and is full of shrub-lined walkways, vibrant flowerbeds, and a lake and garden. During summer months you can enjoy lunchtime concerts with the rest of the city's population. Newman House, on the south side of the green, was home to the Catholic University of Ireland. You can tour the house to see examples of Georgian furniture and interior design.

St. Stephen's Green takes up the block at the top of Grafton St.; Newman House is located on the south side of the park at 85-86 St. Stephen's Green, between Harcourt St. and Earlsfort Terrace, Dublin 2. ☎ *01-706-7422. Take Grafton St. away from Trinity College. DART: Tara St. Station. Bus: 32X, 39X, 41X, 66X, 67X. Admission: Free. Green Open: During daylight hours. Newman House Open: June–Sept Tues–Fri 12:00 p.m.–5:00 p.m., Sat 2:00 p.m.–5:00 p.m., Sun 11:00 a.m.–2:00 p.m. Only open to groups Oct–May. Time: About an hour.*

Trinity College and the Book of Kells
Dublin 2

This college, founded in 1591 by Elizabeth I, remains today an impressive and refined example of Old-World academia. The campus sits in the middle of the busy city, but within its gates everything is composed and quiet. Buildings dating back to antiquity add to the austere atmosphere, and during nice weather students are splayed on the well-kept greens for picnics or studying. You might even imagine the days when former students Samuel Beckett, Oliver Goldsmith, or Edmund Burke rushed across the cobbled walks to class.

Most people visit Trinity for one reason: to see the Book of Kells. And no wonder! This ancient manuscript, painstakingly crafted by monks around 800 A.D., detail the four gospels of the Bible. Written in Latin in ornate script, the book is one of the oldest in the world and includes vividly colored drawings that are not to be missed (though you'll only be able to see one page on any given visit — they flip to the next page once a day). Included in the tour is admission to the Long Room, a vast hall of 200,000 of the college's oldest books. You can also see Ireland's oldest surviving harp and marble busts of famous historical persons.

Main entrance on College St. at the eastern end of Dame St. Dublin 2. ☎ *01-677-2941. Walk two blocks south of the River Liffey from O'Connell St. Bridge; entrance will be on your left. Walk through the front entrance arch and follow signs to the Old Library and Treasury. DART: Tara St. Station. Bus: 15, 15A, 15B, 83, 155 Admission: College grounds: Free; Old Library and Book of Kells: £3.50 ($5.18) adults, £3 ($4.44) students and under 17, free under 12; Open: Mon–Sat 9:30 a.m.–5:30 p.m., Sun 12:00 p.m.–4:30 p.m. Closed for ten days during Christmas holiday. Time: Two and a half hours.*

Kilmainham Gaol
Dublin 8

The place where rebels were jailed and many awaited the firing squad, Kilmainham Gaol (pronounced "jail") is one of the most startling testaments to what Irish freedom fighters endured. Starting in the extremely well-put-together museum, you'll learn about the jail's history, what kind of criminals were held there (much more than just dissidents against England), and how prisoners were treated during the jail's 130-year history. You'll shudder at the dank cells of such famous patriots as Charles Stewart Parnell, Joseph Plunkett, and James Connolly. There's a short movie about the jail shown in the chapel where Plunkett was allowed to marry Grace Gifford just hours before being shot for his part in the 1916 Rising. You can stand in the very spot where many rebels were shot by firing squads — including Connolly, who was so badly injured he couldn't stand up by himself and had to be strapped into a chair to be shot. Kilmainham was used as the set for the Daniel Day Lewis film *In the Name of the Father.*

Inchicore Rd., Kilmainham, Dublin 8. ☎ *01-453-5984. Bus: 79, 90. Admission: £3 ($4.45) adult, £2 ($2.95) seniors, £1.25 ($1.85) student and child. Open: Apr–Sept daily 9:30 a.m.–6:00 p.m., Oct–Mar Mon–Fri 9:30 a.m.–5:00 p.m., Sun 10:00 a.m.–4:30 p.m. Time: Two hours.*

Merrion Square
Dublin 2

This square, one of the most elegant sections of Dublin, is a public garden surrounded by some of the best examples of Georgian architecture you'll run across. The row homes retain their original splendor, and many still have the original doors, knockers, and wrought-iron balconies. You'll see plaques that note the former homes of poet W. B. Yeats (No. 82), playwright Oscar Wilde (No. 1), and Catholic liberator Daniel O'Connell (No. 58). The square served as a soup kitchen in the 1840s, during the Great Famine.

Merrion Square takes up the block directly behind the National Gallery. Take Nassau St. on the south side of Trinity College and continue east for a few blocks till it becomes Merrion Sq. North. DART: Pearse St. Station and head south on Westland Row and Merrion St. Lower. Bus: 5, 7A, 8 Admission: Free. Open: Daylight hours. Time: Twenty minutes.

Dvblinia
Dublin 8

This interactive museum covers Dublin history from the invasion of the Anglo-Normans in 1170 to the mid-sixteenth century. There's lots of interesting information about medieval Dublin's religion, trade, and development. An audiovisual tour through a life-sized display depicts milestones in the city's history, such as the Black Plague. Also, a scale model of Dublin circa 1500 shows what the city looked like at the tail end of the Middle Ages. An added plus to this attraction is St. Michael's Tower, located in the building that houses the Dvblinia Museum. It's one of the highest, most central points open to the public in this low-rise city. From the top you'll get an astounding view of Dublin, and kids will love it! You have to take the tour to get up into it.

High St. (linked to Christ Church), Dublin 8. ☎ *01-679-4611. Bus: 50, 78A. Admission: £3.95 ($5.85) adults, £2.90 ($4.30) children, students and seniors, £10 ($14.80) family of 2 adults and 2 children. Open: Apr–Sept daily 10:00 a.m.–5:00 p.m., Oct–Mar Mon–Sat 11:00 a.m.–4:00 p.m., Sun 10:00 a.m.–4:30 p.m. Time: An hour and a half.*

Dublin Castle
Dublin 2

This impressive building — which really looks less like a castle than any other in the country — was once the seat of English government. Now the castle is purely Irish, home to official state functions like the president's inauguration. Check out the Drawing Room, which features a breathtaking Waterford Crystal chandelier, and the Throne Room, which is believed to hold an original seat of William of Orange. St. Patrick's Hall holds the banners of the knights of St. Patrick and historical ceiling paintings. Note the statue of Justice in the courtyard. See how she faces away from the city? Cynical Dubliners will tell you that was intentional.

Cork Hill, off Dame St., Dublin 2. ☎ *01-677-7129. Bus: 50, 50A, 54, 56A, 77, 77A, 77B. Admission: £2.50 ($3.70) adult, £1.50 ($2.20) students and seniors, £1 ($1.50) under 16. Guided tours are obligatory. Open: Mon–Fri 10:00 a.m.–12:15 p.m. and 2:00 p.m.–5:00 p.m., Sat and Sun 2:00 p.m.–5:00 p.m. Closed for state functions. Time: Forty-five minutes.*

Dublin's Viking Adventure & Feast
Dublin 8

Dublin was actually founded over a thousand years back by Viking invaders, and this attraction gives you a chance to witness their history — live! Interactive and interesting, the Viking Adventure takes you on a journey through time. You'll get to walk the streets of Viking Dublin, talk to its inhabitants, and watch them work. Take a simulated ride on a Viking ship and look over the exhibit of artifacts. It's much more than a museum, letting kids enjoy how they play a part in it all. On Wednesday through Monday you can participate in a huge Viking feast.

Essex St. West, Temple Bar, Dublin 8. ☎ *01-679-6040. DART: Tara St. Station. Bus: 51, 51A, 51B, 79, 90 Admission: £4.75 ($7.05) adults, £3.85 ($5.70) age 18-12, £2.95 ($3.65) age 11-3, £13 ($19.25) family of 2 adults and 4 children. Viking Feast: £35 ($51.80) per person. Open: Mar–Oct Tues–Sat 10:00 a.m.–1:00 p.m. and 2:00 p.m.– 4:30 p.m. Time: An hour and a half (longer if you participate in the feast).*

Guinness Hop Store
Dublin 8

Don't expect a brewery tour (Guinness doesn't offer them), but get ready to enjoy a museum-like atmosphere that tells you about the making of the famous cascading black beer. An audiovisual show provides the story of the history of Guinness. You'll also see how Guinness was stored and transported in its early days, and how the famous ad campaign

Dublin Attractions

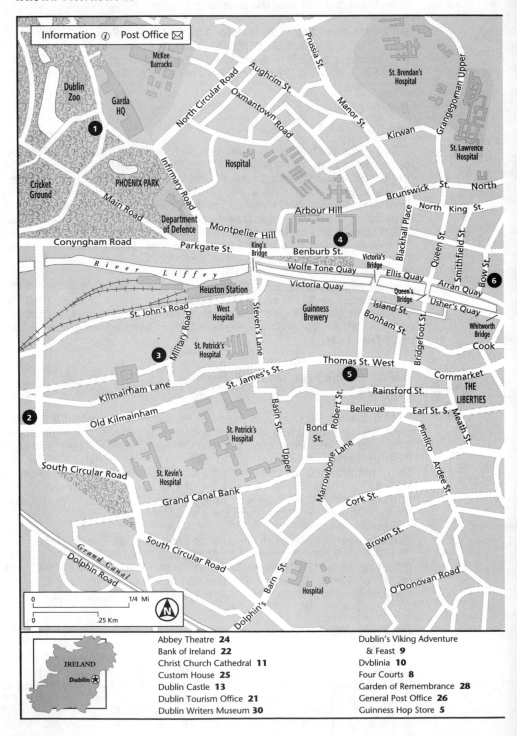

Information ⓘ   Post Office ✉

McKee Barracks
Dublin Zoo
Garda HQ
Cricket Ground
PHOENIX PARK
Main Road
Infirmary Road
Department of Defence
Conyngham Road
Parkgate St.
Montpelier Hill
North Circular Road
Oxmantown Road
Aughrim St.
Prussia St.
Manor St.
Kirwan
St. Brendan's Hospital
Grangegoman Upper
St. Lawrence Hospital
Brunswick St. North
North King St.
Hospital
Arbour Hill
King's Bridge
Benburb St.
Victoria's Bridge
Blackhall Place
Queen St.
Smithfield St.
Bow St.
River Liffey
Wolfe Tone Quay
Ellis Quay
Arran Quay
Heuston Station
Victoria Quay
Queen's Bridge
Usher's Quay
St. John's Road
West Hospital
Steven's Lane
Guinness Brewery
Island St.
Bonham St.
Bridgefoot St.
Whitworth Bridge
Cook
Military Road
St. Patrick's Hospital
Thomas St. West
Cornmarket
THE LIBERTIES
Kilmainham Lane
St. James's St.
Rainsford St.
Bellevue
Earl St. S.
Meath St.
Old Kilmainham
St. Patrick's Hospital
Basin St. Upper
Bond St.
Robert St.
Pimilico
Ardee St.
South Circular Road
St. Kevin's Hospital
Grand Canal Bank
Marrowbone Lane
Cork St.
Brown St.
Grand Canal
Dolphin Road
South Circular Road
Dolphin's Barn St.
Hospital
O'Donovan Road

0   1/4 Mi
0   .25 Km

IRELAND
Dublin ★

Abbey Theatre **24**
Bank of Ireland **22**
Christ Church Cathedral **11**
Custom House **25**
Dublin Castle **13**
Dublin Tourism Office **21**
Dublin Writers Museum **30**

Dublin's Viking Adventure & Feast **9**
Dvblinia **10**
Four Courts **8**
Garden of Remembrance **28**
General Post Office **26**
Guinness Hop Store **5**

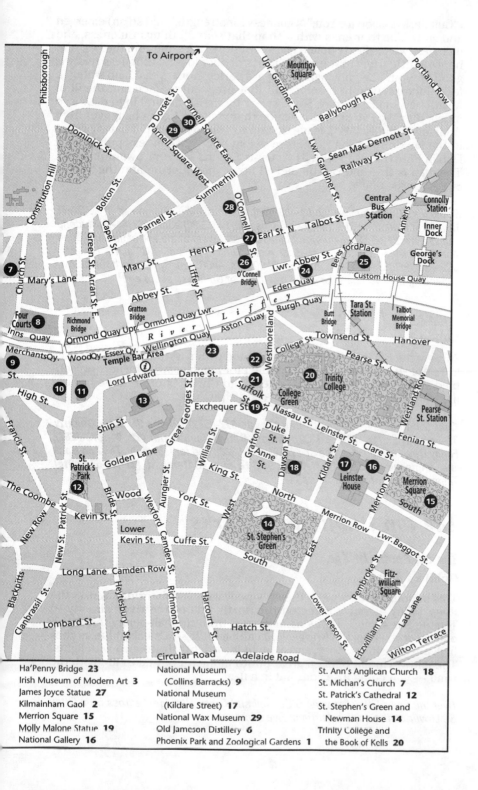

Ha'Penny Bridge **23**
Irish Museum of Modern Art **3**
James Joyce Statue **27**
Kilmainham Gaol **2**
Merrion Square **15**
Molly Malone Statue **19**
National Gallery **16**

National Museum
  (Collins Barracks) **9**
National Museum
  (Kildare Street) **17**
National Wax Museum **29**
Old Jameson Distillery **6**
Phoenix Park and Zoological Gardens **1**

St. Ann's Anglican Church **18**
St. Michan's Church **7**
St. Patrick's Cathedral **12**
St. Stephen's Green and
  Newman House **14**
Trinity College and
  the Book of Kells **20**

("Guinness Is Good for You," "Guinness for Strength," and so on) emerged and grew. The tour ends with a shop that sells all things Guinness, and includes two perfectly pulled glasses of the black stuff from the bar. And here's a little trivia to warm the hearts of beer lovers: Guinness really *is* good for you. The only ingredients are barley, hops, yeast, and water. In fact, doctors used to recommend that pregnant women and the ill of health have a glass a day. Some swear by the all-natural ingredients so much, they'll go so far as to tell you that you don't get a hangover from drinking Guinness! We'll leave that up to you to find out. If having a pint in the faux pub at the Hop Store doesn't cut it, Guinness publishes a Dublin Pub Trail map with 31 "must-try" pubs for your own pub crawl. The map is free and can be picked up at the museum and the Suffolk Street tourist office.

St. James's Gate, Dublin 8. ☎ 01-408-4800. Internet: www.guinness.ie. *DART: Tara St. Station. Bus: 51B, 78A, 123. Admission: £4 ($5.90) adults, £3 ($4.45) students and seniors, £1 ($1.50) under 12; includes two half-pints at the end of the tour. Open: Apr–Sept Mon–Sat 9:30 a.m.–5:00 p.m., Sun 10:30 a.m.–4:30 p.m., Oct–Mar Mon–Sat 9:30 a.m.–4:00 p.m., Sun 12:00 p.m.–4:00 p.m. Time: An hour or two, depending on if you partake in the free pints of Guinness at the end!*

Temple Bar Pub Crawl
Dublin 2

Some of the city's best pubs are all located within a stumble of each other in Temple Bar, making the area perfect for a pub crawl. The narrow, cobbled streets between Trinity College and Christ Church Cathedral are nice paths between some fun and classic pubs.

Auld Dubliner, 24–25 Temple Bar (☎ 01-677-0527); Oliver St. John Gogarty, 57–58 Fleet St. (☎ 01-671-1822); Temple Bar, 47 Temple Bar (☎ 01-672-5287); Foggy Dew, 1 Upper Fownes St. (☎ 01-677-9328); and for late night, The Left Bank Bar, Anglesea St. (☎ 01-671-1822), or O'Brien's, 40 Dame St. (☎ 01-677-8816). Time: Approximately four hours.

The top Dublin landmarks

The Ha'Penny Bridge
Dublin 1 and 2

This famous footbridge — the only pedestrians-only bridge across the River Liffey — has connected the north side of the river directly to Temple Bar since 1816. Its name comes from the half-penny toll that it once cost to cross the bridge. You can't miss it — it's baby blue, arches high over the River Liffey, and at night it's brightly festooned with lights. The midway point offers a great photo moment, but take care with the wind — you could lose your hat in a flash!

Over the River Liffey between O'Connell and Grattan bridges, across from Liffey St. Lower on the north side. Time: Five minutes.

Abbey Theatre
Dublin 1

This modern-looking theater was cofounded by poet and playwright W. B. Yeats in 1898. It's survived riots stemming from outrage to J. M. Synge's *The Playboy of the Western World,* and has showcased the work of some of Ireland's most famous literary voices. Rebuilt in 1966, its lobby walls are lined with portraits of noted people associated with the theater.

Lower Abbey St., Dublin 1. ☎ *01-878-7222. Time: Fifteen minutes.*

Molly Malone Statue
Dublin 1

Sing along now: "In Dublin's fair city, where the girls are so pretty, there once was a girl named sweet Molly Malone. . . ." Inspired by the traditional song "Cockles and Mussels," this statue is a tribute to the fictional Molly Malone, who represents all the women who hawked their wares on Dublin's busy streets in the past. Affectionately known as "The Tart with the Cart," Molly welcomes shoppers at the head of Grafton Street.

Located on the corner of Nassau and Grafton streets. Time: About 30 seconds, unless you take time to sing the whole song.

James Joyce Statue
Dublin 1

This statue pays homage to the wiry, bespectacled man whose inspired words have become the essence of Dublin in the "auld times."

Halfway up O'Connell St., just at the top of Earl St. North, only blocks away from the James Joyce Cultural Centre, 35 North Great George's St. (☎ *01-878-8547), which all true Joyce fans need to visit. Time: A few seconds, unless you decide to recite a sentence or two from* Finnegan's Wake, *which could take a month.*

The Dublin Tourism Office
Dublin 2

The first place you'll want to stop anyway, this fantastic resource is located inside the beautifully restored St. Andrews Church on Suffolk Street. There's endless information to gather and there's a helpful group of people who'll answer all your questions. The Belfry Cafe serves a nice cuppa' (tea, that is), and there are two gift shops with not-too-cheesy stuff. Ironically, the former St. Andrews was closed when the number of parishioners dwindled down to less than a dozen folks, but now it's visited by thousands of tourists every day.

Suffolk St. at Westmoreland, near Trinity. Time: About a half-hour.

Custom House
Dublin 1

This building, a classic example of Georgian architecture, was made obsolete in 1800, a decade after it was built, when customs trading moved to London. The tops of the archways, or keystones, have beautiful, sculpted heads that represent the rivers of Ireland and the Atlantic Ocean. The building is now full of government offices and is closed to the public, but it's enough to just stand in front and look at. Even from across the river, the Custom House presents an impressive view. There's no tour, but there is a visitor centre with pamphlet info and pictures for those who want to learn more about the building.

Custom House Quay, Dublin 1. ☎ *01-878-7660. East of O'Connell facing the River Liffey from the north side. Custom House Visitor Centre Cost: £1 ($1.50). Open: mid-March to Nov Mon–Fri 10:00 a.m.–5:00 p.m., Sat and Sun 2:00 p.m.–5:00 p.m., Nov–mid-Mar Wed–Fri 10:00 a.m.–5:00 p.m., Sun 2:00 p.m.–5:00 p.m. Time: A half-hour.*

Four Courts
Dublin 8

If you have some time, go in and watch imposing barristers with powdered wigs try court cases with perfect, bookish English. You'll be amazed at the difference from home — this is no *People's Court!* You can also get information about the building's history in the entrance. If you're just taking in the sights, tip your head up to the copper-covered dome that rises above a six-column portico. In this are statues of Moses, Justice, and Mercy. This regal building sits on the edge of the River Liffey and you can get a great view of it from the Ha'Penny Bridge.

Inns Quay, west of the O'Donovan Rossa Bridge and facing the River Liffey from the north side. Time: An hour or less.

General Post Office
Dublin 1

Probably the single most striking symbol of the Easter Rising of 1916, the GPO still bears the scars of that violent battle between Irish patriots and the English. You can actually stick your fingers in the holes in the pillars left by gunshots. During the rising, members of the Irish Volunteers and Irish Citizen Army captured the GPO and stayed for a week, holding their enemies barely at bay. From its steps, Patrick Pearse read the Proclamation of the Irish Republic. British persistence forced the rebels out, and 14 leaders were later shot. Inside this cavernous building — still kicking as Ireland's main post office — stands a statue of ancient Irish hero Cuchulainn, which was dedicated to those who died for their part in the rebellion.

North of the River Liffey, halfway up the left-hand side of O'Connell St. Time: A half-hour.

Garden of Remembrance
Dublin 1

This peaceful and orderly garden is dedicated to the men and women who died in the pursuit of Irish freedom. It's hard not to be touched by the serenity of the spot, with its bright flowers and still reflecting pool. There's a telling statue representing the sad myth of the Children of Lir, who were turned into swans by their selfish and cruel stepmother. A symbolic mosaic at the bottom of the pool depicts broken weapons, standing for peace. Eamon de Valera, veteran freedom fighter, opened the garden on the 50th anniversary of the Easter Rising. The location is significant, too; it was where several leaders of the rising were held overnight before being taken to Kilmainham Gaol — and their deaths.

The north end of Parnell Sq. at the top of O'Connell St. Open: Nov–Feb daily 11:00 a.m.–4:00 p.m.; Mar, Apr, Oct 11:00 a.m.–7:00 p.m.; May–Sept 9:30 a.m.–8:00 p.m. Time: Fifteen minutes.

The Bank of Ireland
Dublin 2

Once the Parliament House, the Bank of Ireland is a striking eighteenth-century building. Visit the Irish House of Lords, where Parliament sat before being joined with England's in London. This beautiful chamber features woodwork in Irish oak, period tapestries, and an awesome Irish crystal chandelier dating back to 1765. One thing you'll notice right away: There aren't any windows in the Bank of Ireland! This isn't for security reasons; rather, when it was built, England levied a hefty property tax that increased drastically as the number of windows did. So, to save money, the building was constructed with a single atrium for light and no windows. Have you heard of the phrase "daylight robbery"? You guessed it — it comes from the government's charging for daylight!

2 College Green, Dublin 2. ☎ 01-677-7155. Cost: £1.50 ($2.20) adult, £1 ($1.50) seniors and students. Open: Mon–Wed and Fri 10:00 a.m.–4:00 p.m., Thur 10:00 a.m.–5:00 p.m. Time: Fifteen minutes.

Other fun stuff to do

So, you've loaded up on java, worn out the soles of your walking shoes, and seen all the best sights that we listed in this chapter, huh? Get ready for some more fun stuff.

Museums and galleries

✔ **National Museum (Collins Barracks and Kildare Street branches):** These two museums, which between them house Ireland's finest collection of historical artifacts, are set in two separate parts of the city but are both worth the trip. Highlights from the Kildare Street location include the **National Treasury,** which contains the Ardagh Chalice, the intricately detailed Tara Brooch, and the Cross of Cong dating back to 1123. **"The Road to Independence"** exhibit deals

Temple Bar

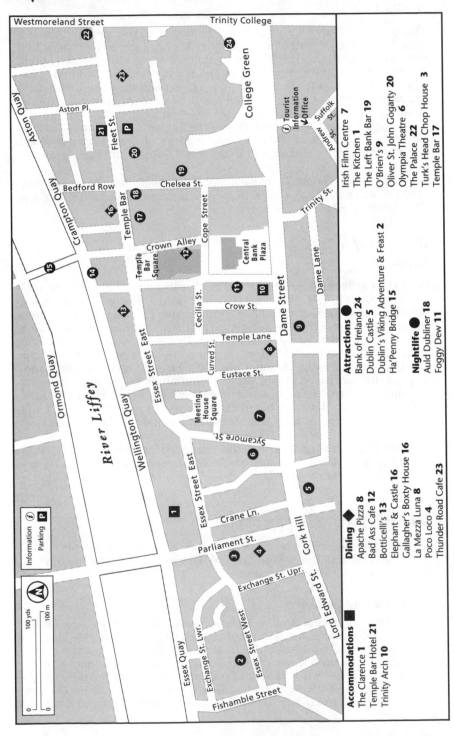

Accommodations ■
The Clarence **1**
Temple Bar Hotel **21**
Trinity Arch **10**

Dining ◆
Apache Pizza **8**
Bad Ass Cafe **12**
Botticelli's **13**
Elephant & Castle **16**
Gallagher's Boxty House **16**
La Mezza Luna **8**
Poco Loco **4**
Thunder Road Cafe **23**

Attractions ●
Bank of Ireland **24**
Dublin Castle **5**
Dublin's Viking Adventure & Feast **2**
Ha'Penny Bridge **15**

Nightlife ●
Auld Dubliner **18**
Foggy Dew **11**

Irish Film Centre **7**
The Kitchen **1**
The Left Bank Bar **19**
O'Brien's **9**
Oliver St. John Gogarty **20**
Olympia Theatre **6**
The Palace **22**
Turk's Head Chop House **3**
Temple Bar **17**

with the turbulent time in Irish history between 1916 and 1921. **Collins Barracks** is the oldest military barracks in Europe, and features pieces of the economic, social, political, and military history of Ireland. Some of the museum's greatest claims are a pocketbook carried by Wolfe Tone while imprisoned in the barracks for his involvement in the 1798 Revolution, gauntlets worn by King William in the Battle of the Boyne, and pieces saved from the wreckage of the *Lusitania*.

Location: Collins Barracks, Benburb St., Dublin 7; Kildare Street branch at Kildare and Merrion Streets, Dublin 2. ☎ **01-677-7444** (for both). DART to Collins Barracks: Connolly Station. Bus to Collins Barracks: 25, 25A, 66, 67, 90. DART to Kildare Street: Pearse Street. Bus to Kildare Street: 7, 7A, 8, 10, 11, 13. Admission: Free. Open: Tuesday through Saturday 10:00 a.m. to 5:00 p.m., Sunday 2:00 p.m. to 5:00 p.m. Guided tours available. Time: Two hours.

✔ **Dublin Writers Museum:** Ireland's love affair with literature and its illustrious legacy is represented in this gorgeous museum. Set in an eighteenth-century mansion, the writers museum exists for anyone with a literary bent. Through books, letters, portraits, and personal items, it explores the lives of Dublin's literary luminaries from the past 300 years — writers like Jonathan Swift, George Bernard Shaw, W. B. Yeats, James Joyce, and Samuel Beckett. Poetry and prose readings and lectures are hosted here as well. There's a specialty bookstore with an out-of-print search service. The on-site restaurant, Chapter One, is excellent.

Location: 18 Parnell Sq. North, Dublin 1. ☎ **01-872-2077.** DART: Connolly Station. Bus: 10, 11, 11A, 11B, 13, 16, 16A, 19, 19A, 22, 22A, 36. Admission: £2.95 ($4.35) adult, £2.50 ($3.70) under 18, £1.30 ($1.90) under 12. Open: June to August, Monday through Saturday 10:00 a.m. to 6:00 p.m., Sunday 11:00 a.m. to 5:00 p.m.; September to May, Monday through Saturday 10:00 a.m. to 5:00 p.m., Sunday 11:00 a.m. to 5:00 p.m. Time: Forty-five minutes.

✔ **The National Gallery:** You might not expect Ireland to be home to a stellar collection of art, but this gallery should change your mind. There is, of course, loads of Irish art, from landscapes — and what scenery to paint! — to portraits. A large portion of the Irish collection is devoted to the work of Jack Yeats, poet W. B. Yeats's brother. There's also art from the major European schools. Some of the most respected pieces are "The Taking of Christ" by Caravaggio, "Castle of Bentheim" by Ruisdael, and "For the Road" by Jack Yeats. Kids will want to spend hours in the interactive gallery — an ingenious set of computers that make it easy and fun to discover any aspect of art. It'll even wow parents.

Location: Merrion Sq. West, Dublin 2. ☎ **01-661-5113.** DART: Pearse Street Station and head south on Westland Row and Merrion Street Lower. Bus: 5, 7A, 8 . Admission: Free, although special exhibits may have a cost. Open: Monday through Wednesday, Friday and Saturday 10:00 a.m. to 5:30 p.m., Thursday 10:00 a.m. to 8:30 p.m., Sunday 2:00 p.m. to 5:00 p.m. Guided tours available. Time: One hour.

✓ **Old Jameson Distillery:** This small but popular museum is housed in part of Jameson's now-unused Bow Street distillery. It traces the history of Irish whiskey distilling from sixth-century monasteries to the present. Finish off the tour with a 40-proof sample of the goods at the Ball o' Malt Bar.

Location: Bow St., Dublin 7. ☎ **01-872-5566.** DART: Connolly Street. Bus: 67, 67A, 68, 69, 79, 90. Admission: £3.50 ($5.20) adults, £3 ($4.45) students and seniors, £1.50 ($2.20) children. Open: Daily 9:30 a.m. to 6:00 p.m. Time: Forty-five minutes.

✓ **Irish Museum of Modern Art:** Grandly sitting at the end of a tree-lined lane, this is one of Ireland's most magnificent seventeenth-century buildings, built in 1680 as a hospital for injured soldiers and still used for its original purpose until 1927. So impressive is this building, when it was finished many lobbied to use it as the campus for Trinity College! Even if you could care less about modern art (and the collection's not exactly extensive), you'll probably enjoy just looking at the building. The Baroque chapel of wood carvings and stained glass is a sight in itself. Exhibits change often, but invariably include Irish and international art. You can also catch a performance there, somtimes theater, sometimes music.

Location: Military Rd., Kilmainham, Dublin 8. ☎ **01-612-9900.** Bus: 79, 90. Admission: Free. Open: Tuesday through Saturday 10:00 a.m. to 5:30 p.m., Sunday 12:00 p.m. to 5:30 p.m. Time: One hour.

✓ **National Wax Museum:** From the very start, with the wax man reading the *Irish Times* in the lobby, you'll be second-guessing your own wits in this place, where history is re-created in life-size and true form! Heroes from Irish antiquity and present day are represented here, and everything is broken down into interesting sections. The replica of DaVinci's "Last Supper" is magnificent, and kids will love the Children's World of Fairytale and Fantasy and the Hall of Megastars. If your kids (or you!) are even slightly skittish, though, steer them away from the Chamber of Horrors — it's amazingly realistic!

Location: Granby Row, Parnell Sq., Dublin 1. ☎ **01-872-6340.** DART: Connolly Street Station. Bus: 11, 13, 16, 22, 22A. Admission: £3.50 ($5.20) adults, £2.50 ($3.70) students, £2 ($2.95) children. Open: Monday through Saturday 10:00 a.m. to 5:30 p.m., Sunday 12:00 p.m. to 5:30 p.m. Time: One hour.

A park and zoo experience

✓ **Phoenix Park and Zoological Gardens:** This is Europe's largest enclosed city park — five times the size of London's Hyde Park! You can drive through it, but if the weather's nice don't pass up the chance to walk, because Phoenix Park is more than just a green spot for picnic lunches: Enclosed within it are the homes of Ireland's president and the U.S. ambassador. The **Zoological Gardens** is the world's third-oldest zoo, and is home to many animals, including the world's most famous lion — the one that roars before every MGM movie. Other sights include the **Papal Cross,** where Pope John Paul II said Mass to a million Irish in 1979, and

Ashton Castle, a seventeenth-century tower house that's now the visitor's centre. Originally a deer park, the area is still home to many deer, so be watchful when driving.

Location: Park Gate, Conyngham Rd.; Phoenix Park Visitor Centre, Dublin 8. ☎ **01-677-0095** Visitor Centre, ☎ **01-677-1425** Zoological Park. To the Park: Bus 37, 38, or 39 to Ashtown Cross Gate. To the Zoo: Bus 10, 25, 26. Admission: Free to park; to zoo ₤5.90 ($8.75) adults, ₤4.20 ($6.20) students, ₤3.20 ($4.75) under 17. The park is open 9:30 a.m. to 5:30 p.m. daily from late March until May and the month of October; 9:30 a.m. to 6:30 p.m. daily from June until September; and 9:30 a.m. to 4:30 p.m. Saturday and Sunday from November to mid-March. The zoo is open Monday to Saturday 9:30 a.m. to 6:00 p.m., Sunday 10:30 a.m. to 6:00 p.m. Closes at sunset in winter. Time: Two and a half hours.

Cathedrals and churches

✔ **Christ Church Cathedral:** This mother of the Church of Ireland in Dublin is also the city's oldest building, first founded in 1038 as a simple wooden church. In 1169 the church was rebuilt by Strongbow, the Anglo-Norman conqueror of Dublin, for Laurence O'Toole, archbishop of Dublin. O'Toole was later canonized as the patron saint of the city. Neither lived to see the completed cathedral, but the remains of Strongbow and the heart of St. Laurence are kept there. There are original medieval tiles in the chapels and a basement crypt keeps the mummies of a cat and rat found in an organ pipe in the 1860s.

Location: Christ Church Place, Dublin 8. ☎ **01-677-8099**. DART: Tara Street Station. Bus: 50, 50A, 78, 78A. Admission: ₤1 ($1.50) adults. Open: Daily 10:00 a.m. to 5:00 p.m. Time: Forty-five minutes.

✔ **St. Patrick's Cathedral:** This church, the national cathedral of the Church of Ireland, is as symbolic and historic as it is impressive and beautiful. Because members of the Church of Ireland live in the Republic as well as Northern Ireland, the cathedral is an important bridge between two groups that are desperately trying to meet on a religious middle ground. The famous satirist Jonathan Swift was a dean of St. Pat's, and now enjoys his final resting place there. Most interesting, though, is the well inside the cathedral. Legend says that it's where St. Patrick baptized converts in the fifth century. Services are given nearly every day, whether there's anyone there or not. The choir section is amazing to behold, as is the great Willis organ, Ireland's largest.

Location: Patrick's Close, Dublin 8. ☎ **01-475-4817**. DART: Tara Street Station. Bus: 50, 54A, 56A. Admission: ₤2 ($2.95) adults, ₤1.50 ($2.20) students, services free. Open: April to October, Monday through Friday 10:00 a.m. to 6:00 p.m., Saturday 9:00 a.m. to 5:00 p.m., Sunday 10:00 a.m. to 4:30 p.m.; November to March, Monday through Saturday 9:00 a.m. to 4:00 p.m., Sunday 10:00 a.m. to 4:30 p.m. Time: Forty-five minutes.

✔ **St. Michan's Church:** Unless you plan to make your next vacation a tour of the ancient pyramids, this may be your best chance to see actual mummies. It's hard to believe, but something unique in the dry air here preserves bodies, and the vaults contain the remains of such people as Henry and John Sheares, leaders of the Rebellion of 1798. In addition to that, the church proudly displays an organ believed to have been played by Handel. The detailed wood carvings of instruments above the choir area are a sight, too.

Location: Church St., Dublin 7. ☎ **01-872-4154.** DART: Tara Street Station. Bus: 34, 70, 80. Admission: £1.50 ($2.20) adult, £1 ($1.50) seniors and students, 50p (75 cents) under 12. Open: Monday through Friday 10:00 a.m. to 5:00 p.m., Saturday 10:00 a.m. to 12:30 p.m. Time: One hour.

✔ **St. Ann's Anglican Church:** In this church, the writer of the creepy novel *Dracula,* Irishman Bram Stoker, married Florence Balcombe, witty playwright and Oscar Wilde's first love. Wolfe Tone, famous rebel, was also married here. There are gorgeous stained-glass windows throughout.

Location: Dawson St., Dublin 2. ☎ **01-676-7727.** DART: Tara Street Station. Bus: 10, 11A, 11B, 13, 20B. Admission: Free. Open: Monday through Friday 10:00 a.m. to 4:00 p.m. Time: A half-hour.

Attractions a little out of town

✔ **Malahide Castle:** This castle was witness to the longevity of one of Ireland's great and wealthy families, the Talbots, who resided here from 1185 to 1973. The architecture of the house is varied, and period furniture adorns the rooms. There's a large collection of Irish portrait paintings, many from the National Gallery. The Great Hall chronicles the Talbots, with portraits of family members and tidbits of information about them. One tragic legend details the morning of the Battle of the Boyne in 1690, when 14 members of the family shared a last meal; by nighttime they had all been killed. The grounds are spectacular, retaining beauty that probably hasn't changed much in the past 800 years. Kids will have a great time at the Fry Model Railway Museum (see next listing) located on the castle grounds.

Location: Malahide. ☎ **01-846-2516.** Irish Rail: Malahide Station from Connolly Station. Bus: 42. Admission: £3 ($4.45) adults, £2.50 ($3.70) under 18, £1.65 ($2.45) under 12; combined tickets available for castle and Fry Model Railway Museum (see later in this section). Open: April to October, Monday through Saturday, 10:00 a.m. to 5:00 p.m., Sunday 11:00 a.m. to 6:00 p.m.; November to March, Monday through Friday 10:00 a.m. to 5:00 p.m., Sunday 2:00 p.m. to 5:00 p.m. Time: An hour and a half.

✔ **Fry Model Railway Museum:** Located on the grounds of Malahide Castle, the Fry Model Railway Museum will entertain kids of all ages — even those with little interest in model trains. The unique collection of handmade trains spans the history of this mode of transportation in Ireland, from the early days of train travel to present day. The collection is the intricate work of Cyril Fry, a railway engineer from the 1920s and '30s, and his attention to detail and craftsmanship is evident in each piece.

Location: Malahide. ☎ **01-846-3779.** Irish Rail: Malahide Station from Connolly Station. Bus: 42. Admission: £2.75 ($4.05) adults, £2.10 ($3.10) under 18, £1.60 ($2.35) under 12; combined tickets available for castle and museum. Open: April to September,

Monday through Friday 10:00 a.m. to 6:00 p.m., Saturday 10:00 a.m. to 5:00 p.m., Sunday 2:00 p.m. to 6:00 p.m.; October to March, Saturday and Sunday 2:00 p.m. to 5:00 p.m. Closed Fridays in April and May. Time: One hour.

✔ **Newbridge House and Park:** Walking around Dublin you've seen plenty of examples of Georgian exteriors, now it's time to see a fine show of Georgian interior. This manor perfectly exhibits the refined quality of the Georgian style, and each room is open to the public. Antique and original furniture fill the rooms, and the house looks pretty much exactly as it did 150 years ago. On the grounds is a traditional farm representative of the time period. It even has animals living on it — kids will love this part!

Location: Donabate. ☎ 01-843-6534. Irish Rail: Donabate Station from Connolly Station. Bus: 33B. Admission: £2.85 ($4.20) adults, £2.50 ($3.70) under 18, £1.55 ($2.30) under 12. Open: April to September, Tuesday through Saturday 10:00 a.m. to 5:00 p.m., Sunday 11:00 a.m. to 6:00 p.m. Closed 1:00 p.m. to 2:00 p.m. Time: An hour and a half.

✔ **National Botanic Gardens:** This is a must for anyone who has a green thumb (or wishes he or she had one). Some of the features of the gardens are an arboretum, a rock garden, and rare Victorian "carpet bedding" — a style of ground cover (like ivy or periwinkle) with spots of colorful flowers interspersed. It's dense and looks impressive. The glass houses (Irish-speak for "greenhouses") contain a large palm house, an alpine house, and a complex for ferns, tropical water plants, and succulents.

Location: Glasnevin, Dublin 9. ☎ 01-837-7596. Bus: 13, 19, 134. Admission: Free. Open: Summer, Monday through Saturday 9:00 a.m. to 6:00 p.m., Sunday 11:00 a.m. to 6:00 p.m.; Winter, Monday through Saturday 10:00 a.m. to 4:30 p.m., Sunday 11:00 a.m. to 4:30 p.m. Time: Forty-five minutes.

✔ **Joyce Tower and Museum:** This tower was made famous in the first scene of *Ulysses,* when Joyce has his main character, Stephen Dedalus, stay here with the character Buck Mulligan. Located on the rocky beach in the quaint town of Sandycove, the tower was built with 11 others in 1804 as protection against a possible invasion by Napoleon. Joyce actually did stay in the tower with his friend Oliver St. John Gogarty (the real model for the fictional Mulligan) at the start of the century, and now the place is officially known as Joyce Tower, and houses such Joycean effects as letters, a walking stick, and a cigar case.

Location: Sandycove. ☎ 01-280-9265. DART: Sandycove Station. Bus: 8. Admission: £2.50 ($3.70) adults, £2 ($2.95) under 18, £1.30 ($1.90) under 12. Open: April to October, Monday through Saturday 10:00 a.m. to 5:00 p.m., Sunday 2:00 p.m. to 6:00 p.m. Time: One hour.

Green on green: Dublin's top golfing spots

✔ **St. Margaret's:** One of the hosts of the Irish Open, this is a new, challenging, and exciting course of the highest standard, with an infamously difficult finishing hole.

Location: Stephubble, St. Margaret's, County Dublin. ☎ 01-864-0400. E-mail: Stmarggc@indigo.ie. Par: 73. Fees: £40 ($59.20) for 18 holes in the summer, £25 ($37) in the winter.

✔ **Portmarnock:** The area was home of the first Irish Open in 1889 and was renovated and reopened in the early 1990s. It's a natural golf course, incorporating the rugged landscape of the region rather than being purpose-built.

Location: 25 minutes from Dublin City Centre, Portmarnock, County Dublin. ☎ 01-846-2968. E-mail: secretary@portmarnockgolfclub.ie. Par: 72. Fees: £65 ($96.20) midweek, £80 ($118.40) weekends.

✔ **Royal Dublin:** Situated on man-made North Bull Island in Dublin Bay, only four miles from Dublin City Centre, it's a championship course that has offered exciting play among great scenery for over 100 years.

Location: North Bull Island, Doillymount, Dublin 3. ☎ 01-833-6346 or 01-833-1236. E-mail: royaldublin@clubi.ie. Internet: www.globalgolf.com. Par: 72. Fees: £65 ($92.20) mid-week, £80 ($118.40) weekends.

Seeing Dublin by Guided Tour

Unless you're traveling with someone who knows the city, sometimes it's worthwhile to take a tour. The tours we've listed here are entertaining and fun.

If you want something more independent, there are lots of self-guided tours you can take in Dublin as well. The **Rock 'n' Roll Trail** focuses on contemporary Irish music like U2, Sinead O'Connor, and Chris de Burgh. The **Georgian Trail** covers five eighteenth-century squares, surrounded by period homes. The **Old City Trail** concentrates on the medieval area of Dublin. And the **Cultural Trail** covers the city's impressive architecture. Maps are available at the **Dublin Tourism Board** on Suffolk Street and generally cost £2.50 ($3.70) each. Give yourself an afternoon for each tour.

Jameson's Literary Pub Crawl

Literature was never so much fun! This is a fabulous idea, done exceptionally well. Two Irish actors combine talent and comedy for 2½ hours of pure entertainment. They'll take you to pubs of literary fame and interesting stops along the way, the whole time superbly acting out tidbits from famous Irish lit. If you pay attention, there's even a chance to win some prizes at the end. We highly recommend this one — it's so good we did it twice!

Tours generally run every evening during the summer starting at 7:30 p.m., and in the winter on Thur and Fri at 7:30 p.m. and Sun at noon and 7:30 p.m. year-round. Tickets can be purchased a half-hour in advance at The Duke (Duke St., off Grafton), where the tour begins. Information: ☎ 01-670-5602. Be sure to call, as times

Attractions around County Dublin

Bellewstown

R152

N2

Skreen

Delvin · Balbriggan

N1

R122

Naul

R127

N3

Garristown

Skerries

Hurley

R130

R130

R122 · R108

R127

R128

R125 · Dunshauglin

Ratoath · Ashbourne

Lusk · Rush

D U B L I N

N1

R154 · R155

Broad Meadow

R126 · ❶ Donabate

Batterstown

Kilsallaghan

Tolka

R156 · N3

Ward · R125

Lambay Island

❷

Dunboyne

R121 · N2 · R108

Ward · R106 · ❸

R124

Maynooth

R157

Kinsaley · Portmarnock

❹

R148

Royal · Canal

Leixlip · River Liffey

M4

Celbridge

Phoenix Park

R107 · R105

❻ · N1 · ❺ · R105 · Howth

R403

M50

Dublin Bay

Ferry to Douglas (Isle of Man), Holyhead and Liverpool

DUBLIN

Newcastle · N7

N11

R118

Grand Canal

Rathcoole

N82

N81 · Tallaght

❼ · **Dun Laoghaire**

Kilteel

Brittas

R114

L93 · R113

Killakee · Stepaside · *Killiney Bay*

Loughlinstown

R115 · R116 · Three Rock Mt.

Kiltiernan

N81

Kilbride

R117 · M11 · **Bray**

Blessington

R759

Enniskerry

R761

Kippure ▲

Fry Model Railway Museum **3**   Portmarnock Golf Course **4**

Glasnevin Cemetery **6**   Royal Dublin Golf Course **5**

Joyce Tower and Museum **7**   St. Margaret's Golf Course **2**

Malahide Castle **3**

National Botanic Gardens **6**

Newbridge House and Park **1**

Airport ✈
Lighthouse
Railway ++++

0 ___ 10 Mi
0 ___ 10 Km

sometimes change seasonally. E-mail: info@dublinpubcrawl.com. Internet: www.dublinpubcrawl.com. Price: £7 ($10.35) adults, £5 ($7.40) students and seniors. Time: About three hours.

Traditional Irish Music Pub Crawl

Learn the story of Irish music while listening to a professional musician perform some of the songs that made the Celts famous. You don't have to know the music beforehand, but you'll probably want to learn some when it's over. You'll be taken to four musical watering holes in the city. A fun evening!

Tours run nightly during the summer and Fri and Sat nights in the winter (no tours in Dec or Jan), leaving from the Oliver St. John Gogarty Pub in Temple Bar (corner of Fleet and Anglesea St.) at 7:30 p.m. We suggest you arrive early. Information: ☎ 01-478-0193. E-mail: musical.pub.crawl@ officelink.eunet.ie. Internet: www.musicalpubcrawl.com. Price: £6 ($8.90) adults, £5 ($7.40) students and seniors. Time: An entire evening.

Historical Walking Tours

This is a great way to get an interesting and historical perspective of the city. Imagine — you'll be learning without even trying! It's called the "Seminar on the Street," and explains the main features of Irish history. The tour is led by history grad students from Trinity and covers Old Parliament House, Dublin Castle, City Hall, Christ Church, and Temple Bar, with entertaining commentary and insight along the way.

Tours run daily at 11:00 a.m. and 3:00 p.m. from May to Sept and Fri, Sat, and Sun at noon from Oct to Apr. Leaves from the front gate of Trinity College on College St., Dublin. Information: ☎ 01-878-0227. E-mail: tours@historicalin sights. ie. Price: £6 ($8.90) adults, £5 ($7.40) students, seniors, and children. Time: Two hours.

Glasnevin Cemetery Walking Tours

Here lie such famous figures as Michael Collins, Charles Stewart Parnell, and Brendan Behan, and you can make it your final stop, too! This is a fine resting place after a day of touring, and you'll learn tons more about Irish history. The grounds feature beautiful sculpture and hand-carved faces of high kings and queens of Ireland. The guide, Shane MacThomas, really knows his stuff.

Tours meet at the main entrance of the cemetery at 2:30 p.m. on Wed and Fri. Information: ☎ 01-830-1133. Internet: www.glasnevin-cemetery.ie. Take Bus 19. 19A, 13, 40, 40A. Price: Free. Time: About an hour.

Hop on–Hop off Bus Tours

We definitely recommend this tour, which is perfect for people who want some tourlike guidance but also want the freedom to take as much time as they want checking out the sights. Pretty much every attraction the city has to offer is at one of the bus stops, and there's commentary throughout. The tour takes an hour and fifteen minutes if you just ride the bus straight through, but you can, as the name says, hop on and hop off, stretching the tour out to a whole day. Some attractions offer discounts for people taking this tour. All tours leave from Dublin Bus, 59 Upper O'Connell St., Dublin 1. ☎ **01-872-0000.** Runs every 30 minutes weekdays and every 15 minutes weekends. Credit cards accepted. Price: £6 ($8.90) adults, £3 ($4.45) child.

Dublin Bus Coastal Bus Tours

The two best tours that cover the outlying areas of Dublin are run by Dublin Bus. The "Coast and Castle Tour" travels north and covers the fishing villages of Dublin Bay, the coastline, and Malahide Castle. It leaves at 10:00 a.m. daily. The "South Coast Tour" covers the port towns of Dun Laoghaire, and Dalkey, Killiney Bay, and the Wicklow Mountains. Leaves at 11:00 a.m. and 2:00 p.m. daily. Each tour costs £12 ($17.75) adult, £6 ($8.90) under 14 and departs from 59 Upper O'Connell St., Dublin 1 (☎ **01-872-0000**).

Suggested one-, two-, and three-day sightseeing itineraries

On **day one,** start off with breakfast at Bewley's on Grafton Street. Next, do some shopping on Grafton Street, the main shopping area in the city, and take in the Molly Malone statue at the end of the street across the street opposite Trinity. Walk around Trinity's campus and see the Book of Kells.

From there, walk over the O'Connell Street Bridge, up to the historic Grand Post Office, back over the Ha'Penny Bridge, and then across Dame Street to grab traditional fish and chips at Leo Burdocks — the most famous chipper in the city.

Next, visit Dublin Castle (across the street from the chipper). Go back across Dame for Christ Church Cathedral and then down the road to St. Patrick's Cathedral.

You've worked up an appetite for traditional Irish fare so it's dinner at Boxty House in Temple Bar and then a pub crawl for Irish music and dancing for as long as you can stay out.

On **day two,** have breakfast at your hotel, filling up for a big walking day. Put on your comfy walking shoes and make a morning stop at a local shop for some fruit, cheese, bread, and a couple beers for an Irish picnic later in the day.

Head out to South Circular Road and make your first stop the Modern Art Museum, and then go across the street to the infamous Kilmainham Gaol.

Your next stop is Phoenix Park and the Dublin Zoo. Take a breather in the park for your picnic. On your way back toward the city, take the Guinness tour and visit the Hop Store.

Back in the city, treat yourself to a nice dinner at the upscale chain Fitzer's — the one on the lovely Merrion Square. In the evening, do the Literary Pub Crawl that starts at Duke's off Grafton Street.

On **day three,** after breakfast make your way to the north side of the River Liffey and pop into the famous Abbey Theatre and the Garden of Remembrance at the top of O'Connell Street. Next head to Parnell Square to see the Dublin Writers Museum and the Wax Museum.

Hop over the Ha'Penny Bridge to Temple Bar and have an authentic pub lunch at one of the pubs, and then head back across the River Liffey to take in the old Jameson Distillery and Collins Barracks.

Have dinner in Temple Bar at the Elephant & Castle. Finally, cross over the Ha'Penny again for upscale cocktails at Zanzibar and Pravda.

Shopping in Dublin

Dublin is the shopping mecca of Ireland. Within the city limits you can easily find all of the those items that have made Ireland famous, like Donegal tweed, Waterford Crystal, Belleek china, and Claddagh rings.

Locating the best shopping areas

There are two main shopping areas in Dublin. The first, on the North side of the River Liffey, is the **Henry Street-Mary Street area,** at the corner of O'Connell at the GPO. Here you'll find a stretch of huge department stores and smatterings of smaller specialty stores. You can find what you need along this gauntlet of stores, even down to the week's groceries. **Moore Street,** just off the main shopping drag, offers a daily open-air market where you'll find plenty of the freshest (and cheapest) fruits and vegetables in the city. You'll hear the high-pitched and perfected lilt of the vendors hawking their wares — a Dublin attraction in its own right.

For the more image-conscious, there's **Grafton Street** on the south side of the River Liffey. Here you'll find trendy boutiques and big-name fashions on a perpetually busy pedestrian street. You'll see some of the same stores as on the north side, but everything will cost more — you pay for being in a chic area. Check out the **Guinness clothing store** or Ireland's chi-chi department store, **Brown Thomas.** Having a cup of tea and people-watching from Bewley's Cafe is a fun and inexpensive way to spend time here — it's like getting your own personal fashion show!

Of course, there are other places to shop aside from these two main areas. If you're looking for funky second-hand fashions, go directly to **Temple Bar,** where you'll also find eclectic jewelry and art, modern home furnishings, and every kind of music there is.

If your idea of shopping consists mostly of pampering yourself, the **Powerscourt Townhouse Shopping Centre,** 59 S. William St., Dublin 2 (☎ 01-679-4144), is for you. This restored Georgian townhouse is home to **The Crafts Council of Ireland.** There are daily piano concerts and shops ranging from clothes boutiques to antique shops.

What to look for and where to find it

Known the world over for its handmade products and fine craftsmanship, Ireland offers many unique shopping opportunities. Dublin, as Ireland's commercial center, is a one-stop source for the country's best wares.

Antiques

There are two main areas of concentration for antique dealers: **Francis Street** (between Thomas Street West and the Coombe) and **Dawson-Molesworth Streets** (between St. Stephen's Green and Trinity College). The following places are some of your best bets for quality and value.

- ✔ **Butler Antiques,** 14 Bachelor's Walk, Dublin 1, along the north quays (☎ 01-873-0296), offers a great variety and some good bargains.

- ✔ **Anthony Antiques,** 7 Molesworth St., Dublin 2 (☎ 01-677-7222), specializes in late nineteenth-century furniture and brass.

- ✔ **Antique Trade Services,** 17 Marks Alley W., Dublin 8, off Francis Street (☎ 01-454-1143), is the place for keen bargain hunters.

Books

Like any section of a city that surrounds a college campus, there are loads of good bookstores near Trinity College. You'll find works of Irish writers that may be hard to find at home.

- ✔ **Waterstone's,** Jervis Centre, Mary St., Dublin 1 (☎ 01-679-1415), is pretty much the Barnes & Noble of the Emerald Isle.

- ✔ **Fred Hanna,** 29 Nassau St., Dublin 2 (☎ 01-677-1255), is a family-run business with an excellent selection and some secondhand books.

- ✔ **Greene's,** 16 Clare St., Dublin 2 (☎ 01-676-2554), was famously mentioned in Joyce's *Ulysses* and boasts a huge Irish literature section.

- ✔ **Books Upstairs,** 36 College Green and Dame St., across from the Trinity College front entrance, Dublin 2 (☎ 01-679-6687), has bargains and a great selection in the arts and humanities.

- ✔ **Cathach Books,** 10 Duke St., off Grafton St., Dublin 2 (☎ 01-671-8676), has one of Dublin's most thorough stocks of Irish literature.

Dublin Shopping

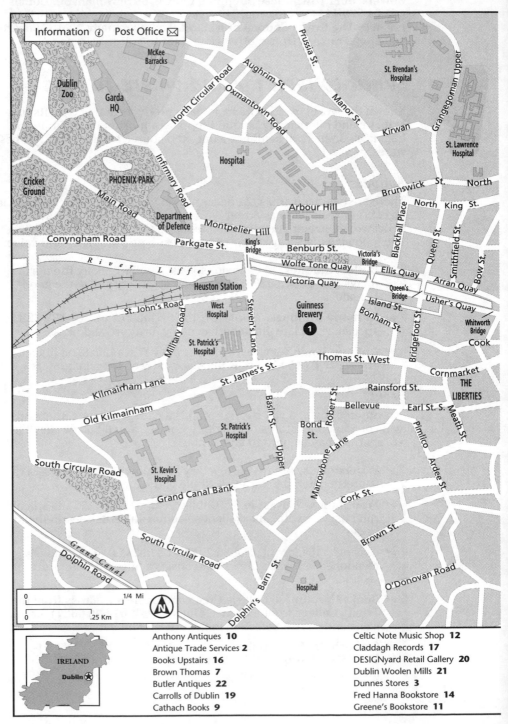

Information ⓘ Post Office ✉

McKee Barracks
Dublin Zoo
Garda HQ
Prussia St.
Aughrim St.
Oxmantown Road
Manor St.
North Circular Road
St. Brendan's Hospital
Grangegorman Upper
Kirwan
St. Lawrence Hospital
Hospital
Cricket Ground
PHOENIX PARK
Infirmary Road
Main Road
Arbour Hill
Brunswick St. North
North King St.
Blackhall Place
Queen St.
Smithfield St.
Bow St.
Conyngham Road
Department of Defence
Montpelier Hill
Parkgate St.
King's Bridge
Benburb St.
Victoria's Bridge
River Liffey
Wolfe Tone Quay
Ellis Quay
Arran Quay
Queen St.
Heuston Station
Victoria Quay
Queen's Bridge
Usher's Quay
Whitworth Bridge
St. John's Road
West Hospital
Steven's Lane
Guinness Brewery
Island St.
Bonham St.
Bridgefoot St.
Cook
Military Road
St. Patrick's Hospital
Thomas St. West
Cornmarket
THE LIBERTIES
Kilmainham Lane
St. James's St.
Rainsford St.
Old Kilmainham
Basin St. Upper
Bellevue
Robert St.
Earl St. S.
Meath St.
St. Patrick's Hospital
Bond St.
Pimlico
Ardee St.
South Circular Road
St. Kevin's Hospital
Marrowbone Lane
Grand Canal Bank
Cork St.
Brown St.
Grand Canal Dolphin Road
South Circular Road
Dolphin's Barn St.
Hospital
O'Donovan Road

0   1/4 Mi
0   .25 Km
N

IRELAND
Dublin ★

Anthony Antiques **10**
Antique Trade Services **2**
Books Upstairs **16**
Brown Thomas **7**
Butler Antiques **22**
Carrolls of Dublin **19**
Cathach Books **9**

Celtic Note Music Shop **12**
Claddagh Records **17**
DESIGNyard Retail Gallery **20**
Dublin Woolen Mills **21**
Dunnes Stores **3**
Fred Hanna Bookstore **14**
Greene's Bookstore **11**

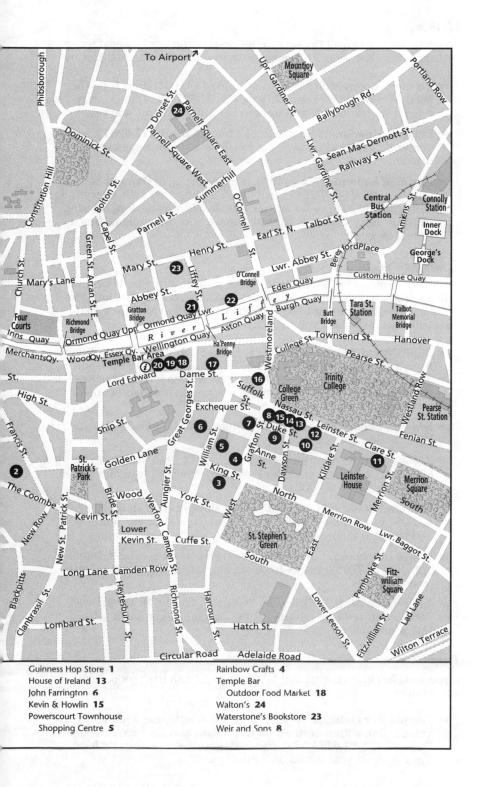

Guinness Hop Store **1**
House of Ireland **13**
John Farrington **6**
Kevin & Howlin **15**
Powerscourt Townhouse
   Shopping Centre **5**

Rainbow Crafts **4**
Temple Bar
   Outdoor Food Market **18**
Walton's **24**
Waterstone's Bookstore **23**
Weir and Sons **8**

Clothes

You don't have to go all the way to the Aran Islands or Donegal for authentic Irish knitwear. At these stores, you can find the real McCoy!

✔ **Dublin Woolen Mills,** 41 Lower Ormond Quay, Dublin 1, on the north end of the Ha'Penny Bridge (☎ **01-677-5014**), has everything from traditional sweaters to kilts, shawls, and scarves.

✔ **Kevin & Howlin,** 31 Nassau St., Dublin 2 (☎ **01-677-0257**), sells authentic handwoven tweed jackets and hats for men and women.

✔ **House of Ireland,** 37 Nassau St., at the corner of Dawson St., Dublin 2 (☎ **01-677-7949**), is a premier shop that sells everything authentically Irish — for a price. You can buy Waterford Crystal, china, jewelry crafted with traditional symbols, woolens, housewares, and more.

Crafts and jewelry

A surge of demand for jewelry and crafts with a Celtic flair is occurring, so craftsmanship is at a premium. If you're looking for the perfect set of wedding bands engraved with the Claddagh symbol or a pendant with the Tara harp, you're sure to find it.

✔ **DESIGNyard Retail Gallery,** 12 E. Essex St., Dublin 2, along Temple Bar's main thoroughfare (☎ **01-677-8453**), stocks exquisite and generally affordable contemporary Irish design jewelry, textiles, glass, and earthenware, all housed in a converted eighteenth-century warehouse.

✔ **Brown Thomas,** 92 Grafton St., Dublin 2 (☎ **01-605-6666**), stocks Irish fashion and giftware.

✔ **Rainbow Crafts,** Westbury Hotel Mall, off Grafton, Dublin 2 (☎ **01-677-7632**), is a great place for European-designed toys and games, and handmade Irish dolls.

✔ **Weir and Sons,** 96 Grafton St., at Wicklow Street, Dublin 2 (☎ **01-677-9678**), sells fine jewelry, Waterford Crystal, silver, leather, and watches in elegant showcases.

✔ **House of Ireland,** Corner of Dawson and Nassau streets, Dublin 2 (☎ **01- 677-7949**), stocks Aran sweaters, Irish tweed and Celtic jewelry.

✔ **John Farrington,** 32 Drury St., Dublin 2 (☎ **01-679-1899**), is a good bet for vintage jewelry, from Georgian silver earrings to Victorian lockets.

Food

If you've fallen in love with that fabulous and fresh Irish food, take some home:

✔ **Temple Bar Outdoor Food Market,** Meetinghouse Square in Temple Bar, with entrances on East Essex and Eustace streets, Dublin 2 (☎ **01-677-2255**), has Irish gourmet and organic food. They're open year-round on Saturdays.

✔ **Dunnes Stores,** St. Stephen's Green Shopping Centre, Dublin 2 (☎ 01-478-0188), stock sausages and vacuum-packed smoked salmon at better prices than you'll find at the airport.

Music and musical instruments

If you're hoping to master the sounds of the traditional session you heard at the pub last night, first you need the instruments. Start with an Irish tin whistle or bodhrán drum (pronounced *bow*-rahn). If you're not that adventurous, just buy a CD!

✔ **Celtic Note Music Shop,** 12 Nassau St., Dublin 2 (☎ 01-670-4157), is a great place to find any type of Irish music, from traditional to contemporary.

✔ **Claddagh Records,** 2 Cecilia St., Temple Bar, Dublin (☎ 01-677-0262), specializes in folk and traditional Irish music.

✔ **Walton's,** 2–5 North Frederick St., Dublin 1 (☎ 01-874-7805), and 69–70 South Great Georges St., Dublin 2 (☎ 01-475-0661), stocks harps, whistles, pipes, bodhráns, and cassettes and books to help you learn to play them.

Souvenirs

You just can't go home empty-handed! Even if it's just a little shot glass or paper model of a Irish cottage, it wouldn't be a vacation without these goofy reminders.

✔ **Carrolls of Dublin,** 4 Merchants Arch, Dublin 2 (☎ 01-671-0047), is the hands-down winner for Irish and Guinness souvenirs, from T-shirts to authentic pint glasses and anything else you can imagine, all at better prices than the many specialty shops.

✔ **Guinness Hop Store,** St. James's Gate, Dublin 8 (☎ 01-408-4800; Internet: www.guinness.ie), stocks all things Guinness, from posters and slippers to clocks and candles.

Hitting the Pubs and Enjoying Dublin's Nightlife

Pubs play an integral part in Irish culture. And nowhere is this better represented than in Dublin. Whether you're looking for a warm and smoky traditional enclave where older patrons know each other by name or you're in search of a sleek, neo-Celtic bar that proudly represents the cosmopolitan edge of the city, Dublin has it all.

James Joyce put it best in *Ulysses,* in this thought that flitted through the head of his character Leopold Bloom: "Good puzzle would be cross Dublin without passing a pub." Rather than make you search out the best among Dublin's 1,000 pubs, we've taken on the pleasant task of finding some of the finest.

Dublin Nightlife

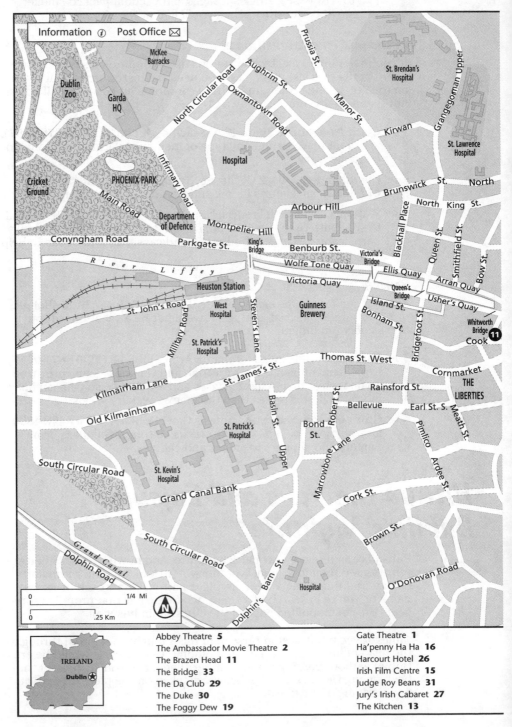

Information (i)   Post Office ✉

McKee Barracks

Dublin Zoo

Garda HQ

North Circular Road

Aughrim St.

Oxmantown Road

Prussia St.

Manor St.

St. Brendan's Hospital

Grangegorman Upper

Kirwan

St. Lawrence Hospital

Cricket Ground

PHOENIX PARK

Infirmary Road

Main Road

Hospital

Brunswick   St.   North

Blackhall Place

North   King   St.

Queen St.

Smithfield St.

Bow St.

Department of Defence

Conyngham Road

Montpelier Hill

Parkgate St.

Arbour Hill

King's Bridge

Benburb St.

Victoria's Bridge

River   Liffey

Wolfe Tone Quay

Ellis Quay

Arran Quay

Heuston Station

Victoria Quay

St. John's Road

West Hospital

Military Road

St. Patrick's Hospital

Steven's Lane

Queen's Bridge

Island St.

Usher's Quay

Guinness Brewery

Bonham St.

Bridgefoot St.

Whitworth Bridge **11**

Cook

Thomas St. West

Cornmarket

THE LIBERTIES

Kilmairham Lane

St. James's St.

Rainsford St.

Old Kilmainham

St. Patrick's Hospital

Basin St.   Upper

Robert St.

Bellevue

Bond St.

Earl St. S.

Meath St.

South Circular Road

St. Kevin's Hospital

Pimlico

Ardee St.

Grand Canal Bank

Marrowbone Lane

Cork St.

Brown St.

Grand Canal

Dolphin Road

South Circular Road

Dolphin's   Barn St.

Hospital

O'Donovan Road

0   1/4 Mi
0   .25 Km

IRELAND

Dublin ★

Abbey Theatre **5**	Gate Theatre **1**
The Ambassador Movie Theatre **2**	Ha'penny Ha Ha **16**
The Brazen Head **11**	Harcourt Hotel **26**
The Bridge **33**	Irish Film Centre **15**
The Da Club **29**	Judge Roy Beans **31**
The Duke **30**	Jury's Irish Cabaret **27**
The Foggy Dew **19**	The Kitchen **13**

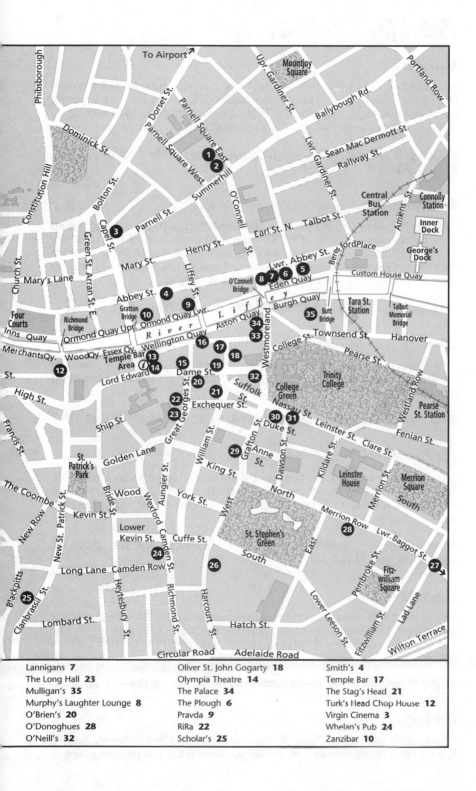

Pub life

Mulligan's

An authentic old Dublin pub and favorite watering hole for the journalists of the nearby *Irish Times* newspaper. JFK drank here as a young European correspondent for the Hearst newspapers in 1945 and again when he visited as president. It's also mentioned in *Ulysses*.

*8 Poolbeg St. (off south quays near O'Connell Bridge), Dublin 2. ☎ **01-677-5582**. Bus: 5, 7, 7A, 7X, 8.*

The Brazen Head

It claims to be the oldest pub in Dublin, and many a pint has been pulled here since its opening in 1198! The unusual name comes from a story about a bold woman who was so curious during one of the country's many rebellions that she stuck her head out of the window — only to have it chopped off! There's live music every night.

*20 Lower Bridge St., Dublin 8. ☎ **01-679-5186**. Bus: 78A, 79, 90.*

Oliver St. John Gogarty

This popular pub is named for a friend of James Joyce who became the model for Buck Mulligan, a flip character in *Ulysses*. Check out the great lunch buffet.

*57–58 Fleet St., Temple Bar, Dublin 2. ☎ **01-671-1822**. Bus: 46, 46A, 46B, 63, 150.*

The Plough

Appropriately across from the Abbey Theatre, this pub was named for Sean O'Casey's *The Plough and the Stars*. The play opens in a pub and dramatizes the Easter Rising of 1916. Drop in for a pint after checking out the theater.

*28 Lower Abbey St., Dublin 1. ☎ **01-874-0971**. Bus: 29A, 31, 31A, 31B, 32, 32A, 37, 38, 42A, 42B, 51A, 70, 70X, 130.*

The Duke

One of Michael Collins's secret meeting places during the independence movement, The Duke is now decorated in a classic Georgian style. The pub features cozy fires, a maze of rooms, and portraits of Irish literary figures.

*9 Duke St. (off Grafton St.), Dublin 2. ☎ **01-679-9553**. Bus: 10, 11A, 11B, 13, 20B.*

O'Brien's

Prominently located on Dame Street and nicely situated between Temple Bar and the Trinity-Grafton Street area, O'Brien's is the perfect place to drop in for a pint while taking in the city. Barkeeps are always friendly and willing to talk, but they do get too busy to chat sometimes. An unusual feature in this Irish pub is a huge fish tank.

40 Dame St., Dublin 2. ☎ *01-677-8816. Bus: 21A, 50, 50A, 78, 78A, 78B.*

The Stag's Head

It's hard to stand out as an exceptional pub in a city that houses nearly 1,000, but The Stag's Head is a landmark. Its Victorian decor includes a massive mahogany bar and stained glass that'll wow you. The food's great — often called the best pub grub in town.

1 Dame Ct., Dublin 2. ☎ *01-679-3701. Bus: 21A, 50, 50A, 78, 78A, 78B. Look for the mosaic stag head inlaid into the sidewalk on Dame St., pointing the way.*

O'Neill's

This is practically a labyrinth of a pub, with many cozy corners and rooms to settle into. Once a hangout of Samuel Beckett's, O'Neill's is now a favorite of students and professors alike, who ramble over from nearby Trinity College. At night it's bound to turn into a noisy, smoky college bar, though, so be warned.

2 Suffolk St. (across from the Dublin Tourism Office), Dublin 2. ☎ *01-679-3614. Bus: 5, 7A, 8, 15A, 15B, 15C, 46, 55, 62, 63, 83, 84.*

The Long Hall

Rumored to have the longest bar in the city, The Long Hall is a gorgeous specimen of a pub. There's a vast array of antique clocks, and plenty of cozy compartments (or "snugs") to get lost in. It backs up to Dublin Castle, so stop in on your way!

51 S. Great George's St., Dublin 2. ☎ *01-475-1590. Bus: 50, 50A, 54, 56, 77.*

Smith's

This is one of the finest bars on the north side of the city, renowned for stunning decor that boasts a marble bar and spiral staircase. You'll feel comfortably lost inside this vast pub, which has two levels. Not a great stop for pub-crawling though — there's not much else nearby worth checking out. So when you go, stay for a few.

9–10 Jervis St., Dublin 1. ☎ *01-873-1567. Bus to Jervis St.: 25, 25A, 26, 39, 39A, 66, 66A, 66B, 67, 67A, 134.*

Scholar's

The spacious bar at Scholar's, a restored all-boy's National School, has a giant screen that offers a perfect view from any seat of the latest football (read: soccer), rugby, hurling, or Gaelic football matches. Many who attended the school in their youth say it's hard to enjoy a pint there!

Donovan's Lane, off Clanbrassil St., below St. Patrick's Cathedral, Dublin 8 (☎ 01-453-2000).

Hip bars

Zanzibar

From the beauty and style of the people inside, you'd think patrons of chic Zanzibar were trying to look as gorgeous as the fabulous decor. It's the hottest of Dublin's hot spots.

35 Lower Ormond Quay, Dublin 1 (facing the River Liffey). ☎ 01-878-7212.

Pravda

The head of the cool department, Pravda is where the fashion-conscious assemble. The decor is grand and Soviet-esque, and there are plenty of couches. Lines reach the Ha'Penny Bridge on weekends.

35 Liffey St. Lower, Dublin 1 (north side of the Ha'Penny Bridge). ☎ 01-874-0076.

Late-night bars

Still up for some partying after last call (at the shocking hour of 11:30 p.m.!)? We personally recommend the following extended-hours pubs:

- ✔ **The Bridge,** 10 Westmoreland St. (directly below O'Connell Street Bridge) Dublin 2. ☎ 01-670-8133.
- ✔ **The Foggy Dew,** 1 Upper Fownes St., Temple Bar, Dublin 2. ☎ 01-677-9328.
- ✔ **Judge Roy Beans,** 45 Nassau St. (across from Trinity College), Dublin 2. ☎ 01-679-7539.
- ✔ **O'Brien's,** 40 Dame St., Dublin 2. ☎ 01-677-8816.
- ✔ **Turk's Head Chop House,** Parliament St., Temple Bar, Dublin 2. ☎ 01-679-9701.
- ✔ **Whelan's Pub,** 25 Wexford St., Dublin 2. ☎ 01-478-0766.

Traditional music venues

Want to hear real Irish music? We suggest the **Traditional Irish Music Pub Crawl** (listed under "Seeing Dublin by Guided Tour," earlier in this chapter), but here are a few pubs where you can listen to the traditional sounds.

- ✔ **O'Donoghues,** 15 Merrion Row, Dublin 2 (☎ 01-676-2807), is a popular singing pub with traditional Irish music every night. No cover.

- ✔ **Temple Bar,** 47 Temple Bar, Temple Bar, Dublin 2 (☎ 01-672-5287), is a place to hear often unrehearsed, impromptu, and exceptional traditional sessions. No cover.

- ✔ **Harcourt Hotel,** 60 Harcourt St. Dublin 2 (☎ 01-478-3677), has traditional music Monday through Wednesday and Saturdays. Occasional cover.

- ✔ **Whelan's Pub,** 25 Wexford St., Dublin 2 (☎ 01-478-0766), has a cozy, wooden interior with an excellent and eclectic mix of live music. Nice atmosphere.

- ✔ **Lannigans,** O'Connell Bridge, Dublin 1, in the Clifton Court Hotel (☎ 01-874-3535), is a candlelit pub with real turf fires and music sessions every night.

Club life

As in most European capitals, clubbing is taken seriously in Dublin and the hot spots are frequented by local fashionistas. Therefore, dress is pretty important, especially at the trendiest, most popular clubs — don't be surprised it you're turned away because of jeans or sneakers. Often there are cover charges (usually between 5 and 10 pounds) and you could need to show an ID. Clubs usually open just when buses stop running (about 11:30 p.m.), so expect to take a cab afterward.

The Kitchen

Frequented by the terminally stylish, The Kitchen is an intimate if cavernous club owned in part by the members of U2, and is one of the better places to be seen, if you don't get lost. It boasts the best deejays and modern music. Located under the Clarence Hotel, it can be found at the end of the long line.

E. Essex St., Temple Bar, Dublin 2. ☎ *01-677-6635.*

RiRa

Probably the most relaxed of the cool clubs, the RiRa offers an atmosphere chill enough to have a conversation in. The music's suited to please everyone, with hip-hop, garage, and soul featured on rotating nights. It's open seven nights a week.

11 Great George's St. South, Dublin 2. ☎ *01-677-4835.*

The Da Club

This small club, located upstairs from a classy bar and restaurant, is known for its diverse nightly offerings: You might find live music, comedy, or a hot new DJ on the bill. Small means small, though — there's only one toilet.

2–5 Johnsons Place, Dublin 2. ☎ *01-670-3137.*

The Palace

A dance-a-holic's dream! Even wallflowers will be lured to the dance floor when the DJ spins favorites from the 1970s and '80s. There's a large round bar in the center and intriguing music memorabilia on the walls. The crowd's often younger than in most clubs in the city.

21 Fleet St., Dublin 2. ☎ *01-677-9290.*

Yes Virginia, there is other nightlife in Dublin

If pubs aren't your thing, you'll still find some mighty fine nightlife in Dublin. From Dublin's legendary theaters to cutting-edge cinema and gut-busting humor, you'll never lack for entertainment. Here are a few things you can do.

See a theatrical show

Dubs have long held theater in high reverence, and today the city's theaters are liable to play host to quality plays that will later find their way to America and England. Check out what's on at Ireland's most famous playhouse, the **Abbey Theatre,** Lower Abbey St., Dublin 1 (☎ **01-878-7222**), where some of the biggest names in drama first flaunted their work. Or try the **Gate,** 1 Cavendish Row, Dublin 1 (☎ **01-874-7483**), which features classic Irish theater and is the place where a traveling Orson Welles got his professional start. If you're in the mood for some lighthearted fare, try the **Olympia Theatre,** 72 Dame St., Dublin 2 (☎ **01-478-2183**), where you'll see big-name bands on European tour. Call or check the *Irish Times* newspaper for details about shows.

Go to the movies

Or, as the Irish say, "the cinema." There are lots of places to catch a flick in Dublin, and all types of film-goers can find a theater that suits them. **The Ambassador,** Parnell St., Dublin 1 (☎ **01-872-7000**), plays only one film at a time, but does so in an old-fashioned theater complete with a balcony and red curtain that opens to a huge screen. **Virgin Cinema,** midway down Parnell St., Dublin 1 (☎ **01-872-8444**), is a streamlined and very modern multiplex, with nine screens and a full-service bar. The **Irish Film Centre,** 6 Eustace St., Temple Bar, Dublin 2 (☎ **01-679-3477**), shows up-and-coming Irish independent cinema, European exclusives, and classics. A place for true film buffs, the IFC is as hip as it gets. There's a cafe, a lively bar, and a book-video shop on the premises (the videos won't play in your VCR at home — they're formatted for European models — so don't waste the money).

Have a laugh

Everybody needs a good laugh, and one of the funnier choices includes **Murphy's Laughter Lounge,** Eden Quay, just off O'Connell on the north side of the River Liffey (☎ **01-874-4611**), for stand-up. On Tuesday nights, hilarious improv that feeds off of the audience can be found at the **Ha'penny Ha Ha,** upstairs at the Ha'Penny Bridge Inn, 42 Wellington Quay in Temple Bar (☎ **01-677-0616**). Prices vary.

Come to the cabaret

Irish variety shows are an extremely popular form of entertainment with tourists, and **Jury's Irish Cabaret,** at Jury's Hotel, Pembroke Road, Ballsbridge (☎ **01-660-5000**), is a great example, featuring Irish music, song, dance, and a few laughs. Runs nightly between May and early October. Dinner begins at 7:15 p.m. and the show at 8:00 p.m. Price: £36.50 ($54) dinner and cabaret, £20 ($29.60) cabaret and two drinks.

Fast Facts: Dublin

Area Code

The area code for Dublin city and county is 01. You only need to dial the area code if you are calling Dublin from outside the city. If you're calling from outside the country you can drop the 0.

Currency Exchange

Currency exchange is available everywhere, and indicated by the sign "Bureau de Change." You can exchange money at travel agencies, hotels, and some post offices, but the best rates are to be found at banks. If you have American Express Travelers Cheques you can exchange them without paying any commission at the **AmEx office,** 41 Nassau St., Dublin 2 (☎ 01- 679-9000). There is a second AmEx exchange location inside the **Dublin Tourism Centre** at St. Andrew's Church on Suffolk St. (☎ 01- 679-9000), open year-round.

Dentists

You can get emergency dental care at the **Dental Hospital,** Lincoln Place, Dublin 2 (☎ 01-612-7200). Prices depend on the care given.

Doctors

See "Hospitals."

Embassies-Consulates

U.S., 42 Elgin Rd., Ballsbridge, Dublin 4 (☎ 01-668-8777); **Canada,** 65 St. Stephen's

Green, Dublin 2 (☎ **01-478-1988**); **U.K.,** 29 Merrion Rd., Dublin 4 (☎ **01-205-3700**); **Australia,** Fitzwilton House, Wilton Terrace, Dublin 2 (☎ **01-676-1517**). **The New Zealand Consulate** is no longer in operation; for emergencies, contact the embassy in London.

Emergencies

Dial ☎ **999** for police, fire, or ambulance.

Eyeglasses

For quick replacement of glasses and contact lenses go to **Vision Express** in the ILAC Centre off O'Connell's St., Dublin 1 (☎ **01- 873-2477**).

Hospitals

The two most prominent hospitals in Dublin are **St. Vincent's Hospital,** Elm Park, Dublin 4 (☎ **01-269-4533**), on the south side of the city, and **Beaumont Hospital,** Beaumont Road, Dublin 9 (☎ **01-837-7755**), on the north side. Emergency care is available to all visitors from outside the EU at a fixed rate of £50 ($74).

Internet

The following internet cafes have World Wide Web access for Hotmail, AOL, and printing capabilities: **Global Internet Cafe,** 8 Lower O'Connell St., Dublin 1 (☎ **01-878-0295**); **Cyberia Internet Cafe,** Temple Lane South, Temple Bar, Dublin 2 (☎ **01-679-7607**; Internet: www.cyberia.ie).

Pharmacies

O'Connell's Pharmacies at 55 Lower O'Connell St., Dublin 1 (☎ **01-873-0427**), and 21 Grafton St., Dublin 2 (☎ **01-679-0467**), have extended hours.

Police

Dial ☎ **999** in case of emergencies. The Dublin Garda (Police) headquarters is at Harcourt Square, Dublin 2 (☎ **01-475-5555**).

Post Office

The **General Post Office (GPO)** is located on O'Connell St., Dublin 1 (☎ **01-872-6666**). Its hours are Mon–Sat 8:00 a.m.–8:00 p.m., Sun 10:00 a.m.–6:00 p.m. Branch offices, called *An Post* and noted with green storefront awnings, are generally open 9:00 a.m.–6:00 p.m., Mon–Sat.

Chapter 12

Easy Trips North of Dublin: Counties Meath and Louth

In This Chapter

▶ Finding the best of the Celtic high crosses

▶ Exploring the Cooley Peninsula

▶ Trying out water sports in the Irish Sea

▶ Running through tombs like Indiana Jones

▶ Visiting the ancient capital of Ireland

Collectively, Counties Louth and Meath are typically known as "the ancient land of the Celts." They're the country's hot spots for visiting prehistoric sites, such as ancient burial mounds and sites where the old Irish High Kings held court. You can easily take day trips from Dublin to both counties, which you may well think of as one destination because they're so complimentary. But, we've also listed a few good hotels in case you want to set up camp for a while.

What's Where? Meath and Louth's Major Attractions

County Meath has a few of the biggest ancient religious and political attractions in Ireland — the ancient tombs of **Newgrange** and **Knowth** and the **Hill of Tara.** The heart of the area is the River Boyne, home of the famous battle of the same name and one of the region's most fought-over by the country's many invaders. All those invaders, from the Normans to the English, left their mark on the area. Other influences, from the ancient High Kings to Christianity, are evident, too. Ruins, religious sites, and exalted meeting places are just some of the evidence of how the area has been molded over the centuries. The history-rich towns of **Kells, Slane,** and **Trim** (with minor attractions like Slane Castle and Trim Castle) are the best towns for a stopover. Some of County Meath's highlights include

✔ **Newgrange and Knowth:** Ancient burial mounds where you can get a feel for really old history.

✔ **The Hill of Tara:** And no, this attraction has nothing whatsoever to do with *Gone With the Wind* — instead, it's the ancient seat of Irish kings.

Counties Meath and Louth

Accommodations
Ballymascanlon House Hotel **3**
Boyne Valley Hotel
  & Country Club **7**
Conyngham Arms **6**
Station House **8**
Dining
Carrick House **9**
The Gables **4**
Jordan's **1**

Attractions
Cooley Peninsula **2**
Hill of Tara **8**
Knowth **7**
Monasterboice **5**
Newgrange Farm **6**
Newgrange **7**
Old Mellifont Abbey **7**

Shopping
Carlingford Adventure
  Centre **1**
Mary McDonald
  Craft Studio **6**

Nightlife
McManus' **3**
O'Hare's **1**
Railway Bar **9**

What **County Louth** lacks in big tourist attractions, it makes up for in history and the charm of small towns like **Dundalk** and **Drogheda.** These towns are the stomping grounds of legends such as Cuchulainn, Queen Maeve, and the great warrior Finn MacCool. Our favorite part of Louth is the far northern area of the beautiful **Cooley Mountains** and **Peninsula** and the town of **Carlingford.** While the rest of the county is not as picturesque as other areas, if you happen to be coming from Northern Ireland and have time to make the short Cooley drive, we guarantee you can have a few picture-worthy moments. So, be sure to catch

- ✔ **Dundalk and Drogheda:** Stop by for a pint in one of these charming little towns.

- ✔ **The Cooley Peninsula:** A gorgeous drive with great views of the Irish Sea and Carlingford Lough.

Touring

Most visitors to **Louth** and **Meath** arrive by car, often on a day trip from Dublin. Take the N2 north toward Slane and the N3 toward Navan and Kells. You can get to most major towns and attractions from these routes — just follow the signs. If you're heading directly to Louth from Dublin, take the N1 north toward Drogheda, Dundalk, and Newry. Most major towns and attractions are along that route. To get to the **Cooley Peninsula** from Dundalk, take the R173, which loops to the town of Newry.

Irish Rail (☎ 01-836-6222) has stops in the **County Louth** towns of **Drogheda** and **Dundalk** from Dublin.

Bus Eireann (☎ 01-836-6111) has year-round routes to **Navan, Kells, Slane,** Drogheda, Dundalk, **Carlingford,** and other smaller towns throughout the area. It also runs a year-round day tour of **Newgrange** and the **Boyne Valley** that begins in Dublin. The tour covers all the major sights, including the **Hill of Tara.** When and where: Runs May to September, Saturday and Sunday; October through April, Thursday and Saturday. Leaves Central Bus Station in Dublin at 10:00 a.m. and returns at 5:45 p.m. Information: ☎ **01-836-6111.** Price: £17 ($25.15) adult, £9 ($13.40) children.

Where to stay in Meath and Louth

Ballymascanlon House Hotel
$$ Dundalk, Louth

Here you can stay in an authentic Victorian mansion for a moderate price. The house retains an Old World ambience, and rooms are in a traditional style, with antiques and Victorian touches. This hotel is a great place for golfers — complete with an 18-hole course on the grounds — and recent renovations have made way for a leisure centre with a pool, jacuzzi, tennis courts, and more. The hotel also features a restaurant that serves local meats, seafood, veggies from the garden, and a bar that generally plays Irish music on the weekends.

Dundalk, Louth. ☎ *042-937-1124. Fax: 042-937-1598. E-mail:* info@ballyma scanlon.com. *Internet:* www.globalgolf.com/ballymascanlon. *By car: N1 from Dublin. Rates: £82–88 ($121.35–$130.25) double. AE, DC, MC, V.*

Boyne Valley Hotel & Country Club

$$$ Drogheda, Louth

Though it's in Louth, this hotel is a great starting point for touring the sites of Newgrange, Knowth, and Mellifont Abbey (all located in nearby Meath). Beautiful gardens and woodlands surround the elegant house and make for a pleasant stroll or a great view from the large atrium. All rooms are spacious and have been smartly refurbished. Amenities for guests include a pool. And the fish dishes served in the restaurant, prepared from the catch of the Boyne River, are fresh enough to almost flop off the plate!

Drogheda. ☎ *041-983-7737. Fax: 041-983-9188. E-mail:* reservations@ boyne-valley-hotel.ie. *Internet:* www.boyne-valley-hotel.ie. *By car: N1 from Dublin. Rates: £100–120 ($148–$177.60) double. AE, DC, MC, V.*

Conyngham Arms

$$ Slane, Meath

Located near Newgrange and Knowth, the Arms is a good base from which to explore the Boyne Valley. The service at this family-run hotel is personable and friendly, and the four-poster beds are a nice touch. You'll think you're staying in a B&B rather than a hotel.

Slane, Meath. ☎ *800-44-UTELL, from the United States; 041-982-4155. Fax: 041-982-4205. E-mail:* conynghamarms@eircom.net. *Internet:* www. destination-ireland.com/conyngham. *By car: N2 from Dublin. Rates: £60–85 ($96.20–$125.80) double. AE, DC, MC, V.*

Station House

$$ Kilmessan, Meath

Located near the Hill of Tara, this unique hotel was built inside an old Victorian railway junction building and uses the old ticket office, luggage room, platforms, and signal box for various hotel functions. The rooms are comfortably furnished, the price is right, and the theme is interesting.

Kilmessan, Meath. ☎ *046-25-239. Fax: 046-25-588. E-mail:* stnhouse@indigo.ie. *To get there: N3 from Dublin (near turn-off for the Hill of Tara). Rates: £50–60 ($74–$96.20) double. AE, DC, MC, V.*

Where to dine in Meath and Louth

Carrick House

$$ **Kells, Meath IRISH**

The food is good, and the price is even better at this family restaurant and lounge. The service is not the swiftest, but they make up for that with generous portions and comfortable seating. The restaurant also has a nice policy of using local, hormone-free beef. This menu features plenty of variety, so everyone will be happy.

Kells (on the main road), Meath. ☎ 046-40-100. By car: Take the N3 from Dublin to Kells. Main courses: £5.50–10.50 ($8.15–$15.55). MC, V. Open: 12:30 p.m.–10:00 p.m. daily.

The Gables

$$$ **Ardee, Louth FRENCH**

This fine and classically French restaurant goes out of its way to spoil you. From the service to the wine, everything is top-notch. It's high-class eating minus all the fuss. Specialties include snails in garlic butter, local prawns, venison, and, yes, pigeon. We must tell you: Pigeon is gamy and doesn't taste at all like chicken. We recommend The Gables for New Yorkers in particular.

Dundalk Rd., Ardee, Louth. ☎ 041-685-3789. By car: R173 from Dundalk. Main courses: £11.50–22 ($17–$32.55). MC, DC, V. Open: Mar-Sep Daily 12:30 p.m.– 5:00 p.m. and 7:00 p.m.–11:00 p.m. Off-season Sun lunch. Closed in Jan.

Jordan's

$$$–$$$$ **Carlingford, Louth IRISH**

Located in a renovated stone warehouse, this Irish restaurant overlooking Carlingford's harbor has excellent dishes made from locally and organically grown ingredients. The interior is classic — with ornate wall fixtures, white tablecloths, and fresh flowers — the service top-notch, and the atmosphere is casual. You can't go wrong ordering one of its award-winning fish dishes.

Newry St., Carlingford, Louth. ☎ 042-937-3827. By car: N2 from Dublin. Main courses: £14.50–24 ($21.45–$35.50). MC, V. Open: Daily 12:30 p.m.–11:00 p.m.

Enjoying the area's top attractions

Bru' na Boinne Visitor Centre (Newgrange and Knowth)
Donore, County Meath

This Visitor Centre has combined two of the best sites in Meath into an historic and archeological stop well worth your time. In addition to Newgrange Tumulus and Knowth, the centre itself contains many interpretive displays about the rich history of the Boyne Valley as well as viewing areas of the Neolithic (New Stone Age) sites. Unlike in the past, you can no longer get direct access to Newgrange and Knowth. You must purchase tickets at the Visitor Centre and take its minibus shuttle to the sites.

More fun than informative, Newgrange Tumulus is a huge, impressively intact round mound — 200,000 tons of earth and stone covering a magnificent and well-preserved 5,000-year-old burial chamber. You enter through a low arch and make your way Indiana Jones-style down the long and narrow stone passage to the central burial chamber. Knowth is an even older and larger tomb, used from the Bronze Age through the Norman periods of Irish history. You can see two burial chambers filled with "tomb art" and 18 smaller satellite tombs with passages. If you have to choose between Newgrange and Knowth, we recommend Knowth — there's more to see inside, even though Newgrange is prettier from the outside.

Over the entrance stone of Newgrange is a roof box opening that allows light to slowly creep back into the burial chamber during the winter solstice, filling the room for about 15 minutes. A sign of the new year or a clue to finding the lost ark? We don't know because tours during the solstice are booked up years in advance.

Off N51, Donore, east of Slane, County Meath. ☎ 041-988-0300. By car: L21 off N1 from Drogheda or N2 from Slane. By bus: Bus Eireann (☎ 01-836-6111) takes a day tour of Newgrange and the Boyne Valley from Dublin. Admission: Centre & Newgrange: £3 ($4.45) adults, £2 ($2.95) seniors, £1.50 ($2.20) students and children, £7.50 ($11.10) family; Centre & Knowth: £2 ($2.95) adults, £1.50 ($2.20) seniors, £1 ($1.50) students and children, £5 ($7.40) family. Centre, Newgrange & Knowth: £5 ($7.40) adults, £3.50 ($5.20) seniors, £2.25 ($3.35) students and children, £12.50 ($18.50) family. Open: June to mid-Sept daily 9:00 a.m.–7:00 p.m., May and mid-Sept to the end of Sept daily 9:00 a.m.–6:30 p.m.; Mar, April, and Oct daily 9:30 a.m.–5:30 p.m.; Nov–Feb daily 9:30 a.m.–5:00 p.m. Restricted access for people with disabilities. Time: Four hours.

Hill of Tara
South of Navan, County Meath

This Stone Age meeting house was once the seat of the High Kings and capital of Celtic Ireland. It looks like something out of the *X-Files* — a large round structure raised from the earth — and the atmosphere is just a bit creepy. The audio-visual presentation is interesting, but walking about this early Christian religious and political site is a close encounter of its own kind.

South of Navan off the main Dublin road (N3), County Meath. ☎ 046-25-903 May–Oct or 041-24-488 Nov–April. By car: From Dublin, take the N3 toward Navan and look for signs beginning about 9 miles before reaching the town. Near the village of Kilmessan. Admission: £1.50 ($2.20) adults and seniors, 60p (90 cents) students and children. Open: mid-June to mid-Sept daily 9:30 a.m.–6:30 p.m., May to mid-June and mid-Sept to Oct daily 10:00 a.m.–5:00 p.m. Restricted access for people with disabilities. Time: Forty-five minutes.

Newgrange Farm
Slane, County Meath

This is your average working Irish farm turned tourist attraction, where the darn-friendly Redhouse family gives a tour of its farm, livestock, garden, and seventeenth-century buildings. You can hold a baby chick, watch a threshing machine in action, see a horse get a new pair of shoes, pet a donkey, and more. This attraction is definitely one for the kids, but adults can enjoy themselves as well, and maybe learn a few pointers for the herb garden at home.

Off N51, Slane, County Meath. ☎ *041-982-4119. By car: N2 from Dublin or N51 from Navan or Drogheda. Admission: £2.50 ($3.70) per person, £9 ($13.40) family. Open: April–Aug Mon–Sat 9:30 a.m.–5:30 p.m. Time: An hour and a half.*

Old Mellifont Abbey
Tullyallen, County Louth

Founded by St. Malachy in 1142, Mellifont was the first Cistercian monastery in Ireland. This historic house of worship was suppressed by Henry VIII, then became a pigsty, and later was the headquarters for William III during the Battle of the Boyne. The site is still a peaceful and tranquil place. The unique *octagonal lavabo* (a washing trough for religious ceremonies) remains intact, along with several of the abbey's arches, all set along the River Mattock. The visitor centre contains examples of masonry from the Middle Ages.

Tullyallen, Drogheda, County Louth. ☎ *041-982-6459 summer, 041-988-0300 winter. By car: N1 from Dublin. Cost: £1.50 ($2.20) adults, £1 ($1.50) seniors, 60p (90 cents) students and children. Open: May to mid-June and mid-Sept to mid-Oct daily 10:00 a.m.–5:00 p.m., mid-June to mid-Sept daily 9:30 a.m.–6:30 p.m. Time: One hour.*

Monasterboice
Collon, County Louth

Throughout Meath and Louth you'll see more Celtic high crosses than you can shake a stick at. These imposing crosses, which began being erected in the eighth century, were status symbols for churches and monasteries. Beginning in the tenth century, they were decorated with biblical scenes. It's thought that the crosses were used as teaching tools for the illiterate to better understand the Bible. Two such remarkable ninth-century decorated High Crosses are the highlights of the sixth-century Monasterboice monastery. Muiredach's Cross, one of the best examples of of the popular Celtic crosses, depicts the Last Judgment and Old Testament scenes. The other cross is one of the largest in Ireland. The rest of the area is rather unassuming, with its standard graveyard, round tower, and church ruins, but Monasterboice remains one of the most important religious sites in Ireland.

Off the main Dublin road (N1) near Collon, County Louth. By car: N1 from Dublin. Cost: Free. Open: Daylight hours. Time: Thirty minutes.

Cooley Peninsula, Louth
Outside Dundalk, County Louth

This peninsula offers a great scenic drive with impressive views of the Irish Sea and Carlingford Lough. At one point, the road actually passes through the mountainside. This attraction is the mythic home of legendary heroes, namely Cuchulainn and Finn MacCool. Dotted along the drive are dolmen, forests, mountains, rivers, and quaint fishing villages. The largest village, Carlingford, is a good place to stop for a stretch and to see the ruins of King John's Castle or to visit the Holy Trinity Heritage Centre. Drive the route in a few hours or hike along Tain Trail out of Carlingford in an afternoon.

By car: R173 loops around the Peninsula, off N1 outside Dundalk. Time: Three hours.

Shopping and other fun stuff to do

✔ **Mary McDonnell Craft Studio** (Slane, County Meath): Mary personally designs fine cushions, quilts, and wall hangings inspired by the legends and folklore of the Boyne Valley. Other treasures include ceramics, candles, leatherwork, and jewelry.

Location: 4 Newgrange Mall, Slane, Meath. (No phone.) By car: N2 from Dublin or N51 from Navan or Drogheda. Time: As long as you like to browse.

✔ **Carlingford Adventure Centre** (Carlingford, County Louth): Great outdoor fun — like windsurfing, kayaking, and sailing on Carlingford Lough or trekking and rock climbing in the Cooley Mountains — is what the Adventure Centre is all about. The centre is fun for the whole family and the best way to experience the area's natural beauty.

Prices and schedules for activities vary. Location: Thosel Street, Carlingford, Louth. ☎ **042-937-3100.** By car: R173 from Dundalk, on the Cooley Peninsula. Open: Year-round. Time: Two hours.

Perusing Pub Life

McManus'

This family-run establishment is like three pubs in one. The Music Bar often hosts spontaneous traditional music sessions that keep your feet tapping. On cold days, make your way to the back Kitchen Bar, an intimate room with brick interior and a warm cast-iron stove. The Secret Beer Garden's outdoor seating area has coal and turf fires burning year-round, as well as the occasional barbecue.

17 Seatown, Dundalk. Louth. ☎ *042-933-1632.*

O'Hare's

As part-grocery, part-pub, O'Hare's is a dying breed of places that combine a local watering hole with a neighborhood convenience store. But this popular place brings in the tourists for an even more unique attraction: the leprechaun in a glass case. That's right, a leprechaun! Judge its authenticity for yourself. The pub also features traditional music on Wednesdays. The pub grub is good, but the house specialty — oysters — is a must-try. Simply scrumptious.

Carlingford (take the first left off the main road and stay to the right until you see the beer garden), Louth. ☎ *042-937-3106.*

Railway Bar

This charming pub is so full of warmth and character that the place often fills up quickly, but fear not: It has a conservatory that opens to a large walled garden out back to handle the overflow.

Kells, Meath. ☎ *046-40-215.*

Fast Facts: Counties Meath and Louth

AREA CODE(S)

042 and 046 for Meath, 042 and 041 for Louth.

EMERGENCIES/HOSPITALS

Dial ☎ **999** for all emergencies. **Louth County Hospital** is on Dublin Rd. in Dundalk (☎ **042-933-4701**).

GENEALOGICAL RESOURCES

In Meath, contact the **Meath Heritage Centre,** Mill St., Trim (☎ **046-36-633**, Fax: 046-37-502). In Louth, contact **MC Research Service,** Seabank, Castlebellingham, Dundalk (☎ **042-937-2046;** Fax: 042-937-2046).

INFORMATION

For visitor information in Meath, go to one of the tourist offices: Trim (☎ **046-37-111**),

Navan (☎ **046-37-426**), Slane (☎ **041-988-4055**), and Kells (☎ **046-49-336**). E-mail: info@meathtourism.ie. The office in Trim is open year-round. For telephone directory assistance, dial ☎ **1190**. For visitor information in Louth, go to the tourist office at Jocelyn St., Dundalk (☎ **042-933-5484;** Internet: www.louthholidays.com), open year-round. They can also provide reservation services. For telephone directory assistance, dial ☎ **1190**.

POST OFFICE

Clanbrassil St., Dundalk, Louth (☎ **042-933-4444**).

Chapter 13

Easy Trips South of Dublin: Counties Wicklow and Kildare

. . . .

In This Chapter

▶ Viewing homes and gardens no magazine could capture

▶ Exploring the Wicklow Mountains and the scenic Wicklow Way

▶ Enjoying high-class dining and accommodations you won't soon forget

▶ Making a pilgrimage to the home of Irish racing

▶ Discovering the history of the area at a pub

▶ Finding out everything you ever wanted to know about steam

. . . .

*I*mmediately south of bustling Dublin, you find the beginnings of all that Irish green you've been hearing about your whole life. While county Wicklow's people trim all that lush greenery into beautiful gardens, County Kildare's citizens tend to feed theirs to the horses — the county is home to dozens upon dozens of horse farms, as well as race tracks.

What's Where? Wicklow and Kildare and Their Major Attractions

County Wicklow is affectionately known as "The Garden of Ireland," and you won't need long to see why. The county begins just barely out of Dublin's limits, but immediately the cityscape gives way to rural roads and stunning scenery. Wicklow makes for a great day trip when staying in Dublin, but the area offers plenty of charming places to stay.

Wicklow's eastern coast is studded with resort areas and harbor towns where you can have a fine seafood dinner and stay in a family-run guesthouse to experience Ireland's famed hospitality. But it's County Wicklow's inland that will amaze you. To really get a feel for the area, you should see it by foot, taking a walk on a stretch of the **Wicklow Way,** a signposted walking path that follows forest trails, sheep paths, and county roads from just outside Dublin all the way to Clonegal.

Nestled among the hills are quaint, not-to-be-missed villages plus some great attractions like

- ✔ **Powerscourt House, Gardens, and Waterfall:** This sweeping estate has some of the finest gardens in all of Europe, as well as a beautifully preserved mansion and Ireland's highest waterfall.

- ✔ **Wicklow Mountains National Park:** Nearly 50,000 acres of Irish nature.

- ✔ **Glendalough Round Tower and Monastery:** St. Kevin built this monastery in the sixth century, and the remains today give a little peek into how the Irish saved civilization.

- ✔ **The National Sea Life:** An aquarium and museum explain life in the ocean and bring you face to face with its wonders.

When you drive into **County Kildare,** you drive into horse country! Horse racing is an integral part of Irish culture, and Ireland is known worldwide for its respectable horse breeding. Much of that reputation stems from the work done with horses in County Kildare, where for years breeders have raised and raced some of the finest thoroughbreds the world has to offer.

For those of you less than enthusiastic about horses, first, some advice: Don't admit it in these parts! Second, the area offers plenty of other interesting things for you to see. For instance

- ✔ **Irish National Stud and Japanese Gardens:** Visitors to this state-run stud farm can walk around the grounds and see the prize-winning horses being groomed and exercised, or visit the Horse Museum or the striking Japanese Gardens — one of the finest outside of Asia — which boast bonsai, bamboos, and cherry trees.

- ✔ **The Curragh:** Ireland's best-known racetrack is often referred to as the Churchill Downs of Ireland.

- ✔ **Celbridge Abbey Grounds:** Sitting along the River Liffey, these grounds were planted by the daughter of the Lord Mayor of Dublin in 1697 for Jonathan Swift.

- ✔ **Castletown House:** This impressive, stately, eighteenth-century house is a standout in Irish architecture.

- ✔ **Steam Museum:** This collection houses locomotive engines dating all the way back to 1797.

County Wicklow

Wicklow is green, green, green, and you can easily hit the highlights in a day or stick around to really get the flavor of the place. Many Dubliners go on vacation in Wicklow, especially in the area around the River Dargle. But that's not what makes the spot so well known. No, what's really given it immortality is its use in drinking songs. After all, can you think of another town name that rhymes so easily with the word "gargle"?

Counties Wicklow and Kildare

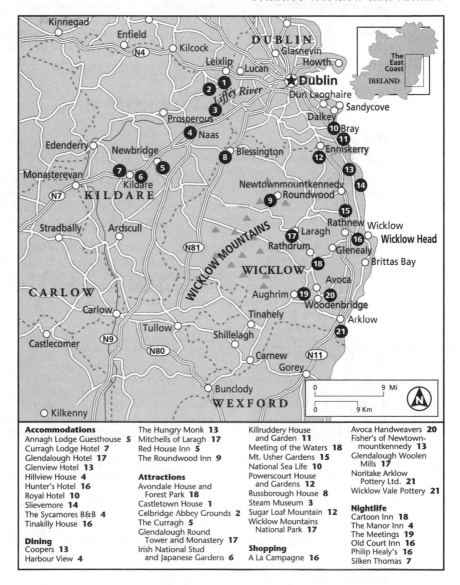

Accommodations
Annagh Lodge Guesthouse **5**
Curragh Lodge Hotel **7**
Glendalough Hotel **17**
Glenview Hotel **13**
Hillview House **4**
Hunter's Hotel **16**
Royal Hotel **10**
Slievemore **14**
The Sycamores B&B **4**
Tinakilly House **16**

Dining
Coopers **13**
Harbour View **4**

The Hungry Monk **13**
Mitchells of Laragh **17**
Red House Inn **5**
The Roundwood Inn **9**

Attractions
Avondale House and
    Forest Park **18**
Castletown House **1**
Celbridge Abbey Grounds **2**
The Curragh **5**
Glendalough Round
    Tower and Monastery **17**
Irish National Stud
    and Japanese Gardens **6**

Killruddery House
    and Garden **11**
Meeting of the Waters **18**
Mt. Usher Gardens **15**
National Sea Life **10**
Powerscourt House
    and Gardens **12**
Russborough House **8**
Steam Museum **3**
Sugar Loaf Mountain **12**
Wicklow Mountains
    National Park **17**

Shopping
A La Campagne **16**

Avoca Handweavers **20**
Fisher's of Newtown-
    mountkennedy **13**
Glendalough Woolen
    Mills **17**
Noritake Arklow
    Pottery Ltd. **21**
Wicklow Vale Pottery **21**

Nightlife
Cartoon Inn **18**
The Manor Inn **4**
The Meetings **19**
Old Court Inn **16**
Philip Healy's **16**
Silken Thomas **7**

Getting to and around Wicklow

If you're arriving by car, take the N11 (which becomes M11 periodically) south from Dublin toward Arklow. You can turn off along this route to reach most major towns and attractions. The **Dublin (Connolly Station)-Rosslare Harbour train line** (☎ 01-703-1843) has stations in Bray, Greystones, Wicklow, Rathdrum, and Arklow. Dublin Area Rapid Transit (DART) extends as far as Greystones. **Dublin Bus** (☎ 01-872-000) runs from City Centre to Dun Laoghaire and the Bray

DART station. **Bus Eireann** (☎ 01- 836-6111) travels year-round between Bray, Wicklow, Arklow, Rathdrum, and Avoca.

Stena Sealink (☎ 01-204-7777) travels from Holyhead, Wales, to Dun Laoghaire six to eight times a day. You can catch the DART or bus or rent a car at the port town.

Where to stay in Wicklow

Hunter's Hotel

$$$ Rathnew

This family-run hotel is one of Ireland's oldest coaching inns, offering views of breathtaking gardens and nearby mountains. Irish dishes, like Wicklow lamb, and fresh vegetables from the hotel's gardens are served in the restaurant. Blazing fires and antique furniture add to its charm.

Newrath Bridge, Rathnew. ☎ *0404-40-106. Fax: 0404-40-338. E-mail:* reception@ hunters.ie. *Internet:* www.hunters.ie. *By car: N11 from Dublin and take a left in Ashford village by the bridge and opposite Ashford House pub. Hunter's is one and a half miles (2km) from Ashford. Rates: £105–120 ($155.40–$177.60) double. AE, DC, MC, V.*

Tinakilly House

$$$ Rathnew

This small country-house hotel brings together every notion you've ever had about the grandeur and friendliness of Ireland. Staying at Tinakilly House may cost a bit more than you'd like to pay, but when your every whim is being catered to and you're lost in the surroundings, you'll be happy you splurged! The hotel is an impressive Victorian home, with rooms that have four-poster beds and overlook gardens that are tended with precision. The menu changes daily, but if you see it, try the turbot with shrimp ravioli and black sesame and soy dressing.

Off the Dublin-Wexford Rd., on R750, Rathnew, Wicklow. ☎ *0404-69-274 or 800-525-4800 from the U.S. Fax: 0404-67-806. E-mail:* reservations@tinakilly. ie. *Internet:* www.tinakilly.ie. *To get there, take the R750 off the main Dublin-Wexford Rd. Rates: £130–180 ($192.40–$266.40) double. AE, DC, MC, V.*

Glenview Hotel

$$$ Delgany

This bright, relaxing hotel is easy to reach — off the N11 and just a half-hour from Dublin. Glenview was recently refurbished, and all the bed-rooms are tasteful and have amenities like pants press and satellite TV. Its best draw is the Woodlands Restaurant, though, which overlooks the hotel's namesake, the scenic glen.

Glen O' The Downs, Delgany. ☎ *01-287-3399. Fax: 01-287-511. E-mail:* glenview@ iol.ie. *By car: 25 minutes south of Dublin off the N11. Rates: £116–150 ($171.70–$222) double. AE, DC, MC, V.*

Royal Hotel and Leisure Centre
$$ Bray

This hotel has it all: luxury for a bearable cost, a prime location in a great town, and tons of extras to tempt you to skip sightseeing. The Royal sits on the picturesque main street of Bray and isn't dubbed a "leisure centre" for nothing. After relaxing in the indoor pool or whirlpool, you can stroll into the hotel's top-grade pub for a meal from the *carvery* (buffet). Rooms are large enough to fit whole families, and the Royal provides child-care, too.

Main St., Bray. ☎ *01-286-2935. Fax: 01-286-7373. E-mail:* royal@regency hotels.com. *By car: N11 to Bray. DART: Bray is 30 minutes from Dublin. Rates: £98 ($145.05) double. AE, DC, MC, V.*

Glendalough Hotel
$$ Glendalough

Any shortcomings to this hotel are made up for by the surrounding vistas. On the whole, it's a charming place. The food served in the impressive dining room is excellent and fresh, and the Glendalough Tavern has some of the best pub food you'll find in a hotel. The rooms are pretty bland and are a letdown compared to the rest of the place, but why would you spend lots of time in your room with so much to see?

On the 755, Glendalough. ☎ *0404-45-135. Fax: 0404-45-142. By car: Take the R755 off the N11. Rates: £60–100 ($88.80–$148) double. AE, DC, MC, V. Closed for Jan.*

Slievemore
$ Greystones

You won't get a better view of Greystones's spectacular beachfront than from Slievemore, an impeccable, white-washed B&B run by a pleasant couple. Step out of the door and take a walk on the beach before having a traditional breakfast in the atrium. This place is a great representation of the quaintness of the town.

The Harbour, Greystones. ☎ *01-287-4724. By car: Follow signs south out of Bray to Greystones village. Rates: £40 ($59.20) double. No credit cards.*

Where to dine in Wicklow

Mitchells of Laragh
$$$$ Glendalough   IRISH

Set in a garden among the Wicklow Mountains, this schoolhouse-cum-restaurant is renowned for its Irish fare and mercurial gourmet menu. While the country-style decor and fireplaces inside are lovely, ask for a table outside in the summer. Among their specialities, the local rack of Wicklow lamb is a must try, as is the homemade ice cream. Yum!

Laragh, Glendalough. ☎ *0404-45-302. By car: From N11/M11 turn right at Kimacanogue to Glendalough. Main courses: £16.50–19.50 ($24.42–$28.85). AE, DC, M, V. Open: 9:00 a.m.–9:00 p.m. daily, Apr–Sept; Wed–Sun 9:00 a.m.–9:00 p.m., Oct–Mar.*

The Roundwood Inn

$$$ Bray   SEAFOOD/IRISH/ECLECTIC

Forget about fish and chips! The Roundwood Inn takes the preparation of seafood to new levels, with careful creations and European flair. Nothing's oversauced or tries too hard to be continental. In fact, the food is a perfect mix of Irish heartiness and worldly sophistication. The Roundwood also serves pub food that's a step above the norm all day. Try the lobster salad.

Main St., Roundwood, Bray. ☎ *01-281-8107. Reservations recommended. By car: Out of Bray take R755 to Roundwood. Main courses: £9.50–17 ($14.05–$25.15). AE, DC, MC, V. Open: Wed–Sat 7:30 p.m.–10:00 p.m., Sun 1:00 p.m.–10:00 p.m. Not wheelchair accessible.*

The Hungry Monk

$$$ Greystones   IRISH/ECLECTIC

Another fabulous place to eat in this little town! The Hungry Monk, a small, candlelit restaurant on the main street, boasts a menu that's as varied as it is good. The roast rack of Aughrim lamb is delicious, and the starters are tempting enough to order as a meal. Portions are generous, no matter what you decide on, so if you don't have a hearty appetite, you'll either be sharing or getting a doggy bag. You can enjoy a romantic meal here, and it's best to leave the kids with a sitter.

Church Rd., Greystones. ☎ *01-287-5759. By car: Follow signs south out of Bray to Greystones village. Main courses: £10.50–16.95 ($15.55–$25.10). M, V. Open: Tues–Sat 7:00 p.m.–11:00 p.m. Sun 12:30 p.m.–8:00 p.m. Not wheelchair accessible.*

Coopers

$$ Greystones   SEAFOOD/IRISH/ECLECTIC

Possibly Greystones's greatest claim to fame, Coopers is a restaurant everyone seems to know about. And for good reason: It's a great place. Because of its proximity to the ocean (waves practically hit the place), it's no surprise the fish dishes are delicious, but the quality extends throughout the entire menu. For starters, try the duck and chicken paté with cumberland sauce, moving on to baked salmon on a bed of aubergines. On weekends it's crowded, so call ahead.

The Harbour, Greystones. ☎ *01-287-3914. Reservations recommended. By car: Follow signs south out of Bray to Greystones village. Main courses: £8.50–10.50 ($12.60–$15.55). AE, M, V. Open: Mon–Sat 5:30 p.m.–11:30 p.m., Sun 12:30 p.m.– 4:00 p.m., 5:30 p.m.–10:00 p.m.*

Exploring Wicklow

As we say earlier in this chapter, gardens and greenery are the big draws here, but Wicklow also has its share of historic houses and monastic sites. In this section we run through the best of them.

The top attractions

Here are a few of our favorite hot spots to hit in Wicklow.

Powerscourt House, Gardens, and Waterfall
Enniskerry

This sweeping estate has some of the finest gardens in all of Europe, maintained with meticulous care and covering 100 acres at the base of a Palladian mansion built in the 1730s by the first Viscount Powerscourt, Richard Wingfield. The house was gutted by a fire in 1974 but was recently rebuilt and is now once again open to the public. The sweeping grounds feature Japanese gardens, a beautiful mosaic of pebbles gathered from the beach in Bray, and classically styled statues throughout. An incredible stairway leads to the circular Triton Lake, which the gardens majestically surround. A crafts center, children's play area, and restaurant on the premises round out the amenities. Also part of the estate is Ireland's highest waterfall, just four miles away.

Off the main Dublin-Wicklow Rd. (N11), Enniskerry. ☎ *01-204-6000. By car: Take the N11 out of Dublin (it becomes the new motorway M11) and follow signs for the garden. By bus: 44 from Dublin to Enniskerry and Alpine Coach (*☎ *01-286-2547), which runs daily buses from Dublin to the gardens. Admission: Garden only: £3.50 ($5.20) adults, £3.20 ($4.75) students and seniors, £2 ($2.95) children under 16; House only: £1.50 ($2.20) adults, £1.30 ($1.90) students and seniors, £1 ($1.50) children under 16; House and Garden: £5 ($7.40) adults, £4.50 ($6.65) students and seniors, £3 ($4.45) children under 16. Open: Garden Mar–Oct 9:30 a.m.–5:30 p.m., Nov–Feb 9:30 a.m.–dusk. Waterfall Mar–Oct 9:30 a.m.–7:00 p.m., Nov–Feb 10:30 a.m.–dusk. Closed for the two weeks prior to Christmas. Time: Two hours.*

Wicklow Mountains National Park
Glendalough

This area, covering nearly 50,000 acres, includes large mountain bogs and protects such wildlife as the rare peregrine falcon. The park centers around the beautiful Glendalough, and the Glendalough Wood Nature Reserve serves as the information and education facilities for the park. In May the park hosts a two-day walking festival.

Glendalough. ☎ *0404-45-425; winter number* ☎ *0404-45-338. By car: N11 to R755 from Dublin; R752 to R755 from Wicklow. The Information Point is located by Upper Lake, R756 off R755. Admission: Free. Information Point Open: May–Aug daily 10:00 a.m.–6:00 p.m., April and Sept Sat and Sun 10:00 a.m.–6:00 p.m. Time: One to three hours.*

Glendalough Round Tower and Monastery
Glendalough

Despite being sacked, pillaged, and destroyed by fire, this monastery has persevered. St. Kevin built the monastery in the sixth century, but Vikings invaded it in the ninth century. A fire swept through the second version at the end of the fourteenth century, and most of what now stands is a restoration from the 1800s. Just beyond the Visitor Centre and through the stone arch is St. Kevin's Church, and the chimney-looking building — the Round Tower at Glendalough — was actually once a bell tower. One of the first things to attract your attention is the position of the door — 10 feet off the ground! The most accepted explanation for this is that the monks put it there for safety. They would climb to the door on a ladder and then pull up the ladder in case of a threat below.

Glendalough. ☎ *0404-45-325. By car: N11 to R755 from Dublin, R752 to R755 from Wicklow. Admission: £2 ($2.95) adults, £1.50 ($2.20) seniors, £1 ($1.50) children and students. Open: Mid-Oct to mid-Mar daily 9:30 a.m.–5:00 p.m., mid-Mar to May and Sept to mid-Oct daily 9:30 a.m.–6:00 p.m., June–Aug daily 9:00 a.m.–6:30 p.m. Time: An hour and a half.*

The National Sea Life
Bray

Much more than an aquarium, this interactive museum breaks boundaries to explain life in the ocean and bring you face to face with its wonders. Two hundred tanks house nearly 700 species of aquatic life! Kids have a ball here, following an adventure trail with clues and puzzles or even picking up real ocean dwellers. The Explore Think Tank is an interactive display, with touch-screens and CD-ROM games. You can come and go all day, taking advantage of the feeding demonstrations and talks.

Bray, Strand Rd. (on the boardwalk). ☎ *01-286-6939. By car: N11 to Bray. DART: The center is a 10-minute walk from the Bray Station. Admission: £4.95 ($7.35) adults, £4.50 ($6.65) senior, £4 ($5.90) students, £3.50 ($5.20) children. Open: Oct–Mar Mon–Fri 12:00 p.m.–4:00 p.m., Mar–Sept daily 11:00 a.m.–6:00 p.m. Time: Two hours.*

Other fun stuff to do
What? The historic houses and gardens that we mention previously aren't enough of a feast for you? Okay, then. Here's some dessert.

✔ **Walk the Wicklow Way:** This 76-mile trail extends from Dublin City to County Carlow. You may not have the time (or energy!) to walk the entire thing, but do drop into parts of it — you won't be disappointed. Beginning in the plains, the trail climbs into the Dublin Mountains and then dips into glens in the high Wicklow Mountains, along the way passing places of historical note, farms, and traditional stone walls that separate land ownership. Those stone walls that separate fields in Ireland began out of a practical necessity to clear the earth of all the rocks in order to make the land suitable for crops and grazing.

To get there: A daily bus runs from Dublin and Waterford to Bunclody near the County Carlow end of the trail (Bus Eireann, Dublin-Waterford Express). Before you go, be sure to pick up a map at a County Wicklow tourism office, through e-mail at eastwest@ eircom.net, or via the Web at http://homepage.eircom.net/ ~eastwest. Time: Varies, depending on distance walked.

✔ **Killruddery House and Garden:** Since 1618, this house has been in the family of the Earls of Meath, but the draw of the place is really the gardens. Kilruddery is one of the earliest gardens in Ireland that still survives, exhibiting the seventeenth-century French style. The garden contains an outdoor theater, foreign trees and shrubs, and a round pond with fountains.

Location: Off the main Dublin-Wicklow road. (N11), Killruddery. ☎ 01-286-2777. By car: Take N11 south from Bray. Admission: £4.50 ($6.65) adults, £3 ($4.45) seniors and students. Garden only: £3 ($4.45) adult, £2 ($2.95) seniors and students. Open: Mid-February to June and September Daily 1:00 p.m. to 5:00 p.m. Garden open April to September. Time: One and a half hours.

✔ **Russborough House:** This house, built in the mid-1700s in the Palladian style, is home of the world-famous Beit Collection of paintings, which includes pieces by Gainsborough, Rubens, and Vernet. Inside you can see a fine selection of furniture, tapestries, porcelain, and silver. Stop by the restaurant, shop, children's playground, and lakeside picnic area.

Location: Off N81, Blessington. ☎ 045-86-5239. By car: From Dublin, take the N7 to Naas and pick up the R410. The house is located where the R410 meets the N81. Admission: Main rooms £4 ($5.90) adults, £3 ($4.45) seniors and students, £2 ($2.95) children under 12. Additional £2.50 ($3.70) for bedroom tour, which includes silver and porcelain displays. Open: June to August daily 10:30 a.m. to 5:30 p.m., September Monday to Saturday 10:30 a.m. to 2:30 p.m., Sunday 10:30 a.m to 5:30 p.m. Time: One hour.

✔ **Mt. Usher Gardens:** More than 5,000 species of plants from all over the world are spread throughout these gardens, located along the River Vartry. Starting from a humble potato patch in 1860, these 20 acres have blossomed into an ocean of flowers, meadows, and waterfalls and are a playground for birds and wildlife. A particularly nice area is where the suspension bridge spans a little waterfall — quite a romantic spot! Also check out the shopping courtyard and the tea rooms.

Location: Off the main Dublin-Wicklow road (N11), Ashford. ☎ 0404-40-116. By car: N11 from Dublin or Rosslare. Admission: £3.50 ($5.20) adults, £2.50 ($3.70) students. Open: Mid-March to October daily 10:30 a.m. to 6:00 p.m. Time: An hour and a half.

✔ **Avondale House and Forest Park:** Built in 1779 and set in a lush valley, this house was the birthplace of one of Ireland's great leaders, Charles Stewart Parnell (1846–91) and is now a museum dedicated to his life and memory. Avondale is also the center of Irish forestry, and its plantations have served as a model for the country. The forest park has long, well-marked walks and a picnic area.

Location: Rathdrum. ☎ **0404-46-111.** By car: Take N11 to R752 to Rathdrum crossroads and follow signs to the house. Admission: £3 ($4.45) adults, £2.75 ($4.07) students and seniors, £1.50 ($2.20) children under 16; Parking fee: £2 ($2.95); Forest Park: Free admission. Open: Mid-March to October daily 10:00 a.m. to 5:00 p.m. Time: An hour and a half.

✔ **Wicklow's Best View:** You can enjoy a really spectacular view from the top of **Sugar Loaf Mountain.** The climb is pretty easy, and you can get to the top in under an hour. You'll be happy you did — on a clear day you can see all the way to Wales!

Location: Near Kilmacanogue. Take R755 off N11.

✔ **Best Spot for a Picnic:** Just beyond Avondale House is the famed **Meeting of the Waters,** where the Avonmore and Avonbeg rivers come together. This spot is so beautiful it inspired Thomas Moore to write: "There is not in the wide world a valley so sweet / as the vale in whose bosum the bright waters meet."

Location: three miles south of Rathdrum heading toward Arklow on the R752 (which becomes the R755 as you leave Rathdrum).

Organized tours

Because Wicklow is so close to Dublin, a number of operators offer bus tours and others take advantage of the area's beauty to offer such interesting options as horse tours and boat tours.

The Wild Wicklow Bus Tour

Go off the beaten track in a little 26-seater Mercedes coach to see the most amazing spots in the Wicklow Mountains, accompanied by excellent and entertaining guides who speak of legends and folklore. The day-long tour includes Dun Laoghaire Harbour, Sandycove, Killiney Bay, Avoca Handweavers, Glendalough, Laragh, and the mountains.

When and where: Tours pick up at three Dublin city hotels and the Dublin Tourism Office between 8:50 a.m. and 9:40 a.m. Thur–Sun, April–Oct. Information: Call Aran Tours. ☎ *01-280-1899. E-mail:* info@arantours.ie. *Internet:* www.aran tours.ie/wildwicklow.html. *Price: £22 ($32.55). Advanced reservations recommended.*

Bus Eireann Bus Tour

Bus Eireann offers three-day tours of the area from Dublin. The **Glendalough & Wicklow Panorama Tour** (Price: £17/$25.15 adult, £9/$13.30 child peak season; £14/$20.70 adult, £7/$10.35 child off-peak) runs year-round, covering the south coast of Dublin, Killiney Bay, Wicklow, Avoca Handweavers, Roundwood, and Glendalough. The **Wicklow Mountains, Glenroe,** and **Ballykissangel Tour** and the **Russborough House & Powerscourt Gardens Tour** each run one day a week June through September. (Price: £17/$25.15 adult, £9/$13.40 child).

When and where: All tours leave from the main station, on Store St. behind the customs building. Information: Bus Eireann. ☎ *01-836-6111. Call for schedule information.*

St. Kevin's Bus Service

St. Kevin's bus service offers tours of Glendalough.

When and where: Leaves from the College of Surgeons, St. Stephen's Green West, Dublin, at 11:30 a.m. daily and returns at 6:00 p.m. The round-trip fare is £10/$14.50. Information: ☎ *01-281-8119.*

Blessington Lake Cruises

The MV *Blessington* offers hour-long cruises of the beautiful lakes serenely set in the foothills of the Wicklow Mountains, with history, geography, and folklore supplied as you go.

When and where: Take Bus Eireann 005, 132, or 391 to Blessington. Cruises are only in the summer. Call for more details. Information: Blessington Lake Cruises, Adventure Centre pier, Blessington. ☎ *045-86-5092.*

Brennanstown Riding School Horseback Tours

Horseback riding around the trails of Sugarloaf Mountain is available.

When and where: Take the DART to the end stop at Bray. Information: Brennanstown Riding School, Holybrook, Kilmacanogue, Bray. ☎ *01-286-3778. Price: £15 ($22.20) an hour for groups.*

Shopping in Wicklow

Wicklow is the home of pottery and knitwear. In fact, **the County Tourism Office in Wicklow** (☎ 0404-66-057) puts out a publication called the "Pottery Trail," with a full list of pottery, crafts, and knitwear locations for all your shopping needs. We list some of the county's top shopping spots here.

A La Campagne

This little shop offers unique items, including gifts, kitchenware, pottery, and glass; plenty of artsy stuff, like candles and holders; and also Irish country pottery. The owner, Stephen Falvin, is often on hand to help pick out a gift or advise on choices.

Main St., Wicklow. ☎ *0404-61-388.*

Avoca Handweavers

Here, in the oldest handweaving mill in Ireland (dating to 1723), you can find Avoca clothing, knitwear, and a wide range of fine Irish crafts.

Avoca Village. ☎ *0402-35-105. Outlet store: Kilmacanogue, near Bray.* ☎ *01-286-7466.*

Fisher's of Newtownmountkennedy

Located in a converted schoolhouse, this shop has tons of men's and women's sporting clothes and accessories, as well as cool items like hip flasks and pool cues.

On R765, off N11, Newtownmountkennedy. Just look for a big pink building before getting into town. No phone.

Glendalough Woolen Mills

In this old farmhouse you can not only find quality wool, but you can also find out how wool goes from sheep to sweater. The jewelry workshop features designs from local monasteries, St. Kevin's medals, Claddagh symbols, and Connemara marble.

Laragh, on the R755. No phone.

Noritake Arklow Pottery Ltd.

Any serious shopper for pottery will find something here, in Ireland's largest pottery factory. Home of Noritake's Celt Craft and Misty Isle lines, this factory puts out everything from earthenware to porcelain in modern and traditional designs and plenty of teapots, tableware, and gifts. The factory offers free tours from mid-June through the third week of July and during the last two weeks of August.

South Quay, Arklow. ☎ 0402-32-401.

Wicklow Vale Pottery

This showroom has a complete range of Avoca Blue hand-painted ceramics and Wicklow Vale Ceramics, and you can arrange a tour of the factory. Ther "olde worlde" coffee shop is good for a cup and some homemade pastry.

Tinnahask in Arklow, left on South Quay. ☎ 0402-39-442.

Hitting the pubs

It's like the philosopher said: Wicklow is in Ireland. There are pubs in Ireland. Therefore, there are pubs in Wicklow. Here are some of the best.

Philip Healy's

This pub is a place where locals meet for a leisurely drink and chat. The high ceilings make it feel open and airy, but the pub has plenty of nooks to settle into if you're looking for some quiet conversation. Healy's is an unpretentious place that serves food but unfortunately doesn't have music. So nip in and have a pint before heading out to tour the Wicklow Mountains.

Main St., Wicklow. ☎ 0404-67-380.

Old Court Inn

You can't miss this pub — it's bright yellow and sits at the center of town. Inside, though, it's quiet and cozy and warm. If you visit during chillier times, expect fireplaces to be blazing. Even in the summer, you'll want to hunker down in an overstuffed booth. This is the place to relax after you've trekked through the outdoors all day.

Main St., Wicklow (near the courthouse). ☎ *0404-67-680.*

The Meetings

Sunken down in the beautiful Vale of Avoca, The Meetings has everything. You can get good food all day and hear music at night — and, when the weather's warm, sit outside on the patio and enjoy a pint while taking in the view. The place is clearly geared to tourists, but that's not necessarily a bad thing. After all, how many pubs provide a Bureau de Change and a craft shop?

Vale of Avoca. ☎ *0402-35-226.*

Cartoon Inn

You may be more interested in the cartoons than your drink in this themed pub, whose interior walls are covered with artwork by famous cartoonists. The Cartoon Festival (no, we're not kidding) is held here in early summer. Food is served during lunchtime.

28 Main St., Rathdrum. ☎ *0404-46-774.*

Fast Facts: County Wicklow

AREA CODE(S)

01, 0404, 0402, and 045.

EMERGENCIES

Dial ☎ **999** for all emergencies. The **main hospital** is in Wicklow (☎ **0404-67-108**).

INFORMATION

For visitor information, go to **the tourist office** at Rialto House, Fitzwilliam Sq., Wicklow (☎ **0404- 69-117**), open year-round. They can also provide reservation services. For telephone directory assistance, dial ☎ **1190**.

County Kildare

Welcome to horse country! You can visit Kildare for a quick afternoon with the ponies or settle down for a night or two at one of the hotels we list, maybe blocking out a little time to visit a historic house or the Steam Museum.

Getting to and around Kildare

By car, take the N7 from Dublin or Limerick to get to Kildare. **Irish Rail** (☎ **01-836-6222**) has daily service to Kildare town, and **Bus Eireann** (☎ **01-836-6111**) services Kildare, Straffan, Celbridge, Newbridge, and other towns throughout the area.

Where to stay in Kildare

Annagh Lodge Guesthouse
$$ **Newbridge**

The newly built Annagh Lodge has pluses you don't generally find in a country guesthouse. With sauna and in-house movies, you may be surprised at the level of pampering. Bedrooms are luxurious, too. This is a good place for those of you interested in outdoor activities — eight golf courses and fishing are all within a close drive.

Naas Rd., Newbridge. ☎ *045-43-3518. Fax: 045-433-538. E-mail:* annaghlodge@ tinet.ie. *Internet:* www.homepage.tinet.ie/~annaghlodge. *By car: N7 from Dublin to Newbridge. Rates: £60–90 ($88.80–$134.10) double. MC, V.*

Hillview House
$$ **Naas**

This lovely guesthouse is situated just far enough from Kildare town to give the feel of country isolation but close enough to be a starting point for touring the best attractions in the area. You'll feel at home and catered to by the Allen family, who runs the house. Having a meal in one of their tearooms is a treat, and the food, served all day, is delicious.

Prosperous, Naas. ☎ *045-86-8252. Fax: 045-892-305. E-mail:* hillview@ tinet.ie. *By car: Prosperous is a village on R403 (between N4 and N7) near Naas. From Naas, take the R409 northwest for a few miles. Rates: £50–70 ($74–$103.60) double. MC, V.*

Curragh Lodge Hotel
$$ **Kildare Town**

This hotel is ideal mainly for its location. Just off the N7 and right in Kildare town, the Curragh Lodge Hotel is close to the Irish National Stud and Japanese Gardens. It has clean rooms, serves food, and has a pub, all for a moderate price.

Dublin Rd., Kildare. ☎ *045-52-2144. By car: N7 from Dublin to Kildare. Rates: £70–90 ($103.60–$134.10) double. AE, DC, MC, V.*

The Sycamores B&B

$ Naas

This is the kind of place you'd love to call home! Noreen Malone's comfortable house is a welcome departure from the sometimes impersonal nature of hotels. The exquisitely manicured lawn hints at the clean and nicely decorated rooms and dining area. The town of Naas is just a five-minute walk away, and the price of this lovely stay-over can't be beat.

Sallins Rd., Naas. ☎ 045-89-7598. By car: N7 from Dublin to Naas. Rates: £34–37 ($50.32–$54.75) double. No credit cards.

Where to dine in Kildare

Red House Inn

$$$-$$$$ Newbridge   IRISH/MEDITERRANEAN

Set in a country house, this award-winning restaurant blends modern and traditional fare in a unique way. From Irish to Mediterranean food, the Red House Inn is good for a quiet and delicious meal.

Newbridge. ☎ 045-43-1657. Reservations recommended. By car: N7 between Naas and Kildare. Main courses: £12.50–26.95 ($18.50–$39.90). AE, DC, MC, V. Open: Tues–Sat 7:00 p.m.–10:00 p.m. Sun (three sittings) 12:30 p.m., 1:00 p.m., and 2:30 p.m.

Harbour View

$$$ Naas   IRISH

The food here is what you expect in Ireland: home-cooked, wholesome, delicious, and served in hearty portions. The menu has something for everyone. Don't let the nondescript exterior fool you; one foot in the door and you know you're in for a meal that will keep you going all day long.

Limerick Rd., Naas. ☎ 045-87-9145. By car: N7 from Dublin to Naas. Main courses: £9.50–16 ($14.05–$23.70). AE, DC, MC, V. Open: Daily 7:30 a.m.–10:00 a.m. and 12:00 p.m.–9:30 p.m.

Exploring Kildare: The top attractions

Irish National Stud and Japanese Gardens
Tully

One of the foremost breeding grounds for famous winning horses, the National Stud is ranked year in and out as one of Ireland's top 20 tourist attractions. Visitors can walk around the grounds and see the horses being groomed and exercised. Also check out the Horse Museum with exhibits on racing, hunting, and show jumping, plus the skeleton of the famed Arkle, the renowned king of hunt racing.

On the same grounds are the striking Japanese Gardens, which boast bonsai, bamboos, and cherry trees. The gardens portray the journey of the life of man, starting with birth and going to eternity, which is represented by a Zen rock garden. In all, the grounds make for a nice way to spend a day.

Kildare. ☎ 045-52-1617. By car: Take N7 from Dublin or Naas. By train: Daily service into Kildare Railway Station. Admission: £5 ($7.40) adults, £3 ($4.45) seniors and students, £2 ($2.95) under 12. Open: Mid-Feb to mid-Nov daily 9:30 a.m.–6:00 p.m. Time: Three hours.

The Curragh
Newbridge

This racetrack, the country's best known, is often referred to as the Churchill Downs of Ireland. Races run sporadically from March to October, but you can be sure to catch a race here at least one Saturday a month. In late June the Curragh is host to the famous Irish Derby.

Dublin-Limerick Rd. (N7), Newbridge. ☎ 045-44-1205. Internet: www.curragh.ie. By car: Take N7 from Dublin or Naas. By train: Daily service into Curragh. Admission: £8–12 ($11.85–$17.75) for most races, £35 ($51.80) for the Derby. Special "Racing by Rail" package for £12 ($17.75) can be purchased at Heuston Station in Dublin and includes coach bus to the race track. Call ahead for upcoming dates. Time: Two hours.

Celbridge Abbey Grounds
Celbridge

These grounds were planted by the daughter of the Lord Mayor of Dublin in 1697 for Jonathan Swift. They rest along the River Liffey and feature Rockbridge, the oldest remaining stone bridge over the river. The grounds also boasts a model railway, picnic area, and donkey rides. The abbey itself is a private residence, so don't expect a tour!

Right on the main road (403) in Celbridge. ☎ 01-627-5508 or 01-628-8161. By car: From Dublin take the N4 west, picking up the R403 several miles out of the city. By train: Daily service into Hazelhatch Station. By bus: 67 and 67A from Dublin. Admission: £2.50 ($3.70) adults, £1.50 ($2.20) seniors and children. Open: Daily 10:00 a.m.–6:00 p.m. Time: One hour.

Castletown House
Celbridge

This impressive, stately house was built in the early part of the eighteenth century for William Connolly, then the Speaker of the Irish House of Commons. Its grandeur is staggering, and it remains a standout in

Irish architecture. The mansion was built in the Palladian style, a Renaissance mode meant to copy the classicism of ancient Rome. The sweeping interior is gorgeously decorated with Georgian furnishings, and the main hall and staircase are covered with intricate plasterwork. Run by the state and open to the public, the house is worth the drive — about ten miles northeast of Naas.

R403, off the main Dublin-Galway Rd., Celbridge. ☎ *01-628-8252. By car: From Dublin take the N4 west, picking up the R403 several miles out of the city. Located on the R403 just before you reach the village of Celbridge. By bus: 67 and 67A from Dublin. Admission: £2.50 ($3.70) adults, £2 ($2.95) seniors and students, £1 ($1.50) children. Open: April–Sept Mon–Fri 10:00 a.m.–6:00 p.m., Sat and Sun 1:00 p.m.–6:00 p.m.; Oct Mon–Fri 10:00 a.m.–5:00 p.m., Sat and Sun 1:00 p.m.–5:00 p.m; Nov Sun 1:00 p.m.–5:00 p.m. Time: An hour and a half.*

Steam Museum
Straffan

Anyone with an interest in locomotion will enjoy this museum. This restored church contains two distinct collections; the first is a cache of eighteenth-century locomotive engines that includes Richard Trevithick's Third Model of 1797, the oldest surviving self-propelled machine in existence. The second has engines from the industrial age. You can find plenty of steam-locomotion literature in the shop.

Off the Dublin-Limerick Rd. (N7), Lodge Park, Straffan, near Celbridge. ☎ *01-627-3155 summer, 01-628-8412 winter. By car: Take the N7 from Dublin or Naas. By train: Daily service into Kildare Railway Station. Admission: £4.50 ($6.65) adults, £4 ($5.90) seniors, students and children. Open: April, May, and Sept Sun 2:30 p.m.–5:30 p.m., June–Aug Tues–Sun 2:00 p.m.–6:00 p.m. Time: Two hours.*

More fun things to do: Go golfing

The 18-hole championship **Kildare Country Club (K-Club)** was designed by Arnold Palmer himself. Location: 17 miles west of Dublin in Straffan. ☎ **01-601-7300.** E-mail: golf@kclub.ie. Internet: www.kclub.ie. Par: 72. Fees: £130 ($192.40) for 18 holes in the summer, £75 ($111) in the winter.

Shopping in Kildare

Unless you're in the market for horse saddles or grooming equipment, Kildare's not a shopping extravaganza. But you can buy souvenirs and Irish handcrafts at a few places in town. Here are a couple of the best.

Kildare Woolen Mills

Like many other woolen mills in the country, this one offers traditional Irish clothing — sweaters and tweeds, as well as local crafts and gifts. It's conveniently right in town.

6 Academy St., Kildare. ☎ *045-52-0190.*

Irish Pewter Mill

In addition to its full selection of original pewter jewelry, this 1,000-year-old mill specializes in crafts like tableware.

On the N9, Timolin, Moone. ☎ *0507-24-164.*

Hitting the pubs

The Manor Inn

This warm and inviting pub is a surprisingly great place to discover the area's history. Pictures and mementos throughout reflect local color and Kildare pride. There's enough information to keep your interest while you wait for some delicious pub grub to come your way. Kids love the children's menu.

On N7, where the N7 meets the N9, 25 Main St. South, Naas. ☎ *045-89-7471. By car: N7 from Dublin to Naas.*

Silken Thomas

The quintessential roadside pub — it's not one of Kildare's hottest spots for nothing, and the second you see this place from the outside you understand why. You can hear music six nights a week and you can fortify yourself with some of Silken Thomas's reputably good food until 8:00 p.m. Stop in for a nicely pulled pint and end up staying all evening.

The Square, Kildare. ☎ *045-52-1695. By car: N7 from Dublin to Kildare.*

Fast Facts: County Kildare

AREA CODE(S)

01, 045, 053, and 0507.

EMERGENCIES/POLICE

Dial ☎ 999 for all emergencies.

GENEALOGICAL RESOURCES

Contact the **Kildare Heritage Project,** c/o Kildare County Library, Newbridge (☎ 045-43-3602; Fax: 045-43-2490; E-mail: cap info@iol.ie; Internet: www. kildare.ie.)

INFORMATION

The **tourist office** in Kildare (☎ 045-52-2696) is open mid-May to Sept. For telephone directory assistance, dial ☎ 1190.

INTERNET

The **Cyberx Internet Cafe** (☎ 01-629-1747) in Maynooth has World Wide Web access for Hotmail and AOL and has printing capabilities.

Chapter 14

The Southeast: Counties Wexford, Waterford, Tipperary, and Kilkenny

· ·

In This Chapter

▶ Traversing the Irish National Heritage Park and the Hook Peninsula

▶ Touring the Waterford Crystal Factory

▶ Visiting Ireland's version of The Rock (the Rock of Cashel, that is)

▶ Reliving history at one of Ireland's top medieval castles

▶ Exploring the Dunmore Caves

▶ Playing at a former Irish Open golf course

· ·

*I*reland's Southeastern counties — Wexford, Waterford, Tipperary (which it's a long way to. . .), and Kilkenny — are often referred to as "the sunny Southeast" because they generally enjoy more sunshine than the rest of the country. They also provide a varied touring experience, whether you're looking to shop at the world-famous Waterford Crystal Factory, visit the huge Rock of Cashel, or play a few rounds of golf at a championship course.

What's Where? The Southeast Counties and Their Major Attractions

Located on the southeastern tip of the country, **County Wexford** makes a nice stop on your tour, especially if nature calls (so to speak). The area's dotted with bird sanctuaries, beaches, and pretty countryside. It's bordered by the Wicklow Hills on the north and the Blackstairs Mountains on the west, and the rest is bound by the Irish Sea. The county is also the home to the Kennedys. Yes, *the* Kennedys: The family of the first Irish-Catholic U.S. president hailed from the town of New Ross.

The Southeast

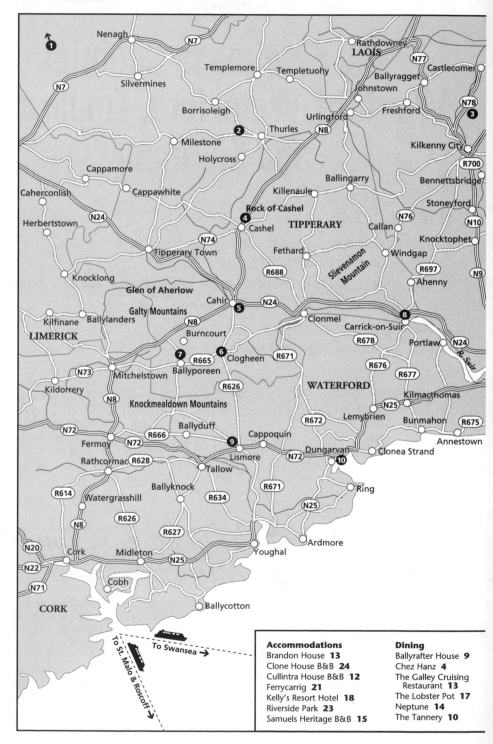

Accommodations
Brandon House **13**
Clone House B&B **24**
Cullintra House B&B **12**
Ferrycarrig **21**
Kelly's Resort Hotel **18**
Riverside Park **23**
Samuels Heritage B&B **15**

Dining
Ballyrafter House **9**
Chez Hanz **4**
The Galley Cruising
  Restaurant **13**
The Lobster Pot **17**
Neptune **14**
The Tannery **10**

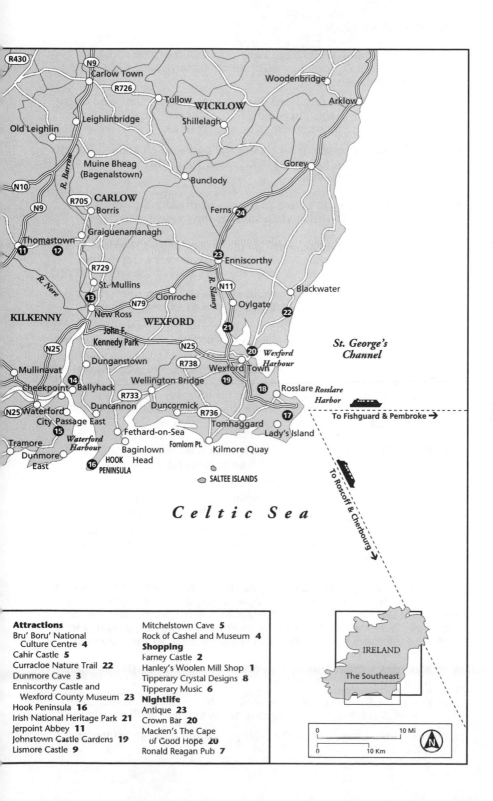

Attractions
Bru' Boru' National
  Culture Centre **4**
Cahir Castle **5**
Curracloe Nature Trail **22**
Dunmore Cave **3**
Enniscorthy Castle and
  Wexford County Museum **23**
Hook Peninsula **16**
Irish National Heritage Park **21**
Jerpoint Abbey **11**
Johnstown Castle Gardens **19**
Lismore Castle **9**

Mitchelstown Cave **5**
Rock of Cashel and Museum **4**
Shopping
Farney Castle **2**
Hanley's Woolen Mill Shop **1**
Tipperary Crystal Designs **8**
Tipperary Music **6**
Nightlife
Antique **23**
Crown Bar **20**
Macken's The Cape
  of Good Hope **20**
Ronald Reagan Pub **7**

IRELAND

The Southeast

0   10 Mi
0   10 Km

Some highlights include

- **The Irish National Heritage Park:** Traces the region's history from its earliest Stone Age settlements through the Celtic, Viking, and Norman periods.

- **Johnstown Castle Gardens:** The gardens, lawns, lakes, and ornamental towers of this fairy-tale castle are worth exploring, as is the agricultural museum that's on the grounds.

- **The Hook Peninsula:** A lovely coastal pathway, an ancient abbey, and a few castles, forts, and lighthouses make this small foot of land well worth visiting.

County Waterford doesn't have an excess of attractions, but the things it has are well worth a visit, such as the following:

- **Waterford Crystal Factory:** The place they make the world-famous crystal offers a tour that shows you every step of the crystal-making process. Afterward, you can visit the factory shop.

- **Reginald's Tower:** This tower, in the heart of Waterford Town, is the only Viking building continuously used since that age.

- **Lismore Castle:** This twelfth-century castle isn't open to the public, but the gorgeous garden and 8,000-acre estate grounds are.

Tipperary is one of the largest counties in Ireland, and it has one of the country's biggest attractions: the Rock of Cashel. This, and some great places to shop, makes it a nice place to wander through. It's not exactly a bustling area, though, so we don't recommend setting up camp here. Just roll on in and see the sights, such as

- **Rock of Cashel:** The limestone Rock of Cashel and the medieval towers and monuments built on and around it are among the country's most awesome archeological sites.

- **Mitchelstown Cave:** You can explore about a half-mile of caverns on this tour, while tour guides explain their formation.

- **Cahir Castle:** This castle, one of Ireland's largest and best preserved, is the one that was used as the set for John Boorman's film *Excalibur*.

In the past, **County Kilkenny** often made it onto visitor itineraries only because it's one of the counties people would drive through on their way out of Dublin. These days, though, Kilkenny county and town are fighting to become a destination to reckon with by putting money into restoring the more historic sights in the area, such as the following:

- **Kilkenny Castle:** This twelfth-century medieval castle sits among beautiful sculptured gardens.

- **Dunmore Cave:** These large, well-lit chambers and passageways are natural formations of limestone dating back millions of years.

- **Jerpoint Abbey:** One of the best-preserved monastic ruins in Ireland.

County Wexford

County Wexford was the heartbeat of the 1798 rebellion, when Irish rebels took a brave stand against the strong arm of the Brits, and it was at Vinegar Hill, near Enniscorthy, where 20,000 rebels were massacred by English cannons, effectively ending the rebellion. **Wexford Town** is a fairly attractive harbor town, but not the best town for a lengthy stay. The river's edge is kind of industrial-looking and driving around town, along one-way streets the width of a supermodel's waist, can be frustrating. There's so much to see in the county, though, you shouldn't pass it up.

Getting to and around County Wexford

If you're driving from Dublin, take the N11 (which becomes M11 periodically) south to Enniscorthy and Wexford; from Wexford take the N25 west to New Ross. Most attractions are along this route. A fast and cost-effective shortcut across Waterford Harbour between Passage East, County Waterford, and Ballyhack, County Wexford, is provided by **Passenger East Car Ferry** (☎ **051-38-2480**). It runs Sunday through Friday year-round, and will save you a lot of time driving around. Cost per vehicle: £6 ($8.90) round trip, £4 ($5.90) one way.

The Dublin (Connolly Station)-Rosslare Harbour line of **Irish Rail** (☎ **01-836-6222**) has stations in Rosslare, Wexford, and Enniscorthy. **Bus Eireann** (☎ **01-836-6111**) travels year-round to Wexford, Enniscorthy, Rosslare, New Ross, and other towns throughout the area.

There's a chance that you may arrive in Ireland via Wexford. **Stena Sealink Line** (☎ **01-204-7777**) has passenger and car ferries from Fishguard, Wales, to Rosslare Harbour Ferryport. **Irish Ferries** (☎ **01-855-2222**) has service from Pembroke, Wales, to Rosslare. Irish Ferries also makes trips between Rosslare and the French towns of Le Havre, Cherbourg, and Roscoff. Call for more details.

Walking is the best way to get around County Wexford's towns. Even the largest town, Wexford, is easily walkable.

Where to stay in County Wexford

Kelly's Resort Hotel
$$$ Rosslare

Situated along a five-mile stretch of sandy beach, this family-run hotel is truly a resort accommodation. You'll be spoiled by the two pools, indoor and outdoor tennis courts, and crazy golf and croquet grounds — though you won't exactly feel like you're in the Emerald Isle as you sip cocktails on the beach. It's not far from the ferry port, and in the spring Kelly's hosts special activities like wine tastings.

Rosslare. ☎ ***053-32-114.*** *Fax: 053-32-222. E-mail:* kellyhot@iol.ie. *By car: Take N25 from Wexford. Rates: £98–132 ($145.05–$195.35) double. AE, MC, V.*

Ferrycarrig
$$$ Wexford

This has one of the best locations of all Ireland's hotels, perched over the River Slaney estuary. The rooms and facilities (including a health club, pool, and two water-side restaurants) are unbeatable and the staff is friendly and warm. There's not a bad view in the house. Ferrycarrig also has the cool, on-premises Dry Dock Bar, where you'll be tempted to sit and relax the entire time.

Ferrycarrig Bridge, Wexford. ☎ ***053-20-999.*** *Fax: 053-20-982. E-mail:* ferrycarrig@ griffingroup.ie. *By car: Take N11 from Wexford toward Enniscorthy. Rates: £100–300 ($148–$444) double. AE, DC, MC, V.*

Brandon House
$$ New Ross

This Victorian country manor, sitting on sculpted grounds at a high point overlooking the River Barrow, offers only the warmest of welcomes. Rooms are tastefully decorated and the building has been renovated to offer all modern conveniences. Check out the Library Bar — it's charming and popular with New Ross locals.

Located right on the N25, just on the outskirts of New Ross. ☎ ***051-42-1703.*** *By car: Take N25 from Wexford, just outside New Ross. Rates: £50–80 ($74–$118.40) double. AE, DC, MC, V.*

Riverside Park
$$ Enniscorthy

The county's newest hotel, Riverside Park is situated on the banks of the River Slaney. It's difficult to miss coming in or out of town, given its beautiful brick-and-glass sea wall and round tower. From the moment you walk in and see the amazing foyer till you check out your spacious room (almost all have a fantastic view) you will know you've made the right choice. You're pretty much guaranteed to thoroughly enjoy your stay, especially if you wander into the unique Mill House pub — what a great hotel bar!

The Promenade, Enniscorthy. ☎ ***054-37-800.*** *Fax: 054-37-900. E-mail:* riversideparkhotel@eircom.net. *By car: On the N11 just outside Enniscorthy. Rates: £85 ($125.80). AE, DC, MC, V.*

Clone House B&B
$ Enniscorthy

This 300-year-old farmhouse set in the picturesque countryside is a quiet getaway spot, and it's almost a surprise to realize it's also close to golf,

Wexford Town

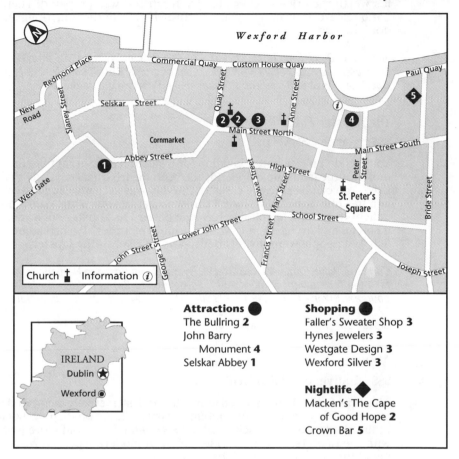

Wexford Harbor

Commercial Quay   Custom House Quay
Paul Quay
Redmond Place
New Road
Slaney Street
Selskar Street
Quay Street
Anne Street
Main Street North
Cornmarket
Abbey Street
Main Street South
West Gate
Rowe Street
High Street
Mary Street
Peter Street
St. Peter's Square
Brida Street
Lower John Street
School Street
John Street
George's Street
Francis Street
Joseph Street

Church ✝ **Information** ⓘ

Attractions ●
The Bullring **2**
John Barry
    Monument **4**
Selskar Abbey **1**

Shopping ●
Faller's Sweater Shop **3**
Hynes Jewelers **3**
Westgate Design **3**
Wexford Silver **3**

Nightlife ◆
Macken's The Cape
    of Good Hope **2**
Crown Bar **5**

IRELAND
Dublin ★
Wexford ◉

beaches, and area attractions. The best things about this place are the comfy beds and the Breens, the lovely couple who run the house. They're wonderfully knowledgeable about the area and are eager to help you decide where to go and what to see.

Ferns, Enniscorthy. ☎ *054-66-113. By car: Off the N11 between Enniscorthy and Gorey. Rates: £50 ($74) double. No credit cards.*

Where to dine in County Wexford

The Galley Cruising Restaurant
$$$$ **New Ross   IRISH**

You can enjoy your meal while nestled into the heated salon of a riverboat cruising along the picturesque Barrow and Nore rivers. It's a wonderful experience. The menu of mainly Irish fare is limited and not cheap, but it's worth the price — everything is fresh and well-prepared. There's a bar on board as well. Give yourself three hours for the tour, Gilligan, and don't be late!

New Ross Quay, New Ross. ☎ *051-42-1723. By car: West on N25 from Wexford. Main courses: £20–24 ($29.60–$35.50). Cost of cruise: £10 ($14.80). No credit cards. Open: Leaves at 6:00 p.m. and 7:00 p.m. daily. Reservations required.*

The Lobster Pot
$$$ Carne   SEAFOOD

You couldn't pick a better location for a seafood restaurant than this, the most southeastern tip of Ireland, between the Irish Sea and Lady's Island Lake. You can be sure the catch of the day was actually caught that day, and has only traveled a stone's throw to get to your plate. Gastronomic delights and rural hospitality have garnered The Lobster Pot awards for its menu and excellent pub. What should you order? We had some tasty fish, but people were raving about — what else? — the lobster.

Carnsore Point, Carne. ☎ *053-31-110. By car: From Rosslare Harbour or Wexford take the N11 toward Kilmore and follow signs to Carne or Lady's Island. Main courses: £12.95–15.95 ($19.15–$23.60). AE, DC, MC, V. Open: June–Sept daily 12:00 p.m.–10:00 p.m., Oct–Dec and Feb–May Tues–Sun 12:00 p.m.–10:00 p.m. Closed Jan. Reservations required.*

Neptune
$$$ Ballyhack   SEAFOOD

This is as fine a bistro as you'll find in Ireland, attractively decorated with an ever-changing lineup of contemporary Irish art on display. Located in the shadow of Ballyhack Castle, it's growing more and more popular with the tourists. Expect gourmet meals at moderate prices. We recommend the poached hake in lobster sauce.

Ballyhack. ☎ *051-38-9284. By car: Take the R733 west from Wexford or south from New Ross. Main courses: £10.50–15 ($15.55–$22.20). AE, DC, MC, V. Open: Mid-Mar to mid-Nov Tues–Sat 6:00 p.m.–10:00 p.m. and Mon in July and Aug.*

Exploring County Wexford: The top attractions

Irish National Heritage Park
Ferrycarrig

This informative and attention-grabbing place traces the region's history from its earliest Stone Age settlements through the Celtic, Viking, and Norman periods. Visitors receive maps that take them through to 14 historical sites. Re-creations of castles, boats, homes, and dolmen, guides in period dress, and audio-visual presentations bring the dynamic history of Ireland to life. Everything is hands-on, so it's a great place for the kiddies. Set on a wooded 35-acre site overlooking the Slaney River, the heritage park also has a Celtic-themed restaurant and craft shop on the grounds.

Off the Dublin-Wexford road (N11), Ferrycarrig. ☎ *053-20-733. By car: A few miles west of Wexford off the N11 at Ferrycarrig. Admission: £5 ($7.40) adults, £4.50 ($6.65) seniors, £4 ($5.90) students, £2 ($2.95) children ages 4–12, £11.50 ($17) family. Open: Apr–Oct daily 9:30 a.m.–6:30 p.m. Time: About two hours.*

Johnstown Castle Gardens
Wexford Town

Only the entrance to this fairy-tale castle is open, but the gardens, lawns, lakes, and ornamental towers are worth exploring. There is an agricultural museum with displays on the potato and everything you ever wanted to know about the Great Famine (but were afraid to ask). The museum also houses a collection of antique farm tools and large-scale replicas of blacksmith and cooper's workshops. What's a cooper? A barrel maker — a good trade in the land of whiskey and stout.

Bridgetown Rd., off Wexford-Rosslare Rd. (N25), Wexford Town. ☎ *053-42-888. By car: A couple miles east of Wexford off the R733. Castle Grounds admission (only charged May–Oct): £3 ($4.45) per car or £1.50 ($2.20) per adult pedestrian, 50p (75 cents) student and child pedestrian. Museum admission: £2.50 ($3.70) adults, £1.50 ($2.20) students and children, £8 ($11.85) family. Gardens Open: Daily 9:00 a.m.– 5:00 p.m. Museum Open: Mon–Fri 9:00 a.m.–5:00 p.m. Sat and Sun 2:00 p.m.–5:00 p.m. Closed weekends Nov–Mar. Time: All attractions, two hours; the rest, about a half-hour each.*

Hook Peninsula

There is so much to see on this small clubbed foot of land (in southwest County Wexford) that it's worth spending the afternoon driving and walking the lovely Slí Charman (Wexford's Coastal Pathway) to the end and back, provided you have the time and it's the peak season (as a few places close for the winter). Highlights include the richly ornamented **Tintern Abbey,** near Saltmills, with its maze of ancient paths, walled gardens, fortified bridge, and church ruin (£1.50/$2.20 adults, £1/$1.50 seniors, 60p/89 cents children and students); **Ballyhack Castle** (☎ 051-38-9468) with displays on the Crusades (£1/$1.50 adult, 50p/74 cents children and students); **Slade Castle** (☎ 051-38-9454), an amazing fortress ruin near the **Hook Head Lighthouse,** one of the oldest lighthouses in Europe (£3.50/$5.20 adults, £2.50/$3.70 children and seniors); and **Duncannon Fort** (☎ 051-38-9454), built to fend off attacks from the Spanish Armada.

By car: Tintern Abbey, Ballyhack, and Duncannon are off R733. To get to Hook Head, go south toward Fethard on R734 from New Ross. Park in Fethard and walk the coastal path to Slade Castle, the Lighthouse, and even on to Duncannon. Time: Varies, depending on distance you go, but give it a couple of hours.

Top landmarks in Wexford Town

The Bullring
Wexford Town

The location of the first declaration of independence for the Irish Republic, during the Rebellion of 1798 (commemorated by the Pikeman statue). The area's name comes from the bloody sport of bull-baiting that took place here in the seventeenth century.

Off Quay St., Wexford Town.

Selskar Abbey
Wexford Town

This is said to be one the oldest houses of worship in Wexford, and was probably built during the Crusades. It's noted for being where King Henry II spent 40 days of penance for his part in the death of Thomas à Becket, the martyred Archbishop of Canterbury.

Abbey St., Wexford Town.

John Barry Monument
Wexford Town

"Who's John Barry?" you ask. No less than the father of the American Navy! He bravely went to the colonies and signed up for the Revolutionary War to fight against the British. He was captain of the famous ship *Lexington,* and was appointed by George Washington as commander-in-chief of the brand-spanking-new U.S. Navy.

Crescent Quay, Wexford Town.

Other fun stuff to do

- ✔ **Curracloe Nature Trail:** Free and informative maps are available on this excellent nature trail through the seashore dunes. Located eight miles north of Wexford, this public and sheltered sandy beach is fun for the whole family. To get to the beach: Take the R742 five miles out of Wexford Town.

  Information: Wexford County Council. ☎ 053-42-211. Time: One hour.

- ✔ **Curracloe House Equestrian Holiday Centre:** Do you like horsin' around? Well, this centre, seven miles from Wexford, is for you. It's great for all levels of equestrian experience (even none), and there are horses available for touring the Curracloe beaches or the dunes and wildlife of the Wexford Sloblands.

  Location: Curracloe. By car: Take the R742 ten minutes out of Wexford town and look for the big sign to the Centre. Information: ☎ 053-37-241. Time: Depends on which tour you choose, but generally a couple of hours.

✔ **Enniscorthy Castle and Wexford County Museum:** Witness the town's turbulent history and learn about the castle's traditional place in the town over the centuries. The castle is well preserved, and the museum contains historical, religious, industrial, and agricultural artifacts from the nineteenth and twentieth centuries. There's a really complete display dealing with the 1798 uprising — an exceptionally big piece of history in these parts, given the town's participation.

Location: Castle Hill, Enniscorthy. ☎ **054-35-926.** By car: North of Wexford off the N11 or east of New Ross off the N30. Admission: £3 ($4.45) adults, £2 ($2.95) students and seniors, 50p (75 cents) children, £7.50 ($11.10) family. Open April to September, 10:00 a.m. to 6:00 p.m.; October to November and February to March 2:00 p.m. to 5:30 p.m. Closed December and January. Time: Forty-five minutes.

Organized tours

✔ **Walking Tours of Wexford:** You can see the sights of Wexford town on this tour, lasting one and a half hours to two hours, "depending on how interested everyone is." Book ahead — the number of tours and time of departure depends on how many people are involved.

When and where: Generally given daily between 11:30 a.m. and 2:30 p.m. year-round. Meets at the Westgate Heritage Tower, William Street, Wexford. ☎ **053-46-508.** Price: £3 ($4.45) adults, £1 ($1.50) for children.

✔ **Galley Cruising:** Travel the calm and brackish waters of the River Barrow for a relaxing tour of the countryside. When and where: June through August, leaves at 3:00 p.m. daily from New Ross Quay, 15 miles from Waterford on N25. ☎ **051-42-1723.** Price: £5 ($7.40). Optional tea and snack, additional £6 ($8.90). No credit cards.

Shopping in County Wexford

Faller's Sweater Shop

Far from the Aran Islands, this shop nonetheless specializes in authentic Aran knitwear — sweaters mostly, but also accessories like scarves and hats.

29B N. Main St., Wexford Town. ☎ *053-24-659.*

Hynes Jewelers

This shop carries leading brands of watches and gifts, but specializes in Celtic jewelry and claddagh rings.

17 North Main St., Wexford Town. ☎ *053-22-736.*

Westgate Design

A large selection of Irish giftware, from wool clothing to pottery, is the highlight of this little shop.

22 North Main St., Wexford Town. ☎ *053-23-787.*

Wexford Silver

A family of silver- and goldsmiths run this shop, which sells finely crafted pieces, perfect for gifts or keepsakes.

115 N. Main St., Wexford Town. ☎ *053-21-933.*

Pub life in County Wexford

Macken's The Cape of Good Hope

As you venture into Wexford's famous Bullring area, you're sure to do a double take when you see Macken's: The awning over the entrance advertises a bar, undertaker, and grocery. And it's no joke — you can have a pint, pick up a loaf of bread, and make funeral arrangements in one convenient stop! Irish rebels made Macken's a popular meeting place over the centuries, and mementos from their struggles line the walls. Definitely a place like none other.

The Bullring, Wexford Town. ☎ *053-22-949.*

Crown Bar

The oldest pub in Wexford Town, the Crown was formerly a stagecoach inn and is full of antique memorabilia. Dueling pistols and other weapons from the revolutionary days of yore might be the main draw for many who pop in, but the locals go there for the excellent drink and town gossip.

Monck St., Wexford Town. ☎ *053-21-133.*

Antique

The black-and-white exterior makes this traditional pub easy to recognize. Inside, it's a dark and cozy public house full of revolutionary antiques. Check out the famous weapons of the Pikeman of the 1798 uprising. The balcony is a nice spot for sitting outside when the weather's nice.

14 Slaney St., Enniscorthy. ☎ *054-33-428.*

Fast Facts: County Wexford

AREA CODE(S)

051, 053, 054, and 055.

EMERGENCIES/HOSPITAL

Dial ☎ **999** for all emergencies. **Wexford General Hospital** is on New Town Rd., Wexford (☎ **053-42-233**).

GENEALOGICAL RESOURCES

Contact the County Wexford Heritage Research Centre, Yola Farmstead Folk Park, Tagoat. ☎ **053-32-610.** Fax: 053-32-612. E-mail: wexgen@iol.ie.

INFORMATION

For visitor information, go to the **tourist office** at Crescent Quay, Wexford (☎ **053-23-111,** open year-round). It can also provide reservation services. Seasonal offices (open June–Sept) are in Enniscorthy at the **Town Centre** (☎ **054-34-699**) and **Rosslare Harbour Terminal Building** (☎ **053-33-232**). Another great source is the Web site: www.wexfordtourism.com/. For telephone directory assistance, dial ☎ **1190.**

POST OFFICE

The **main post office** is on Anna St., Wexford. ☎ **053-22-587.**

County Waterford and Waterford City

The name Waterford certainly sounds appropriate for a place on the shores of two rivers, but the name actually comes from the Danish for "weather haven," which is funny: We don't know what the Viking invaders who named it were used to in terms of weather, but Waterford sure gets plenty of rain!

Speaking of invaders, Waterford is the only city in Ireland that was spared Oliver Cromwell's brutal and bloody 1649 attack, though not through lack of effort. He attempted to invade Waterford from two routes, through Hook Head and Crooke Village — neither of which are direct or easy ways to enter Waterford. Both tries failed, and from that we get the expression about doing something "by Hook or Crook" — when you resort to unconventional and extreme tactics to get something done.

County Waterford isn't exactly chock-full of a zillion things to see and do, but the things it's got — such as **Waterford City** itself and the famous **Waterford Crystal Factory** — are amazing in their own right and more than worth the stop. The main part of Waterford City runs along the River Suir and has a wonderful medieval feel to it, with its narrow alleyways and the remains of its city wall. The major attraction downtown is the richly historic **Reginald's Tower** (Waterford Crystal is a few miles out of town), there are several nice restaurants and hotels, and while the city has become cosmopolitan thanks to modern shopping and commerce, it's still very much part of the "auld worlde."

Getting to and around Waterford City

If you're driving, take the N25 from Cork or Wexford or N7 to N9 from Dublin to get to Waterford City. Lismore is on the N72 off the N25. A fast and cost-effective route across Waterford Harbour, between Passage East, County Waterford (10 miles east of Waterford), and Ballyhack, County Wexford (20 miles west of Wexford), is provided by **Passenger East Car Ferry** (☎ 051-38-2480). It runs year-round, Sunday through Friday. Cost per vehicle: £6 ($8.90) round trip, £4 ($5.90) one way.

Irish Rail (☎ 051-87-401) services Waterford at Plunkett Station, located next to the Ignatius Rice Bridge. **Bus Eireann** (☎ 01-87-9000) travels year-round to Waterford, Lismore, and other major towns in County Waterford. In Waterford City, buses arrive at Plunkett Station, next to the Ignatius Rice Bridge. Bus Eireann also has a tour bus out of Dublin covering the River Barrow and the Waterford Crystal Factory. It leaves Dublin's main bus terminal at 9:30 a.m. and returns at 9:00 p.m. on Wednesdays, June through October. Cost is £25 ($37) adults, £17 ($25.15) child. The cost includes lunch and a boat tour of the River Barrow.

Waterford is an easily walkable city. Stroll up the Quays toward Reginald's Tower, take a right, and you'll be in the heart of town. You will need a car to get out to the Waterford Crystal Factory, though, unless you take a taxi (available in the city and mostly found at Plunkett Station on the Quay; call **Parnell Cabs** at ☎ 051-87-7710 if you need one to pick you up). If you're parking your car here you'll need parking disks, which you can buy at local shops near the block you're parking on or at the tourist office. Hotels in the city centre generally have their own parking areas.

Where to stay in Waterford

Tower
$$ Waterford City

Here is a three-star hotel that leaves nothing for want. Facing Reginald's Tower and situated next to the river, the Tower is in the heart of the city and is the flagship branch of the Tower Hotel Group. The rooms are large and have wide windows that open to the lovely breezes that come off the water. The finest rooms face the river and allow you to watch the water traffic slowly tug by. The indoor pool and gym are nice amenities and the huge Adelphi Riverside Lounge is a nice spot for a nightcap.

The Mall, Waterford City. ☎ *800-448-8355, from the United States; 051-87-5801. Fax: 051-87-0129. E-mail:* tower@iol.ie. *To get there: It's across the street from Reginald's Tower, near The Quay. Rates: £95–105 ($140.60–$155.40) double. AE, DC, MC, V.*

Waterford City

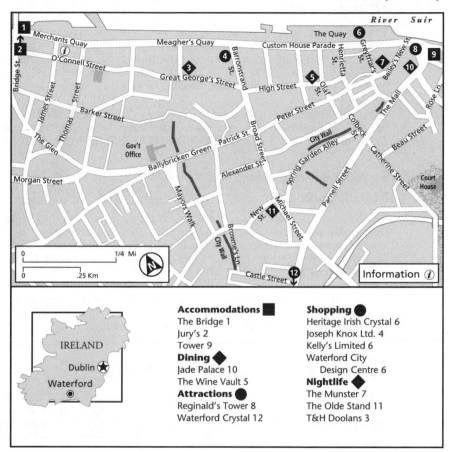

Accommodations ■
The Bridge 1
Jury's 2
Tower 9
Dining ◆
Jade Palace 10
The Wine Vault 5
Attractions ●
Reginald's Tower 8
Waterford Crystal 12

Shopping ●
Heritage Irish Crystal 6
Joseph Knox Ltd. 4
Kelly's Limited 6
Waterford City
  Design Centre 6
Nightlife ◆
The Munster 7
The Olde Stand 11
T&H Doolans 3

IRELAND
Dublin ★
Waterford ●

The Bridge
$$ Waterford City

This three-star hotel overlooking the River Suir is one of the oldest in Waterford, but has been refurbished to provide every modern comfort. The Bridge is what an old Irish hotel should be: run like a tight ship by the Treacy family but with a friendly, jovial atmosphere. Three in-house restaurants can serve up just about anything you want.

1 The Quay, Waterford City. ☎ ***051-87-7222.*** *Fax: 051-87-7229. E-mail:* bridgehotel@ tinet.ie. *Internet:* www.bridgehotel.com. *To get there: Take The Quay to the foot of the Ignatius Rice Bridge. Rates: £66–90 ($97.70–$134.10) double. AE, DC, MC, V.*

Jury's
$$ Waterford City

There's a great view of Waterford and the River Suir from this hotel on a mountain. The rooms are decorated Victorian style and are spacious, and if you can't fully relax there, try the indoor heated pool, the sauna, or the steam room. The Jury's hotel chain always delivers, and this branch in Waterford is no exception.

Ferrybank (across the river bank from city centre), Waterford. ☎ *051-83-2111. Fax: 051-83-2863. E-mail:* info@jurys.com. *To get there: Take Rice Bridge, from The Quay, across the River Suir. Rates: £95–105 ($140.60–$155.40) double. AE, DC, MC, V.*

Samuels Heritage B&B
$ Ballymacode

This beautiful family home is set on 30 acres of farm and garden land overlooking the River Suir. The rooms are all non-smoking and en suite; televisions are available upon request. Close proximity to beaches and four 18-hole golf courses. A nice touch is having your breakfast outdoors if the weather's nice.

Dunmore Rd., Ballymacode, Waterford. ☎ *051-87-5094. By car: Take Cork Rd. from city centre three miles to Dunmore, beyond the Regional Hospital and Orpens Pub, on the left. Rates: £36 ($53.30) double. No credit cards.*

Where to dine in Waterford

Turn that smile upside down with some blaa! More upscale restaurants may not serve this local specialty, but Waterford locals enjoy their *blaa* (meat, onion, tomato, and lettuce on a roll). Sounds a little blah, but it'll perk you up! The best blaa we had was at Munster's (see the "Pub life in Waterford City" section, later in this chapter).

In addition to the places we list later in the chapter, you can also combine your dinner with a river cruise aboard the **Galley Cruising Restaurant.** Although you catch the boat on the River Barrow in New Ross, County Wexford (see "Other fun stuff to do" in the Wexford section), the trip takes you down to the River Suir and through County Waterford.

The Wine Vault
$$$ Waterford City   SEAFOOD

Not just a place for excellent oysters, mussels, and fresh prawns, the Vault has historical appeal and is a must-stop for wine enthusiasts. This cavernous yet cozy stone-walled casual restaurant is the former home of Waterford mayor and wine merchant James Rice. Currently, the wine list runs to as many as 250 selections. The Vault's wine shop has an excellent range and you can buy souvenir glasses with the Vault's logo

(Bacchus, the Greek god of wine). Try a white wine with the house speciality, panache of seafood in a tarragon and lobster bisque sauce.

Lower High St., Waterford City. ☎ *051-85-3444. E-mail:* bacchus@tinet.ie. *Main courses: £11–18.75 ($16.30– $27.75) . AE, V. Open: Mon–Sat 12:30 p.m.– 2:30 p.m., 5:30 p.m.–10:30 p.m.*

Jade Palace
$$–$$$ Waterford City CHINESE

Chinese food? In Ireland? Yes. Authentic, mouth-watering, you'll-eat-too-much Cantonese and Szechuan in downtown Waterford. This is the kind of place where you tell the manager what you think you'd like and let him decide for you. Your choice of silverware or chopsticks. The steamed fish with ginger is excellent.

3 The Mall, Waterford, next to Reginald's Tower in city centre. ☎ *051-85-5611. Main courses: £8–14.95 ($11.85–$22.15). Service charge of 10 percent added. AE, MC, V. Open: Mon–Fri. 12:30 p.m.–2:30 p.m., Sun 1:00 p.m.–3:00 p.m., daily 5:30 p.m.– midnight.*

Ballyrafter House
$$$$ Lismore SEAFOOD

You know you can expect good seafood from a restaurant if the local fishermen recommend it, and Ballyrafter House is no exception. It's got a great view of the riverside Lismore Castle, and it's the little touches, like fresh-cut flowers from the garden or the pub's many photographs of smiling fishermen and their big catches, that make this place so memorable. The smoked Blackwater Salmon is delicious and is one of its most popular dishes.

Right on the N72, Lismore. ☎ *058-54-002. By car: From Waterford or Cork take the N25 to the N72 at Dungarvan. Main courses: £22 ($32.55) for five courses. AE, DC, MC, V. Open: Mar–Dec daily 1:00 p.m.–2:30 p.m. and 7:30 p.m.–9:30 p.m.*

The Tannery
$$$$ Dungarvin SEAFOOD

This old leather tannery has been converted into a stylish, contemporary restaurant. The kitchen is wide open so patrons can watch chef Paul Flynn in action. The interior is minimalist — white dishes on unadorned light-wood tables. The roasted red pepper soup with basil aoili is an excellent starter to the delicious crispy cod cakes. Desserts are too tantalizing to pass up.

10 Quay St., Dungarvan. ☎ *058-45-420. By car: From Waterford or Cork, take the N25. Main courses: £20–22 ($29.60–$32.55) for five courses. No credit cards. Open: Tues–Thur 12:30 p.m.–2:30 p.m., 6:30 p.m.–10:00 p.m.; Fri and Sat 12:30 p.m.–2:30 p.m., 6:30 p.m.–10:30 p.m.*

Exploring County Waterford: The top attractions

Waterford Crystal Factory
Kilbarry

What makes crystal shine brighter than regular glass? It's the lead, of course! Seems odd, but the addition of a lead oxite called red litharge gives crystal that characteristic gleam. That's the first thing you'll learn in the surprisingly interesting tour of the Waterford Crystal Factory. You'll be shown every step of the meticulous process that goes into making the world-renowned Waterford Crystal, from the blowing to the cutting to the detail decorating. And talk about a stressful job: The Waterford Crystal Factory has a six-step screening process for every piece that's made. Only perfect pieces of crystal make it out of the factory, which means 45 percent are destroyed for minor flaws! The glass blowers and craftsmen only get paid for perfect pieces. Sometimes on the Waterford Crystal tour you get to see one-of-a-kind pieces in production, like the Millennium Ball that fell in Times Square at midnight, 2000, or the Super Bowl's Vince Lombardi Trophy, which we saw them working on. After the tour you can stop in the Waterford Crystal Gallery to stock up.

Kilbarry (five minutes out of Waterford). ☎ *051-37-3311. By car: From Waterford, take the main road to Cork (N25); the factory is five miles outside town on the right. Admission: £2 ($2.95) for tour. Open: Apr–Oct tours daily 8:30 a.m.–4:00 p.m., showroom daily 8:30 a.m.–6:00 p.m.; Nov–Mar tours Mon–Fri 9:00 a.m.–3:15 p.m., showroom Mon–Fri 8:30 a.m.–6:00 p.m. Time: Two hours.*

Reginald's Tower
Waterford City

Recently refurbished, this small but significant landmark in the heart of Waterford City is worth the three-story climb to the top. The tower, which is the only Viking building continuously used since that age, has seen a lot of history and worn many hats. The ground and first floors were built around the beginning of the thirteenth century, and the top floors were built as many as 300 years later. Besides being the main tower for the old city walls, the building was the wedding chapel for Norman chief Strongbow, as well as a place for minting money, an ammunition dump, and a police station. If these walls could talk. . .

The Quay, Waterford City. ☎ *051-30-4220. Admission: £1.50 ($2.20) adult, £1 ($1.50) child. Open: Apr and May Mon–Fri 10:00 a.m.–1:00 p.m. and 2:00 p.m.–6:00 p.m., Sat 10:00 a.m.–1:00 p.m.; June–Oct Mon–Fri 10:00 a.m.–8:00 p.m., Sat 10:00 a.m.– 1:00 p.m. and 2:00 p.m.–6:00 p.m. Time: A half-hour.*

Lismore Castle
Lismore

This castle was originally built in the twelfth century and was owned by Sir Walter Raleigh in the sixteenth century. Raleigh never actually lived in his castle, which is a shame for him; it rests on a beautiful spot high above the River Blackwater and the view is incredible. The castle itself isn't open to the public, but the gorgeous 8,000-acre estate and garden are, and there's plenty to see.

Lismore. ☎ 058-54-424. By car: From Waterford or Cork take the N25 to the N75 in Dungarvan. Admission: £3 ($4.45) per person. Open: Apr–Sept daily 1:45 p.m.– 4:45 p.m. Time: An hour and a half.

Organized tours

✔ **Waterford Tourist Services Walking Tours:** Lasting an hour, this tour covers four national monuments, including Reginald's Tower and the Wine Vault Restaurant (see "Where to dine in Waterford City").

Where and when: Leaves from the Granville Hotel (Meagher Quay), March to October daily at 12:00 p.m. and 2:00 p.m. Information: ☎ 051-87-3711 or 051-85-1043. Price: £3 ($4.45) adults, free for children.

✔ **Galley Cruising:** Travel the calm and brackish waters of the River Suir estuary and have a relaxing tour of the countryside.

Where and when: June to August daily 3:00 p.m., Waterford Harbour, next to the Custom House Parade. Information: ☎ 051-42-1723. Price: £5 ($7.40). The optional tea and snack is an additional £6 ($8.90). No credit cards.

Shopping in Waterford City

Heritage Irish Crystal

The other authentic, hand-blown crystal makers in town; excellent quality but not as big or famous as its counterpart — Waterford Crystal.

67-68 The Quay, Waterford City. ☎ 051-84-1787.

Joseph Knox Ltd.

Established in the eighteenth century, this gift shop stocks Celtic jewelry, English and Irish china and crystal, porcelain, and linen.

3–4 Barronstrand St., Waterford City. ☎ 051-87-2723.

Kelly's Limited

At 150 years old, it's one of the oldest businesses in town, selling crafts, linens, Waterford Crystal, and Belleek pottery.

75 The Quay, Waterford City. ☎ 051-87-3557.

Waterford City Design Centre

Everything you could be looking for is under one roof: gifts, designer Irish clothing, handcrafted ceramics, jewelry, candles, linen, lace, glass and more.

44 The Quay, Waterford City. ☎ 051-85-6666.

Waterford Crystal Gallery

This is the most famous showroom of crystal in the world. It's two floors of only the best.

Kilbarry (five minutes out of Waterford). ☎ 051-873-311. By car: Take the main Cork Rd. (N25). Open: Mon–Fri 8:30 a.m.–6:00 p.m. Plus Nov–Mar, Sat 8:30 a.m.–6:00 p.m.

Pub life in Waterford City

T&H Doolans

The oldest tavern in Waterford, Doolans has long been considered the best establishment in the area. This black-and-white eighteenth-century pub opens onto a pedestrian street in the center of town and has excellent traditional music sessions every night, warm fires, delicious pub grub, warm welcomes, and a cheerful crowd. Oh, and the stout is perfect as well. What's the T&H stand for? That's for you to find out.

31 George's St., Waterford City. ☎ 051-87-2764.

The Munster

The Munster (also known as Fitzgerald's) is superbly decorated with Waterford Crystal , antique mirrors, and wood walls taken from the old Waterford toll bridge. There are many sections to this Old-World bar and restaurant, and it's a good place to get to know the locals after you find you've been seeing the same ol' tourist faces over and over. Traditional music kicks up on weekends mostly.

Bailey's New St., Waterford City. ☎ 051-87-4656.

The Olde Stand

This Victorian Pub — or rather, pubs (there are two downstairs and one upstairs) — is a fine place for a pint or a meal. There's a restaurant upstairs, but you can have a casual meal downstairs as well. Everyone raves about the steak and the fresh seafood dishes. We liked the well-pulled Guinness and the chatty bartender who enjoyed our company as much as we did his.

45 Michael St., Waterford City. ☎ 051-87-9488.

Fast Facts: County Waterford

AREA CODE(S)

051, 052, 058.

EMERGENCIES/POLICE

Dial ☎ **999** for all emergencies. **Regional Hospital** (Cork Rd., Waterford, ☎ **051-87-3321**). Late-night **Pharmacy: Mulligans** (Dunmore Rd., Waterford, ☎ **051-84-3700**) is open till 9:00 p.m. Mon–Sat and 6:00 p.m. on Sundays.

GENEALOGICAL RESOURCES

Contact the **Waterford Heritage Survey,** Jenkins Lane, Waterford. ☎ **051-87-6123** or 051-87-3711. Fax 051-85-0645. E-mail: mnoc@iol.ie.

INFORMATION

For visitor information go to the **tourist office** at 21 The Quay (☎ **051-87-5788**), open year-round. It can also provide reservation services. For telephone directory assistance, dial ☎ **1190.**

INTERNET

Voyager Internet Cafe, Parnell Court, Parnell St. (☎ **051-84-3843**), has Internet access for Hotmail, AOL, and printing capabilities.

POST OFFICE

The **main post office** is on Parade Quay, Waterford City (☎ **051-74-444**).

County Tipperary

Even though it's one of the largest counties in Ireland, Tipperary isn't exactly a bustling area, so we don't recommend setting up camp here (and for that reason haven't provided any lodging choices). Tipperary does have one of the country's largest attractions, though: the **Rock of Cashel.** This, and some great places to shop, makes it a nice place to wander through.

While you're moseying around and hitting the pubs, you're likely to hear the song "It's a Long Way to Tipperary," a happy yet plaintive tune about an Irishman in England missing his home. The song was actually composed by Englishman Jack Judge — a man who'd never been to Ireland in his life! He chose the town's name for his song simply because it made the basis of a good rhyme. But the song is perhaps best known by Americans as the tune the cast of *The Mary Tyler Moore Show* sang as they left the station for the last time.

Getting to and around County Tipperary

If you're coming by car, take the N8 from Cork or Dublin (via N7) to Cashel and Cahir. Take the N24 from Limerick or Waterford to Tipperary and Cahir. **Irish Rail** (☎ **01-836-6222**) services Tipperary, Cahir, and Carrick-on-Suir, and **Bus Eireann** (☎ **01-836-6111**) travels year-round to Tipperary, Cahir, Cashel, and Carrick-on-Suir, as well as other major towns in County Tipperary.

Where to dine in County Tipperary

Chez Hanz
$$$$ Cashel FRENCH

This is French cuisine at its finest, as evidenced by the number of patrons who flock to this converted Baptist chapel. From the black-and-white uni-formed waitstaff to the artistic dishes, everything is professional and to the nines. The portions are surprisingly large, the famous Cashel blue cheese finds its way into many dishes, and the fresh desserts are to die for. Don't be afraid to try something you never had before, like the mussel gratin — everything is simply top notch.

Rockside, Cashel. ☎ 062-61-177. To get there: Just look for the giant rock. The restaurant is located below it. Main courses: £22–25 ($32.55–$37). MC, V. Open: Tues–Sat 6:30 p.m.–10:00 p.m. Closed Jan. Reservations required.

Angela's Wholefood Restaurant
$ Clonmel INTERNATIONAL

Angela's Wholefood Restaurant offers scrumptious, substantial fare at remarkable value. The blackboard menu may include custom-made breakfast omelets, spicy Moroccan lamb stew, savory tomato-and-spinach flan Provençal, homemade soups and sandwiches made to order, and an array of delicious salads. The food is vibrant, fresh, and appreciated by the bustling patrons who line up with trays in hand, from barristers (in garb) to baby-sitters.

Clonmel. ☎ 052-26-899. To get there: 14 Abbey St. in Clonmel. Breakfast menu £2–4 ($2.95–$5.90); lunch menu £1.60–5.50 ($2.35–$8.15). No service charge. No credit cards. Mon–Fri 9:00 a.m.–5:30 p.m., Sat 12:00 p.m.–5:00 p.m.

Exploring County Tipperary: The top attractions

Rock of Cashel and Museum
Cashel

Sure, it's big, but even so, you might be wondering, "What's so important about Cashel?" Here goes: Legend places St. Patrick in Cashel for his famous explanation of the Holy Trinity. He is said to have shown pagans a shamrock, pointing out that the three leaves represent the Father, Son, and Holy Ghost. In the eleventh century, Ireland's most important High King, Brian Ború, was crowned King of Ireland here (which explains the presence beside the rock of the Brú Ború National Culture Centre — see later in the chapter).

Today, the limestone Rock of Cashel is one of the country's most awe-some archeological sites. The Round Tower is perhaps the oldest and most remarkably well preserved building of its kind. Irish Romanesque-style Cormacs Chapel, located on a dramatic outcrop, is ornate with carved beasts and human figures. The unique St. Patrick's Cross (a replica — the original is in the museum) has the carved figure of St. Patrick on one side and Jesus on the other. The roofless cathedral is the largest building on the Rock and was never restored after being set fire (along with the villagers hiding inside) by Oliver Cromwell's men. The museum, housed in the beautifully restored Hall of Vicars, the old choir residence, has great views for photos and contains stone carvings and silver religious artifacts.

Cashel. ☎ 062-61-437. By car: Take N8 from Dublin or N74 east from Tipperary. Admission: £3 ($4.45) adults, £2 ($2.95) seniors, £1.25 ($1.85) children, £7.50 ($11.10) family. Open: Mid-Mar to mid-June daily 9:30 a.m.–5:30 p.m.; mid-June to mid-Sept daily 9:00 a.m.–7:30 p.m.; mid-Sept to mid-Mar daily 9:30 a.m.–4:30 p.m. Time: One hour.

Brú Ború National Culture Centre
Cashel

Located next to the Rock of Cashel, the Culture Centre has advanced family-research facilities but is more popular for the music, theater, and craft exhibits it hosts. The resident group of entertainers has represented Ireland all over the world and was even on *Good Morning America*. Brú Ború means "Palace of King Brian Boru."

Rock of Cashel. ☎ 062-61-122. By car: Take N8 from Dublin or N74 east from Tipperary. Admission: Free. Evening performance: £8 ($11.85) or £25 ($37) for dinner and show. Open: Mon–Fri 9:00 a.m.–5:00 p.m. Folk theater performances 9:00 p.m. (dinner at 7:00 p.m.), June–Sept Tues–Sat. Time: Varies, depending on event.

Mitchelstown Cave
Cahir

You can explore three massive caverns full of cool stalactites and stalagmites with biblical names like the Tower of Babel and the Shroud of Turin. Tour guides explain the formation of the caves and describe features and wall markings as they take you through nearly a half-mile of caverns. **Note:** The caves can get quite chilly, so wear your new Aran sweater.

Burncourt, Cahir. ☎ 052-67-246. By car: Go west of Tipperary off the N7. Admission: £3 ($4.45) adults, £2.50 ($3.70) seniors, £1 ($1.50) children. Open: Daily 10:00 a.m.–6:00 p.m. Time: Up to two hours.

Cahir Castle
Cahir

The castle, one of Ireland's largest and best preserved, sits on an island in the middle of the River Suir. The walls and towers are in near-pristine condition and the interior is fully restored. The audio-visual presentation is interesting as well, covering the history of the castle. Attention movie buffs: The castle was used as the set for John Boorman's film *Excalibur*.

Cahir. ☎ *052-41-011. By car: Off the N8 from Cashel or Cork or N24 from Tipperary. Admission: £2 ($2.95) adults, £1.50 ($2.20) seniors, £1 ($1.50) students and children. Open: Mid-Mar to mid-June and mid-Sept to mid-Oct daily 9:30 a.m.–5:30 p.m.; mid-June to mid-Sept daily 9:00 a.m.–7:30 p.m.; mid-Oct to mid-Mar daily 9:30 a.m.–4:30 p.m. Time: One hour.*

Organized tours

✔ **Cashel Heritage Tram Tour:** This company provides tours of Cashel's historic sites as well as entry to the Cashel Heritage Centre and Bolton Library.

Where and When: Leaves from the Heritage Centre (see earlier in this chapter). You can hop on and off where you please. Operates June through September, Tuesday through Saturday, 12:00 p.m. to 6:00 p.m. Information: ☎ **062-62-511.** Price: £3 ($4.45) adults, £1.50 ($2.20), for students.

Shopping in County Tipperary

Farney Castle

Uniquely located inside a medieval castle, this knitwear and porcelain shop has Jacob sweaters (from the undyed colored fleece of the rare Jacob sheep), jackets, and fine porcelain figurines and ornaments.

Near Thurles and Holycross, on the R503 from the N8. No phone.

Hanley's Woolen Mill Shop

Located next to the weaving factory in Ballyartella, Hanley's has a fantastic collection of tweed, knitwear, pottery, glassware, and gift items. The Mill Shop provides weaving demonstrations and complimentary tea and coffee.

Ballyartella, Neagh (take the R495 to Dromineer and turn right toward Ballycommon). No phone.

Tipperary Crystal Designs

A band of rebel craftsmen left Waterford Crystal in 1988 and set up this enterprise, where they produce the same top-quality stuff they did under their former label. These folks are so good they're the only Irish crystal producer to supply the prestigious Tiffany & Co. They give free tours Monday through Friday from April to September.

Carrick-on-Suir. ☎ *051-64-1188. By car: Take the N24 from Waterford, located next to Dovehill Castle. Showroom hours: winter, Mon–Fri 9:00 a.m.–5:15 p.m., Sat 9:30 a.m.–4:45 p.m., Sun 11:00 a.m.–4:45 p.m.; summer, Mon–Sat 9:00 a.m.–6:00 p.m., Sun 11:00 a.m.–5:30 p.m.*

Tipperary Music

Watch *bodhráns* (traditional Irish drums) being made and wander through the showroom full of other traditional instruments, plus Irish music books, CDs, and crafts.

Main St., Clogheen. ☎ *052-65-307. By car: Take the R668 from Lismore or Cahir or the R665 from Mitchelstown or Clonmel.*

Pub life in County Tipperary

Ronald Reagan Pub

Pints are pulled with a special "trickle-down" tap method that seems to have staved off the inflationary cost of beer at this pub that is, in fact, named after the President himself. In 1984, Ronnie visited Ballyporeen, hometown of his great-grandfather, and the pub/gift shop/shrine has photos of the historic visit on the walls and mementos for sale. More hype than hop, but an interesting stop.

Main St., The Square, Ballyporeen. ☎ *052-67-133.*

Fast Facts: County Tipperary

AREA CODE(S)

051, 052, 062, and 067.

EMERGENCIES/POLICE

Dial ☎ **999** for all emergencies.

GENEALOGY RESOURCES

Contact the **Brú Ború Heritage Centre**, Rock of Cashel (☎ **062-61-122**; Fax: 062-62-700), or the **Tipperary Heritage Unit**, The Bridewell, Michael St., Tipperary (☎ **062-52-757**; E-mail: thu@iol.ie).

INFORMATION

For visitor information, go to the seasonal **tourist offices** at Town Hall, Main St., Cashel (☎ **062-61-333**), open Apr–Sept; or James St., Tipperary (☎ **062-51-457**), open May–Sept. For telephone directory assistance, dial ☎ **1190**.

County Kilkenny

Often tourists stop in Kilkenny only because they have to drive through it to get to Dublin. They may stop to see **Kilkenny Castle** or have a pint at the **Marble City Bar,** but often they then just drive on. That could soon change— recently Kilkenny county and town have made an effort to restore some of the historic sights in the area in hopes of becoming a more popular destination. We've listed only the top attractions and most interesting things to see in the time you have, but we've also included a couple of great accommodations and some shopping areas if you choose to extend your stay in County Kilkenny. You won't be disappointed if you do. Kilkenny is fast becoming the preferred route from Dublin, chosen over the naturey route of Wexford or the crystal capital of Waterford.

Getting to County Kilkenny

By car, take the N7 to N9 to N10 south from Dublin or the N9 north from Waterford to Kilkenny City. **Irish Rail** (☎ **01-836-6222**) services Kilkenny and Thomastown. **Bus Eireann** (☎ **01-836-6111**) travels year-round to Kilkenny and other towns in County Kilkenny, and also has a tour bus out of Dublin covering Kilkenny, Jerpoint Abbey, and the Nore Valley. It leaves Dublin's main bus terminal at 9:30 a.m. and returns at 7:00 p.m. on Wednesdays, June through October. Cost: £17 ($25.15) adults, £9 ($13.40) child.

Where to stay in County Kilkenny

Butler House
$$ Kilkenny Town

This wonderful house was once part of Kilkenny Castle, and the castle gardens are in back as proof. The three-story, ivy-covered house overlooks the town's main street, and each of the 14 rooms is decorated individually, tastefully, and comfortably. You couldn't ask for a better location — just stepping out of the front door puts you in the perfect place to start off exploring the city. If you decide to stay in (and we could hardly blame you) you can ask for a VCR and movie from the collection at the front desk.

16 St. Patrick St., Kilkenny Town. ☎ ***056-65-707.*** *Fax: 056-65-626. E-mail:* res@ butler.ie. *Internet:* www.butler.ie. *By car: Take the N7 to N9 to N10 from Dublin to Kilkenny. Rates: £89–99 ($131.70–$146.50) double. AE, DC, MC, V.*

Cullintra House B&B
$ Inistioge

A finely built farmhouse among trees and farmland, this place seems a million miles from everything even though it's just five or six miles from Jerpoint Abbey and close to Kilkenny. Relax by the fireplace in the living

Kilkenny Town

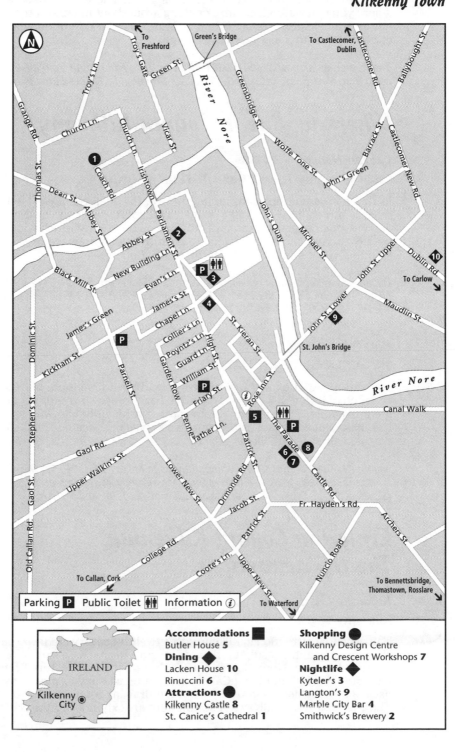

To Freshford
Green's Bridge
To Castlecomer, Dublin

Troy's Ln.
Troy's Gate
Green St.
Castlecomer Rd.
Ballybought St.

River Nore
Greensbridge St.
Castlecomer New Rd.

Grange Rd.
Church Ln.
Vicar St.
Wolfe Tone St.
Barrack St.

Church Ln.
Church Rd.
Irishtown
John's Green

❶

Thomas St.
Dean St.
Abbey St.
Parliament St.
John's Quay
Michael St.

❷

Black Mill St.
New Building Ln.
Evan's Ln.
P ♿

James's St.
❸

James's Green
Chapel Ln.
❹
John St. Lower
John St. Upper
Dublin Rd.
To Carlow
❿

Dominic St.
Collier's Ln.
Poyntz's Ln.
St. Kieran St.
John St. Lower
Maudlin St.

Kickham St.
Parnell St.
Garden Row
Guard Ln.
William St.
High St.
P
❾

Stephen's St.
Friary St.
St. John's Bridge

River Nore

♿
Rose Inn St.
(i)
Canal Walk

❺
The Parade
P

Gaol Rd.
Father Ln.
❽

Upper Walkin's St.
Lower New St.
❻ ❼
Castle Rd.

Gaol St.
Ormonde Rd.
Patrick St.
Fr. Hayden's Rd.
Archers St.

Old Callan Rd.
Jacob St.

College Rd.
Patrick St.
Nuncio Road

To Callan, Cork
Coote's Ln.
Upper New St.
To Waterford
To Bennettsbridge, Thomastown, Rosslare

Parking **P** Public Toilet ♿ Information (i)

IRELAND

Kilkenny City

Accommodations ■
Butler House **5**
Dining ◆
Lacken House **10**
Rinuccini **6**
Attractions ●
Kilkenny Castle **8**
St. Canice's Cathedral **1**

Shopping ●
Kilkenny Design Centre
  and Crescent Workshops **7**
Nightlife ◆
Kyteler's **3**
Langton's **9**
Marble City Bar **4**
Smithwick's Brewery **2**

room or take a stroll down to the River Nore. There's a conservatory where you can watch local foxes milling around out back, and there are nature trails leading from the house. Your host, Mrs. Cantlon, goes the extra distance to make you feel at home.

The Rower, Inistioge. ☎ 051-42-3614. By car: Take R700 south from Kilkenny or north from New Ross. Rates: £40–50 ($59.20–$74) double. No credit cards.

Where to dine in County Kilkenny

Lacken House
$$$$ **Kilkenny Town** **IRISH/INTERNATIONAL**

In this handsome but unassuming house, the McSweeneys (husband Eugene is the chef, wife Breda is the wine expert) serve the best in Irish and international cuisine and will advise you on exactly which wine goes best with your meal. Try the lamb with the tansy mousse or the outstanding vegetable soup with nettle pesto. *Bon appetit!*

Dublin Rd., Kilkenny (just outside of town). ☎ 056-61-085. By car: Take the N7 to N9 to N10 from Dublin to Kilkenny. Main courses: £23 ($34.05) fixed-price dinner. AE, DC, MC, V. Open: Tues–Sat 7:00 p.m.–10:30 p.m.

Rinuccini
$$$ **Kilkenny Town** **ITALIAN**

You surely didn't expect to come to Ireland for Italian food, but there's so much of it (and it's so good) that it's hard to pass it by. Rinuccini is a great example. This quaint restaurant is run by an Italian who specializes in homemade pasta dishes, but also serves veal, seafood, and steaks. It's just across from Kilkenny Castle.

Number 1, The Parade, Kilkenny Town (opposite Kilkenny Castle). ☎ 056-61-575. By car: Take the N7 to N9 to N10 from Dublin to Kilkenny. Main courses: £8.95–13.50 ($13.25–$20). AE, DC, MC, V. Open: Daily 12:30 p.m.–2:30 p.m. and 6:00 p.m.–11:30 p.m.

Exploring County Kilkenny: The top attractions

Kilkenny Castle
Kilkenny Town

The principal attraction in Kilkenny, this twelfth-century medieval castle sits among beautiful sculptured gardens and a formal rose garden on the shore of the River Nore. Guided tours take you through restored rooms, including the 150-foot Long Gallery (which boasts masterpieces by the likes of Dutch master Van Dyck), a library, drawing room, and bedrooms. The castle's Butler Gallery houses modern art exhibits and the National

Furniture Collection is like no other in the world. There is also a large outdoor children's play area.

The Parade, Kilkenny. ☎ 056-21-450. By car: Take the N9 north from Waterford or take the N7 to N9 to N10 out of Dublin. Admission: £3 ($4.45) adults, £2 ($2.95) seniors, £1.25 ($1.85) students and children. Open: Apr–May daily 10:30 a.m.–5:00 p.m., Oct–Mar Tues–Sat 10:30 a.m.–5:00 p.m., June–Sept daily 10:00 a.m.–7:00 p.m. Time: An hour and a half.

Dunmore Cave

Ballyfoyle

These large, well-lit chambers and passageways are natural formations of limestone dating back millions of years. Viking coins and other artifacts are on display. It was here in 928 A.D. that the Vikings discovered and slaughtered more than 1,000 Irish villagers. The skeletal remains of 40 people who were probably hiding from the raids have been found. You can walk the catwalks through the chambers and make the deep descent down.

Off Castlecomer Rd. (N78), Ballyfoyle (not Dunmore Village, as the name might imply). ☎ 056-67-726. By car: Seven miles north of Kilkenny on the N78 (the Kilkenny–Castlecomer Rd.). Admission: £2 ($2.95) adults, £1.50 ($2.20) seniors, £1 ($1.50) students and children. Open: Mar–June Tues–Sat 10:00 a.m.–4:00 p.m., Sun 2:00 p.m.–4:00 p.m.; July–Sept daily 10:00 a.m.–6:00 p.m. Inaccessible for wheelchairs. Time: About an hour.

Jerpoint Abbey

Thomastown

This Cistercian abbey is considered one of the best-preserved monastic ruins in the country and houses Celtic crosses and unique stone carvings of knights and dragons. There's a ton to see as you tiptoe through the graveyard and fifteenth-century cloister grounds. The small visitor center provides information about the history of the carvings and abbey.

Off the Waterford Rd. (N9), Thomastown. ☎ 056-24-623. By car: It's off the N9. Admission: £2 ($2.95) adults, £1.50 ($2.20) seniors, £1 ($1.50) children. Open: Apr–May daily 10:30 a.m.–5:00 p.m.; Oct–Mar Tues–Sat 10:30 a.m.–5:00 p.m., Sun 11:00 a.m.–5:00 p.m.; June–Sept daily 10:00 a.m.–7:00 p.m. Time: Forty-five minutes.

More fun stuff to do

✔ **Enjoy Kilkenny's best view:** Climb the Round Tower of St. Canice's Cathedral for the best view of the city and beyond. There's a small charge and you have to climb all the way to the top, so you'll sweat for this photo op, but we think it's worth it.

Location: Off St. Canice's Place. Time: Twenty minutes.

✔ **Golf Kilkenny's top course:** Mount Juliet was host of the Irish Open from 1993 to 1995. The lakes and waterfalls make a picturesque backdrop to this course, called the "Augusta of Europe" and voted the best inland course in Ireland.

Location: On the N9 Waterford-Dublin Rd, Thomastown, County Kilkenny. ☎ **056-73-000.** Par: 72. Fees: £70 ($103.60) mid-week, £75 ($111) weekends.

✔ **Join a walking tour:** On one of Tynan's Walking Tours, local historian Pat Tynan will take you through the old streets of Kilkenny, mapping out the medieval history of the town.

Location: Tours depart from the Tourist Office, Shee Alms House, Rose Inn St., Kilkenny. ☎ **056-65-929.** Price: £3 ($4.45) adults, £2 ($2.95) seniors and students, £1 ($1.50) children. Daily March to October; Tuesday to Saturday November to February. Time: One hour.

Shopping in County Kilkenny

The tourism office puts out a publication called the "Craft Trail Map," which includes the pottery of Nicholas Mosse, later in the chapter, plus more shops throughout Kilkenny.

Kilkenny Design Centre and Crescent Workshops

Located in the courtyards of Kilkenny Castle, these workshops stock the best in clothing, ceramics, and linens, as well as local gifts.

Castle Yard, Kilkenny. ☎ *056-22-118.*

Nicholas Mosse

Expert craftsman Mosse uses the River Nore to produce the electricity to fire his pots, and each piece is hand thrown. The earthenware clay pottery, sold as individual pieces or in sets, is designed and detailed for elegance and makes a nice addition to any kitchen. The customer service is outstanding and the shop also stocks linens, baskets, and home accessories.

Bennettsbridge. ☎ *056-27-105. By car: R700 south from Kilkenny.*

Upper Court Manor

Home to the country's largest collection of antique furniture, housed in one of Ireland's finest eighteenth-century mansions. It will ship large items to your home.

Freshford. ☎ *01-32-174. By car: R693 north from Kilkenny.*

Pub life in County Kilkenny

Kilkenny is home to one of Ireland's own brews: Smithwick's, a thick red ale. The brewery, on Parliament Street (☎ **056-21-014**), churns out this tasty brew as well as an American favorite, Budweiser (which is an import here!). You can't get a tour of the brewery but they do have an audio-visual display and tasting session, Monday to Friday at 3:00 p.m., June through August.

Kyteler's

The best feature of this haunting old coaching inn is the outdoor court-yard, where you can enjoy your pint and the weather (the former more predictably good, the latter iffy). The place is named for Dame Alice Kyteler, a woman who, along with her maid, was accused of witchcraft after the mysterious deaths of Alice's four husbands. Alice escaped punishment; the maid burned at the stake. There's an effigy of a witch in the window frame.

27 St. Kieran's St., Kilkenny. ☎ *056-21-064.*

Langton's

This place is a four-time winner of the National Pub of the Year award. You'll find comfortable seating inside the recently renovated interior and a garden enclosed by old city walls outside. Good conversation and friendly faces fill the many small pub sections, each individually decorated. There's toe-tapping, hand-clapping music and dancing four nights a week, as well as a popular Tuesday disco night.

69 John St., Kilkenny. ☎ *056-65-133.*

Marble City Bar

The oldest and most famous pub in Kilkenny gets its name from the local limestone, but gets its reputation from great service and a friendly atmosphere. Of course you'll spend your carousing time inside one of Marble City's four floors of snugs and bars, but the outside Edwardian facade of brass and carved wood lit by gas lamps is an attraction in itself.

66 High St., Kilkenny. ☎ *056-62-091.*

Fast Facts: County Kilkenny

AREA CODE(S)

056 and 0505.

EMERGENCIES/POLICE

Dial ☎ **999** for all emergencies.

GENEALOGY RESOURCES

Contact the **Kilkenny Archaeological Society,** 16 Parliament St., Rothe House. ☎ **056-22-893**. Fax: 056-51-108.

INFORMATION

For visitor information go to **Shee Alms House,** Rose Inn St., Kilkenny. ☎ **056-51-500.** Open year-round. It can also provide reservation services. For telephone directory assistance, dial ☎ **1190.**

INTERNET

Compustore, Unit 12, Market Cross Shopping Centre, High St., Kilkenny (☎ **056-71-210),** has Internet access for Hotmail, plus printing capabilities.

POST OFFICE

The **Kilkenny District Post Office** is at 73 High St., Kilkenny. ☎ **056-21-813.**

Part IV
The South

"Let me ask you a question. Are you planning to kiss the Blarney Stone, or ask for its hand in marriage?"

In this part . . .

Counties Cork and Kerry make up what may be
Ireland's most visited region. And that's not just by
chance. Once you spend some time here, you, too, will see
why visitors flock to it year after year.

We start with Cork City, a bustling, cosmopolitan city with
a small-town feel. This is a great place to set up camp for
exploring the south's many historical attractions and natural wonders. If shopping for great Irish products strikes
your fancy even a little bit, you could build up a big head
of shopping steam in these parts. And let's not forget West
County Cork — home of Kinsale, Ireland's mecca for gourmet food lovers. If all this isn't enough to get you excited,
have we mentioned that County Cork is home to the
Blarney Stone as well? For details, turn to Chapter 15.

County Kerry has long been Ireland's hottest tourist spot,
in part due to the charming, picturesque town of Killarney.
The county is also well known for the Ring of Kerry, a 110-
mile route lined with endless scenic views of the mountains and sea, and dotted with charming Irish towns and
villages. Add to this the amazing Killarney National Park, a
few museums, an amazing recreation of a medieval town,
and a chance to swim with the world's friendliest dolphin.
What more could you ask from a vacation destination? All
this and more is covered in Chapter 16.

Chapter 15

County Cork

County Cork occupies the eastern half of Southern Ireland, and has the country's second-largest city (Cork City), one of its most beautiful golf courses (at the Old Head of Kinsale), a host of historical sights, and, bar-none, the most famous rock on the island: the Blarney Stone. Pucker up!

Many travelers breeze into Cork City, look around, stop at Blarney Castle on the way out for a quick kiss, and then head right for Killarney, but to that we say: BIG MISTAKE. The stretch of coast from the lovely seaside town of Kinsale to the tip of Bantry Bay is just too beautiful to pass up. Our advice: Stick around a while. And because East Cork is a good strategic starting point from which to explore the entire Southern Coast of Ireland, we've given you plenty of great options for accommodations.

What's Where? County Cork's Major Attractions

Cork City has the cosmopolitan atmosphere you would expect from the second-largest city in the Republic, yet unlike Dublin, Cork hasn't lost any of its small-town friendliness. This dichotomy mixes architecture of auld and a history of political activism with contemporary shopping and dining that's spread into the city like wildfire. You'll also find attractions like

✔ **St. Finbarre's Cathedral:** Before Cork existed as a city, the area was a monastic settlement established by St. Finbarre in 606. This cathedral stands on the site of his original monastery and university, and offers informative tours.

✔ **Old English Market:** This pretty, Old-World stone-floored market has been in use for over 200 years.

Outside the city, in **East County Cork,** lie some of the really big attractions you come to this area for, especially

✔ **Blarney Castle and the Blarney Stone:** Visit the castle, kiss the rock! Legend says kissing the rock is better for your public-speaking skills than a night course at your local community college.

✔ **Fota Wildlife Park:** Lions and tigers and bears (and cheetahs, ostriches, and giraffes)! Fota is a little bit of the wild world, where you can check out the animals with no bars between you.

✔ **Jameson Heritage Centre:** Home of Jameson's Midleton Distillery — the largest distillery in Ireland — which produces many different whiskies. You can tour the place and then sample some of the product yourself.

✔ **Cobh, The Queenstown Story:** The story of Cobh and the part it played in Irish emigration and the stories of the *Titanic,* the *Lusitania,* and more are all detailed in this fascinating exhibit.

The lovely seaside town of **Kinsale** is known as "the Gourmet Capital of Ireland," and we've included some of the best dining you'll find among the town's narrow, winding streets, which are dominated by **Charles Fort,** Ireland's largest fortification.

West County Cork is the epitome of the quaint Ireland you see on postcards and television commercials. It's full of small fishing villages, joyful pubs, and marvelously interesting history. With everything from fortified towers to inspiring gardens, you won't be in want of things to do and see, like

✔ **Mizen Head:** At the very tippy-tip of this point you'll get priceless views of the wild Atlantic waves and the jagged rocks.

✔ **Bantry House and Gardens:** 250 years old at this writing, Bantry House contains a unique collection of tapestries, furniture, and art from around the world, and its exquisite Italian gardens overlook Bantry Bay.

✔ **Garinish Island:** Take the ferry over from Glengariff and what do you find? An uninhabited 37-acre island that was bare rock before someone brought in hundreds of tons of topsoil and planted an exotic Italian garden.

County Cork

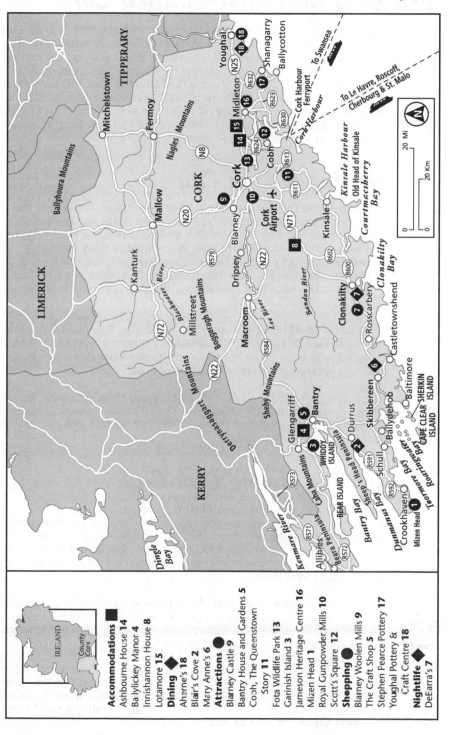

Accommodations ■
Ashbourne House **14**
Ballylickey Manor **4**
Innishannon House **8**
Lotamore **15**
Dining ◆
Aherne's **18**
Blair's Cove **2**
Mary Anne's **6**
Attractions ●
Blarney Castle **9**
Bantry House and Gardens **5**
Cosh, The Queenstown
  Story **11**
Fota Wildlife Park **13**
Garinish Island **3**
Jameson Heritage Centre **16**
Mizen Head **1**
Royal Gunpowder Mills **10**
Scott's Square **12**
Shopping ●
Blarney Woolen Mills **9**
The Craft Shop **5**
Stephen Pearce Pottery **17**
Youghal Pottery &
  Craft Centre **18**
Nightlife ◆
DeEarra's **7**

Cork City and East County Cork

County Cork has always been associated with the sea. In 1669, Quaker leader William Penn, founder of the state of Pennsylvania, sailed to America from Cork Harbour. It was also the last port of call for the first steamship to cross the Atlantic westward, *The Sirius,* in 1838. Appropriately, Cork's coat of arms contains the inscription *Statio Bene Fide Carinis* — "safe harbour for ships." The nearby village of **Cobh,** in addition to being the jumping-off point for most of the Irish who emigrated to America, was also the last port of call ever for the most famous ship to ever cross the Atlantic, the *Titanic.*

Getting to Cork City

To get to **Cork City** by car, take the N25 west from Waterford; the N20 south from Limerick; and the N22 east from Kilkenny. The towns of East Cork are located off the N25. If you're coming to Cork City from the east, you can save lots of time by taking the **Cork Harbour Crossing Car Ferry** (☎ 021-81-1223) between Cobh on the east side of the bay and Ringaskiddy (ten miles south of Cork) on the west side. The scenic trip only takes about five minutes and runs year-round, 7:15 a.m. to 12:30 a.m. daily.

Irish Rail (☎ 021-50-4888) services Cork City, Fota, and Cobh regularly, and **Bus Eireann** (☎ 021-50-8188) services Cork City, Cobh, Youghal, and other cities throughout County Cork daily. The main bus depot is located at the **Travel Centre,** Parnell Place, Cork.

You can travel right to Cork from Britain and France as well. **Swansea Cork Ferries** (☎ 021-27-1166) sails to Cork from Swansea, Wales. **Brittany Ferries,** 42 Grand Parade, Cork (☎ 021-27-7801), sails from Roscoff and LeHavre, France.

Getting around Cork City

Cork City can be confusing to find your way around, specifically because the River Lee forks and creates two sets of quays (wharfs or piers). Although the streets are not as narrow as in most towns, the one-way streets can be frustrating when you're carried across a bridge you don't mean to cross or you see where you want to go but can't quite seem to get there.

Most of the smaller roads and alleys are open exclusively to pedestrian traffic. If you're in Cork City to see the sights and do some shopping, just park when you get downtown and see the city by foot. (Parking in Cork City runs on a paper disk system. Disks can be purchased at small shops on each block for 50p. There's also a multistory parking garage in Cork City at Lavitt's Quay.) Most of the attractions and shopping lie on the island between the two tributaries. **St. Patrick's Street** is the city's hub for shopping, and **Oliver Plunkett Street** is the main place for a Cork City pub-crawl. If you end up needing a taxi in town, call **Taxi Co-op** (☎ 021-27-2222).

Cork City

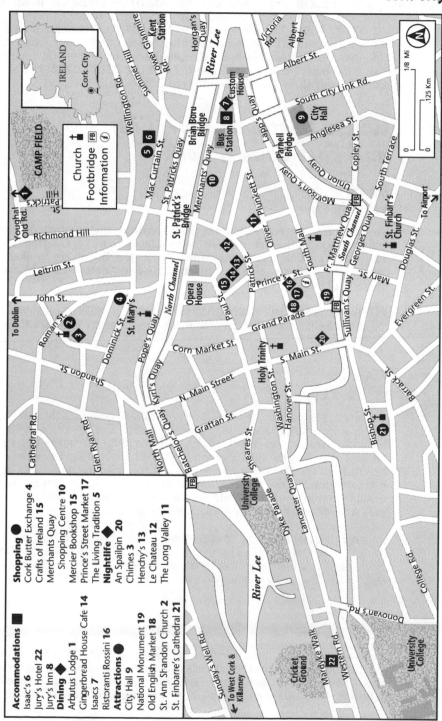

IRELAND

Cork City

Church ✝
Footbridge FB
Information ⓘ

CAMP FIELD

River Lee

Accommodations ■
Isaac's **6**
Jury's Hotel **22**
Jury's Inn **8**
Dining ◆
Arbutus Lodge **1**
Gingerbread House Cafe **14**
Isaacs **7**
Ristranti Rossini **16**
Attractions ●
City Hall **9**
National Monument **19**
Old English Market **18**
St. Ann Shandon Church **2**
St. Finbarre's Cathedral **21**

Shopping ●
Cork Butter Exchange **4**
Crafts of Ireland **15**
Merchants Quay
Shopping Centre **10**
Mercier Bookshop **15**
Prince's Street Market **17**
The Living Tradition **5**
Nightlife ◆
An Spailpin **20**
Chimes **3**
Henchy's **13**
Le Chateau **12**
The Long Valley **11**

It's best to have a car for getting to and from attractions and towns in East Cork. Car rental companies include **Great Island Car Rentals,** MacCurtain St., Cork (☎ **021-50-3536**), and Rushbrooke, Cobh (☎ **021-81-1609**). **Bus Eireann** (☎ **021-50-8118**) also operates local service around Cork City to neighboring towns like Blarney, Cobh, and Fota. Most buses leave from the Parnell Place Bus Station. If you need a taxi in the outlying towns, call **Castle Cabs** (☎ **021-38-2222**) in Blarney and **Harbour Cabs** (☎ **021-81-4444**) in Cobh.

Where to stay in Cork City and East County Cork

Isaac's
$$ Cork City

Rustic charm, a literary theme, a great location, and a courtyard garden featuring a beautiful waterfall are the highlights of this comfortable hotel. The rooms are uniquely (some oddly) decorated, but all are comfortable. This oasis of a hotel also has apartments and hostel rooms to accommodate all income levels.

48 MacCurtain St., Cork City. ☎ *021-50-0011. Fax: 021-50-6355. To get there: Above the north channel, take a right off of St. Patrick's Hill. Rates: £58–64 ($85.85–$94.70) double. AE, MC, V.*

Jury's Inn
$$ Cork City

The service is par for the course and rooms are comfortable, but there's nothing exceptional about Jury's Inn — except the low price. A flat rate for up to three adults or two adults and two children makes this a good deal for traveling families. Even though the high-rise inn faces the north tributary of the River Lee, the view's not tremendous, and there are no extra amenities like its out-of-town sister hotel — Jury's Hotel (see next in this section) — although there's a decent casual restaurant and it's only a block away from the Cork City bus station.

Anderson's Quay, Cork City. ☎ *021-27-6444. Fax: 021-27-6144. Internet: www. jurys.com. E-mail: info@jurys.com. To get there: Between the Custom House and bus station at the mouth of the north channel. Rates: £47–57 ($68.55–$84.35) up to three adults or family of four. AE, DC, MC, V.*

Jury's Hotel
$$$ Cork City

As at all the jewels in the Jury's Hotel crown, the service here is professional and efficient and the rooms are modern and cookie-cutter standard. The major feature that makes this one stand out is the enclosed grounds, featuring a walking path, pool, and outdoor sunbathing. The amenities are what you're paying for when you compare the price to the downtown Jury's Inn (mentioned in the previous entry) to this one, located about three minutes outside the city.

Western Rd., Cork City. ☎ *021-27-6622. Fax: 021-27-4477. Internet:* www.jurys. com. *E-mail:* info@jurys.com. *To get there: Take Lancaster Quay from city centre, which becomes Western Rd. Rates: £110($162.80) double. AE, DC, MC, V.*

Ashbourne House
$$ Glounthaune

This ideal country house was once called Harmony Lodge, a fitting name for a peaceful retreat that's right on the tourist route. Cork City is only ten minutes away and the Fota Wildlife Park (see "Exploring East County Cork," later) is just five minutes from here. Golfers will appreciate the proximity to four 18-hole courses. Every inch of this place is flawless, from four-poster beds to the tiny fireplace-warmed bar to the large and relaxing Oakroom lounge. Look out any window and see the award-winning gardens and verdant grounds. All this harmony overlooks the River Lee and is attended to by a small but competent staff.

Glounthaune, Cork. ☎ *021-35-3319. Fax: 021-35-4338. E-mail:* ashbournehh@ eircom.net. *Internet:* www.homepage.eircom.net/~ashbournehh. *By car: From Cork, take the N25 east for ten minutes and look for signs for Glounthaune on the left. Rates: £64–86 ($94.70–$127.30) double. No credit cards.*

Lotamore
$$ Tivoli

This 20-room Georgian-manor-turned-guesthouse functions like a four-star hotel and is beautifully furnished with antiques. It's only ten minutes from Cork City centre — just far enough to be a quiet respite from the beaten path yet in easy reach to Cobh, Fota Island, Blarney, and several golf courses. You can't beat the price for the pampering you'll receive. If you get sick, worry not, as the manor is run by two doctors. The estate overlooks the River Lee and castle ruins.

Tivoli, Cork. ☎ *021-82-2344. Fax: 021-82-2219. E-mail:* lotamore@iol.ie. *By car: East off the main road to Waterford (N25). Rates: £50–61 ($74–$90.30) double. AE, MC, V.*

Where to dine in Cork City and East County Cork

Before we take you into some of Cork's best restaurants, we feel it's our duty to introduce you to the local specialties — because if you're a picky eater, there's a lot of Cork cuisine you might not like. Food in East County Cork can be a little tricky — and perhaps a little disgusting. Cork people love their local dishes, but you might not. You should know these handy translations: *crubeens* are pig's feet, *Drisheens* are local blood sausage, and *tripe* is animal stomach. Does that sound good to you? If not, we've got some nice Italian restaurants listed for you.

Gingerbread House Cafe

$$$ **Cork City** **CAFE**

Good food, bread that's baked in-house, and probably the best slow-roasted coffee you'll find in Ireland are yours for the taking in this little cafe. The modern, open dining area looks out onto a pedestrian square in the heart of town. In an effort to break out of its breakfast and lunch, coffee-house-crowd niche, the Gingerbread has created an impressive full menu that extends through dinnertime and has one of the best wine selections in Cork City.

Paul St. Plaza, Cork City. ☎ *021-27-6411. To get there: One block north of Patrick St. Main courses: £5.50–10.50 ($8.15–$15.55). AE, MC, V. Open: Mon–Wed 8:30 a.m.–9:30 p.m., Thur–Sat 8:30 a.m.–10:30 p.m.*

Isaacs

$$ **Cork City** **INTERNATIONAL-PIZZA**

An informal and trendy restaurant that doesn't act like it. Like Cork City itself, Isaacs is an amalgam of contemporary and traditional. Located in a converted Victorian warehouse with a vaulted ceiling, Isaacs has red brick walls adorned with local art pieces. But this place isn't all atmosphere; the international cuisine is reliably delicious too. We recommend the specialty pizzas.

48 MacCurtain St., Cork City. ☎ *021-50-3805. To get there: Above the north channel, take a right off of St. Patrick's Hill. Main courses: £5.50–12.95 ($8.15–$19.15). AE, MC, V. Open: Mon–Sat 10:00 a.m.–10:30 p.m., Sun 6:30 p.m.–9:30 p.m.*

Ristoranti Rossini

$$ **Cork City** **ITALIAN**

Quintessentially Italian, down to the elegant blue plates and matching blue candles dripping over chianti bottles, this charming and authentic restaurant is located down one of the side streets off Oliver Plunkett Street. The pasta is homemade by the chef and you can't go wrong with the speciality *Italia de la Casa* — pasta and seafood with the chef's own sauce creation. If you don't have a pleasant meal here, you just don't like Italian food, period.

34 Princes St., Cork City. ☎ *021-27-5818. To get there: Between Oliver Plunkett St. and South Mall. Main courses: £5.40–11 ($8–$16.30). MC, V. Open: Mon–Sat 12:00 p.m.–3:00 p.m. and 6:00 p.m.–12:30 a.m., Sun 5:00 p.m.–12:00 a.m.*

Arbutus Lodge

$$$–$$$$ Montenotte   IRISH-FRENCH-INTERNATIONAL

You'll find the best in local dishes here, up a hill just outside Cork City —
tripe, crubeens, and ham with cabbage, as well as French and interna-
tional cuisine. The meals are gourmet, the decor relaxing, the service
friendly, and the wine list extensive, so don't be afraid to ask your server
for recommendations. The lobster, straight from the tank, is exceptional
and tender, and not so big that the meat gets tough.

St. Luke's Hill, Montenotte, Cork. ☎ ***021-50-1237.*** *To get there: North on St. Patrick's
Hill from the north channel. Main courses: £15–19.45 ($22.20–$28.80). AE, DC, MC,
V. Open: Mon–Sat 1:00 p.m.–2:30 p.m., 7:00 p.m.–9:30 p.m.*

Aherne's

$$$ Youghal   SEAFOOD

This port town restaurant has a reputation for serving the freshest and
tastiest seafood in this part of the country. Don't expect a lot of fanci-
ness and formality with your dishes: The chef is more concerned about
taste than presentation. New Englanders may never order cod back
home again after having it at Aherne's. The seafood chowder is
unmatched as well. If you're really hungry, go for the award-winning six
fish-four shellfish platter.

163 N. Main St., Youghal. ☎ ***024-92-424.*** *To get there: Take the main road to Waterford
(N25), and then turn off onto Main St. Main courses: £11.50–16.95 ($17–$25.10). AE,
DC, MC, V. Open: Tue–Sun 11:00 a.m.–8:00 p.m.; Mon in July and Aug.*

Exploring East County Cork

The really big attractions in East County Cork are outside Cork City. We
detail a few of the finest in the following sections.

The top attractions and monuments

Blarney Castle
Blarney

You've just got to see this place, one of the greatest tourist attractions in
Ireland. The seat of the Munster province, Blarney is one of the most fortified castles in Ireland — its walls are 18 feet thick in some parts. But
the highlight of your self-guided romp through this seventeenth-century
castle is of course, the Blarney Stone, located at the top of the castle.
The world's most famous rock allegedly imparts eloquence, or "the gift
of gab," to those daring enough to contort upside down from the parapet
walk and kiss it. It's a real feat to lean back into nothing and tip your head
to kiss that smooth rock — it may even be a little frightening to people
afraid of heights (or germs!). It's customary to tip a pound to the guy who

holds your legs, and you may want to give it over *before* he holds you over the far-away courtyard.

Don't leave Blarney without seeing the enchanted castle grounds. You'll go through odd foliage, ancient trees, and mystic stones along this walk, and even wander through a witch's kitchen and leprechaun-sized tunnel!

Wondering just where the old "gift of gab" lore stems from? Well, we've all heard some blarney in our lives, but the person who did it best (and first) was the charismatic Lord of Blarney, Cormac McDermot McCarthy. When Queen Elizabeth was asking all Irish lords to effectively sign over their land to the crown, McCarthy was determined not to. For every demand the Queen made, he responded with eloquent letters that claimed undying loyalty and dripped with flattery, although he had no intention of giving in to her demands. After receiving yet another crafty letter, the Queen, exasperated, explained that it was "all blarney" and that the Lord never meant what he said or did what he promised. So, today, anyone who uses a lot of eloquence and empty phrases and play-fully deceives or exaggerates is said to be talking "blarney."

Off the N20, Blarney. ☎ *021-38-5252. By car: Off the N20 north of Cork City, head-ing toward Limerick. By bus: Bus Eireann from Cork £1.65 ($2.70) one way, £2.60 ($3.85) round trip. Admission: £3 ($4.45) adults, £2 ($2.95) children. Open: June–Aug Mon–Sat 9:00 a.m.–7:00 p.m., Sun 9:30 a.m.–5:30 p.m.; May and Sept Mon–Sat 9:00 a.m.–6:30 p.m., Sun 9:30 a.m.–5:30 p.m.; Oct–Apr Mon–Sat 9:00 a.m.–dusk, Sun 9:30 a.m.–sundown. Not accessible by wheelchair. Time: Two to three hours.*

Fota Wildlife Park
Carrigtwohill

A bit of the African savanna in Ireland, and more. View 70 species of exotic wildlife without any cages between you and the animals (except for the cheetahs — Fota's the world's largest breeder of this endangered species). See ostriches, zebras, giraffes, monkeys, and kangaroos. There's a train tour that takes you around the park. Also check out the arboretum, snack, and gift shops. This is a perfect place for the kids.

Carrigtwohill, Cork Harbour. ☎ *021-81-2678. To get there: ten miles from Cork City toward Cobh off the N25. Admission: £3.80 ($5.60) adults, £3.40 ($5) students, £2.30 ($3.40) children and seniors, £15 ($22.20) family. Open: Apr–Oct Mon–Sat 10:00 a.m.–5:00 p.m., Sun 11:00 a.m.–5:00 p.m. Time: An hour and a half.*

Jameson Heritage Centre
Midleton

Journey through the history of Irish whiskey! You'll see a great audio-visual presentation and parts of the restored eighteenth-century distill-ery, including the largest Pot Still in the world, able to hold an intoxicating 30,000 gallons! Midleton Distillery is the largest in Ireland, producing many different whiskies, including Jameson and Tullamore Dew. At the end of the tour you get to sample some of the smoothest whiskey ever made. The souvenir shop will sell you anything from a shot glass to a bottle of the Water of Life.

Distillery Rd., off Main St., Midleton. ☎ *01-872-5566 (Dublin number). To get there: Off the N25, east of Cork City and west from Youghal. Admission: £3.50 ($5.20) adults, £1.50 ($2.20) children. Open: Mar–Oct daily 10:00 a.m.–6:00 p.m.; Nov–Feb Mon–Fri 10:00 a.m.–6:00 p.m. with tours departing at 12:00 p.m. and 3:00 p.m. Time: Two hours.*

Cobh, The Queenstown Story
Cobh

Cobh Harbour was the main point of departure for thousands of starving Irish on their way to the United States during the Great Famine. Annie Moore, along with her two brothers, left Cobh for America and became a footnote in the history books: She was the first immigrant ever to be processed at Ellis Island. At this top attraction, you'll learn all about Cobh's part in the emigration, as well as the town's history. Elsewhere in this guide we've tended to ignore all the sleep-inducing attractions that focus on small-town history, but the presentation Cobh puts on is fascinating and shown with several dramatic exhibitions throughout this restored Victorian Railway Station and Customs Hall. The most interesting exhibits detail the experiences of an Australian-bound convict ship and the ill-fated tragedies of both the *Titanic* and the *Lusitania* — both of which made Cobh their last port of call.

In case you skip this attraction, here are a few tidbits: The word *Cobh* means "cove," in Gaelic, which makes sense, as the town's obviously a little cove for Cork's harbor. But in the mid-1800s, the town was renamed Queenstown after a visit from Queen Victoria. Later, when the novelty of having a queen drop by wore off (or after she'd been dead long enough), the town's original name was restored.

Cobh Railway Station, Cobh. ☎ *021-81-3591. To get there: Off the N25, east of Cork City and west from Youghal. Admission: £3.50 ($5.20) adults, £2 ($2.95) children, £10 ($14.80) family of two adults and three children. Open: Daily 10:00 a.m.–6:00 p.m. Time: One hour.*

The top Cork landmarks

St. Finbarre's Cathedral
Cork City

This cathedral was built on the site of the monastery and university that served the settlement St. Finbarre established here in 606 — long before Cork City existed. Interesting highlights of the cruciform (cross-shaped) cathedral include the one-of-a-kind underground church organ, zodiac symbols on the stained glass, and gilded ceilings. You'll get more out of your visit to this French Gothic-styled Protestant cathedral if you take the short but informative tour, rather than see it alone.

Dean St., Cork City. ☎ *021-32-2993. To get there: Take Bishops St. from Sullivan Quay. Admission: Free, £1 ($1.50) for the tour. Open: Mon–Fri 10:00 a.m.–1:00 p.m. and 3:00 p.m.–5:30 p.m. Time: A half-hour.*

Royal Gunpowder Mills
Ballinollig

Between 1794 and 1903, these mills — the largest of their type in Europe — manufactured and supplied gunpowder to European armies. So important were they that when Napoleon threatened the United Kingdom (which then included Ireland), the British government sent an envoy to control and protect the mills. Today the site, set along the pretty banks of the River Lee, is an excellent attraction, with guided tours through the canal- and tree-lined complex ending at a functioning water-powered mill wheel.

Right off the N22 in Ballinollig (look for the signs). ☎ 021-87-4430. To get there: Only five minutes west of Cork on N22 toward Killarney. Bus Eireann from Cork £1.35 ($2) one way, £2.30 ($3.40) round trip. Admission: £3 ($4.45) adults, £2.50 ($3.70) students and seniors, £1.80 ($2.65) children, £8 ($11.85) family. Open: Mar–Oct daily 10:00 a.m.–6:00 p.m. Time: One hour.

Scott's Square
Cobh

An impressive and sobering memorial stands in honor of the 1,195 people who died aboard the *Lusitania* when it was hit by a German torpedo off the Irish coast in 1915. The sinking prompted America's entry into World War I.

Cobh Harbour, on the square right by the water. The little road that takes you onto the Island from the N25 ends at the village.

City Hall
Cork City

Lit up every night in spectacular glory and reflected off the river, this is where JFK gave a speech during his historic visit to Ireland in 1963.

On Albert Quay, between Anglesea St. and the South City Link Rd., Cork City.

Old English Market
Cork City

This pretty, Old-World stone-floored market was originally the Root Market (from 1788 to 1862). The area was destroyed by fire in 1980. The market you see today contains the original cast-iron fountain, columns, and railings. Meats, fish, vegetables, fruit, and some Irish delicacies (like tripe and Drisheens) are sold at numerous stands throughout the market.

Between Grand Parade and Princes St.

National Monument

Cork City

A unique and grand memorial to the Irish patriots who lost their lives in the struggle for independence between 1798 and 1867.

At the river end of Grand Parade, Cork City.

Cork's best view

Until 1986, when they were repaired, each of the four clock faces on the tower of **St. Ann Shandon Church,** on Church Street, gave a different time, earning it the nickname "The Four-Face Liar." Today, you can stop in anytime Monday through Saturday 10:00 a.m. to 5:00 p.m., climb the bell tower, and see the city's best view. And, there's an added attraction: You get to ring the bells yourself!

Church St., Cork City.

Organized tours

- ✔ **Bus Eireann Heritage Tour:** Visits Blarney, Cobh, and Midleton. Sundays in July and August. Leaves from Cork Bus Station at 10:00 a.m. and returns 10:00 p.m.

  Information: ☎ **021-50-8188.** Price: £14 ($20.85) adult, £10 ($14.80) child.

- ✔ **Bus Eireann Open-Top City Tour:** Visits all the major city sites. This tour leaves from Cork Bus Station regularly between June and September. The tour lasts three hours.

  Information: ☎ **021-50-8188.** Price: £6 ($8.90) adult, £3 ($4.45) child.

Shopping in Cork City and East County Cork

Cork is a diverse city for shopping. From the highbrow stores on Patrick's Street to the eclectic mix of small retail shops along Oliver Plunkett Street, you'll find everything from designer clothing and linen to gourmet cheese and homemade crafts. Patrick Street is the location of Cork's only mall, the **Merchants Quay Shopping Centre,** home to 40 shops and the upscale department stores Roches and Marks & Spencer. There are two main markets in Cork as well. The **Cork Butter Exchange** (John Redmond Street) is a cobblestone rotunda housing many craft workshops and summertime music sessions. The **Prince's Street Market** is a grand old indoor market with gourmet delights of all kinds, but with an emphasis on fish.

Here are a few of our favorite shops in the area.

Blarney Woolen Mills

The original in a string of famous stores. In addition to the wares (cashmere sweaters, tweeds, hats, and signature wool sweaters), this one has several craft demonstrations you can watch — including handweaving, of course.

Near Blarney Castle, off the N20, Blarney. ☎ *021-38-5280. Bus: Bus Eireann from Cork, £1.65 ($2.45) one way, £2.60 ($3.85) round trip.*

Crafts of Ireland

Local crafts galore: glass, leatherwork, pottery, toys, weaving, and much more.

11 Wintrop St. (one block from Patrick St.). ☎ *021-27-5864.*

The Living Tradition

One of the best traditional music shops in Ireland, with a large variety of bodhráns, tin whistles, and sheet music.

40 McCurtain St., Cork City. ☎ *021-50-2040.*

Mercier Bookshop

A wide selection of titles from Irish history to cult fiction. It also stocks the complete collection of the Cork-based Mercier Press, Ireland's oldest independent publishing house.

18 Academy St., Cork City. ☎ *021-27-5040.*

Stephen Pearce Pottery

Unique handmade earthenware, handblown Simon Pearce glass, linen, and jewelry.

On the R629. Shanagarry. ☎ *021-64-6807.*

Youghal Pottery & Craft Centre

One of the single largest selections of pottery styles under one roof, specializing in the colorful and unique smoke-fired Raku pottery. It stocks knitwear, crafts, and gifts as well.

Foxhole. Take the N25 east from Cork. Foxhole is just a little beyond Youghal — you don't even realize you've left Youghal — and the pottery centre is the biggest thing going on there; there are signs for it on the N25. ☎ *024-91-222.*

Pub life in County Cork

The Long Valley

This quixotic watering hole is popular with college students and locals, but things never get out of hand under the watchful, motherly eye of Mrs. Moynihan. She might even let you peek at the list of celebs who have visited The Long Valley through the years. Always fun, and always good music playing.

10 Wintrop St., at the corner of Oliver Plunkett (across from the General Post Office), Cork City. ☎ 021-272-144.

Henchy's

Perhaps the highlight of this stylish pub is the legitimate snug (a separate room where women were once relegated to drink), which has its own entrance. The mahogany bar and stained glass are staples of a traditional pub, but the frequent poetry readings aren't. Henchy's has all of the above.

40 Saint Luke's St., Cork City. ☎ 021-50-7833.

An Spailpin

Low ceilings, plenty of brickwork, and traditional music six nights a week make An Spailpin (that's "The Loft" for you non-Gaelic speakers) one of the best pubs in town. It's also one of the oldest pubs in Cork, and the old-time furnishings help prove it. An Spailpin is located opposite the Beamish Brewery, which should give you a good idea what you should order.

28 S. Main St., Cork City. ☎ 021-27-7949.

Le Chateau

Centrally located in the heart of Cork and built more than 200 years ago, this labyrinthine Victorian-decorated pub with an inexplicably French name is one of the oldest and most-favored places in town. City memorabilia is featured prominently throughout the many sections and snugs. And the Irish coffee is legendary.

93 Patrick St., Cork City. ☎ 021-27-0370.

Chimes

This is a popular working-class pub and the best place to watch a football or hurling match on the telly. We suggest you drink the local beers — smooth Murphy's or sharp Beamish. Foot-stomping accordion music usually plays on weekends.

27 Church St., Cork City. ☎ 021-30-4136.

Fast Facts: Cork City and East County Cork

AREA CODE(S)

021, 022, 024.

EMERGENCIES-POLICE

Dial ☎ **999** for all emergencies. **Cork Regional Hospital** is on Wilton Rd. ☎ **021-54-6400.**

GENEALOGY RESOURCES

Mallow Heritage Centre, 27–28 Bank Place, Mallow. ☎ **022-21-778.** Fax: 022-20-276.

INFORMATION

For visitor information go to **Aras Fáilte, Tourist House,** Grand Parade (near Oliver

Plunkett St.), Cork. ☎ **021-27-3251.** Open year-round. E-mail: user@cktourism.ie. It can also provide reservation services. For telephone directory assistance, dial ☎ **1190.**

INTERNET

FutureKids Internet Centre, South Douglas Rd. (☎ **021-89-3800**), has Internet access for Hotmail, AOL, and printing capabilities.

POST OFFICE

The **General Post Office** in Cork is on Oliver Plunkett St. ☎ **021-27-2000.**

Kinsale and West County Cork

If you've ever seen quaint postcards or television commercials of Ireland, **West Cork** will look familiar to you. It's full of the small fishing villages and joyful pubs that probably come to mind when you think of the Emerald Isle. But it has more than just scenery to offer — in County Cork you can see fortified towers, stroll through inspiring gardens, or explore a former earl's estate.

You can also feast on some of the finest cuisine available in Ireland at the port city of **Kinsale,** which is known as "the Gourmet Capital of Ireland." In this section, we include information on some of the best dining you'll find among the ancient buildings rising throughout the town's narrow, winding streets.

Getting to Kinsale and West County Cork

To get to Kinsale by car, take the R600 south from Cork or the R605 south from Inishannon. The N71 links Cork to most of the major towns in West County Cork. **Bus Eireann** (☎ **021-50-8188**) travels year-round to Kinsale, Bantry, and other major towns in West County Cork. Bus Eireann also has a special day-trip bus to Kinsale from Cork from April to mid-September. Price: £3.80 ($5.62) round trip.

Kinsale

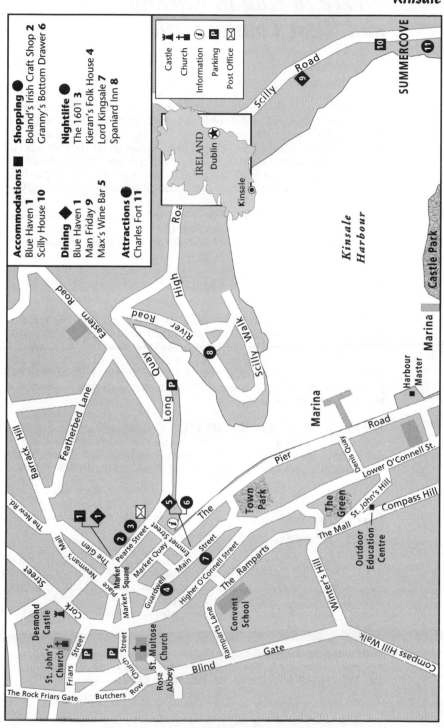

Accommodations ■
Blue Haven **1**
Scilly House **10**

Dining ◆
Blue Haven **1**
Man Friday **9**
Max's Wine Bar **5**

Attractions ●
Charles Fort **11**

Shopping ●
Boland's Irish Craft Shop **2**
Granny's Bottom Drawer **6**

Nightlife ●
The 1601 **3**
Kieran's Folk House **4**
Lord Kingsale **7**
Spaniard Inn **8**

Castle
Church
Information
Parking
Post Office

IRELAND
Dublin
Kinsale

SUMMERCOVE

Scilly Road

Kinsale Harbour

Castle Park

Marina

Harbour Master

Marina

Road

Pier

Denis Quay

Lower O'Connell St.

Marina Road

High Road

River Road

Scilly Walk

Quay

Long

Eastern Road

Featherbed Lane

Barrack Hill

The New Rd.

Street

The Glen

Newman's Mall

Market Place

Market Square

Pearse Street

Emmet Street

Market Quay

Guardwell

Main Street

Higher O'Connell Street

The Street

Town Park

The Green

St. John's Hill

Compass Hill

The Mall

Outdoor Education Centre

Winter's Hill

The Ramparts

Ramparts Lane

Convent School

Gate

Blind

Rose Abbey

St. Multose Church

Church Street

Butchers Row

The Rock Friars Gate

St. John's Church

Friars Street

Desmond Castle

Cork Street

Compass Hill Walk

Where to stay in Kinsale and West County Cork

Scilly House
$$$ **Kinsale**

A lovely mix of Irish and American styles, Scilly House is decorated with antique pine, folk art, and American quilts. The hotel's restaurant serves Californian cuisine and the lovely library and wine bar has a grand piano and hearty fire. The rooms are spacious, uniquely decorated, and all non-smoking. The bedroom suites, dining rooms, and three patios all over-look the sea, Charles Fort, and the house's professional gardens. Ask your host to tell you the hotel's haunting tale of the White Lady.

Scilly, Kinsale. ☎ *021-77-2413. Fax: 021-77-4629. To get there: From Kinsale, take Scilly Rd. (R600) toward the Charles Fort. Once you cross the bay, Scilly House is on the right. Rates: £100–130 ($148–$192.40) double. AE, MC, V. Closed Nov–Mar.*

Actons
$$–$$$ **Kinsale**

Three stories high and contemporarily furnished with big beds, Actons has exceptional amenities, like an indoor heated pool, gym, and solarium. Pay the extra £10 ($14.80) for a sea view overlooking Kinsale's beautiful harbor and yachting marina — it's worth it. An outdoor breakfast is another nice feature, and if you like your morning meal, you can take your lunch or dinner at the hotel's excellent Captain's Table restaurant, which is also quite good.

Pier Rd., Kinsale. ☎ *021-477-2135. Fax: 021-477-2231. E-mail:* info@ actonshotelkinsale.com. *Internet:* www.actonshotelkinsale.com. *To get there: Take the N71 to R605 if coming from West Cork (Clonakilty) direction and R600 from Cork City direction. Rates: £76–130 ($112.50–$148) double. AE, DC, MC, V.*

Blue Haven
$$–$$$ **Kinsale**

There's nothing fishy about this award-winning hotel, located on the site of Kinsale's old fish market. Its townhouse-style interior, rooms decorated with local crafts, and a super-friendly staff combine to make the Blue Haven the quintessential small-town accommodation. It was recently expanded and refurbished, and is centrally located in the heart of town.

3–4 Pearse St., Kinsale. ☎ *021-77-2209. Fax: 021-77-4268. E-mail:* bluhaven@ iol.ie. *To get there: Pearse St. becomes Long Quay at the harbour. Rates: £80–150 ($118.40–$222) double. AE, DC, MC, V. Closed Jan.*

Ballylickey Manor
$$–$$$$ **Ballylickey**

One of the few great accommodations overlooking Bantry Bay, this seventeenth-century manor house is flanked by modern cottages, an outdoor heated pool, and a private fishing area. Standard and luxury rooms are available, but all guests will enjoy the pretty grounds and views.

Ballylickey, Bantry Bay. ☎ *027-50071. Fax: 027-50-124. E-mail:* ballymh@ tinet.ie. *To get there: From Bantry Town go three miles north on the N71 toward Glengarriff. Ballylickey Manor in on the left, facing the water. Rates: £130–220 ($112.50–$325.50) double. AE, DC, MC, V. Closed Nov–April.*

Innishannon House
$$–$$$ **Innishannon**

Innishannon House boasts of being "the most romantic hotel in Ireland." While the romance pretty much depends on you, the top-shelf wine cellar, fine dining, woodland walks, river's-edge locale, rose garden, and rooms with Irish country house decor will undoubtedly help things along. There's boating and private salmon and trout fishing available.

On the N71 in Innishannon, west of Cork and east of Clonakilty. ☎ *800-44-UTELL in the United States; 021-77-5121. Fax: 021-77-5609. E-mail:* innishannonhotel@ tinet.ie. *Internet:* www.iol.ie/hotels. *To get there: Take the N71 west from Cork and east from Clonakilty. Rates: £75–130 ($110–$148) double. AE, DC, MC, V. Closed Jan–mid-Mar.*

Where to dine in Kinsale and West County Cork

Man Friday
$$$ **Kinsale   SEAFOOD**

Like most of Kinsale's top restaurant picks, the specialty here is seafood, caught locally and served up fresh. The wood-and-stone decor give the place a warm and cozy feel. The portions are huge, the sole is perfectly grilled to the bone, and the desserts are piled high. These are the kind of meals you might dream about if you were stranded on an island eating nothing but coconuts and seaweed.

On the Skilly Rd., Skilly, Kinsale. ☎ *021-77-2260. To get there: On the Skilly Rd. Main courses: £9–15 ($13.40–$22.20). AE, MC, V. Open: Daily 7:00 p.m.–10:30 p.m., Sun 12:30 p.m.–3:00 p.m.*

Blue Haven

$$–$$$ **Kinsale** **ECLECTIC**

Look for the ornate blue-and-gold clock above the entrance to this multi-award-winning restaurant. Once you enter, you'll notice the maritime theme and sky-lit dining area. The atmosphere is not the least bit stuffy and the menu has a large range, making this a good place to bring the whole family. There's everything from seafood pancakes, pasta, and lamb stew to farmyard duck and local venison.The house specialty is oak-chip-roasted salmon. Next door is Blue Haven's wine and cheese shop, so you can take some of their favorites (and yours) home.

3 Pearse St., Kinsale. ☎ 021-77-2209. To get there: Pearse becomes Long Quay by the harbour. Main courses: £4.25–16.50 ($6.30–$24.40). AE, DC, MC, V. Open: Daily 7:45 a.m.–10:30 a.m., 12:30 p.m.–3:00 p.m., and 7:00 p.m.–10:30 p.m. Closed two weeks in mid-Jan.

Max's Wine Bar

$$ **Kinsale** **CONTEMPORARY IRISH**

Located in the heart of Kinsale, this small and unassuming restaurant is one of the best gourmet dining experiences you'll have in the area — the *Irish Independent* newspaper put it best when it wrote, "No visit to Kinsale is complete without a visit to Max's." The scallops poached in vermouth and cream is heavenly, and the rack of lamb with red wine and rosemary sauce is unforgettable.

Main St., Kinsale. ☎ 021-77-2443. To get there: One block from harbour. Main courses: £6.50–12.50 ($9.60–$18.50). MC, V. Open: Daily 12:30 p.m.–3:30 p.m. and 6:30 p.m.–10:30 p.m. Closed Nov–Feb.

Blair's Cove

$$$$ **Darrus** **SEAFOOD**

For starters, let's talk about the starters — a host of delicious options, arranged buffet-style for you to pick and choose among. Then come the main-course options, mostly fish and meat, all grilled to perfection. And finally, the piano becomes a dessert tray, with a vast array of to-die-for sweet delectables. Go for the complete package, because you'll probably only get to eat here once in your life (twice if you're lucky). The Cove is on the water side and has an open terrace for summer dining. During the off-season, you can have a romantic meal in a candlelit stone barn.

Barley Rd., Durrus. ☎ 027-61-127. To get there: One mile from Durrus on the road to Barleycove. Main courses: £22–28 ($32.55–$41.45). AE, DC, MC, V. Open: Mar–June and Sept–Oct Tues–Sat 7:00 p.m.–9:30 p.m., July–Aug Mon–Sat 7:00 p.m.–9:30 p.m.

Mary Anne's

$$$ **Skibbereen** **SEAFOOD**

Although located in a traditional 150-year-old pub, Mary Anne's doesn't just serve up the old standards of pub grub. A shared treasure of the locals and visitors in the pleasant small town of Castletownshed, this is known as *the* place to go for top-notch seafood. Popular dishes include filleted sole with Mornay sauce glaze, scallops meunière, and deep-fried prawn (large shrimp). Also delicious and popular are the local West Cork cheeses.

Castletownshed, Skibbereen. ☎ 028-36-146. To get there: N71 to Skibbereen and then five miles south on the Castletownshed Rd. (R596). Main courses: £12–19.50 ($17.76–$28.86). MC, V. Open: Tues–Sun 12:30 p.m.–2:00 p.m. and 6:00 p.m.–10:00 p.m. Closed Tues during winter.

Exploring Kinsale and West County Cork: The top sights

In this section, we list the big attractions in West County Cork, but if you've a mind to skip the forts, gardens, and the like for a good game of golf, the **Old Head Golf Links** beckon (☎ **021-77-8444**; E-mail: info@oldheadgolf.ie; Internet: www.oldheadgolflinks.com). This brand-new, challenging course is located on a stunning outcrop of land surrounded by the Atlantic Ocean, just south of Kinsale. Par is 72 and greens fees are £50 ($74) in summer, £45 ($66.60) in winter.

Charles Fort

Kinsale

Ireland's largest fortification is impossible to miss when you're in Kinsale, because it guards the city. The nicest way to get there is along a neat coastal path. The classically star-shaped fort was in continual use from 1677 until it was destroyed in 1922 during the Irish Civil War.

☎ 021-77-2263. To get there: Scilly Rd. or coastal walk from Kinsale. Admission: £2 ($2.95) adults, £1.50 ($2.20) seniors, £1 ($1.50) students and children, £5 ($7.40) family. Open: Mid-April to mid-June Mon–Sat 9:00 a.m.–5:00 p.m., Sun 9:30 a.m.– 5:30 p.m.; mid-June to mid-Sept Mon–Sun 9:00 a.m.–6:00 p.m.; mid-Sept to Oct Mon–Sat 9:00 a.m.–5:00 p.m. Restricted access for the disabled due to uneven terrain. Time: About an hour.

Mizen Head

The Visitor Centre and the Fog Signal Station on the very tippy-tip of this point are exciting additions to an already popular spot, where you'll get priceless views of the wild Atlantic waves and the jagged rocks of Ireland's most southwesterly point. Take your pictures, and then walk the station grounds, including the keeper's house, observation area, and engine room. Then traverse the famous suspension bridge and the "99 Steps" to the top of Mizen Head. Set down as far as you can go on the Bantry Peninsula, Mizen Head seems a little out of the way, but it's an exhilarating stop regardless of a little drive.

Mizen Head. ☎ *028-35-115 or 028-35-591. To get there: From Skibbereen, take the N71 to the R592 in Ballydehop to the R591 in Toomore and follow the signs for Mizen Head. (You don't really know you're on the R591. You begin seeing signs for Mizen back in Skibbereen and you're basically just following the signs to get there.) Admission: £2.50 ($3.70) adults, £1.75 ($2.60) students and seniors, £1.25 ($1.85) under 12, free for under 5, £7 ($10.35) family of two adults and three children. Open: June–Sept daily 10:00 a.m.–6:00 p.m.; mid-Mar to May and Oct daily 10:30 a.m.–5:00 p.m.; Nov to mid-Mar Sat and Sun 11:00 a.m.–5:00 p.m. Time: A half-hour, not including the drive, which takes about an hour from Skibbereen.*

Bantry House and Gardens
Bantry

This mostly Georgian house was built in 1750 for the earls of Bantry. Every room contains a unique collection of tapestries, furniture, and art from around the world, all carefully collected by the Earl of Bantry. The stately home and exquisite Italian gardens overlook Bantry Bay. The highlights include the Rose Room, Dining Room, and Rose Garden. If you fall in love with this pleasant brigadoon (and have deep pockets), you can stay overnight in the expensive (up to £95 per night) B&B. (Call the number in the following paragraph for more information.)

On the N71, Bantry. ☎ *027-50-047. By car: On N71 between Glengarriff and Skibbereen. By bus: Eireann Bus from Cork, £8.80 ($13) round trip. Admission: £6 ($8.90) adults, £4.50 ($6.65) seniors, £4 ($5.90) students, free under 12. Open: Mar–Oct daily 9:00 a.m.–6:00 p.m. Time: Two hours.*

Garinish Island

This little island is an amazing and rare sight — an Italian garden of rare trees and shrubs set along walkways and pools, and all propped out in the sea on an uninhabited 37-acre island. Before the owner brought hundreds of tons of topsoil to grow the exotic plants, the island was bare rock. Half the fun is the short journey getting there on one of the small ferries that service the island.

Ilnacullin (Garinish Island). ☎ *027-63-040. To get there: The Blue Pool Ferry leaves from the harbour in Glengarriff every half-hour or so and takes 15 minutes to reach the island. Ferry prices are £5 ($7.40) adults, £4 ($5.90) students and seniors, £1.50 ($2.20) children. Admission: £2.50 ($3.70) adults, £1.75 ($2.60) seniors, £1 ($1.50) children and students, £6 ($8.90) family. Open: June–Sept daily 10:00 a.m.–6:00 p.m.; mid-Mar to May and Oct daily 10:30 a.m.–5:00 p.m.; Nov to mid-Mar Sat and Sun 11:00 a.m.–5:00 p.m. Time: An hour and a half, including ferry trip.*

Organized tours

✔ **Bus Eireann Day Tour:** This tour visits Bantry, Glangarriff, Kenmare and more. It leaves at 11:00 a.m. from Cork Bus Station on Fridays only, June through August, and it returns at 8:15 p.m.

Information: ☎ **021-50-8188.** Price: £14 ($20.85) adult, £10 ($14.80) child.

✔ **Harbour Queen Boat Tour:** Leaving from Glengarriff, the *Harbour Queen* makes trips to Garish Island and hosts seal-watching cruises to Seal Island from March to October.

Call for prices and times of departure. Information: ☎ 027-63-116.

Shopping

Boland's Irish Craft Shop

From the pretty to the pretty unusual, Boland's has a variety of items — Aran vests, Kinsale smocks, ceramic sheep, and miniature paintings.

Pearse St., Kinsale. ☎ *021-77-2161.*

The Craft Shop

The best of everything: pottery by Nicholas Mosse and Stephen Pearse, glass by Jerpoint Glass Studio, silver jewelry by Linda Uhleman, plus candles, leatherwork, book binding, baskets, and more.

Glengarriff Rd., Bantry. ☎ *027-50-003.*

Granny's Bottom Drawer

Traditional linen and lace: pillowcases, placemats, tablecloths, and all the rest, all handwoven with delicate care.

53 Main St., Kinsale. ☎ *021-77-4839.*

Pub life in Kinsale and West County Cork

Spaniard Inn

The best part of the Spaniard is a whole lot of outdoor seating that overlooks the harbor. Inside there's cozy turf and log fires and traditional, jazz, folk, and blues music. This fisherman-theme pub is built over the ruins of a castle and named in honor of Don Juan del Aquila, commander of the Spanish fleet and ally to the Irish during the Battle of Kinsale in 1601.

Skilly, Kinsale. ☎ *021-77-2436.*

The 1601

The front bar is essentially a memorial to the town's most famous battle, and the back bar doubles as an art gallery. The pub grub menu is always changing but the locals assure us that it never falls short of "superb."

Modern and traditional music plays on Mondays and Tuesdays. The Irish lost the Battle of 1601, but this great bar reminds us who won the war.

Pearse St., Kinsale. ☎ *021-77-2529.*

Kieran's Folk House

Who doesn't come to Kieran's? This place is popular with both locals and visitors (a rare combination in itself) as well as with the angling and diving crowds. Small but vivacious, it really kicks up on the weekends, when live music is featured. If you're hungry, the Bacchus Brasserie serves up some delicious dishes (although it's only open April to October).

Guardwell, Kinsale. ☎ *021-77-2382.*

DeBarra's

From top to bottom and inside and out, everything about this lovely traditional pub is authentic. The musicians hail from the local Irish-speaking area (called a *Gaeltacht*) and you'll see hand-painted signs and old-fashioned whiskey jars. People come far and wide to enjoy the ambience of one of County Cork's finest pubs.

Main St., Clonakilty. ☎ *023-33-381.*

Lord Kingsale

A classic black-and-white exterior pub, the Kingsale is a romantic little spot, with small snug areas, music on weekends, and even poetry readings. There's delicious home-cooked food served all day long and a comfortable, lived-in atmosphere that draws a pleasant, subdued crowd.

4 Main St., Kinsale. ☎ *021-77-237.*

Fast Facts: Kinsale and West County Cork

AREA CODE(S)

021, 027, and 028.

EMERGENCIES-POLICE

Dial ☎ **999** for all emergencies.

INFORMATION

For visitor information go to the **tourist office at Town Hall**, Skibbereen (☎ **028-21-788**), open year-round. It can also provide reservation services. A seasonal **tourist office in Kinsale**, on Pier Rd. (☎ **021-77-2234**), is open Mar–Oct. For telephone directory assistance, dial ☎ **1190**.

Chapter 16

County Kerry

County Kerry, located at the bottom of Ireland, is home to some of the country's most spectacular scenery, including the famous Ring of Kerry. It's also got Ireland's two highest mountains, Carrantuohill and Mount Brandon, as well as some great golf courses, pubs, and charming towns, like Killarney, Kenmare, and Tralee.

What's Where? County Kerry's Major Attractions

One glance at the picturesque, whimsical **Killarney** and you'll know why it's probably Ireland's most visited town. Charming streets lined with pubs, restaurants, hotels, and shops give way to outlying areas of breathtaking scenery, courtesy of the surrounding:

- **Killarney National Park:** The drive around the three lakes and towering mountains that make up the park is one of the best time investments you can make in Ireland.

- **Muckross House and Gardens:** This stirring Victorian mansion is one of Ireland's finest stately manors, and provides a venue for traditional craftsmen.

- **Ross Castle:** Built in the 1400s, this castle is the perfect example of the home of an Irish chieftain during the Middle Ages, when the chieftain kings ruled the area.

County Kerry

CLARE

Atlantic Ocean

River Shannon
Tarbert Ferryport

Ballybunion
R551
Tarbert

Mouth of the Shannon
R552

Kerry Head
Listowel

Ballyheige
LIMERICK

N69

Ballyheige Bay
R551

Tralee Fenit Spa **Tralee**
2 *Bay* N21
Mt Brandon ▲ Blennerville
R560
Camp **1**
Ballyferriter Slieve Mish Mountains
Dunquin Annascaul N23
4 Ventry **Dingle** Castlemaine
3 R561 Farranfore Airport ✈
R559 Inch Farranfore
Slea Head Killorglin N22
GT. BLASKET **5** R563
ISLAND *Dingle Bay* *Caragh* R562 **Killarney** N72
Glenbeigh **7** *Lough*
Ring of Kerry *Lough* **14**
VELENTIA ISLAND **8** Carrauntoohil▲ *Leane*
N70 *Lough* N22 **6**
10 9 Cahirciveen **KERRY** *Guitane*
Portmagee **11** R565 R567 N71 Kilgarvan R569
R566 *Lough* MacGillycuddy's Reeks
Ballinskelligs *Currane* Sneem *Ring of Kerry* Kenmare
SKELLIG Waterville **13** Parknasilla R571
ROCK *Ballinskelligs Bay* **12**
Caherdaniel *Kenmare River* Lauragh
Caha Mountains

CORK

IRELAND

County Kerry

Atlantic Ocean

0 ————— 12 1/2 Mi
0 ————— 12.5 Km
Ⓝ

Accommodations	Waterside Restaurant	**Shopping**
Alpine House **3**	& Coffee Bar **3**	Brian de Staic **3**
Captains House **3**	**Attractions**	Irish Crafts and Gifts **3**
Connors **3**	Blasket Centre **4**	Pat's Craft Shop **8**
Oakley House **1**	Conor Pass **3**	**Nightlife**
Pax House **3**	Derrynane House	Bianconi **5**
Scarriff Inn **12**	National Historic Park **12**	Caitin Baiters **9**
Towers Hotel **7**	Fungi the Dolphin	Dick Mack's **3**
Dining	boat docks **3**	The Dingle Pub **3**
Beginish Restaurant **3**	Kerry Bog Village Museum **7**	Natterjack **2**
The Blue Bull **13**	Killarney National Park **6**	O'Flaherty's **3**
Doyles Seafood Bar **3**	The Skellig Experience **10**	The Point Bar **9**
The Forge Restaurant **3**	Skellig Islands boat docks **11**	

The drive around the **Ring of Kerry** is one of the most scenic and gratifying you'll make during your trip around Ireland. The 110-mile route is along the Iveragh Peninsula, providing endless and beautiful views of the sea, mountains, and quaint towns. Most people make the drive counterclockwise, beginning in Killarney or Killorgan and going around to the picturesque town of **Kenmare,** where you can enjoy fine hotels, restaurants, shopping, and pubs. Other attractions in the area include:

- ✔ **The Skellig Experience:** Ten miles off the coast of the Iveragh Peninsula lie the Skellig Islands, **Skellig Michael and Little Skelling,** two impossibly steep and rocky little points on which a community of Irish monks built a monastery in the sixth or seventh century. A sea cruise from the center circles the rocks, but you can also visit Skellig Michael via ferry from Ballyskellig.

- ✔ **Kenmare Heritage Centre and Heritage Trail:** The town of Kenmare has an interesting story to tell, and the Heritage Centre tells it, from a display on lacemaking to the local effects of the Great Famine.

- ✔ **Derrynane House National Historic Park:** This beautiful home was where the Great Liberator, Daniel O'Connell, lived for most of his life.

- ✔ **Kerry Bog Village Museum:** C'mon, don't tell us you've never wanted to visit a bog? In addition to displays on peat bog, there's thatched-roof cottages, a blacksmith's forge and house, a stable, and a dairy house.

Northwest of Killarney and the Ring, **Tralee** is the capital town of County Kerry, and a pleasant place to stay overnight. It's the home of the **Rose of Tralee Festival,** and you'll also find plenty of culture, as well as, of course, a pub or two. From here you can set off on a driving tour of the **Dingle Peninsula,** just north of the Ring of Kerry, which offers historic sights and stunning mountain and seacoast scenery all the way to the town of **Dingle,** a vibrant fishing port full of shops, pubs, seafood restaurants, and an astounding natural beauty. Some Dingle Peninsula highlights include:

- ✔ **Kerry the Kingdom:** Ever wanted to know what life was like in Kerry in the fifteenth century? Here's your chance. Kerry the Kingdom includes a very realistic re-creation of a medieval street as well as a museum.

- ✔ **The Aqua Dome:** Let's talk about pure fun here. Under a big dome there's a main pool, kiddie pool, and sky-high waterslides, as well as a sauna dome, a steam room, a cool pool, and a sunbed.

- ✔ **Fungi the Dolphin:** Fungi the Dolphin has lived in the waters around Dingle since 1984. Today, you can ride a fishing boat out for a visit or even put on a wet suit and take a dip with him.

- ✔ **Blasket Centre:** For years, there was an isolated, Irish-speaking community on the Blasket Islands, off the coast of the Dingle Peninsula. The islands were abandoned in the 1950s, but at this cultural centre you can learn all about the islands and the former inhabitants.

Killarney Town and Killarney National Park

A stay in Killarney epitomizes what it is to travel in Ireland. In fact, one glance at picturesque, whimsical Killarney Town and you'll know why it's a popular place to visit. And if the town itself isn't enough to keep you occupied, it makes a great base for seeing the amazing mountain scenery of the region.

Getting to Killarney

If you're coming by car from Dublin, follow signs for N7 south to Limerick and then N21 or N69 (Coast Road) to Tralee. The Dingle Peninsula extends to Dingle via R559. **Irish Rail** (☎ **064-31-067** or 066-26-555) services Killarney from Dublin, Limerick, Cork, and Galway. Trains arrive daily at the Killarney Railway Station, Railway Road, off East Avenue Road. **Bus Eireann** (☎ **064-34-777**) operates daily scheduled trips from all over Ireland to Killarney. The bus depot is across from the train station.

Getting around Killarney

This compact town is entirely walkable. There's a "Tourist Trail" that takes you past all the best sights and attractions in the town. Just follow the signs, or get a pamphlet about the trail at the tourist office (see "Fast Facts: Killarney" later in this chapter for the address). If you have a rental car with you, we suggest you just park it at your hotel until you're ready for a day trip to Killarney National Park. Most accommodations offer free parking for guests, but there's also street parking. During the day you'll need to display a parking disc in your car. Parking is 30p (48 cents) an hour; discs are available at shops and hotels. There's no bus service within the town, but you can get a taxi if you need one at the taxi rank on College Square, between 8:00 a.m. and midnight. Otherwise, call **O'Callaghan's Cab & Chauffeur Service** (☎ **064-37-555**) or **Dero's Taxi Service** (☎ **064-31-251**).

Where to stay in Killarney

Killarney Park Hotel
$$$ Killarney

Every inch of this luxurious hotel says, "Pamper me." This place is for people who want comfort, class, and a taste of Old-World refinement. It's not exactly a place for kids. The lobby alone has many plush areas to relax (whether in front of a fire or not), including an ornate and fully stocked library where you can plan out your day over a cuppa' tay. The Garden Bar maintains traditional stylings, with wood everywhere and strategically placed fireplaces and snugs. You'll be amazed at the breakfast, served in a vaulted dining room complete with life-sized portraits and plush, high-backed chairs. This hotel definitely is worth a splurge.

Killarney

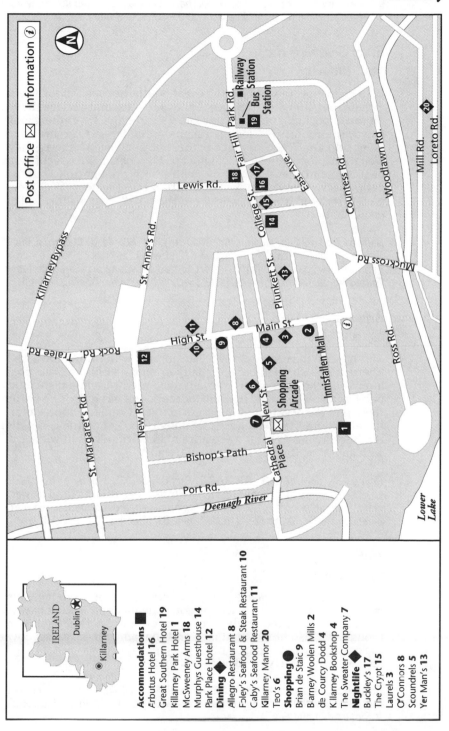

Post Office ⊠   Information *i*

N

Railway Station
Bus Station
Park Rd.
Fair Hill
Lewis Rd.
College St.
Killarney Bypass
St. Anne's Rd.
Plunkett St.
Main St.
High St.
Rock Rd. Tralee Rd.
New Rd.
St. Margaret's Rd.
New St.
Shopping Arcade
Cathedral Place
Bishop's Path
Port Rd.
Deenagh River
Innisfallen Mall
East Ave.
Countess Rd.
Muckross Rd.
Woodlawn Rd.
Mill Rd.
Loreto Rd.
Ross Rd.
Lower Lake

IRELAND
Dublin ★
● Killarney

Accommodations ■
Arbutus Hotel **16**
Great Southern Hotel **19**
Killarney Park Hotel **1**
McSweeney Arms **18**
Murphys Guesthouse **14**
Park Place Hotel **12**

Dining ◆
Allegro Restaurant **8**
Foley's Seafood & Steak Restaurant **10**
Gaby's Seafood Restaurant **11**
Killarney Manor **20**
Teo's **6**

Shopping ●
Brian de Staic **9**
Barney Woolen Mills **2**
de Courcy Dodd **4**
Killarney Bookshop **4**
The Sweater Company **7**

Nightlife ◆
Buckley's **17**
The Crypt **15**
Laurels **3**
O'Connors **8**
Scoundrels **5**
Yer Man's **13**

Kenmare Place, Killarney. ☎ *064-35-555. Fax: 064-35-266. E-mail:* info@ killarneyparkhotel.ie. *To get there: Located between the railway station and the Cineplex. Rates: £150–240 ($223.50–$355.20) double. AE, DC, MC, V.*

Great Southern Hotel

$$$ Killarney

With its manor-house style, the Great Southern doesn't look like part of a chain, but after you experience the amenities and service they lavish on you, it becomes obvious they know the routine. Everything looks polished, the rooms overlook gorgeous grounds, and the breakfast is a diner's dream! There's a piano in the lobby and even hallways have tiny side rooms for a smoke or a nightcap. All rooms have tea-coffeemaking facilities, and there's a leisure centre with pool and jacuzzi, a baby-sitting service, and a cocktail bar with a conservatory. You'll feel completely isolated from the world, but the hotel's just a short walk to the center of town.

Railway Rd., off East Avenue Rd., Killarney. ☎ *800-44-UTELL, from the United States or 064-31-262. Fax: 064-31-642. E-mail:* res@killarney.gsh.ie. *Internet:* www.gsh.ie. *To get there: Located between the railway station and the Tourist Office. Rates: £114–150 ($169.85–$223.50) double. AE, DC, MC, V.*

Arbutus Hotel

$$ Killarney

This hotel in the center of town is decorated with traditional Irish luster. There are plush, high-backed chairs around an old-time turf fire in the lobby, and the rooms are large and decorated with fine taste. Buckley's pub has an oak-paneled bar, and local opinion has it that the bartenders there pull the best pint of Guinness in town. Good traditional music fills the air nightly. The Arbutus is a family-run hotel (three generations of the Buckley family), and the entire staff is friendly and willing to help with anything. It really is a taste of Ireland.

College St., Killarney. ☎ *064-31-037. Fax: 064-34-033. E-mail:* arbutushotel@ eircom.net. *To get there: From Main St., turn onto Plunkett St. (it only goes one way). Plunkett becomes College and the hotel is at the roundabout where College meets Lewis Rd. Rates: £66–110 ($98.34–$163) double. AE, DC, MC, V.*

McSweeney Arms

$$ Killarney

If you're not the extravagant type, and a simple place to lay your head is fine, then this is the place for you. The location is mainly what you pay for — it's perfect, right in the center of town. Don't get us wrong, though: It's also homey and nice and the family that runs it covers all the bases. One of the highlights is the great food in the restaurant, beginning with the hearty breakfasts and on to savory dinners.

College St., Killarney. ☎ *064-31-211. Fax: 064-34-553. To get there: Located at the roundabout in the town center. Rates: £60–100 ($89.40–$149) double. AE, DC, MC, V. Closed Jan and Feb.*

Park Place Hotel

$ **Killarney**

Okay, so the rooms could use a facelift and the bathrooms aren't pala-
tial, but this place offers a lot for the price. Not only is it right in the
heart of town, but the rooms are big enough to fit an entire family (some
have three beds). The restaurant offers delicious food, and even during
the off-season the breakfast is huge and varied. All rooms have television and tea-making facilities. The owners are delightful people, and
you'll enjoy chatting with them about your home in America — they've
got family in the South.

High St., Killarney. ☎ *064-31-058. Fax: 064-34-454. To get there: From the center of
town, take Main St. to High St. Rates: £40–55 double. ($59.60–$81.95) AE, DC, MC, V.*

Murphys Guesthouse

$ **Killarney**

This is one of those ideal places that you'll remember long after coming
home. A great and (therefore) popular pub downstairs makes it the perfect place to have a guesthouse — at the end of the night, after a few
pints and music, you just go upstairs to your bed! The owners are
friendly and will ensure you enjoy yourself. All rooms are newly refurbished but still retain that Old-World ambiance. You'll even think you're
in someone's home once you taste the food. And parents, take note:
They've got a baby-sitting service and children's menu.

18 College St., Killarney. ☎ *064-31-294. Fax: 064-34-507. E-mail:* info@murphys
bar.com. *To get there: Go through the roundabout and down College St. £40–50
double. ($59.60–$74.50) AE, DC, MC, V.*

Where to dine in Killarney

There are some who say that because Killarney tourists are pretty
much hungry captives in the town, there's isn't much incentive for
restaurants to try very hard to make food palatable. We don't necessarily agree; there's loads of really good places to get delicious and
varied food. Here are our top picks.

Gaby's Seafood Restaurant

$$$ **Killarney   SEAFOOD**

Make this stop for the finest seafood in Killarney. It's well known for its
lobster dishes, but the Kerry shellfish platter takes the cake. The rustic
brickwork and wooden floors make for pleasurable surroundings. And
enjoying dinner in the raised dining area is a welcome break from sitting
amid the chaos of some restaurants. The excellent food, which includes
tons more than vittles from the sea, is complimented by the diverse wine
list from Gaby's cellar. Altogether, you're practically guaranteed a great
meal — and you might not even mind what it'll cost you.

27 High St., Killarney. ☎ *064-32-519. To get there: Follow Main St. until it becomes High St. Main courses: £13.95–16.95 ($20.80–$25.25). MC, V. Open: Tue–Sat 12:30 p.m.–2:30 p.m., Mon–Sat 6:00 p.m.–10:00 p.m.*

Foley's Seafood & Steak Restaurant
$$$ Killarney   SEAFOOD-IRISH

The elegant black and white exterior of Foley's is an adequate indicator of what to expect inside. It's primarily a seafood restaurant, but it's the land-lubber's food that will surprise you. The menu changes all the time, but it's not everywhere you can count on such meat entrees as duck or pheasant. Whatever you choose, you'll be blessed with homemade brown bread — delicious. Even vegetarians will enjoy a fabulous meal at Foley's.

23 High St., Killarney. ☎ *064-31-217. Main courses: £8.95–14.50 ($13.35–$21.60). MC, V. Open: 12:30 p.m.–2:30 p.m. and 6:00 p.m.–10:00 p.m.*

Allegro Restaurant
$$ Killarney   PIZZA-IRISH

Like its sister take-out version down the street, Allegro makes a mean pizza! But here you can get much more, from salads to traditional Irish eats. Prices are unbeatable, especially for the good food and huge portions. Fresh ingredients and homemade dough make for incredible pizza. The single-serve pizzas can feed two, even if you're extra-hungry. The house wine is surprisingly good, and sinking into an oversized booth is rewarding after a day of seeing sights!

9 High St., Killarney. ☎ *064-32-816. Main courses: £4.95–9.50 ($7.40–$14.15). MC, V. Open: 5:00 p.m.–10:30 p.m.*

Teo's
$$ Killarney   ECLECTIC

A restaurant to satisfy any taste, whether it be for Greek, Italian, or French cuisine, or even a tangy Szechuan stir-fry. Teo's covers it all, with plenty of vegetarian food, too. Italian dishes make up the bulk of the menu, but there are plenty of other Southern European influences throughout that give the food zest — and if you don't want anything very exotic, you can always count on standard (and tasty) spaghetti and lasagna. Teo's is also a good place for a light meal before dinner hours.

13 New St., Killarney. ☎ *064-36-344. Main courses: £4.95–8.95 ($7.40–$13.35). MC, V. Open: 12:00 p.m.–10:30 p.m.*

Killarney Manor
$$$$ Killarney   IRISH

Here's your big chance to have dinner in an authentic vintage manor, in the most authentic way — just like it was in the nineteenth century. Of course there's electricity and you'll arrive by car, but nearly everything else is the same. You become part of the act in this entertaining (and appetizing) feast, as guests of "Lord and Lady Killarney" in their stately home. You'll start with a welcome drink in the imposing Gallery Room and then move into the Great Hall for a five-course meal. All the while, the captivating sounds and poetry of the auld days are played for you. The rousing after-dinner entertainment is characteristic of a great Irish house — you'll really feel like an honored guest when the players sing and dance for you. It's fun! It's exciting! It's dinner! Older kids will love it.

Loreto Rd., Killarney (about two miles out from town). ☎ *064-31-551. Open nightly Apr–Oct. Dinner is served from 7:45 p.m.–10:00 p.m. The cost is £28 ($41.45). Reservations are not required but are a good idea in the summer.*

Exploring Killarney and Killarney National Park: The Top Attractions

Killarney Town is a "wander around, do some shopping, and have a pint" kind of place, but the outskirts are another matter entirely, providing some of the most amazing things to see in all Ireland, including the beautiful Killarney National Park and the famed Lakes of Killarney. The drive around the lakes is one of the best time investments you can make in Ireland, so it's best to set aside a day to focus on it by itself. In autumn, you'll pass mountains covered with beautiful purple heather — the subject of many an Irish song. A curve in the road might open up to a deep and far-reaching valley dotted with brooks and goats. You'll want to spend more time outside of the car than in it.

If you get a yen to do the golf thing while you're in the midst of all this green, visit the **Killarney Golf and Fishing Club.** Home of the 1991 and 1992 Irish Open Championship, this course is nestled among the beautiful Lakes of Killarney and below the majestic Macgillycuddy's Reeks mountains. It's on Mahony's Point, Killarney (☎ **064-33-899;** E-mail: kgc@iol.ie). Par is 72, and the greens fees are £38 ($56.25).

Killarney National Park
Outside Killarney

Three thrilling lakes surrounded by towering mountains comprise this state-owned park. A well-defined (but occasionally dippy and curvy) road winds throughout the park, making for an incredible drive. There are plenty of places to park and take pictures, or even do a little climbing. Be careful not to drive too fast or you'll pass the parking areas before you know it. Without stopping, the drive takes just over an hour, but undoubtedly you'll stretch it out for hours — there's just so much to see and do within the park's limits.

Killarney National Park

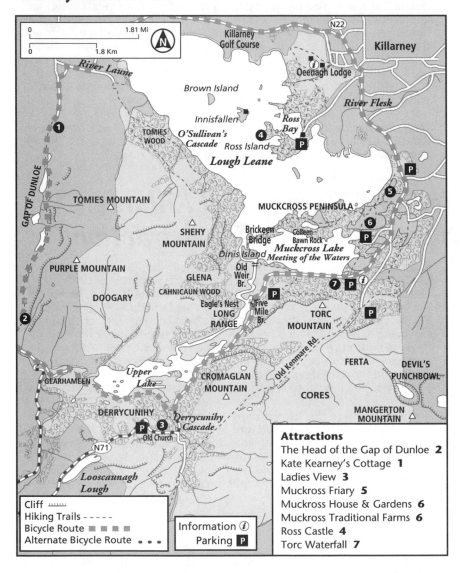

Just inside the park, about a mile in on the left, is parking for **Torc Waterfall.** Only a few steps into the forest and you see the bottom of it, but don't be fooled and think that's it. The waterfall trail is easy to walk, and will take you to the top of the mountain and the head of the falls. From here (about an hour's climb) you'll get the most exhilarating view of the lakes.

Continuing on, you'll pass **Ladies View,** which is marked by a pretty large parking area. Definitely stop for the view: It's extraordinary. How did it get its name? In the 1800s Queen Victoria of England made a momentous trip to Killarney and took her entourage through what's now the National Park. Along the way, the Queen's ladies in waiting were so overcome with marvel at the landscape from this particular spot, they stopped for a Kodak moment (sans the camera). From that moment on the spot's been known as "Ladies View."

About midpoint in the park is **Moll's Gap,** where the mountains are highest. Here you can stop for a bite to eat (there's a cafe-bakery, but it's also a good spot for a picnic if you've brought some grub with you) or some shopping before heading down. The park drive dumps you in the town of Kenmare (see "Tralee and the Dingle Peninsula," later on in this chapter). You don't have to go back through the park to return to Killarney; there's a route that bypasses the mountains.

Killarney. ☎ *064-31-440. To get there: Take Kenmare Rd. (N71) out of town. Signs indicate the park (and guide throughout it). Admission: Free. Open: Daylight hours.*

Muckross House, Gardens, and Traditional Farm
Killarney National Park

This Victorian mansion is within the National Park and is one of Ireland's finest stately manors. The decor of the home, down to tiny furnishing details, silently explains the lifestyle of the gentry of the mid-nineteenth century. The downstairs basement portrays the harsher environment of the life of the domestic servants. Today, you can watch traditional craftsmen weaving, bookbinding, and making pottery at Muckross. There are landscaped grounds, known for their rhododendrons and azaleas, and a traditional farm that preserves the way things were run before modern conveniences. Restricted accessibility for the disabled.

Killarney National Park, Killarney. ☎ *064-31-440. To get there: Take Kenmare Rd. (N71) out of town. Admission: For either Muckross House or Farm £3.80 ($5.65) adults, £2.70 ($4.05) seniors, £1.60 ($2.40) children and students, £9 ($13.40) family. Combined ticket £5.50 ($8.15) adults, £4 ($5.90) seniors, £2.75 ($4.05) children and students, £14 ($20.85) family. House Open: Mid-Mar to June, Sept and Oct daily 9:00 a.m.–6:00 p.m.; July and Aug daily 9:00 a.m.–7:00 p.m.; Nov to mid-Mar daily 9:00 a.m.–5:30 p.m.; Farm Open: June–Sept daily 10:00 a.m.–7:00 p.m.; May daily 1:00 p.m.–6:00 p.m.; mid-Mar to Apr and Oct Sat and Sun 2:00 p.m.–6:00 p.m. Time: Two to three hours.*

Ross Castle
Killarney

This castle stronghold was probably built in the 1400s by a member of the O'Donoghue Ross clan, and today serves as a perfect example of the home of an Irish chieftain during the Middle Ages, when the chieftain kings ruled the area. The castle itself looks a lot like a huge tower, and is surrounded by a wall with four smaller towers at each corner — clearly, fortification was a priority. Inside is an admirable collection of furniture from the sixteenth and seventeenth centuries. This was the last place in the province of Munster to surrender to Cromwell in 1652. The castle sits on a peninsula that projects onto Lough Leane, and you can rent boats from here to explore the lake, Killarney's largest.

Ross Rd., Killarney. ☎ *064-35-851. To get there: Head south from town, on Ross Rd. Admission: £2.50 ($3.70) adults, £1.75 ($2.60) seniors, £1 ($1.50) children and students, £6 ($8.90) family. Open: Apr daily 11:00 a.m.–6:00 p.m.; May and Sept daily 10:00 a.m.–6:00 p.m.; June–Aug daily 9:00 a.m.–6:30 p.m.; Oct Tues–Sun 10:00 a.m.–5:00 p.m. Time: An hour and a half.*

Organized tours

If you want the information of a guided tour but could do without the guide, the **Killarney Tourist Trail** takes you through the town's most interesting parts, keeping you on track through a series of signposts. Tour begins at the Killarney of the Welcomes tourist office on Beech Road (for information, call ☎ **064-36-622**), and takes about two hours if you walk at a leisurely pace.

If you're looking to go off the beaten trail on your own, pick up **Simple Pocket Maps for Walkers and Cyclists in Killarney** at the Killarney of the Welcomes office or the Killarney Tourist office at Town Hall (see "Fast Facts: Killarney" later in this chapter). These are concise color maps that will guide you into some of the area's hidden and delightful scenery. If you want to cover any of these routes by bike, you can rent a mountain bike, tandem, touring cycle, or kid's bike by the day or week from **O'Neill Cycle Store Rent-A-Bike,** 6 Plunkett St., Killarney (☎ **064-31-970**). This is a popular option, so call ahead to be sure they'll have a bike for you.

✔ **Killarney Highlights Bus Tour:** This bus tour takes you to the main sights around Killarney. You'll see the lakes, Ross Castle, Muckross House and Gardens, and Torc Waterfall, and then head up to the Gap of Dunloe.

Where and when: May to September daily at 12:30 p.m. The tour takes about three hours and departs from Dero's Tours office at 22 Main St., Killarney. Information: ☎ **064-31-251.** Price: £9 ($13.50) per person.

✔ **Gap of Dunloe and Lakes of Killarney Horse Cart Tour:** This is the real way to see the spectacular Kerry mountains, up close and personal! You can't take cars through the Gap of Dunloe, so you'll get a bus to famous local beauty Kate Kearney's Cottage, once her inn but now home to craft and coffee shops. From there you'll take a horse or a pony cart (depending on your own daring!) for the seven miles through the famous Gap. You'll get lunch at Lord Brandons Cottage and then hop on a boat for a tour of the Lakes of Killarney. You'll stop at Ross Castle before taking a boat back to town. It takes a full day, and really is an adventure.

Where and when: Runs year-round at varying times. Information: Castlelough Tours Ltd., 7 High St. ☎ **064-32-496.** E-mail: `loch@tinet.ie`. Price: £13 ($19.25) per person for bus and boat (plus a small fee for lunch).

✔ **Jaunting Car Tour:** These horse-drawn buggies are as much a part of Killarney as the lakes and mountains. The drivers will take you through the town or as far as the Gap of Dunloe. They'll go into the Killarney National Park as far as Muckross House and

Torc Waterfall, too. The drivers are characters, and pretty persua-
sive — even if you had no intention of taking one, you could find
yourself bouncing in the back of a buggy with a blanket snug
around your legs.

Where and when: There's no phone number or central place to
find a jaunting car, but you can find them all over town — or
rather, they'll find you. Price: It's not like there's a meter in the
cart, so check with the tourist office or your hotel; they'll tell you
what price to expect for where you're going. To be on the safe
side, have the driver quote a price before heading out. The going
rate when we were there last ranged from £3 to £6 per person.

✔ **The Pride of the Lakes Waterbus Tour:** You can take a trip
around Lough Leane, Killarney's largest lake, in a luxurious passenger cruiser.

Where and when: Tours leave from the pier at Ross Castle, from
April to October, and last about an hour. Information: Castlelough
Tours, 7 High St., Killarney. ☎ 064-32-496. Internet: www.
castlelough-tours.com. Price: £5 ($7.40) per person.

Shopping in Killarney

Killarney provides plenty of places for buying Irish treasures. You'll
find the best shopping right in town, but there are some exceptions,
like handweavers smack dab in the middle of the mountains. Some of
the best, for value and selection, are listed in this section.

Avoca Handweavers

This vast shop has a huge selection of sweaters and tweeds for men and
women. Also unique pottery and crafts, and plenty of souvenirs.

Molls Gap (midway through the Killarney National Park). ☎ *064-34-720.*

Blarney Woolen Mills

Here you'll find quality Irish items, from real Aran knit sweaters to linen
and tweed. You can even watch sweaters being handframed and knit.

10 Main St., Killarney. ☎ *064-34-843.*

Brian de Staic

This handcrafted jewelry ranks among the most respected in Ireland.
Goldsmith de Staic is renowned for his work, which captures the best of
Celtic design.

18 High St., Killarney. ☎ *066-33-822.*

de Courcy Dodd

You'll find fine antiques of all kinds for serious collectors and people just dabbling at de Courcy Dodd.

68 New St., Killarney. ☎ *064-31-351.*

Killarney Bookshop

A comprehensive collection of both Irish and worldwide authors. Be sure to ask about its mail-order catalog you can have sent to your home.

32 Main St., Killarney. ☎ *064-34-108.*

The Sweater Company

If you're in the market for just sweaters and hand knits, this is the place for you. From cardigans to pullovers, you'll get the finest Irish knitwear here.

3 New St., Killarney. ☎ *064-35-406.*

Pub-crawling in Killarney

Killarney has been welcoming tourists for years now, and the town has perfected the art of making strangers feel welcome. Music, too, plays a huge part of the Killarney pub scene. So settle in and enjoy!

Yer Man's

If you've been touring around Ireland for a while, you've probably heard people referring to *yer man* (as in, "I was talking to *yer man* the other day . . ."), and by now you're wondering who this incredibly popular guy is. Well, he's the fella Americans might call *this guy* (for example, "I was talking to this guy the other day...."). You might also hear yer man's feminine counterpart, *yer won*. This tiny place, with its blazing turf fires, sawdust on the floor, and light emanating from the candles on low-rising tables, is a true Irish pub catering to yer man, yer won, and you. There's nothing pretentious about it. Everyone knows each other (and so will you, by the end of the evening), and there's always a pickup game of chess being played in a corner. Things are a bit low-key here; you're more likely to hear Celtic or jazz background music than stirring rebel ballads.

24 Plunkett St. (below The Strawberry Tree restaurant), Killarney. ☎ *064-32-688.*

Buckley's

Locals say this pub pulls the best pint of Guinness in town, and we agree — try for yourself. The interior is oak paneled and turf fires burn, making it cozy and welcoming. As the story goes, Publican Tim Buckley had spent some time in New York, and in the 1920s returned to Ireland, deeply missing his hometown. So, he created the bar to combine all the great things he missed about Ireland while in the States. Maybe that's why it exudes Irish comfort. There's pub grub served all day, and music plays every night in the summer.

College St., Killarney. ☎ *064-31-037.*

Laurels

This pub offers more than meets the eye. If you stick around until the music begins, you'll understand why Con O'Leary's place has been dubbed "The Singing Pub." It really comes to life once the music starts. When the back room opens up the pub doubles in size. Soon it seems like everyone's raising their pints to one another. Music's scheduled from April to October. A rousing good time!

Main St., Killarney. ☎ *064-31-149.*

O'Connors

Wood from floor to ceiling adds to the decor of this old-style pub. Stools and tables low to the floor and wonderful stained glass throughout add to the ambience. A friendly place, where locals meet and tourists drop in, the pub has been run by the O'Connor family for three generations. Good soup and sandwiches are served all day.

7 High St., Killarney. ☎ *064-31-115.*

Going clubbing in Killarney

If you prefer club hopping to pub-crawling, fear not! Killarney has some cool places to dance the night away or simply see and be seen.

The Crypt

A lot of effort was put into decorating this club, which really does look like a medieval crypt, but in a surprisingly tasteful and cool way. There's a big dance floor, but mainly clubbers convene around the bar and look good.

College Sq., Killarney. (Located in the Towers Hotel.) Open nightly in the summer; weekends off-season. ☎ *064-31-038.*

Scoundrels

The focus of this club is dance, dance, dance. Most of the place is taken up by a huge dance floor in the center, and the rest of the club resembles an overcarpeted 1970s venue, though it's so dark inside that the dated decor hardly matters. With the jumpy music the DJs spin, you'll be dancing too much to care!

New St. (below Eviston House Hotel), Killarney. ☎ *064-31-640.*

Music venues

Most pubs in town have traditional music nightly during the spring and summer. Another customary form of Irish entertainment is the cabaret, a variety show featuring folk music and sing a-longs. "An Evening In Killarney" is one cabaret hosted by Great Southern Hotel, Railway Rd., off East Avenue Rd., Killarney (☎ 064-33-911), July and August on Monday, Wednesday, and Friday at 8:45 p.m.

Fast Facts: Killarney

AREA CODE

Most numbers have the area code 064.

CURRENCY EXCHANGE

In addition to the standard Bureau de Change, travel agencies, and hotels, you can change money at the **American Express office** on Kenmare Place (open from Mar through Oct).

EMERGENCIES

Dial ☎ **999** for all emergencies.

GENEALOGICAL RESOURCES

Contact the **Killarney Genealogical Centre,** Cathedral Walk, Killarney (☎ 064-35-946).

INFORMATION

For visitor information go to **Killarney of the Welcomes,** on Beech Road (☎ 064-36-622), or the **Killarney Tourist Office,** in the Town Hall, Church Place, off Main St. (☎ 064-31-633). Both are open year-round and provide many brochures. A great resource is the free publication *Where: Killarney,* which includes useful information like maps, events, and entertainment. It's available at most hotels and guesthouses in town.

POST OFFICE

The **Killarney Post Office** (☎ 064-31-051) is on New St.

Kenmare and the Ring of Kerry

The drive around the Ring of Kerry, a 110-mile route along the Iveragh Peninsula, is one of the most scenic and gratifying you'll make during your trip around Ireland, varying from town to town and providing endless and beautiful views of the sea, mountains, and quaint towns. (See the Cheat Sheet at the front of this book for a map of the Ring of Kerry.)

The standard route begins in **Killorglin,** known as the gateway to the Ring. Next comes **Glenbeigh,** a town partially surrounded by a ring of mountains. At **Rossbeigh** you'll first catch sight of the Atlantic, and then comes the town of **Cahirsiveen,** where you're likely to stop for a bite to eat. **Portmagee** is a pretty fishing harbor where you cross the bridge to **Valentia Island. Ballinskelligs** is a *Gaeltacht,* or Irish-speaking area, that has an Irish college where children can attend summer classes to learn the language.

Waterville, the next town on the Ring, is known as a fishing resort, but there's plenty of other sporting attractions to divert you from the drive. In **Caherdaniel** you can see the home of Daniel "The Liberator" O'Connell, and nearby **Castlecove** is loaded with sandy beaches. The lovely village of **Sneem,** one of our favorite little towns, has mountain and river scenery and is a haven of peace and quiet. **Parknasilla** benefits from the Gulf Stream, and has a (comparably) warm climate and even subtropical plants! Finally, the Ring of Kerry ends in the picturesque town of **Kenmare,** where you'll enjoy fine hotels, restaurants, shopping, and pubs.

The Ring is traditionally driven counterclockwise, beginning in Killarney or Killorgan and going around to Kenmare. During the peak tourist seasons you'll encounter a good number of other drivers along this route. So, if you want to avoid the crowds, begin in Kenmare and go clockwise — that way, you'll be going against the traffic.

Getting to and around Killarney and the Ring

By car, take the N70 south from Tralee, or the N71 southwest from Killarney. A car's the best way to get to the Ring of Kerry, and the best way to see it all. **Bus Eireann** (☎ **064-34-777**) has limited service from Killarney to Cahersiveen, Waterville, Kenmare, and a few other towns on the Ring of Kerry.

Where to stay in Kenmare and along the Ring

Stretching about 110 miles, the Ring of Kerry is short enough to drive in a single day, but there are lots of things to see and do throughout the peninsula, and the coastline is dotted with places to stay overnight.

Lansdowne Arms Hotel

$ **Kenmare**

This is a stylish and classy hotel for people looking for a little pampering. It was established as Kenmare's first hotel by Earl Shelburne, and it's obvious the family that runs the place still takes pride in the title. Rooms are big and elegantly furnished, and everything that Kenmare has to offer is just a stone's throw away.

Main St., Kenmare. ☎ *064-41-368. Fax: 064-41-114. E-mail:* lansdowne@ kenmare.com. *To get there: Hotel located where the N70 and N71 meet, in the center of town. Rates: £35–50 ($52–$74) double. MC, V. Closed Nov–Mar.*

Foley's Shamrock

$ **Kenmare**

This B&B has everything: location, food, drink, and comfort, all for a reasonable price. Set in the heart of Kenmare, Foley's is the kind of place Ireland is known for. It's small, so Ms. Foley can care for you personally, and it's within walking distance to golf, horseback riding, and fishing. The restaurant serves Irish and international food (but there are some really great places to eat in town). The downstairs pub is a place that makes you feel secure and snug the second you walk inside.

Henry St., Kenmare. ☎ *064-42-162. Fax: 064-41-799. E-mail:* foleyest@iol.ie. *To get there: Where the N70 and N71 meet. Rates: £36–51 ($53.30–$75.50) double. MC, V.*

Wander Inn
$ Kenmare

This charming B&B might have a silly name, but the O'Sheas, the couple in charge, take their job seriously. You'll feel very welcome and comfortable here, and each room is decorated uniquely with antiques. Rooms all have a TV and phone. If a pint is what you're after, there are two (count 'em, two) pubs in the B&B to choose from, both with traditional music every night. You can get a picnic lunch for the road, and the owners will even organize guided tours of the area.

2 Henry St., Kenmare. ☎ *064-41-038. Fax: 064-41-318. To get there: Located where the N70 and N71 meet, in the center of town. Rates: £40–50 ($59.20–$74) double. MC, V.*

Towers Hotel
$$ Glenbeigh

This elegant hotel is a great place to spend the night after the first leg of your drive around the Ring. Sandy beaches and towering mountains are just a short walk away, and there's fishing and golfing nearby. The hotel's classy restaurant creates superb seafood dishes, and the traditional pub draws locals, so even if you just go in for a bite you'll get to see a real slice of this part of Kerry.

Glenbeigh. ☎ *066-976-8212. Fax: 066-976-8260. To get there: Right off the N70, between Killarney and Cahirsiveen. Rates: £76–94 ($112.50–$139.10) double. AE, DC, MC, V. Closed Nov–Mar.*

Scarriff Inn
$ Caherdaniel

You'll get a fantastic view of Derrynane Harbor from this family-run inn, located on the Ring of Kerry and offering a perfect place to rest your weary head after a long day of sightseeing. There's a seafood restaurant that offers full meals or just nibblers, and even a bar. If you decide to stay for a while, you can explore the countryside from here. Whether it's fishing, diving, or plain relaxation you're looking for, this is a fine spot to set up camp.

Caherdaniel. ☎ *066-947-5132. Fax: 066-947-5425. To get there: On the N70. Rates: £39.90–45.90 ($59.05–$67.95) double. MC, V. Closed Nov to mid-Mar.*

Where to dine in Kenmare and along the Ring

One thing you'll notice about Kenmare is the number of restaurants in this small town. It's chock full o' them! We don't want you to have to go through them all until you find a great place, though, so we've taken the burden upon ourselves. We don't want to think about the number of hours we had to spend on the Stairmaster to work it all off. . .

The rest of the Ring is a bit more spotty in terms of places to eat, so we've picked out one of the best.

d'Arcy's

$$$ Kenmare IRISH

Get ready for real gourmet Irish food, prepared with fresh ingredients by a talented chef. This is the kind of food that's changing stereotypes about Ireland's culinary capabilities — it's not just meat and potatoes anymore. Choose from baked sea trout in puffed pastry with smoked salmon or loin of Kerry lamb with eggplant, tomato, and garlic. The kitchen accommodates vegetarians, too. The dining room has a big, open fireplace that creates a welcome, cozy climate.

Main St., Kenmare. ☎ *064-41-589. To get there: In the center of town. Main courses: £9.50–16.95 ($14.05–$25.10). MC, V. Open: Mar–Oct daily 6:00 p.m.– 10:00 p.m.; Nov–Feb Wed–Sat 7:00 p.m.–9:30 p.m. Closed Mon Sept–June.*

Purple Heather

$-$$ Kenmare HAUTE PUB

Here's a switch: hearty, delicious pub grub with a haute cuisine edge. Perfect for a light meal or snack and guaranteed not to be ordinary. Tasty seafood salads, vegetarian omelettes, soups, and platters piled high with farmhouse cheese are just some of the offerings. It's situated in the heart of town, too.

Henry St., Kenmare. ☎ *064-41-016. To get there: In the center of town. Main courses: £3.50–9.95 ($5.20–$14.75). No credit cards. Open: Mon–Sat 11:00 a.m.–7:00 p.m.*

Virginia's Restaurant and Wine Bar

$$ Kenmare IRISH

Chef and owner Virginia Harrington specializes in traditional and modern Irish food at good prices. Seafood dishes are a staple of the menu, which uses only fresh local produce. Meals are succulent and imaginative, like the house special: supreme of chicken stuffed with farmhouse cheese.

36 Henry St., Kenmare. ☎ *064-41-021. To get there: In the center of town. Main courses: £7.95–12.95 ($11.75–$19.15). MC, V. Open: Mon–Sat 5:00 p.m.–9:30 p.m., Sun 12:30 p.m.–9:30 p.m.*

The Blue Bull
$$$ Sneem   SEAFOOD-IRISH

This quaint roadside restaurant is known throughout County Kerry for its fresh seafood. There's also steaks and hearty soups, and specials include traditional Irish dishes. Check out the bar inside, where good pub grub is served all day long. Stick around after dinner for some Irish music in the pub.

South Sq., Sneem. ☎ *064-45-382. To get there: On the Ring of Kerry, 15 miles west of Kenmare. Main courses: £9.50–14.95 ($14.05–$22.15). AE, DC, MC, V Open: Apr–Oct 6:00 p.m.–10:00 p.m.*

Exploring Kenmare and the Ring: The Top Attractions

In this section we take you to a forbidding island where Irish monks helped save civilization, to a historic home and a cultural center, and then we dump you in a bog. If you want to add a little golf to round out the experience, visit **Waterville Golf Links,** Newrath, Waterville (☎ **066-74-102**), the course to the stars. It's scenic, overlooking the Atlantic, but more importantly, it's where Bob Hope and Sean Connery play when they're in Ireland. It's a par 71 course, and greens fees are £50 ($74).

The Skellig Experience
Valentia Island

At this heritage center, located close to the Ring of Kerry, you'll learn all about the two Skellig Islands off the coast of the Ring, which were once the home of monks. The Skellig Experience, located on the beautiful Valentia Island, explains the life and work of early Christian monks on Skellig Michael and how the lighthouses of the islands guided seafarers. You'll also learn about the sea birds and sea life in and around the Skellig Rocks, and there's a stone theater (where you'll watch a video about the islands) and a place to get a light lunch.

Skellig Heritage Centre, Valentia Island. ☎ *066-76-306. E-mail:* user@ cktourism.ie. *Internet:* www.ireland.travel.ie. *To get there: Only seven miles from the Ring of Kerry (N70). Take the R565 to Portmagee and Valentia Island. The Heritage Centre is just across the bridge from Portmagee as soon as you cross over onto Valentia Island. Admission: £3 ($4.45) adults, £2.70 ($4) seniors and students, £1.50 ($2.20) children under 12. Open: Apr–June and Sept daily 10:00 a.m.–7:00 p.m.; July–Aug daily 9:30 a.m.–7:00 p.m. Time: Two hours.*

Sailing to the Skelligs
Portmagee

You can take a boat out to the larger of the Skellig Islands, Skellig Michael.

The trip takes about 45 minutes and costs £20 ($29.60) per person. Ferries run Apr–Sept daily, leaving between 10:00 a.m. and 11:00 a.m. (weather permitting, so call the evening before to make sure). For a ferry from Portmagee to Ballyskellig (on Skellig Michael), call Joe Roddy (☎ 066-9474-268).

Kenmare Heritage Centre and Heritage Trail
Kenmare

Kenmare has an interesting story to tell, and the Heritage Centre tells it. You'll begin with the Kenmare Lace Exhibition and lacemaking displays, and then learn the history of the town. Afterward, visit the historical sites listed on the Heritage Trail map you'll receive. The walk takes about 40 minutes, and everything is pretty close to the town centre.

Market Sq. (within the Tourist Office), Kenmare. ☎ 064-41-233. To get there: From Killarney, take the N71 south or from Bantry take the N71 north. Market Street is located in the village centre. Admission: £2 ($2.95) adults, £1.50 ($2.20) students and seniors, £1 ($1.50) children under 12, £5 ($7.40) family. Open: Easter–Sept Mon–Sat 10:00 a.m.–6:00 p.m., Sun 11:00 a.m.–5:00 p.m. Time: Forty minutes.

Derrynane House National Historic Park
Caherdaniel

This beautiful home was where the Great Liberator, Daniel O'Connell, lived for most of his life. The lawyer and politician fought for the repeal of anti-Catholic laws, and the home is now a museum that displays many personal pieces from his life and career and includes a 25-minute video. The house sits on gorgeous grounds along the coast.

Right off the Ring, in Caherdaniel. ☎ 066-9475-113. To get there: From Killarney, take the Ring of Kerry (N70) to Caherdaniel. You will see a sign one mile north of the village for parking. Admission: £2 ($2.95) adults, £1.50 ($2.20) seniors, £1 ($1.50) students and children, £5 ($7.40) family. Open: Oct–Apr Tues–Sun 1:00 p.m.–5:00 p.m.; May–Sept Mon–Sat 9:00 a.m.–6:00 p.m., Sun 11:00 a.m.–7:00 p.m. Time: About an hour.

Kerry Bog Village Museum
Glenbeigh

This is a slice of life in Kerry in the 1800s, featuring thatched-roof cottages, a blacksmith's forge and house, a stable, and a dairy house. You'll also see the homes the craftspeople of the area, including a laborer, a turf-cutter, a thatcher, and a tradesman. Of course, there's plenty of freshly cut turf lying about, coming from the bog; it was once a huge part of Irish life, used as heating fuel. Inside the home are authentic pieces from across County Kerry.

Ring of Kerry Rd. (N70), Glenbeigh. ☎ 066-976-9184. To get there: From Tralee, take the Ring of Kerry (N70) south to Glenbeigh. Follow signs from the village. Admission: £2.50 ($3.70) adults, £1.50 ($2.20) students, £1 ($1.50) children. Open: Mar–Nov daily 9:00 a.m.–6:00 p.m.

Organized tours

If you'd like to take a break from driving around the Ring, one of these tours will give you a day off.

- ✔ **Bus Eireann Day Tour:** Bus Eireann makes a day tour of the Ring of Kerry.

  Where and when: From Cork Bus Station, daily between May and September leaves 10:00 a.m. and returns 10:00 p.m. Information: ☎ **021- 50-8188.** Price: £14 ($20.85) adult, £10 ($14.80) child.

- ✔ **Seafari Scenic & Wildlife Cruises:** See Kenmare Bay aboard this covered and heated cruising boat, which holds up to 150 people. For two hours you'll get an informed tour of the history, geography, and geology of the area. You might even see some sea otters, gray seals, and herons. There are evening music cruises during the high season, and you can purchase food and drink on board.

  Where and when: Leaves from Kenmare Pier, Kenmare. Departs every two hours beginning at sunrise, April to October. Information: ☎ **064-83-171.** Price: £10 ($14.80) adults, £8 ($11.85) students, £5 ($7.40) children.

- ✔ **The Kerry Way Self-Guided Walking Tour:** This self-guided walk goes throughout the Ring of Kerry and is for seasoned walkers only!

  Where and when: Pick up maps at a tourist office in Killarney or Kenmare (see "Fast Facts: Kenmare and the Ring of Kerry" later in this chapter).

Shopping

There are plenty of small craft shops along the Ring of Kerry, but the best shopping is in the town of Kenmare. You'll find a variety of speciality shops and souvenir stores, and plenty of what the town is known for: Kenmare lace.

Cleo

This women's shop has stylish Irish clothes, and is noted for colorful tweeds and linen.

2 Shelbourne Rd., Kenmare. ☎ *064-41-410.*

Nostalgia

The finest collection of the famed Kenmare lace, in tablecloths, bed linens, doll clothes, and more.

27 Henry St., Kenmare. ☎ *064-41-389.*

Pat's Craft Shop

One-stop shop for souvenirs and crafts, with crystal, china, clothes, and more.

Kells Post Office, between Glenbeigh and Cahirsiveen on the Ring. ☎ *066- 9477-601.*

Quills Woolen Market

Fine selection of Irish crafts, like Aran sweaters, Donegal tweeds, and Waterford Crystal.

The Square, Kenmare. ☎ *064-32-277. Outlet store at North Sq., Sneem.* ☎ *064- 45-277.*

Pub life

Bianconi

This will probably be your first stop along the Ring of Kerry. An interesting little pub, Bianconi's offers good Irish lunches — you can even splurge on some smoked salmon or oysters. There's folk music most evenings, and you can count on a friendly welcome from the staff.

Right on the N70 (near where it meets the N72), Killorglin. ☎ *066-61-146.*

Caitin Baiters

This thatched-roof pub is as authentic as they get, and inside you'll enjoy hearty food and a well-pulled pint, both at reasonable prices! Some nights (it's hit and miss) there are music sessions.

Kells Bay, Cahirsiveen (from the town's main street, follow the turnoff to Kells Bay; it's on that little road). ☎ *066-947-7614.*

The Point Bar

If the weather's good, this is the place to be. Sitting outside on the patio sipping a pint and looking out at the water is simply idyllic. If you're hungry, there are plenty of good, fresh seafood dishes, served 12:30 p.m–3:00 p.m. and 6:30 p.m.–9:30 p.m.

On the road to Renard Point (off the Ring road) in Cahirsiveen, just a minute or two from the N70). ☎ *066-947-2165.*

Fast Facts: Kenmare and the Ring of Kerry

AREA CODE

Most numbers on the Ring of Kerry have the area code 064.

EMERGENCIES

Dial ☎ **999** for all emergencies.

INFORMATION

For visitor information go to the **Kenmare Tourist Office** at Market Sq. (☎ **064-41-233**).

For telephone directory assistance, dial ☎ **1190**.

INTERNET

Tanamara Ltd., Mountain Ash, Gortalinney, Kenmare (☎ **064-41-358**), offers Internet access.

Tralee and the Dingle Peninsula

You'll begin your exploration of the Dingle Peninsula (just north of the Ring of Kerry) in **Tralee,** the quaint "Gateway to Kerry." This is the capital town of County Kerry, a pleasant place to stay overnight, and the home of the world famous **Rose of Tralee Pageant,** the highlight of the annual Festival of Kerry. The festival lasts for five days and includes concerts, street entertainment, and horse races leading up to the beauty-talent contest that names the Rose herself.

From Tralee you can set off on a driving tour through Castlemaine, Inch, and Annascaul before reaching **Dingle,** the primary town of the peninsula. Don't pass by this gem of a town before taking in all that it has to offer (which invariably means at least a night's stay). The town is small, but chock full of the things that epitomize Ireland: shops, pubs, seafood restaurants, and an astounding natural beauty. All these explain its popularity as a tourist locale. But tradition's been preserved, too: Dingle is one of the few remaining Gaeltachts, or Irish-speaking areas.

The drive around the Dingle Peninsula affords some sights you might not expect to see in Ireland. The first weird thing you'll probably notice are palm trees. *Palm trees?* It's true; the Gulf Stream sweeps up to the peninsula and its warm waters provide fertile ground for palm trees. Next, you'll notice sandy, clean beaches that lie tucked between jagged coves. At the very tip of the peninsula is Slea Head, where the land rounds out and you'll get spectacular views of the ocean and Blasket Island. Don't pass up the chance to see these sights!

Tralee

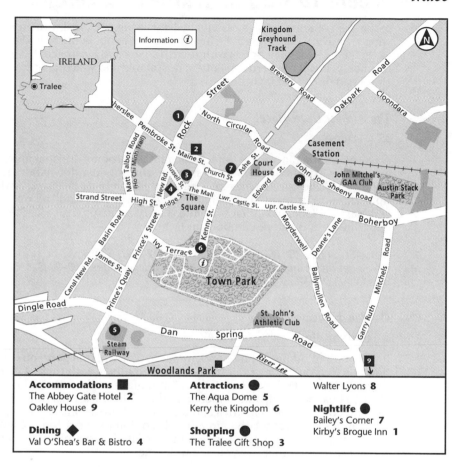

Accommodations ■
The Abbey Gate Hotel **2**
Oakley House **9**

Dining ◆
Val O'Shea's Bar & Bistro **4**

Attractions ●
The Aqua Dome **5**
Kerry the Kingdom **6**

Shopping ●
The Tralee Gift Shop **3**

Walter Lyons **8**

Nightlife ●
Bailey's Corner **7**
Kirby's Brogue Inn **1**

Getting to and around Tralee and the Dingle Peninsula

If you're coming by car from Dublin, follow signs for N7 south to Limerick and then N21 or N69 (Coast Road) to Tralee. To get to Dingle at the head of the Dingle Peninsula, take the R559. Trains to Tralee arrive daily from Dublin, Cork, and Limerick to the railway station on **John Joe Sheehy Road** (☎ **066-712-3522**). There is no train that goes to Dingle. Buses arrive in Tralee daily from all over Ireland at the Bus Eireann depot on John Joe Sheehy Road. **Bus Eireann** provides service to Dingle daily; the depot is on Upper Main Street (☎ **066-712-3566**).

Where to stay in Tralee and Dingle

In this part of Kerry you've essentially left the big city (well, you know what we mean) and entered the heartland. You're not going to find much along the lines of huge hotels with room service and leisure centers. But fear not, you will run across plenty of hospitable and welcoming places to stay. Read on for our favorites.

The Abbey Gate Hotel

$$ Tralee

A real all-in-one place. The hotel is elegant and rooms are spacious, and everyone's extremely helpful. To sweeten the pot, just downstairs is the quite good Vineyard Restaurant. Using only fresh local produce, it whips up Irish and European meals that everyone will like. And the pub, The Old Market Place, has open fires and a cozy atmosphere — a nice stop after dinner and before climbing up to bed.

Maine St., Tralee. ☎ *066-712-9888. Fax: 066-712-9821. E-mail:* abbeygat@iol. ie. *To get there: located right in the center of town. Rates: £50–98 ($74–$145.05) double. AE, DC, MC, V.*

Oakley House

$ Ballymullen

If you don't mind being just barely outside of town, this gorgeous guest-house is for you. It's a grand restored period house with tons of character and charm. Tralee is less than a ten-minute walk, and the house is close to beaches, golf, and horseback riding. There's a guest lounge with tea- and coffeemaking facilities and television. Here, rooms are much like those in a home, rather than in a hotel (so don't expect tons of amenities), but you'll appreciate the hominess of it. The couple who run the house are certain to make you feel welcome.

Ballymullen, south of Tralee along the N70. ☎ *066-712-1727. Fax: 066-712-1727. To get there: Right on the N70. Rates: £36–40 ($53.30–$59.20) double. MC, V.*

Alpine House

$ Dingle Town

This is a guesthouse that people rave about. The sizable rooms offer all the best pluses, like tea- and coffeemaking facilities, hair dryers, direct-dial phones, and central heating (sure beats huddling next to a radiator on chilly days!). Plus, you have use of a roomy guest lounge and can enjoy the hospitality of the O'Shea family. The heart of Dingle Town is only a two-minute walk. There's a wide choice for breakfast, too.

Mail Rd., Dingle Town. ☎ *066-915-1250. Fax: 066-915-1966. To get there: Off the main road (N86). Rates: £34–50 ($50.30–$74) double. MC, V.*

Captains House
$ **Dingle Town**

Once you step over the footbridge and enter the yard of the Captains House you'll think you've entered a new world. Hospitality reigns at this family-run B&B. Even breakfast is delightful, featuring homemade bread and preserves in a room overlooking the flawless and award-winning gardens. The rooms are pleasant and the rest of the house is interestingly decorated with the spoils of the now-retired Captain's voyages.

The Mall, Dingle. ☎ *066-915-1531. Fax: 066-915-1079. E-mail:* captigh@tinet. ie. *Internet:* http://homepage.tinet.ie/~captigh/. *To get there: Located right in the center of town. Rates: £46–50 ($68.10–$74) double. AE, DC, MC, V. Closed Jan–mid-Mar.*

Connors
$ **Dingle Town**

For the price and location, Connors is a great place to stay in Dingle. It's been refurbished, and rooms have TV, clock radio, hair dryer, and tea- and coffeemaking facilities. None of the rooms are exactly enormous, but they are all comfortable and homey. There's a choice of breakfast foods and you can even get a packed lunch to take with you on the road. Main Street is only a hop away, and pubs and restaurants are right there.

Dykegate St., Dingle. ☎ *066-915-1598. Fax: 066-915-2376. To get there: Just up from the harbor. Rates: £36–50 ($53.30–$74) double. AE, MC, V.*

Pax House
$ **Dingle Town**

The first thing that you'll notice about this place is the view — it's spectacular. Overlooking the water, with mountains looming in the distance, Pax House will tempt you to just lounge around on its comfortable balcony all day. Inside, everything's meticulously decorated, and rooms are gorgeous. A gourmet breakfast will welcome you in the morning.

Upper John St., Dingle. ☎ *066-915-1518. Fax: 066-915-2461. E-mail:* paxhouse@ iol.ie. *Internet:* www.kerrygems.ie/pax. *To get there: In the center of town. Rates: £45–90 ($66.50–$133) double. MC, V. Closed Nov–Feb.*

Where to dine in Tralee and Dingle

Visiting a place right on the water pretty much promises you'll find plenty of good seafood, and the restaurants on the Dingle Peninsula won't fail you. From elegant to simple, the dishes in these parts are delicious — you'll *sea.*

Val O'Shea's Bar & Bistro
$$ Tralee IRISH

Looking for some hearty, real Irish food? Look no further. Don't expect bland pub food; the chefs focus on creating traditional Irish meals at a high standard, and there are vegetarian dishes, too. Expect soups and salads that will fill you up, and fresh seafood dinners that will surprise you. Despite the full bar and a pretty extensive wine list, it's not exactly a chi chi place — you'll be comfortable with the whole family, and you won't drop too large a chunk of change in the process.

6 Bridge St., Tralee. ☎ *066-712-1559. To get there: In the center of town. Main courses: £4.50–9.95 ($6.65–$14.75). MC, V. Open: Daily 12:30 p.m.–2:30 p.m. and 6:30 p.m.–10:00 p.m.*

Beginish Restaurant
$$$ Dingle Town SEAFOOD

Seafood is in order when you come to this classy restaurant. That's the easy choice; if it's not too busy you can pick between the cozy old dining room with the huge fireplace or the serene conservatory looking out on the gardens. Then you have to decide among such imaginative dishes as scalloped wild salmon with tarragon sauce or a seafood medley of mussels, *prawns* (tiny shrimp), scallops, and monkfish in a liqueur broth.

Green St., Dingle Town. ☎ *066-9151-588. To get there: In the town centre. Main courses: £9.95–16.95 ($14.75–$25.10). AE, DC, MC, V. Open: Tues–Sun 12:30 p.m.– 2:15 p.m., 6:00 p.m.–10:00 p.m. Closed mid-Nov to mid-Mar.*

The Forge Restaurant
$$$ Dingle Town IRISH

This popular restaurant is a family haven. Not only are the prices reasonable, but it also has a special menu for kids. The menu covers seafood, steaks, and vegetarian dishes, and all meals are made with fresh local produce. The Forge is family-run and popular with tourists and locals alike. The Fentons also own and run Fenton's Restaurant on Green Street, which offers great food but doesn't cater to the whole family.

Holyground Rd., Dingle. ☎ *066-915-1209. To get there: Just up from the Main St. Main courses: £8.50–16.95 ($12.60–$25.10). AE, DC, MC, V. Open: Daily 12:30 p.m.– 2:30 p.m. and 6:00 p.m.–10:30 p.m. Closed mid-Nov to mid-Mar.*

Doyles Seafood Bar
$$$ Dingle Town SEAFOOD

If you're looking for lobster, look no further. Here, when you have the speciality of the house, you pick it out of a tank in the bar. And you won't be disappointed! The rest of the menu depends daily on the fresh seafood caught by local fishermen. So while you can't always depend on a certain dish, you can be sure whatever you get will be fresh. The dining room is cozy, with plenty of brick and stone, and you might feel like you're eating in someone's wide-open kitchen.

John St., Dingle. ☎ *066-915-1174. To get there: In the center of town. Main courses: £11.50–18 ($17–$26.65). AE, DC, MC, V. Open: Mon–Sat 6:30 p.m.– 10:00 p.m. Closed mid-Nov to mid-Mar.*

Waterside Restaurant & Coffee Bar
$$–$$$ Dingle Town   CAFE-IRISH

The Waterside combines a place to have a refreshing light lunch or coffee with a perfect summertime dinner restaurant. At lunch, you can slip in while walking around the marina for a cup of joe and a pastry or a delicious Dingle seafood salad sandwich. Then, come back for a relaxing dinner in the conservatory. If the weather's nice, you can even eat *alfresco* on the patio. Young and daring chef John Dillon is a master with innovative Irish dishes, and fresh local produce underscores the entrees.

Quay St., Dingle Marina. ☎ *066-9151-458. To get there: At the marina. Main courses: £8.95–13.50 ($13.25–$20). MC, V. Open: Cafe: Easter–Sept 10:00 a.m.– 6:00 p.m. Restaurant: June–Aug 7:00 a.m.–10:00 p.m. Closed Oct–Easter.*

Exploring Tralee and Dingle Peninsula: The Top Attractions

In this section we'll take you down a medieval street, to a domed pool, and out into the ocean to swim with a dolphin. If your idea of fun leans more toward *duffing* (golfing), though, there are a couple good choices in the area. On Sandhill Road you'll find **Ballybunion** (☎ 068-27-146; E-mail: bbgolfc@iol.ie), a seaside club with two fine 18-hole, par-71 courses. The Old Course is the more challenging of the two and the newer course was fashioned by the legendary Robert Trent Jones. Greens fees are £55 ($81.40). The par-71 **Tralee,** located at West Barrow, Ardfert, in Tralee (☎ 066-713-6379), is the original European Arnold Palmer-designed course. This up-and-coming course is staged before an amazing backdrop, boxed in by river, the sea, and the crumbling castles of Ardfert. Greens fees are £45 ($66.60).

Kerry the Kingdom
Tralee

This is your chance to really witness life in the Middle Ages — on a busy market day in 1450, to be exact. Once you enter the gates you'll walk down a street re-created to look, smell, and sound just like it did centuries ago. The museum comes next, allowing you to look closely at many of the elements the market day highlighted. There are artifacts, scale models, and video presentations to fully explain what life was like in Kerry in the fifteenth century. The rest of the county's history doesn't go unnoticed, either. Kerry's progression through time, starting 7,000 years ago, unfolds before you. This place is loaded with interactive displays and interesting presentations.

Ashe Memorial Hall, Denny St., Tralee. ☎ 066-712-7777. To get there: Located in the same building as the Tourist Office. Admission: £4.20 ($6.29) adults, £2.50 ($3.70) children, £13 ($19.24) family. Open: Mid-Mar–Oct daily 10:00 a.m.–6:00 p.m., Aug daily 10:00 a.m.–7:00 p.m., Nov–Dec daily 12:00 p.m.–7:00 p.m. Time: An hour and a half to two hours.

The Aqua Dome
Tralee

Fun for the whole family! Kids can splash around in the kiddie pools, fly down the sky-high slides, or really get berserk in the raging rapids — all under one roof. Meanwhile, adults can relax in the sauna dome, which has two saunas, a steam room, a cool pool, and a sunbed. The main pool is for the whole family, and next door is an over-16-only "health suite" (which is really just a spot with hot tubs and a relaxing place to read the paper). There's so much to do in the Aqua Dome, whether you're looking to chill out or get rid of some pent-up energy. There's also a restaurant and shop inside, and at night the dome is amazingly lit up.

Dingle Rd., Tralee. ☎ 066-712-8899, 24-hour info line; 066-29-150. To get there: Next to the steam railway heading out of town. Admission: Prices vary, depending on length of stay. Children, student, and family rates. Open: June–Aug daily 10:00 a.m.–10:00 p.m., Sept–May, phone for details. Time: As long as you want!

Fungi the Dolphin
Dingle

Dingle's most famous resident, Fungi the Dolphin, is friendlier and more accessible than those at larger water parks! The water around Dingle is tinged with the Gulf Stream, so Fungi's arrival in 1984 wasn't a huge surprise. But when the super-friendly mammal stayed long enough to be named by local fishermen, people knew he'd made a home. Today, the colorful fishing boats bobbing at the Dingle Pier are waiting to ferry you out to see the gregarious dolphin, who will jump up and greet you. One warning: Don't lean over too far. You don't want to explain that you got a black eye from a dolphin! The trip takes about an hour. **The Fungi the Dolphin Tour** also arranges actual encounters with Fungi. You can rent everything you need (wet suit, mask, snorkel, and fins) for £14 ($20.85), plus another £10 ($14.80) for the boat ride. The morning swim with Fungi is from 8:00 a.m.–10:00 a.m.

The Pier, Dingle. ☎ 066-9151-967. To get there: At the waterfront. Cost: £6 ($8.90) adults, £3 ($4.45) children. There is a kiosk at the pier where you buy tickets. Open: Daily 10:00 a.m.–5:00 p.m. Time: One hour (boat ride only).

Blasket Centre
Dunquin

This heritage center celebrates the Blasket Islands, a group of islands headed by the Great Blasket. On it, a number of Irish people lived in isolation from the world, speaking Gaelic and penning some of the greatest Irish-language literature. In the 1950s the island was abandoned when

Isolation and loneliness drove the inhabitants out. At the very tip of the Dingle Peninsula stands the Blasket Centre, where you can learn all about the islands and the former inhabitants. Through displays, exhibits, and a video presentation you'll come to understand the phenomenon of the people who lived there and enriched Irish literature; there's also a bookshop specializing in Irish literature on the premises.

Dunquin, Tralee, County Kerry. ☎ *066-915-6025. To get there: At the tip of the Dingle Peninsula on the R559. Admission: £2.50 ($3.70) adults, £1.75 ($2.60) seniors, £1 ($1.50) children and students, £6 ($8.90) family. Open: Easter–June daily 10:00 a.m.–6:00 p.m.; July and Aug daily 10:00 a.m.–7:00 p.m.; Sept and Oct daily 10:00 a.m.–6:00 p.m. Time: One hour.*

Conor Pass
Outside Dingle Town

Don't miss the spectacular view from Conor Pass, outside Dingle Town. A twisty, white-knuckle drive up to this spot will reward you with an astonishing view. Once you reach the top, you're at the dead center of the peninsula, and between lush mountains you'll see Brandon Bay and Dingle Bay on either side. Even if it's a bit foggy when you get up there, don't rush off — the fog comes and goes. The drive down the other side of the mountain is equally scary, and if you're squeamish, don't look left — there's nothing there!

To get there: Take Saint's Rd. out of Dingle Town.

Rose of Tralee Pageant-Festival of Kerry
Tralee

Tralee is home to the famous Rose of Tralee pageant, the highlight of the Festival of Kerry, a weeklong celebration at the end of August. Countries from across the globe send a representative to vie for the crown, given to the woman with the most "inner radiance," talent, and social graces. Much more than a beauty contest, the picking of the Rose of Tralee honors hard-working, well-rounded (so to speak) women. People from all over Ireland await the festival; the entire town of Tralee is closed off to let half a million people converge and transform it into a big party. There's theater, clowns, face painting, and of course music and merriment. If you'll be in Ireland while the festival's on, don't miss the chance to join the party!

Contact the Rose of Tralee Festival Office at ☎ *066-712-1322 for more information.*

Organized tours

In addition to the organized tours in this section, you can take self-guided tours in Tralee. Check out the **Walk Information Centre,** 40 Ashe St., Tralee (☎ **066-712-8733**), for details on self-guided walks, maps, and books on the Tralee and Kerry area. It's open Monday through Saturday from 8:30 a.m. to 6:00 p.m.

- **Bus Eireann Tour:** This tour runs a day tour of Killarney, Inch Strand, Dingle, and Tralee.

  Where and when: From Cork Bus Station. Leaves daily at 10:00 a.m. and returns 9:30 p.m., July and August only. Information: ☎ 021-50-8188. Cost: £14 ($20.85) adults, £10 ($14.80) children.

- **Sciuird Tours Bus and Walking Tour:** For anyone interested in archeology, this tour is for you. It lasts two to three hours and is run by an expert who'll show you four or five monuments from the Stone Age to Middle Ages. You'll take a short bus trip and do some easy walking.

  Where and when: Tours begin at the Tourist Office at the head of the Pier of Dingle. Information: Holy Ground, Dingle. Price: £8 ($11.85) per person. May to September, daily 10:30 a.m. and 2:00 p.m.

Shopping

You'll find the most shopping in the heart of Dingle and Tralee towns. But there are some great pottery shops along roadsides throughout the Dingle Peninsula; just drop in when you come across them.

The Tralee Gift Shop

Here's where you can get all those kitschy gifts you promised to bring home, like ceramic cottages and locally made crafts.

Russell St., Tralee. ☎ *066-712-4233.*

Walter Lyons

This is the largest antique and secondhand store in Ireland, and doubles as a flea market. The owners welcome browsers, too.

JJ Sheehy Rd., Tralee. ☎ *066-712-2603.*

Brian de Staic

Unique, handcrafted jewelry made by the artist in his studio-workshop in Dingle. Pieces highlight Celtic art, and you can watch jewelry being made in the studio.

Studio Shop, The Wood, Dingle. ☎ *066-915-1298. Outlet store on Green St., Dingle.*

Irish Crafts and Gifts

From souvenir gifts to keepsakes for yourself, from Waterford Crystal to sweaters to books, this is one-stop shop.

Green St., Dingle. ☎ *066-915-1433.*

Pub life

Local color is a staple of the pub scene in this part of County Kerry. The small but bustling little town of Tralee has pubs galore to suit tourist tastes. And in Dingle, tradition reigns; so often, locals will be chatting to each other in their mother tongue, Gaelic.

Dick Mack's

Undoubtedly one of Ireland's quaintest pubs, Dick Mack's retains an aura of times gone by — years ago, pubs often doubled as bars and groceries; this one doubled as bar and cobbler, and one side of the place still holds the leather-working tools of the late owner. There's a great little snug at the end of the bar side, and an authentic back room that once served as the kitchen. Apparently, when Tom Cruise and Nicole Kidman stayed in Dingle while filming *Far and Away*, they fell in love with the place. Many other stars have stopped in for a pint, leaving their mark on the street out front. See for yourself!

Green St., Dingle Town. ☎ *066-915-1960.*

Kirby's Brogue Inn

This bright-yellow alehouse has dubbed itself "your landmark in Tralee." Given the great atmosphere and food, it probably will be. It's quaint exterior gives way to a wonderful old pub inside, where you'll hear traditional sessions and jazz in the summers, and where you can nosh on glorified pub grub all day — steaks and seafood barside are quite a treat.

Rock St., Tralee. ☎ *066-712-3221.*

Bailey's Corner

You'll find it hard to pass by this inviting corner pub without stopping in. During the day, this busy place serves up delicious food, and the robust crowd it draws only adds to the atmosphere. At night, Bailey's becomes a drinking pub, so don't expect any rousing music to disturb you or your pint-drinking.

Ashe St., Tralee. ☎ *066-712-6230.*

The Dingle Pub

Facing the harbor and easily distinguished by the green-and-white shamrock outside, this place is just what it sounds like: the pub that represents Dingle. Inside, it seems as if nothing's changed in generations, and you can relax in the laid-back atmosphere, all of which is what you'll encounter in the town itself. Stop in for a pint and a talk with the locals.

Main St., Dingle Town, at the harbor. ☎ *066-915-1370.*

O'Flaherty's

You can count on the music in O'Flaherty's to be good — the owner is one of the frequent performers! Check out the posters and clippings that line the walls to get a real feel for Dingle Town. Everything about this place screams "authentic," and the locals who frequent it don't bother speaking English for the tourists' sake. It's big and open, and because of the stone-flagged floor, doesn't exactly get cozy until it gets full. Stop in for a real taste of Ireland.

Bridge St., Dingle Town. ☎ *066-915-1983.*

Natterjack

This pub hearkens back to days of old, and it's a perfect place to stop in for a bite and a refreshing pint after the drive to the north end of the peninsula. Natterjack has held on to authentic ways of old, concentrating more on good music and food than the latest trend in decor. There's a children's menu, and a beer garden in summertime. Don't pass up this old-fashioned pub!

The West End, Castlegregory. ☎ *066-713-9491.*

Fast Facts: Tralee and Dingle Peninsula

AREA CODE

The main area code for Tralee and Dingle is 066.

EMERGENCIES-HOSPITAL

Dial ☎ 999 for all emergencies. In Tralee, the **Tralee General Hospital** on Killarney Rd. (N22) (☎ 066-7126-222). In Dingle, the **Dingle District Hospital** on Upper Main St. (☎ 066-9151-455).

INFORMATION

For visitor information go to the tourist office at **Ashe Memorial Hall,** Denny St., Tralee (☎ 066-712-1288), which is open year-round. For visitor attraction information call ☎ 066-712-7777. The office can also provide reservation services. For telephone directory assistance, dial ☎ 1190.

INTERNET

Computronics Cyber Suite, 33 Ash St., Tralee (☎ 066-712-9794), and **DingleWeb,** Lower Main St., Dingle (☎ 066-52-477), both have Internet access for Hotmail and AOL, plus printing capabilities.

Part V
The West and Northwest

We've been through the thin and the thick of it
So lost that we're thoroughly sick of it
   Our errors so far
   Leave us in Erin go braugh
It's Limerick, the town that we're looking for.

In this part . . .

In this region, you'll find that legendary Irish hospitality just about everywhere you go. You'll also find the lush countryside that inspired some of the most famous Irish ballads and rebel songs like "Galway Bay," "It's a Long, Long Way From Clare To Here," and "Sean South of Garryowen."

We start this section with Counties Limerick and Clare, in Chapter 17. The dilapidated Limerick City author Frank McCourt describes in *Angela's Ashes* is largely a thing of the past. Today, the city sucessfully strikes that difficult balance of mixing old and new, with enough historic sights, fantastic restaurants, and elegant hotels to satisfy discriminating travelers. County Clare is also well worth a visit. This is where you'll find Bunratty Castle as well as the stunning Cliffs of Moher.

You could say that County Galway is a mini-version of the country — a wonderful combination of a major city, quaint small towns, and outdoor wonders — but that might really anger a lot of people who think their own county is just as grand, so we'll pretend the subject never came up. But given all the county's assets, we will say we think you should make a visit here a priority. Turn to Chapter 18 for more details.

Poetry and film fans alike should be excited about a visit to Counties Mayo and Sligo (covered in Chapter 19). John Ford's classic Irish romance *The Quiet Man* was filmed in beautiful Mayo, and you can hardly swing a fisherman's sweater in Sligo without hitting a tribute to the great W. B. Yeats. This region was once the source of divine inspiration as well — Crough Patrick (in County Mayo) is said to be where St. Patrick fasted and prayed for 40 days.

In the last chapter of this section (Chapter 20) we tell you about County Donegal, Donegal Town (a great place to just walk around), the highest sea cliffs in Europe, a couple of impressive castles, a ring fort, and some of the freshest seafood you can get anywhere.

Chapter 17

Counties Limerick and Clare

· ·

In This Chapter

▶ Making a pilgrimage to the literary world of Frank McCourt

▶ Hunting for historical artifacts in the Hunt Museum

▶ Eating in a thatched hut

▶ Visiting the famous Cliffs of Moher

▶ Touring the Burren

▶ Walking through prehistoric Ireland

▶ Learning to do the *Riverdance*. . . sort of

· ·

*F*or years, Counties Limerick and Clare were the first places visitors to Ireland saw, because all international flights used to go to Shannon Airport. Nowadays Dublin Airport has snagged a lot of that business, but whether you fly in directly or visit as part of the typical clockwise swing from Dublin south through Cork and Kerry and then up to Galway, Limerick and Clare have more than enough history, culture, and positively Irish sights to justify your investment of time.

What's Where? Limerick and Clare's Major Attractions

In recent years, **Limerick City** has risen from near dilapidation to achieving a cosmopolitan flair that might soon make it the Dublin of the West. It can't be denied that Pulitzer Prize-winning author Frank McCourt has finally brought this city to the forefront of tourism, but what you'll be surprised to see is how different the Limerick of today is from the Limerick McCourt remembers from his youth.

Counties Limerick and Clare

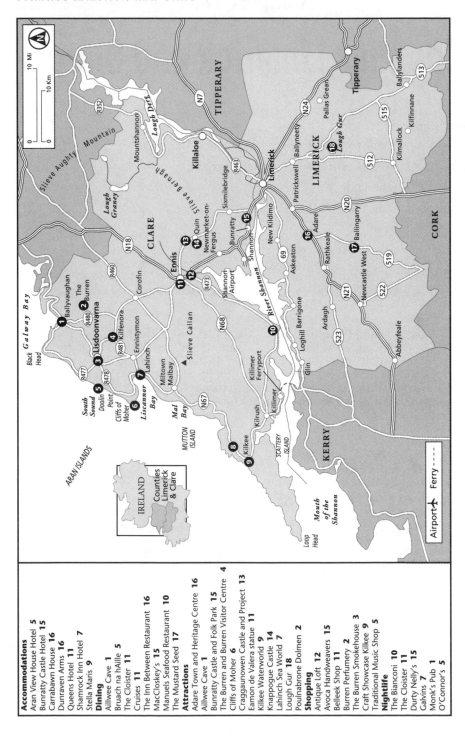

Accommodations
Aran View House Hotel **5**
Bunratty Castle Hotel **15**
Carrabawn House **16**
Dunraven Arms **16**
Queens Hotel **11**
Shamrock Inn Hotel **7**
Stella Maris **5**

Dining
Aillwee Cave **1**
Bruach na hAille **5**
The Cloister **11**
Cruises **11**
The Inn Between Restaurant **16**
MacCloskey's **15**
Manuels Seafood Restaurant **10**
The Mustard Seed **17**

Attractions
Adare Town and Heritage Centre **16**
Aillwee Cave **1**
Bunratty Castle and Folk Park **15**
The Burren and Burren Visitor Centre **4**
Cliffs of Moher **6**
Craggaunowen Castle and Project **13**
Eamon de Valera statue **11**
Kilkee Waterworld **9**
Knappogue Castle **14**
Lahinch Sea World **7**
Lough Gur **18**
Poulnabrone Dolmen **2**

Shopping
Antique Loft **12**
Avoca Handweavers **15**
Belleek Shop **11**
Burren Perfumery **2**
The Burren Smokehouse **3**
Craft Showcase Kilkee **9**
Traditional Music Shop **5**

Nightlife
The Bianconi **10**
The Cloister **11**
Durty Nelly's **15**
Galvins **7**
Monk's Pub **1**
O'Connor's **5**

Some of the major sights in Limerick City and the surrounding area include

- **King John's Castle:** This castle is known as one of the finest examples of a fortified Norman structure in Ireland.

- **Hunt Museum:** Even the most reluctant museum-goer will be wowed by the art at the Hunt, whose collection is destined to be ranked among Europe's finest.

- **Lough Gur:** This incredible mass of prehistoric remnants includes burial mounds, a wedge tomb, and a 4,000-year-old stone circle, all explained at the interpretive centre.

- **Adare Town and Heritage Centre:** Adare is that picturesque town of thatched-roof cottages, narrow streets, and ivy-covered churches that you thought only existed in movies and on post-cards. The Heritage Centre explains how the beautiful village evolved.

County Clare often gets lost somewhere between the dazzle of Counties Galway and Kerry, but people who skip this county are missing out on some of Ireland's best attractions. Clare doesn't boast any large cities, but it's dotted with quaint towns and villages that serve nicely as stopovers and starting points for sightseeing. The narrow streets of Ennis, the main town in the county, are lined with places to stay and see. The tiny towns of Ennistimon, Kilkee, and Lahinch have nothing if not character; the pubs, restaurants, and shops are reason enough to drop in and stay awhile. If you've flown into Shannon Airport, you're in the heart of County Clare anyway and all of the following sights are a short, attractive drive away:

- **Bunratty Castle and Folk Park:** Built in 1425, Bunratty is today one of Ireland's most authentic medieval castles. Bunratty Folk Park is a re-creation of an Irish village of the nineteenth century.

- **Knappogue Castle:** This imposing fifteenth-century castle has been extraordinarily refurbished, and the interior is overflowing with antiques and period furnishings.

- **A Medieval Feast:** Both Bunratty and Knappogue castles host medieval-style banquets, full of meat, mead, and music, plus story-telling and more, and speaking of more . . .

- **The Cliffs of Moher** (pronounced "more"): Rising in places more than 700 feet above the crashing Atlantic and stretching for miles in both directions, these incredible cliffs offer a view of the Clare coast, the Aran Islands, and, on a clear day, mountains as far away as Kerry and Connemara.

- **The Burren:** This vast expanse of limestone, stretching as far as the eye can see, is home to unique plants and animals, massive neolithic tombs, and a maze of underground caves.

- **Aillwee Cave:** Located on the Burren (or rather, beneath it), this cave has ancient stalagmites and stalactites, bridges that span frighteningly deep chasms, and an underground waterfall.

✔ **Craggaunowen Castle and Project:** Ever wonder about life during the Bronze Age? You can see it firsthand here, with actors performing daily tasks in costume, a guide describing life in a ring fort, an Iron Age roadway and cooking site, and a restored castle.

✔ **Kilkee Waterworld:** This indoor underwater playground has pools that swirl and churn and some that gush with geysers.

✔ **Lahinch Sea World:** At this fascinating Atlantic aquarium you'll come face to face with creatures from the Irish coast, like sharks, lobsters, rays, and Conger eels. There's even a touch pool, where kids can plunge their hands into the water and feel the (less-threatening) underwater life.

County Limerick and Limerick City

County Limerick has never exactly been the tourist hub of the country, but most visitors to Ireland end up there at some point in their travels. Whether you're heading north to Galway, west to Clare, or south to Kerry, Limerick is sure to be a stopover — and a worthwhile one, too. The area is rich with history, culture, and distinctly Irish sights, from lush scenery to city and townscapes.

In *Angela's Ashes,* author Frank McCourt described **Limerick City** as a place wracked with poverty, unemployment, alcoholism, and rain — lots of rain. "Out in the Atlantic Ocean," he wrote, "great sheets of rain gathered to drift slowly up the River Shannon and settle forever in Limerick. . . The rain drove us to the church — our refuge, our strength, our only dry place. At Mass, Benediction, novenas, we huddled in great damp clumps, dozing through priest drone, while steam rose again from our clothes to mingle with the sweetness of incense. Limerick gained a reputation for piety, but we knew it was only the rain."

Rain is rain, of course, but you'll be surprised to see how different in all other respects the Limerick of today is from the Limerick McCourt remembers from his youth. In recent years the city has pulled itself up from near dilapidation to become a bustling place full of great restaurants and hotels, all sharing space with historic sights. A stroll along the River Shannon offers a striking vista of the city, and the imposing sight of King John's Castle is never far from view.

Getting to and around Limerick

Shannon International Airport (☎ 061-47-1444), located on the N19, off the N18, south of Ennis and 15 miles west of Limerick, has direct flights from the United States, through Aeroflot, Continental, American Airlines, Delta, and Aer Lingus. Aer Lingus also has flights from all areas of Ireland. Several airlines have flights from England (see "Knowing who flies where" in Chapter 6 for more information).

Limerick City

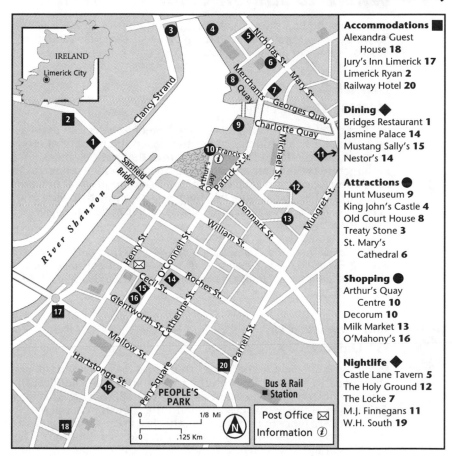

Accommodations ■
Alexandra Guest
House **18**
Jury's Inn Limerick **17**
Limerick Ryan **2**
Railway Hotel **20**

Dining ◆
Bridges Restaurant **1**
Jasmine Palace **14**
Mustang Sally's **15**
Nestor's **14**

Attractions ●
Hunt Museum **9**
King John's Castle **4**
Old Court House **8**
Treaty Stone **3**
St. Mary's
Cathedral **6**

Shopping ●
Arthur's Quay
Centre **10**
Decorum **10**
Milk Market **13**
O'Mahony's **16**

Nightlife ◆
Castle Lane Tavern **5**
The Holy Ground **12**
The Locke **7**
M.J. Finnegans **11**
W.H. South **19**

If you're coming by car, Limerick can be reached by the N20 from Cork, the N21 from Tralee, N24 from Tipperary, N7 from Dublin, or N18 from Ennis and Galway. There are rental car-company desks at Shannon Airport's Arrivals Hall. All the major car rental companies listed in Chapter 7 are represented there.

Irish Rail (☎ **061-31-5555**) services Limerick from Dublin, Cork, Killarney, and other cities throughout Ireland. Trains arrive at Colbert Station, Parnell St., Limerick. **Bus Eireann** (☎ **061-31-333**) has daily service to Limerick City and most towns in County Limerick. For 24-hour automated time schedules out of Limerick, call ☎ **061-31-9911**.

Limerick City is best seen on foot. Park near King John's Castle (for free!) and hoof it from sight to sight. (Parking elsewhere in Limerick City requires disks that can be purchased at local shops.) A car is your best way of getting to the major attractions throughout the county, though Limerick has local bus service that covers the city's suburbs, running from Colbert Station on Parnell St. Taxis can also be picked up at Colbert Station or by calling **Top Cabs** (☎ **061-32-8011**).

Where to stay in County Limerick

In and around Limerick City there are a number of nice places to stay. So whether you prefer to be in the heart of the city or out in the 'burbs, we've got a place for you.

Limerick Ryan
$$–$$$$ Limerick City

Set just outside of the city, this classy hotel has a section that has been around since 1780. Additions have increased the number of rooms and transformed the Ryan into a lovely hotel that echoes times past. The architecture is Georgian, and the grounds are carefully groomed. There's the Ardhu Restaurant (taking its name from the original building), the staid Ardhu Bar, and a more laid-back sports bar with a giant television screen to watch the game. Breakfast is buffet style and is served until noon for you late-risers.

Ardhu House, Ennis Rd., Limerick. ☎ **800-44-UTELL**, *from United States; 061-45-3922. Fax: 061-32-6333. E-mail:* ryan@indigo.ie. *To get there: Take Ennis Rd. (N18) from the Sarsfield Bridge in town. Rates: £70–220 ($103.60–$325.60) double. AE, DC, MC, V.*

Jury's Inn Limerick
$$ Limerick City

Much like a Ramada in the States, this hotel is your standard, comfortable place to stay, and though the rooms are rather nondescript, the place is located in the heart of city. Best of all, though, kids stay free. This is one of the few places in Ireland that doesn't charge per person, so if there are more than two of you, this is a great value (rooms accommodate up to three adults or two adults and two children). There's a parking garage (that you pay to use), an informal restaurant, and a pub.

Lower Mallow St., Limerick. ☎ **061-20-7000**. *Fax: 061-40-0966. E-mail:* info@jurys.com. *To get there: In the city centre, just over the Shannon Bridge (N18). Rates: £88–102 ($130.25–$150.95) double. AE, DC, MC, V.*

Alexandra Guest House
$ Limerick City

This elegant Victorian house sits among a row of classy homes just a few minutes' walk from city centre, on Limerick's main street. Here, rooms are big and comfortable and there's a guest lounge to relax in and enjoy a cup of tea or coffee. The lovely couple who run the guesthouse are happy to organize day tours, and they have nonsmoking rooms — rare. Another nice treat, if you've had you're share of greasy breakfasts, is the healthy meal option you can choose.

O'Connell Ave., Limerick. ☎ 061-31-8472. Fax: 061-40-0433. To get there: O'Connell Ave. is an extension of O'Connell St. from city centre. Rates: £26–45 ($38.50–$66.60) double. MC, V.

Railway Hotel

$ Limerick City

If being in the center of the city is a priority for you, the Railway Hotel is your best option in Limerick. It's across the street from the bus depot and (surprise!) the train station. The Collins family runs the place and is sure to welcome you and ensure your comfort — you can expect personal attention. Rooms are comfy and nicely furnished, and the bar downstairs offers good, hot lunches. From here, you can easily walk to the sights in Limerick City and then (if you're not driving, or want a break) catch a bus for a day tour of your next destination.

Parnell St., Limerick. ☎ 061-41-3653. Fax: 061-41-9762. To get there: Across from the bus-railway station, corner of Parnell and Davis streets. Rates: £44–52 ($65.10–$76.95) double. AE, DC, MC, V.

Dunraven Arms

$$$ Adare

Other hotels are going to seem like roughing it after you stay in the luxurious Dunraven Arms, built in 1792 and surrounded by the well-preserved thatched cottages of little Adare, often called the prettiest village in all of Ireland. The charm of the village is carried into the hotel, where the Old World lives on. Rooms are exquisite, with beautiful antique furniture and even a dressing room. Modern day does seep into some parts, though: There's a pool, steam room, and gym for guests' use.

Main St. (N21), Adare. ☎ 800-44-UTELL, from United States; 061-39-6633. Fax: 061-39-6541. E-mail: dunraven@iol.ie. To get there: From Limerick City, take the N18 southwest on the N21. Rates: £126–157 ($186.50–$232.35) double. AE, DC, MC, V.

Carrabawn House

$ Adare

Attention to detail and warm hospitality are the cornerstones of this luxurious guesthouse. It's not a thatched-roof cottage, but it is a comfortable, roomy house that you're sure to feel welcome in. It's right on Adare's main road, putting all of County Limerick's attractions practically at the doorstep. Rooms are fully equipped with conveniences: television, phone, hair dryer, and tea and coffee.

Killarney Rd. (N21), Adare. ☎ 061-39-6067. Fax: 061-39-6925. To get there: From Limerick City, take the N18 southwest on the N21. Rates: £40–60 ($59.20–$88.80) double. MC, V.

Where to dine in County Limerick

Bridges Restaurant

$$–$$$ **Limerick City** **IRISH-INTERNATIONAL**

Plenty of greenery and light make this dining area relaxing, bright, and cheery, and because it's nestled comfortably in Jury Hotel's lobby, you'll be hard-pressed to miss it. This restaurant is essentially informal, but the quality of the food belies that. The menu is pleasantly varied, and features traditional Irish meals as well as international dishes. There are plenty of lighter options for the not-so-hungry, and Bridges is extremely family friendly.

Jury's Hotel, Ennis Rd., Limerick. ☎ 061-32-7777. To get there: Across the Sarsfield Bridge from city centre. Main courses: £8.50–13.95 ($12.60–$20.65). AE, DC, MC, V. Open: Daily 7:00 a.m.–10:30 a.m., 12:00 p.m.–2:30 p.m., and 6:00 p.m.–10:15 p.m.

Nestor's

$$–$$$ **Limerick City** **QUASI-AMERICAN**

Let the brass rails and wood paneling found throughout this exceptional restaurant be a good indicator of what to expect: classy atmosphere and a tasteful menu. Whether you choose the traditional restaurant or Cafe Bar, you'll get friendly service and delicious, varied food. The restaurant features steaks (the house specialty), Tex-Mex, and pizza, while the Cafe serves continental French (don't be fooled by the fancy title; it's standard cafe-Irish luncheon fare). After 8:00 p.m., you can often enjoy musical accompaniment with your dinner. The quasi-American menu makes this a good place for kids (American ones, at least).

O'Connell St., Limerick. ☎ 061-31-7334. To get there: In city centre. Main courses: £8.50–18.50 ($12.60–$27.40). MC, V. Open: Daily 12:00 p.m.–11:00 p.m.

Jasmine Palace

$$ **Limerick City** **CHINESE**

You've had Chinese food before — most likely from a white paper container with little metal handles. Now's your chance to see what Chinese food can really be. The Irish have a passion for Asian food, and Jasmine Palace delivers (so to speak). Not only is the food fantastic, but the crisp table linens and silver cutlery holders really add to the ambiance. Best of all, this meal will be affordable! (A word to the wise: If you're really starving, get some soup as a starter, because service can be slow.)

O'Connell Mall, O'Connell St., Limerick. ☎ 061-41-2484. To get there: Between Cecil and Roaches streets in the city centre. Main courses: £6.75–12.50 ($10–$18.50). AE, DC, MC, V. Open: Mon–Thurs 5:00 p.m.–12:00 a.m., Fri and Sat 5:00 p.m.–12:30 a.m., Sun 1:00 p.m.–3:00 p.m. and 5:00 p.m.–12:00 a.m.

Mustang Sally's

$$ Limerick City TEX-MEX

South of the border meets the Emerald Isle at Mustang Sally's, Ireland's award-winning Tex-Mex restaurant. The inside resembles any Mexican cantina worth its salt (the kind that rims margarita glasses, that is) and the food is as authentic. When you've had your share of shepherd's pie and lamb stew at other places, drop in here for a memorable enchilada.

103 O'Connell St., Limerick. ☎ 061-40-0417. To get there: In city centre. Main courses: £5.25–12 ($7.75–$17.75). AE, DC, MC, V. Open: Mon–Fri 5:00 p.m.– 11:00 p.m., Sat and Sun 1:00 p.m.–11:30 p.m.

The Mustard Seed

$$$$ Adare IRISH

The surroundings are gorgeous enough to distract your attention, but even endless gardens and a beautiful country manor can't take away the impact of the food at The Mustard Seed. Nothing's thrown together here, and creativity flows. You'll spend a bit more than at many other places mentioned in this book, but you'll get a true gourmet meal in return. Organic vegetables and cheeses are the foundation of the meals, which range from intriguing meatless entrees to savory poultry dishes. The atmosphere is calming and soft arias fill the room.

Echo Lodge, Ballingarry, Adare. ☎ 069-68-508. To get there: From Limerick City, take the N18 southwest to Adare, and then the R519 south for ten minutes. Main courses: £30 fixed price ($44.40). AE, MC, V. Open: Daily 7:00 p.m.–10:00 p.m. Closed Sun and Mon in winter.

The Inn Between Restaurant

$$ Adare SEAFOOD-IRISH

Some thatched-roof cottages offer more than backdrop for great pictures — The Inn Between, for instance. The cheery yellow thatched cottage is nestled between a row of others. Walking in, you might think you're entering a granny's warm kitchen. But soon the bright, airy atmosphere takes over and you're ready to settle in for a great meal. If you're good and hungry, try the always good Inn Between burger, served with fries and homemade relish. If you're looking for something a little less hands-on, there's plenty of more upscale meals, and the Inn's particularly proud of its fish dishes. In the warm months you can sit out back in a lovely courtyard.

Main St. (N21), Adare. ☎ 061-39-6633. To get there: From Limerick City, take the N18 southwest on the N21; the Inn is in the center of the village. Main courses: £6.75–11.50 ($10–$17). AE, DC, MC, V. Open: Daily 10:00 a.m.–10:30 p.m.

Exploring County Limerick: The top attractions

This section includes the big sights in and around Limerick City, as well as some big-time city landmarks.

Hunt Museum
Limerick City

Located in Limerick's beautifully refurbished Custom House, the Hunt's art collection was generously donated by the Hunt family, and includes many world-class pieces that occasionally go out on loan to international exhibitions. The range of art is extremely wide, with Picasso to da Vinci sculptures; medieval paintings, jewelry and crystal; Egyptian, Greek, and Roman pieces; and a great deal of Irish art from as far back as prehistoric times. There's a fabulous shop in the lobby that sells classy souvenirs, and the museum restaurant serves light meals.

The Custom House, Rutland St., Limerick City. ☎ *061-31-2833. To get there: Next to Arthurs Quay, on the River Shannon. Admission: £3 ($4.45) adults, £1.50 ($2.20) students and children. Open: Tues–Sat 10:00 a.m.–5:00 p.m., Sun 2:00 p.m.–5:00 p.m. Time: Two hours.*

King John's Castle
Limerick City

This sturdy, impressive fortress on the River Shannon's banks was the brainchild of King John, who commissioned it in 1210, and whose name will forever be linked with it in the public mind (even though its real name is Limerick Castle). Clearly a place built to keep people out rather than hold court or host lavish parties, this castle is known as one of the finest examples of a fortified Norman structure in Ireland. Fierce war defenses sit in the courtyard (and how often do you get to manhandle a real battering ram?), and you can get a great view of the city from the corner towers. The interior has been completely restored. To get a really complete understanding of the castle's function over the centuries, check out the interpretive centre. Models, displays, and graphics combine to explain the past, and the show "The Story of Limerick" explains the turbulent history of this city in an interesting way.

Nicholas St., Limerick. ☎ *061-41-1201. To get there: East of the Thomond Bridge, corner of Nicholas and Castle streets. Admission: £3.50 ($5.20) adults, £2 ($2.95) students and children. Open: Daily 9:30 a.m.–5:30 p.m. Time: An hour and a half.*

Lough Gur
Southeast of Limerick City

If you're at all interested in prehistoric times, Lough Gur is for you. There are burial mounds, a wedge tomb, and the highlight: the 4,000-year-old Great Stone Circle. Evidence shows this Stone Age settlement was thickly settled in 3000 B.C., but what's left is now this archeological "park" of sorts. The interpretive centre is housed in authentic-looking Stone Age huts right on the location of the original settlement. Inside are models of unearthed tools, weapons, and pottery, plus audio-visual displays. There are regular walking tours of the area, but you're welcome to walk around on your own (and save the cost of entering the interpretive centre).

Lough Gur. ☎ 061-36-1511. To get there: Seven miles southeast of Limerick City off the N24 and R513. Museum admission: £1.90 ($2.20) adults, £1 ($1.50) students. Open: Mid-May–Sept daily 10:00 a.m.–6:00 p.m. Time: Forty-five minutes.

Adare Town and Heritage Centre
Adare

Thatched-roof cottages, narrow streets, ivy-covered churches — the Ireland you dreamed about but figured was an exaggeration of the movies, right? Think again. The picturesque town of Adare is just that, and more. Just a short drive outside of Limerick City, Adare takes great pride in being one of the prettiest villages in the country, if not *the* prettiest. The town history, like its past owners and how it came to be such a quaint and clean place (a concerted effort was put into its renovation), is all explained at the Adare Heritage Centre. In this attractive building is a walk-through display of the town history, plus a model of how Adare looked in the Middle Ages. A 20-minute video also presents the town as it is today — which is interesting, but we suggest you spend the time seeing the real thing instead. Stop into the craft and knitwear shops, and pop into the cafe for some fresh-baked bread. There are books available if you want to learn more about the area.

Main St., Adare. ☎ 061-39-6666. To get there: From Limerick City, take the N18 southwest on the N21; the centre is in the middle of the village. Admission: £2 ($2.95) adults, £1 ($1.50) seniors, students, and children. Open: May–June, Sept and Oct daily 9:00 a.m.–6:00 p.m.; July–Aug daily 9:00 a.m.–7:00 p.m. Time: An hour and a half.

Top Limerick City landmarks

Treaty Stone

This noble slab of limestone is reportedly where the Treaty of Limerick was signed in 1691, ending the bloody Siege of Limerick led by William of Orange. Catholic King James II was defeated, so this stone also marks the sad end of his reign.

Across the Thomand Bridge, facing King John's Castle across the Shannon.

St. Mary's Cathedral

Built in 1172, this is the oldest building in Limerick City. Inside are many beautiful carvings in black oak. Mass is said daily.

Bridge St., one block south of King John's Castle on Nicholas St.

Old Court House

One of the most salacious trials in Ireland's history, the famous Colleen Ba'n trial occurred more than a century ago, but it could be in any of today's newspapers. The case involved the body of a young woman found on the banks of the Shannon. Turns out she was a servant girl, and her murderer was a wealthy landowner. The high-profile case was tried in Limerick's Old Court House, and people came from far and wide to follow it. A public hanging followed, in the center of the city. But the sad fate of Colleen Ba'n resonated among people across the country, and a play was written about the case. An opera followed suit, but presumably because Limerick didn't make for a sexy enough set, it was renamed *The Lilly of Killarney.*

Bridge St., one block south of King John's Castle, across from St. Mary's Cathedral.

Organized tours

Historical walking tours

Led by experienced tour guides, these are two informative and interesting 90-minute tours, one of King's Island (really just a jut of land over the Shannon) and the other of St. Mary's Parish (including Merchant's Quay, St. Mary's Cathedral, King John's Castle, the Treaty Stone, and much more).

Where and when: Leave from St. Mary's Action Centre, 44 Nicholas St., Limerick, daily at 11:00 a.m. and 2:30 p.m. Information: ☎ 061-31-8106. Price: £4 ($5.90) per person, £7.50 ($11.10) family.

Self-guided walking tours

The Tourist Office has two interesting self-guided walking trail maps. The English Town Walk covers the southern part of town and the Viking and Norman influence there. The New Town Walk covers the development of Limerick since the mid-eighteenth century.

Information: Tourist Office, Arthur's Quay, Limerick. ☎ 061-31-7522. Price: One booklet covers both tours and costs £1.50 ($2.20).

Gray Line bus tour

Gray Line runs a full-day comprehensive tour covering the areas around Limerick, the Cliffs of Moher, the Burren, Bunratty Castle, and Galway Bay.

Where and when: Leaves Arthur's Quay, Limerick at 10:00 a.m. daily from May until Oct. Information: ☎ 061-41-3088. Price: £27 ($39.95).

Bus Eireann bus tour

A city "Open Top Tour" with commentary that includes the city's medieval and Georgian history, rivers, bridges, and King John's Castle.

Where and when: Leaves daily from Limerick Tourist Office, Arthur's Quay, June– Aug. Information: ☎ 061-31-3333. Price: £5 ($7.40) adults, £4 ($5.90) seniors and students, £2.50 ($3.70) for children, £12 ($17.75) for a family of two adults and four children.

Angela's Ashes bus tour

Covers the sites and areas from Frank McCourt's Pulitzer prize-winning book, like South's Pub, St. Joseph's Church, and Leamy's School.

Where and when: Tour leaves twice a day Mon–Sat June–Aug. Information: Tourist office, ☎ 061-31-7522. Price: Call for current prices.

Shopping

Limerick, like nearly all of Ireland's major cities, is a hub of shopping for the surrounding region. The main city thoroughfares, O'Connell Street and William Street, are lined with small shops and department stores. You won't find a load of places that sell souvenirs, though. The shopping here is vast and varied, but it mainly suits the needs of the people who live here.

There are two major shopping areas in Limerick City — one new and one old. The **Milk Market** (corner of Wickham and Ellen streets) is a restored medieval marketplace. Bordered by the original city walls, this quaint area offers country produce on Saturdays and local arts and crafts on Fridays. Stalls and open-fronted shops make up the market, where you can find quality secondhand clothes and books, too. The city's real shopping gets done at **The Arthur's Quay Centre,** a modern mall in the heart of town. Inside this open, multistoried mall are 30 stores and places to eat, plus little cafes and child-care facilities.

Here are a couple other, more specific picks.

O'Mahony's

A great selection of books, maps, and stationery so you can catch up on your Joyce or write friends back home in style.

120 O'Connell St., Limerick City. ☎ 061-41-8155.

Decorum

Small but high-quality selection of glassware, pottery, mirrors, rugs, candles, and potpourri.

Arthur's Quay Centre, Limerick City. ☎ 061-41-975.

Pub life

W. H. South

Made famous by Frank McCourt's *Angela's Ashes,* this pub still basks in the glory bestowed by the Pulitzer prize-winning author. The walls bear witness to newspaper accounts of the local uproar that occurred when the book was published (many Limerick natives objected to the negative light it shone on their city). Of course, there are also those that consider McCourt the local boy who made good. Star element aside, South's is a gorgeous pub, all wood and snugs, and always buzzing with people. During the day, hot and delicious lunches are served, and the soup is consistently good.

The Crescent, O'Connell St., Limerick City. ☎ *061-31-8850.*

The Holy Ground

Welcome to the world's only bar in a graveyard! That's right, a corner of the Holy Ground backs up to an old graveyard and a section of it actually sits in it. It was once the home of the graveyard's sexton (or keeper), but was later transformed into a pub (and later still, it was featured on the television program, *Ripley's Believe It or Not*). It's a thrill to go in, have a pint, and be able to say you drank in a graveyard, but that's about the only draw. It's pretty cramped (a few notches above cozy), and although regulars are used to tourists eagerly filing in, they're not always ready to open up to a chat. Go on in; it's a rare opportunity to (legally) be part of something so macabrely weird.

1 Church St., south off of John's Sq., Limerick City. ☎ *061-41-2583.*

Castle Lane Tavern

This beautiful tavern's decor (a medieval recreation, in sort of a Disney way) is so detailed and authentic-looking you might be tempted to summon the barmaid with a hearty "Beer Wench!" but we don't recommend it. We do suggest you grab a drink and maybe some soup or a sandwich and settle into one of the comfortable sunken benches or stools. The tavern is right next to King John's Castle and just down a cobbled alleyway. The whole area gives the pleasant feeling of being in a time warp.

Nicholas St. (next to St. John's Castle), Limerick City. ☎ *061-31-8044.*

The Locke

Dating back to 1724, The Locke is one of Limerick City's oldest and best pubs, and it's got a great location, too, right on the bank of the river, amid some of the city's oldest landmarks — the Old Custom House (now the Hunt Museum) and the Old Court House. When weather permits, there's seating across the street on the quay. Inside, you can warm up at the open fires and listen to traditional music every Tuesday and Sunday night. Hot, home-cooked food is served until 6:00 p.m.

3 George's Quay, Limerick City. ☎ *061-41-3773.*

M.J. Finnegans

Beautifully stylized to echo an old-world appeal, this pub combines elegance with homey comforts. Inside you'll be surrounded by brickwork, wood, stone, and almost distracting vintage decor. If you're hungry, you're in luck; the food is especially good and above the usual pub grub standards, and steaks and seafood are a specialty. There's seating outside for nice weather, so you can enjoy your pint next to a blossoming rose garden. Those of you who've tackled James Joyce's *Finnegans Wake* and recognize the name, you're right on — the tavern is a kind of homage to the opus. Finnegans is just outside of Annacotty on the main Dublin Road.

Dublin Rd., Annacotty (take the N7 south from the city). ☎ *061-33-7338.*

Fast Facts: County Limerick

AREA CODE(S)

061, 063, 068, and 069.

EMERGENCIES-HOSPITAL

Dial ☎ **999** for all emergencies. **St. John's Hospital** is on St. John's Sq., Limerick (☎ **061-41-5822**).

GENEALOGY RESOURCES

Contact the **Limerick Regional Archives,** The Granary, Michael St. ☎ **061-41-0777;** Fax: 061-41-5125.

INFORMATION

For visitor information, go to the **tourist office at Arthur's Quay,** Limerick (☎ **061-31-7522**),

or **Shannon Airport** (☎ **061-47-1664**). Both are open year-round. They can also provide reservation services. For telephone directory assistance, dial ☎ **1190.**

INTERNET

Websters Internet Cafe, 44 Thomas St., Limerick (☎ **061-31-2066**), has Internet access for Hotmail and AOL, plus printing capabilities.

POST OFFICE

The General Post Office is on Post Office Ln., off Lower Cecil St., Limerick (☎ **061- 31-4636**).

County Clare

Sadly, visitors to Ireland are often so drawn by the giant tourist magnets known as Counties Galway and Kerry that they ignore County Clare completely. Well, listen up: We're going to change that, because we don't want you to miss out on Clare's attractions, which we think are among Ireland's best. Think about it — where else can you poke around in completely restored and furnished castles from the Middle Ages (**Bunratty** and **Knappogue**), see prehistoric villages and nineteenth-century towns come to life (**Craggaunowen Castle** and **Bunratty Folk Park**), walk across a unique natural phenomenon (**the Burren**), stand on the precipice of cliffs that will take your breath away (**the Cliffs of Moher**)? And that's just for starters. The county is dotted with quaint towns and villages that serve nicely either as stopovers or starting points for sightseeing.

Getting to and around County Clare

Shannon International Airport (☎ 061-47-1444), located on the N19, off the N18, south from County Clare's main town of Ennis and 15 miles west of Limerick, has direct flights from the United States through Aeroflot, Continental, American, Delta, and Aer Lingus. Aer Lingus also has flights from all areas of Ireland, and several airlines have flights from England. See Chapter 6 for more information.

If you're coming by car, take the N18 north from Limerick or south from Galway to Ennis. There are rental car-company desks at Shannon Airport's Arrivals Hall representing all the major car rental companies listed in Chapter 7. The **Shannon Ferry Ltd.** runs a car ferry connecting Tarbert, County Kerry, with Killimer, County Clare, bypassing Limerick. It runs year-round between 7:30 a.m. and 9:00 p.m. (until 7:00 p.m. October through March) and costs £7 ($10.35) one way, £10 ($14.80) round trip.

Irish Rail (☎ 065-40-444) services Ennis at the Ennis Rail Station on Station Road. All routes run through Limerick. **Bus Eireann** (☎ 065-682-4177) travels year-round to Ennis, Ballyvaughan, Doolin, Kilkee, and most towns in County Clare.

Where to stay in County Clare

Bunratty Castle Hotel
$$–$$$ Bunratty

This bright yellow Georgian hotel is in the center of Bunratty village, with the famed Bunratty Castle pub Durty Nelly's just across the street. The hotel is new and all rooms are tastefully decorated in Irish traditional style. Rooms have every convenience, including air conditioning — pretty rare in Ireland. Everyone is friendly and willing to help, and from here County Clare's best sights are only a short drive. Kathleen's Irish pub is pleasant and serves food, and you're likely to run across plenty of people to chat with.

Bunratty. ☎ 061-70-7034. To get there: Off the N18 between Limerick and Ennis. Rates: £79–150 ($116.90–$222) double. AE, DC, MC, V.

Aran View House Hotel
$$ Doolin

Built in 1736, this gorgeous Georgian house overlooks some of Ireland's most fabulous vistas — you can see the Cliffs of Moher and the Aran Islands while you're being pampered. Rooms are big and tasteful, and the house sits on 100 acres of farmland. The restaurant is comfortable and full of atmosphere, and fish is the house specialty. Horse riding, golf, and fishing are all close, too.

Coast Rd., Doolin. ☎ 065-707-4061. Fax: 065-707-4540. To get there: On the road to the Cliffs of Moher, R487 northwest from Lahinch or southwest from Lisdoonvarna. Rates: £60–110 ($88.80–$162.80) double. AE, DC, MC, V. Closed Nov–Mar.

Shamrock Inn Hotel
$$ Lahinch

This little hotel, located in the heart of the pretty seaside resort town of Lahinch, is pleasant and has it all. Rooms are nicely decorated and have a TV, hair dryer, and tea and coffee. The restaurant is popular in town, which is no surprise. It's cozy and relaxing, the menu is varied, and they're happy to cater to your tastes. In the pub, food is served during the day and music lilts at night.

Main St., Lahinch. ☎ 065-708-1700. Fax: 065-708-1029. To get there: Take the N85 northwest from Ennis. Rates: £60–80 ($88.80–$118.40) double. AE, MC, V.

Queens Hotel
$$ Ennis

Everything about this hotel is perfectly charming. Old World hospitality reigns, and the style is traditional Irish. From here, in the center of Ennis, all of County Clare's sights are only a stone's throw. The bedrooms are completely decked out, with TV, video player, and radio. At the famous Cruise's Pub and Restaurant (which adjoins the hotel), you'll find home-cooked Irish food and traditional music nightly.

Abbey St., Ennis. ☎ 065-682-8963. Fax: 065-682-8628. E-mail: stay@ irishcourthotels.com. *To get there: In city centre. Rates: £60–110 ($88.80–$162.80) double. AE, DC, MC, V.*

Stella Maris
$ Kilkee

This small, family-run guesthouse located in the heart of town perfectly reflects the quaintness of Kilkee. Open peat fires burn inside, or you can sit out on the veranda overlooking the bay. The staff is friendly and welcoming, and concerned with making your stay a good one. The bar features traditional music and hearty, home-cooked food.

O'Connell St., Kilkee. ☎ 065-905-6455. Fax: 065-906-0006. To get there: Take N67 south from Ennistimon or N68 southwest from Ennis. Rates: £40–56 ($59.20–$82.90) double. AE, MC, V.

Where to dine in County Clare

MacCloskey's
$$$$ Bunratty IRISH

This restaurant has been called one of the finest in Ireland by visitors and natives alike. Set in the downstairs of a nineteenth-century mansion,

MacCloskey's is intimate and cozy, and great care is taken to ensure you enjoy everything about the meal. The food is Irish in spirit, with traditional and nouveau flair. Mussels in champagne, crab crepes, and duck a l'orange are some house specialities. Finish off with one of the incredible desserts — go on, do it!

Bunratty Mews House, Bunratty. ☎ *061-36-4082. To get there: Off the N18 north of Limerick. Main courses: £26 fixed price ($38.50). AE, DC, MC, V. Open: Mar–Dec Tues–Sat 7:00 p.m.–9:30 p.m.; July and Aug daily 6:30 p.m.–9:30 p.m. Reservations required.*

Manuels Seafood Restaurant

$$$ Kilkee SEAFOOD

Locally caught fish is the highlight of the menu here, and from the huge windows overlooking the Atlantic you can see just where your dinner's coming from. The nautical decor is nice and the food is even better. Indulge in lobster or salmon, or show your land-lubbing side with a steak or chicken dish. Dinner is often made and delivered to your table by the owners.

On the N67, Corbally, Kilkee. ☎ *065-905-6211. To get there: One mile north of Kilkee on the road to the Cliffs of Moher (N67). Main courses: £8.50–18.50 ($12.58–$27.40). DC, MC, V. Open: April–mid-Sept daily 6:30 p.m.–10:30 p.m. Reservations required.*

The Cloister

$$$ Ennis SEAFOOD

Delicious food is served all day at this restaurant, which sits in the shadow of an ancient abbey. The interior is warm and refined, and turf fires burn. The daytime menu features local mussels, fresh fish, and lively sandwiches. The quality of the food becomes obvious when the place fills up at night with people who clearly come time and again. For dinner try the warm farmhouse cheese salad or Ballyvaughan mussels. Meals come with fabulous bread — you'll be tempted to stuff yourself before your meal even comes.

Club Bridge, Abbey St., Ennis. ☎ *065-682-9521. To get there: It's in the Ennis town centre. Main courses: £11–16 ($16.30–$23.70). AE, MC, V. Open: Daily 12:00 p.m.– 10:30 p.m.*

Bruach na hAille

$$$ Doolin SEAFOOD

This cottagelike restaurant offers a simple menu, but the food is delicious. Local seafood is the highlight of the fare, and it's prepared in a unique way. Everything's incredibly fresh and from the area. Seafood's not the only thing on the menu, but don't miss the baked seafood au gratin or fillet of sole in cider with shellfish cream sauce.

On the coast road, Roadford, Doolin. ☎ *065-707-4120. To get there: Drive through Doolin north along the coast road (R479) one mile. Main courses: £8.90–14 ($13.15–$20.85). No credit cards. Open: Apr–Oct daily 6:00 p.m.–9:30 p.m.*

Cruises

$$ Ennis IRISH

Stone walls and open fires characterize this homey restaurant and pub, and you're sure to get a hot, hearty meal. Pub grub ranges from club sandwiches and seafood soups to the house special — the thick, meaty Friars Irish Stew. Expect more selection at night, when meals become quite sophisticated, from seafood and steaks to vegetarian offerings. Often, music sessions erupt during dinner, but aren't so noisy that they'll interrupt your enjoyment of the meal.

Abbey St., Ennis. ☎ *065-684-1800. To get there: Ennis town centre, next to the Queens Hotel. Main courses: £6.40–13.50 ($9.45–$20). AE, DC, MC, V. Open: Daily 12:30 p.m.–10:30 p.m.*

Exploring County Clare

In addition to the top attractions listed in the following entries, there are some other sites that are worth the time it takes to just buzz by and take a look. And then, of course, there's golf. . .

The top attractions

Bunratty Castle and Folk Park

Bunratty

This formidable castle, built in 1425 and pillaged many times over, is one of Ireland's biggest attractions. It's one of the most authentic medieval castles in the country, and great care has been taken to ensure the interior is as it was in the fifteenth century, with furnishings and tapestries that replicate the era. Great halls and tiny stairways characterize the castle, and the dungeon is so eerie you just might get a serious spook unless you bring someone down there with you. On the castle grounds is the Bunratty Folk Park, a re-creation of a nineteenth-century Irish village. You can poke your head into farmhouses, a blacksmith's forge, and a watermill, and go down a typical village street that has it all: pub, post office, school, pawn shop, doctor's house, printers, hardware shop, and more. The pub, Mac's, is real! Stop in for a bite and a drink. This really is an awesome and complete reproduction — don't miss it.

Bunratty. The short exit ramp off the N18 takes you to the entrance of the castle. ☎ *061-36-1511. To get there: On the N18 north of Limerick. Admission: £5 ($7.40) adults, £4.50 ($6.65) seniors and students, £2.50 ($3.70) children. Open: June–Aug daily 9:00 a.m.–7:30 p.m.; Sept–May daily 9:30 a.m.–5:30 p.m. Time: At least two hours.*

Knappogue Castle

Quinn

This imposing fifteenth-century castle has seen its share of history. Built by the McNamaras, it was the pride of the tribe, which dominated the area for 1,000 years. But the stronghold had its troubles too. In the 1700s Cromwell's troops occupied the castle for ten years, and during the War of Independence (1920s) revolutionary forces camped within its walls.

The castle has been extraordinarily refurbished, and the interior is overflowing with antiques and period furnishings.

Just off the Ennis-Killmury roads, Quinn. ☎ *061-36-8103. To get there: Off the R469 southeast from Ennis. Admission: £2.40 ($3.55) adult, £1.60 ($2.40) children. Open: May–Oct daily 9:30 a.m.–5:30 p.m. Time: One hour.*

The Cliffs of Moher
On the Atlantic Coast

"Spectacular" doesn't begin to describe the view from these breathtaking cliffs. At places they rise more than 700 feet above the crashing Atlantic, and stretch for miles in both directions. On the highest cliff is O'Brien's Tower, built in the 1800s as a viewing point for tourists. From the tower you can see the span of the Clare coast, the Aran Islands, and, on a clear day, mountains as far away as Kerry and Connemara. When it's sunny, the cliffs take on a purple hue (hence the "Purple Cliffs of Moher" of story and song), and when the wind and rain blow in, it can be a bit harrowing up there. There's a lovely little shop and tearoom in the visitor centre.

Be extremely careful when walking along the cliffs! There are no rails separating you from the rocks far below, and sometimes wind gusts can push you around, so take extreme care when approaching the edges. Watch kids carefully, too. They might be tempted to climb down to some lower cliff shelves, but it's not at all a good idea.

Off the R478 on the Atlantic coast. ☎ *065-708-1565. To get there: R487 northwest from Lahinch or southwest from Lisdoonvarna. O'Brien's Tower Admission: £1 ($1.50) adult, 60p (90 cents) children. Parking: £1 ($1.50). Open: May–June daily 9:00 a.m.–6:30 p.m.; July–Aug daily 9:00 a.m.–9:00 p.m.; Sept–April daily 9:30 a.m.–6:00 p.m. O'Brien's Tower opens a half-hour later and closes a half-hour earlier than regular times. Time: Forty-five minutes.*

The Burren and Burren Visitor Centre
Kilfenora

Don't miss this absolute phenomenon of Ireland — a vast expanse of limestone, as far as you can see, and the home to unique plants and animals. The name Burren comes from the Irish for "rocky place," and that's pretty much what it is. You won't find any bogs or pastures in this area of Ireland. Still, man settled here ages ago, a fact proved by the massive neolithic tombs located in the area. The distinct spread of limestone covers a maze of underground caves where water drains from the ground. Plants that otherwise only live in the Arctic and Mediterranean thrive here, thanks to the limestone and the climate. And 26 species of butterflies have been seen here, including one that's indigenous to the area, the Burren Green. From various spots on the Burren, you can see for miles and get views of Clare and Galway Bay. The Burren Display Centre is a good reference and helps explain this amazing area.

The Burren Display Centre is located in Kilfenora. ☎ *065-7088-030. To get there: Take the R476 southeast from Lisdoonvarna. Centre admission: £2.20 ($3.25) adult, £1.60 ($2.35) seniors, £1 ($1.50) children. The Centre is open: July and Aug daily 9:30 a.m.–7:00 p.m., Mar–Oct daily 10:00 a.m.–5:00 p.m. Time: One hour.*

You've been invited to the castle for a feast!

History comes alive at night when Bunratty and Knappogue castles stage their medieval banquets, complete with a feast of food and lively entertainment. At **Bunratty,** the Earl of Thomond hosts the amazingly authentic evening, beginning with a cup of honey mead, heading into a delicious feast, and finishing with period entertainment. The banquet at **Knappogue** celebrates the women of Celtic Ireland, both historical and mythical — queens, saints, and sinners. The entertainment centers around storytelling, singing, and music, all masterfully done, leaving you haunted and enchanted.

Bunratty's Golden Vale farmhouse also hosts **Traditional Irish Nights,** which are banquets taken down a notch, but no less fun and delicious. Here you won't dine with royalty, but rather with the *Fear an Tí,* or man of the house. You'll be very welcome to have a homey meal (Irish stew) and wine with the head of the Golden Vale farmhouse within the Folk Park, and listen to traditional music that's likely to get your toes tapping. Irish instruments, like the pipes and bodhrán (drum), accompany singers and dancers for your entertainment. A fun, lively night!

For reservations to either Bunratty or Knappogue, call **Shannon Medieval Castle Banquets** at ☎ **061-360-788.**

Aillwee Cave
The Burren

You'll get a better understanding of the effects of the Burren on the land once you climb into the depths of Aillwee Cave. Your guide will take you down into this vast cave, where you'll see ancient stalagmites and stalactites, cross bridges that span frighteningly deep chasms, and get wet from the crashing underground waterfall. And you'll be taken into the eerie hibernation chamber of the extinct brown bear. Once back above ground you can shop in the many craft shops selling minerals, fossils, and handmade gifts. There's a dairy where you can watch cheese being made and a tearoom where light snacks are served. There's also a terrace, where you can have a drink and enjoy the view.

The Burren, Ballyvaughan. ☎ *065-707-7036. To get there: Off the R480 south of Ballyvaughan. Admission: £4.75 ($7.13) adult, £3.75 ($5.63) students, £2.75 ($4.13) children. Open: July and Aug daily 10:00 a.m.–6:30 p.m.; mid-Mar to Nov daily 10:00 a.m.–5:30 p.m. Time: Two hours.*

Craggaunowen Castle and Project
Quinn

Ever wonder about life during prehistoric times? You can see it first-hand here, where the life and times of man during the Bronze Age comes alive. Yabba-dabba-doo! You'll see actors performing daily tasks in costume, a guide describing life in a ring fort, and an Iron Age roadway and cooking site. Probably the most interesting site is the *crannóg,* a man-made home made from mud and reeds, sitting right in the middle of a lake (a type of construction that helped protect against enemy pillage). The project surrounds Craggaunowen Castle, the restored home to an impressive furniture collection from the Hunt Museum in Limerick.

Quinn. ☎ 061-36-7178. To get there: Ten miles east of Ennis off the R469. Admission: £4 ($5.90) adult, £2.75 ($4.05) children. Open: Apr–Oct 10:00 a.m.–6:00 p.m. Time: An hour.

Kilkee Waterworld
Kilkee

This indoor underwater playground is hours of fun for the whole family. Drop the kids in the Tommy Turtles Pool or Bubbles & Currents while you relax in The Lazy River. There are pools that swirl and churn and some that gush with geysers. The Dolphin's Rest serves snacks.

Esplanade, East End, Kilkee. ☎ 065-905-6855. To get there: Take N67 south from Ennistimon or N68 southwest from Ennis. Admission: Varies on length of stay; there are adult and children prices. Open: Mar–Oct daily 10:00 a.m.–7:00 p.m. Time: Varies.

Lahinch Sea World
Lahinch

This fascinating Atlantic aquarium will entertain all ages. You'll come face to face with creatures from the Irish coast, like sharks, lobsters, rays, and Conger eels. Kids love the touch pool, where they can plunge their hands into the water and feel underwater life. There's a fisherman's cabin, lobster breeding station, and regular feeding sessions. Want a chance to swim like the fishes? Lahinch Sea World also has a huge indoor heated pool, jacuzzi, sauna, and kiddie pool! The souvenir shop is well stocked, and the cafe serves light meals and snacks.

The Promenade, Lahinch. ☎ 065-708-1900. To get there: West of Ennistimon on the N67. Admission: Aquarium Only £3.95 ($5.85) adult, £3 ($4.45) seniors and students, £2.50 ($3.70) children, £11.50 ($17) family of two adults and three children. Pool and Aquarium £6.25 ($9.25) adult, £4.95 ($7.35) seniors and students, £3.95 ($5.85) children, £16.95 ($25.10) family of two adults and three children. Open: June–Aug daily 9:00 a.m.–9:30 p.m. Time: Two hours.

The top landmarks

Poulnabrone Dolmen
The Burren

These structures are ancient burial monuments, dating back 6,000 years. They're a prominent aspect of the Burren, and more people photograph this landmark than almost any other in Ireland. Go on — stand under the humongous stone and pretend like you're holding it up. Say "Cheese!"

The Burren. To get there: Off R480 south from Ballyvaughan.

Eamon de Valera Statue

Ennis

Eamon de Valera, Irish freedom fighter, president, and prime minister, is honored with a bronze statue in the Ennis town park. De Valera was born in New York; his American citizenship kept him from facing the firing squad after his part in the Easter Rising of 1916.

Ennis. To get there: In the town park off Gort Rd. (R352).

Other fun things to do

- ✔ **Golfing at the Lahinch Golf Club:** Now you're golfing in Ireland! High elevations provide amazing views of sea and valley and local goats are known to cross the fairway. There are two 18-hole courses here, and one is a championship course.

  Lahinch, County Clare. ☎ **065-708-1003.** Par: 72. Fees: ₤25 ($37) midweek, ₤30 ($44.40) weekends.

- ✔ **Dancing Irish-style:** Some people spend their whole lives learning those magnificent Irish dance steps. Lucky for you, it only takes a night . . . sort of. Every Wednesday in Ennis between May and October there's Irish dancing, and you're welcome to come and learn a few steps. Who knows? Drop in on enough sessions and you could be the next Michael Flatley!

  Fees: ₤1.50 ($2.20). For information call Dick O'Connell (☎ **065-20-996**). Venue changes periodically.

Organized tours

DolphinWatch Boat Tour

A fun and informative two-hour boat trip among a resident group of friendly bottleneck dolphins. And the boat is equipped with a hydrophone to listen to dolphins communicate underwater.

Runs daily May–Sept, weather permitting. You must book ahead. Leaves from the port village of Carrigaholt. Information: ☎ 065-905-8156 or 088-258-4711. Price: £10 ($14.80) adults, £6 ($8.90) children (children under five are not permitted).

Healy's bus tours

This is the best coach tour of the sights of County Clare, covering the Burren, Poulnabrone Dolmen, the Cliffs of Moher, Aillwee Cave, and more for a bargain of a price.

Departs from Salthill Tourist Office (on the main road next to the Atlanta Aquarium) at 9:45 a.m. and Galway Tourist Office (Merchants Rd.) at 10:00 a.m. Returns 5:00 p.m. Runs daily in summer. Call for schedule in off-season. Information: ☎ 091- 77-0066 or 088-259-0160. Tickets can be purchased on the bus or at the Galway and Salthill tourist offices. Price: £10 ($14.80) adults, £8 ($11.85) students, £5 ($7.40) children.

O'Neachtain bus tours

This tour rivals the Healy tour by covering several extra sights, such as Lisdoonvarna and Leamanah Castle. But this tour takes the same amount of time as the other — and therefore allows you less time at each place. It's a tradeoff.

Departs from Salthill Tourist Office (see previous entry) at 9:55 a.m. and Galway Tourist Office (stop marked "O'Neachtain") at 9:45 a.m. Returns 4:45 p.m. Information: ☎ *091-56-5056. Price: £10 ($14.80) adults, £8 ($11.84) students, £5 ($7.40) children.*

Shopping

Antique Loft

Interesting and unique pieces of all varieties, styles, and periods.

Clarecastle (south of Ennis and north of Limerick on the N18). ☎ *065-41-969.*

Avoca Handweavers

This is the newly relocated and bigger shop housing the famous clothing and accessories from the Avoca Mill in County Wicklow.

Bunratty (off the N18 north of Limerick). ☎ *061-36-4029.*

Belleek Shop

More than crafts, this is the best store in the area for Waterford Crystal, china, Irish tweed, and cashmere fashions. They have top-notch customer service as well.

36 Abbey St., on the corner of Francis St. in the Ennis city centre. ☎ *065-682-9607.*

Burren Perfumery

The oldest perfumery in Ireland, Burren Perfumery uses local flora to create unique fragrances.

Carron (take the R480 to the Carron turnoff; shop is located just north of town). ☎ *065-89-102.*

The Burren Smokehouse

This gourmet store and visitor centre sells the finest smoked Irish Atlantic salmon. They own the neighboring pub, The Roadside Tavern, which serves up freshly smoked salmon, trout, mackerel, and eel.

Lisdoonvarna, on the N67 south of Ballyvaughan and north of Ennistimon. ☎ *065-74-432.*

Craft Showcase Kilkee

The store is new but the crafts, from ceramics and sheepskin rugs to Celtic jewelry and basketware, are as authentic and traditional as you'll find.

O'Connell St., Kilkee (on the main Kilkee-Kilrush Road, on the right from Kilkee city centre). ☎ *065-56-880.*

Traditional Music Shop

The best shop in the area for Irish instruments (like an authentic tin whistle), plus a large variety of Irish music on CD and cassette — a little traveling music for the rental car!

Doolin, off the N67 west of Lisdoonvarna. ☎ *065-74-407. Closed mid-Oct through Mar.*

Pub life

Durty Nelly's

No trip to Clare is complete without a stop into this world-famous pub. Since 1620 this tavern has been a thirst-quencher for everyone from the guards who once protected Bunratty Castle to the tourists who explore it today. The interior looks like it hasn't changed over the centuries, with the sawdust-strewn floors, low lighting from lanterns, and traditional music sessions that commence at any time in any room of the pub. There's seating outside for nice days, and a pretty good restaurant upstairs.

Next to Bunratty Castle, County Clare (take N18 north from Limerick). ☎ *061-36-4861.*

Galvins

You won't be able to sit still in this interesting pub — there's too much to see. Don't worry, they're used to people wandering around with a pint and looking at the pictures that line the walls. When it was built in 1840, stones from the nearby shore were used in the construction. It's a great place to hear music, and musicians passing through the area often drop in to play.

Church St., Lahinch (in the center of town). ☎ *065-81-045.*

O'Connor's

If the prospect of hearing Irish music plays any part in your choice of pubs, then O'Connor's is for you. This is one of the premier spots in the country for traditional sessions, and fans travel from all over to hear them. The family has run this combination pub and market for more than 150 years. The pub sits amid a row of thatched fisherman cottages and really comes to life at night.

Doolin, off the N67 west of Lisdoonvarna. ☎ *065-707-4168.*

The Cloister

This pub sits next to the famed Ennis friary, and in the summer you can sit outside within arm's length of the landmark. Inside, the pub is comfortable and homey, and pub grub is served all day.

Abbey St., Ennis (in the center of town). ☎ *065-682-9521.*

The Bianconi

Friendly service is a staple of this beautiful pub, decorated with plenty of hard wood and comfortable seats. The food is good, and the attention to quality is clear. Prices are great, too. There's music on weekends.

Kildysert (take the N18 to the R473 south; it's on the shore of the River Shannon). ☎ *065-683-2266.*

Monk's Pub

A taste of the olde world is retained here, where peat fires burn and rustic furnishings invite you to take a seat. It's right on the water, and good pub grub is served all day. Music fills the air most nights.

Ballyvaughan (take the R476 to the R480 north from Ennis). ☎ *065-707-7059.*

Fast Facts: County Clare

AREA CODE(S)
061 and 065.

EMERGENCIES-POLICE
Dial ☎ 999 for all emergencies.

GENEALOGY RESOURCES
Contact the **Clare Heritage Centre**, Church St., Corofin (☎ 065-683-7955).

INFORMATION
For visitor information go to **the tourist office** at Clare Rd., Ennis (☎ 065-28-366), open

year-round. They can also provide reservation services. For telephone directory assistance, dial ☎ 1190.

INTERNET
MacCools Internet Cafe, Brewery Lane, Ennis (☎ 065-682-1988), and **Kilrush Internet Cafe**, The Monastery, Kilrush (☎ 065-51-061), have Internet access for Hotmail and AOL, plus printing capabilities.

Chapter 18

County Galway and Galway City

●●●

In This Chapter

▶ Getting to the Aran Islands

▶ Exploring the vast and amazing Connemara National Park

▶ Riding the rides in Salthill

▶ Navigating Kylemore Abbey

▶ Shopping for your Aran sweater and everything else on your list

▶ Pub-crawling through Galway

●●●

*N*ot making it to every major county in Ireland is no crime, but County Galway's just plain too great to pass up. It's one of the few counties that combines a major city, great small towns, and a healthy dose of scenic outdoors. Given all of its assets, Galway should head your "To Do" list.

What's Where? Galway's Major Attractions

Galway City comes first, serving as the gateway to the rest of the county. This is a major city in Ireland, with as great a variety of places to eat, sleep, drink, and shop as any city worth visiting. But don't be fooled: Inside that city veneer is the heart of a small town, with all the welcome and approachability that implies. Amazingly, while keeping apace of fast-moving progress of the day, Galway manages to hold onto the easygoing way of the Irish: It's both a buzzing college town and a star on the European stage of cities.

Anchored by **Eyre Square** (Eyre is pronounced "air"), a pretty park surrounded by hotels and pubs, the city's picturesque streets stretch down to the harbor. It's said that Christopher Columbus made his last European stop here before setting sail on his famous trip for the New World. Today most people don't arrive by galleon, but tourism is still huge here. Even so, there's nothing tacky about the city. Discriminating shoppers won't be disappointed by the quaint little stores; and pubs and restaurants accommodate city dwellers and visitors alike.

County Galway

Accommodations ■
Alcock and Brown Hotel **3**
Hotel Carraroe Best Western **6**
O'Grady's Sunnybank
    Guesthouse **3**
Dining ◆
Mitchell's Restaurant **3**
O'Grady's **3**

Attractions ●
Aran Islands **7**
Connemara National Park and
    Visitors Centre **2**
Coole Park **10**
Derrygimlagh Bog **4**

Dunguaire Castle **9**
Kylemore Benedictine Abbey **1**
Salthill **8**
Thoor Ballylee **11**
Shopping ●
Roundstone Music **5**
Nightlife ◆
E.J. Kings **3**

Galway's not exactly known for its attractions or major historical sites, but the city itself is enough of a draw. Among other things, it supposedly has more stone carvings of mermaids than any other place in Ireland. Mermaids? Sure. Mermaids play an integral part in Irish folklore, often representing something that's alluring but dangerous. Galway, being such a sea town, has apparently taken them to heart. You can see some in the window of St. Nicholas's, in the center of town. According to legend, if you happen to see a real mermaid sitting on a rock, it means bad luck is coming your way. So don't stare out at the rocks too long! Instead, spend your time walking around the city, which you can cover easily in an hour or so — though if you don't stay overnight you won't get the chance to dip into Galway's vibrant pub scene.

Galway City

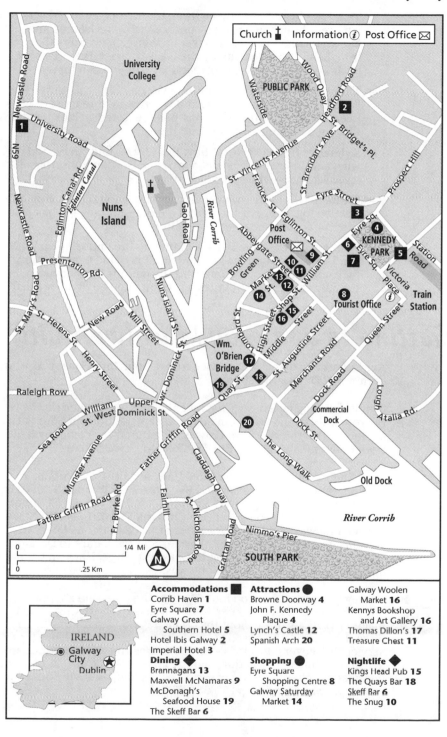

Church ✝ Information ⓘ Post Office ✉

University College

PUBLIC PARK

Newcastle Road

University Road

N59

Waterside

Wood Quay

Headford Road

St. Brendan's Ave.

St. Bridget's Pl.

Prospect Hill

1

2

Eglinton Canal Rd.

Eglinton Canal

Newcastle Road

Nuns Island

✝

Gaol Road

River Corrib

St. Vincents Avenue

Frances St.

Eglinton St.

Fyre Street

Eyre Sq.

3

4

KENNEDY PARK

Station Road

Presentation Rd.

St. Mary's Road

St. Helens St.

New Road

Nuns Island St.

Mill Street

Abbeygate Street

Bowling Green

Post Office ✉

Market St.

Shop St.

William St.

Eyre Sq.

6

7

5

Victoria Place

9

10

11

13

12

14

High Street

Middle Street

15

16

St. Augustine Street

8 Tourist Office

ⓘ

Train Station

Henry Street

Raleigh Row

William St. West

Upper Dominick St.

Lwr. Dominick St.

Lombard St.

Wm. O'Brien Bridge

17

Quay St.

18

19

St. Augustine Street

Merchants Road

Dock Road

Queen Street

Lough Atalia Rd.

Sea Road

Munster Avenue

Father Griffin Road

Claddagh Quay

20

Dock St.

Commercial Dock

The Long Walk

Old Dock

Father Griffin Road

Fr. Burke Rd.

Fairhill

St. Nicholas Road

Grattan Road

Nimmo's Pier

River Corrib

SOUTH PARK

IRELAND

Galway City

Dublin

0   1/4 Mi
0   .25 Km

Ⓝ

Accommodations ■
Corrib Haven **1**
Eyre Square **7**
Galway Great
    Southern Hotel **5**
Hotel Ibis Galway **2**
Imperial Hotel **3**
Dining ◆
Brannagans **13**
Maxwell McNamaras **9**
McDonagh's
    Seafood House **19**
The Skeff Bar **6**

Attractions ●
Browne Doorway **4**
John F. Kennedy
    Plaque **4**
Lynch's Castle **12**
Spanish Arch **20**
Shopping ●
Eyre Square
    Shopping Centre **8**
Galway Saturday
    Market **14**

Galway Woolen
    Market **16**
Kennys Bookshop
    and Art Gallery **16**
Thomas Dillon's **17**
Treasure Chest **11**
Nightlife ◆
Kings Head Pub **15**
The Quays Bar **18**
Skeff Bar **6**
The Snug **10**

Moving out from Galway City, the major attractions include

- ✔ **The Aran Islands:** On these three isolated islands, old ways flourish even though many, many people visit. The islands are best known for the thick, cabled wool fishermen sweaters that come from here. **Rossaveal,** along the Galway coast, is the closest harbor and will be the shortest boat trip you can take.

- ✔ **Thoor Ballylee:** Located south of Galway City, this tower was poet W. B. Yeats's summer home, and where he wrote most of his work. Everything about the place has been restored to look just like it did when the famous poet lived here.

- ✔ **Kylemore Benedictine Abbey:** Built by an English tycoon for his wife, and today the home of a group of Belgian nuns, this abbey looks like a storybook castle.

- ✔ **Clifden:** This little town is the unofficial capital of Connemara. Nestled in a valley at the foot of a mountain range, it has a number of great accommodations for visitors.

- ✔ **Connemara National Park:** Combining the imposing mountains of the Twelve Bens range, boglands that provide peat for the area's fuel, unique flora and fauna, and the famous Connemara ponies, the 5,000-acre park provides a breathtaking day's scenic driving.

Getting to and around Galway City

Aer Lingus has daily local service from Dublin into Galway Airport, in Carnmore (☎ 091-75-5569).

If you're driving to Galway City, take the N18 from Limerick, the N4 and N6 from Dublin, and N17 from Sligo. Most attractions in County Galway are located off the N59 from Galway. The rental car company in downtown Galway is **Budget** (☎091-56-6376), on Eyre Square.

Irish Rail (☎ 091-56-144) services Galway daily from Dublin. The Ceannt Station is off Eyre Square. **Bus Eireann** (☎ 091-56-2000) travels year-round to Galway (Ceannt Station) and most towns in County Galway. The private coach service **CityLink** (☎ 091-56-4163) travels between Galway and Dublin for a better price than Bus Eireann. CityLink departs from Galway's Forster St. Coach Park to Dublin Airport and leaves from Dublin to Galway at SuperMacs on O'Connell St., Dublin. Price: £10 ($14.80) one way.

Galway City is best seen on foot. Many of the pubs and shopping areas are not accessible at all by car. Naturally, a car is best for getting to the major attractions throughout the county. Parking in Galway City requires disks that can be purchased at local shops. Galway also has a local bus service that covers the city's suburbs. Buses run along Eyre Square and go to Connemara, Salthill, and the coast. Call ☎ 091-56-2000 for information. Alternatively, taxis can be picked up on Eyre Square or by calling **Galway Taxi Co-op** (☎ 091-56-1111).

Getting to and around the Aran Islands

The most common way to get to the Arans is by ferry. **Aran Ferries** (☎ 091-56-8903), located at the Galway Tourist Office off Eyre Square, operates ferries that depart from the Galway Docks. Price: £18 ($26.65). Ferries also depart from Rosaveal Pier in Connemara. Price: £15 ($22.20). If you'd rather fly, **Aer Arann** (☎ 091-59-3034) takes off from Connemara Airport, Inverin, near Galway. Interestingly, the ten-minute flight is the shortest scheduled flight in the world. Price: £35 ($51.80) round trip.

You can't bring your car to the Arans, and there are no car rentals, so once you've reached the islands you have a couple choices. You can rent a bike at **Rothar Arainn Teo,** Frenchman's Beach, Kilronan (☎ 091-61-132), which is what we recommend. You can also hire a driver and minibus (Hernon Aran Tours, ☎ 099-61-001 or 099-61-109) or a bumpy horse and cart (Cyril Flaherey, ☎ 099-61-001).

You can also tour the Arans by foot. There are walking-tour maps available at the **tourist office** (☎ 099-61-263). Each route takes a couple of hours.

Where to Stay in County Galway

Galway Great Southern Hotel

$$$ Galway City

A room on one of the higher floors of this incredibly refined hotel will give a view of the entire city and beyond. From the heated rooftop pool you might fool yourself with giddy joy and think you can see all the way to England! This hotel, overlooking Eyre Square and amid the city's best offerings, was built in 1845 and is an elegant example of Victorian style. The spacious lobby and sitting rooms are nice just to look at, with high ceilings and detailed furnishings like crystal chandeliers and fireplace marble from the nearby hills of Connemara. Rooms are exquisite, furnished with style and attention, and with every amenity thinkable. There are special low rates for children and a baby-sitting service is available. If you're looking for fine dining, book a table at the Oyster Room. For a more relaxed meal, stop into O'Flaherty's Pub. The food is excellent and the atmosphere matches it.

15 Eyre Sq., Galway City. ☎ *800-44-UTELL, from the United States; 091-56-4041. Fax: 091-56-6704. E-mail:* res@galway.gsh.ie. *To get there: On the south side of the square. Rates: £116–174 ($171.70–$257.50) double. AE, DC, MC, V.*

Eyre Square

$$–$$$ Galway City

This newest addition to the Galway hotel scene puts as much care and detail into its 45 rooms as it does its exquisite lobby, so amble in off the street to get an idea of what's in store. If being in the thick of things matters to you, this hotel will fit the bill: It's facing Eyre Square, but you still might not venture out to nearby pubs and restaurants with the hotel's Red Square Bar staring you down: There you can have a carvery lunch or nice dinner, and then stick around for some drinks and music later. All rooms are comfortably furnished with the usual standards.

Forster St., Galway City. ☎ *091-56-9633. Fax: 091-56-9641. To get there: Off the south side of Eyre Sq. Rates: £60–140 ($88.80–$207.20) double. AE, DC, MC, V.*

Imperial Hotel

$$ Galway City

The best thing about the Imperial is how inexpensive it is for such an incredible location. It's probably the cheapest place on Eyre Square, Galway City's centerpoint. From here, you're only feet from the bus depot, train station, main shopping streets, restaurants, and pubs. Inside, you'll find quality and subdued elegance, and we beg you not to be put off by what seems like the lobby of a second-rate hotel. It's a little cramped and maybe hasn't been redecorated in a few years, but the rooms really make up for that. They're all big and tastefully decorated, and the spacious, modern bathrooms are a treat in a country full of tiny ones. The hotel's pub, called Blakes Bar but locally known as the "Meeting Place," is a nice place for a drink and some local color.

Eyre Sq. ☎ *091-56-3033. Fax: 091-56-8410. To get there: On the north side of the square. Rates: £60–110 ($88.80–$162.80) double. AE, DC, MC, V.*

Hotel Ibis Galway

$ Galway City

Don't expect luxurious rooms and a pampering staff at this run-of-the-mill hotel, but it does stand out because, unlike most hotels and guesthouses, the Ibis charges per room rather than per person, meaning up to two adults and two children can stay in a room for the cost of a couple. For that reason, the Ibis is an extremely economical choice. Rooms have all the standard amenities, like television and tea and coffee, and there's also a restaurant with a pretty varied menu. The hotel's just blocks from the city centre, too.

Headford Rd., Galway City. ☎ *091-77-1166. Fax: 091-77-1646. To get there: On the north side of the city; Headford becomes St. Vincent's Ave. near the River Corrib. Rates: £38–45 per room ($56.25–$66.60). AE, DC, MC, V.*

Corrib Haven

$ Galway City

If, at this point in your traveling, you stay at Corrib Haven, there are two things you'll probably notice straightaway. First, the showers are exceptionally powerful, given the general absence of water pressure throughout Ireland; secondly, the beds are about as comfortable as we like to think they'll be in heaven. This wonderful new guesthouse is located just out of Galway City, on the way to Connemara and the Aran Islands, so it makes a convenient stopover. This is a B&B run with the professionalism of a hotel, and there's even a menu to choose from at breakfast.

107 Upper Newcastle, just outside Galway City. ☎ *and Fax:* **091-52-4171.** *To get there: On the N59 just out of Galway City. Rates: £36–60 ($53.30–$88.80) double. MC, V.*

Hotel Carraroe Best Western

$$ Carraroe

West of Galway City, this might be one of the quieter areas of the country, but you (and especially the kids) won't be in want of things to do at this hotel. There's an outdoor swimming pool, game room, play area, and tennis court, and boats leave daily for the Aran Islands from the nearby Rossaveal Harbour. You'll get a taste of tradition in the little village of Carraroe, where Irish music is taken very seriously and Old-World values hold sway. This family-run hotel has a staff that's friendly and hospitable. If you've got questions about touring Connemara, just ask; they're helpful and knowledgeable.

Carraroe, near Rossaveal. ☎ **091-59-5116.** *Fax: 091-59-5187. To get there: From Galway take the R336 west to the R343 south into Carraroe. Rates: £60–80 ($88.80–$118.40) double. AE, MC, V. Closed Oct–April.*

Alcock and Brown Hotel

$$ Clifden

Clifden is a quaint village famous for being near the landing spot of Alcock and Brown, who completed the first transatlantic flight in 1919. It's now a perfect liftoff location for touring the spectacular Connemara National Park, which it's situated at the base of. The Alcock and Brown Hotel is a wonderful family-run hotel known for its fantastic restaurant. The inside is modestly and very tastefully furnished, and rooms are quite nice. The bar is comfortable and often filled with people relaxing after a day of sightseeing.

Clifden, Connemara. ☎ **095-21-206.** *Fax: 095-21-842. E-mail:* alcockandbrown@ eircom.net. *Internet:* www.alcockandbrown-hotel.com. *To get there: Take the N59 northwest from Galway or southwest from Westport. Rates: £58–74 ($85.85–$109.50) double. AE, DC, MC, V.*

O'Grady's Sunnybank Guesthouse

$ Clifden

This first-rate guesthouse is sure to surprise you. How often do little family-run B&Bs have heated pools, a sauna, a sunbed, and a tennis court? Having scoured the country, we can categorically say, "Not many." This gorgeous period home even has a fish pond and little waterfall in the landscaped gardens. The inside of the house is just as fantastic. It's only feet from the town centre, too. You'll be doing yourself a favor by staying here.

Church Hill, Clifden. ☎ *095-21-437. Fax: 095-21-976. To get there: Take the N59 northwest from Galway or southwest from Westport. Rates: £46–60 ($68.10–$88.80) double. MC, V. Closed Nov–Feb.*

Pier House

$ Lower Kilronan, Inishmore, Aran Islands

Located on a small island, you're pretty much guaranteed a view of the water from anywhere; but from a room in the Pier House, you'll get that and more. Only feet from the harbor, this guesthouse is a lovely place to stay while visiting the Aran Islands. Sandy beaches, pubs, and restaurants are all a short walk away, and the ocean breeze will make its way into your room's open window at night. Rooms are quite nice, and it's obvious that great care goes into ensuring a guest's comfort. Given all of this, you can't beat it for the price.

Lower Kilronan, Inishmore, Aran Islands. ☎ *099-61-417. Fax: 099-61-122. E-mail:* pierh@iol.ie. *To get there: See "Getting to and around the Aran Islands" earlier in this chapter. Rates: £40–44 ($59.20–$65.10) double. MC, V. Closed Nov–Feb.*

Where to Dine in County Galway

Brannagans

$$$ Galway City   INTERNATIONAL-ECLECTIC

Versatility is at the heart of this little restaurant, where the menu spans the globe. You're practically guaranteed to find what you're craving, whether it be a steak, pizza, pasta, seafood, or Asian cuisine. Best thing about it is that it's all done surprisingly well. You might think a place with so many offerings overdoes it, not managing to create any one thing that's noteworthy, but that's not the case here. The fajitas are especially good, with plenty of meat and sauteed veggies to cram into warm tortillas. The atmosphere is cozy and wonderful, with brick and pine and giving you the feeling that you're in someone's spacious kitchen.

36 Upper Abbeygate St., Galway City. ☎ *091-56-5974. To get there: Near Lynch's Castle. Main courses: £10–15 ($14.80–$22.20). MC, V. Open: Daily 5:00 p.m.–10:30 p.m.*

The Skeff Bar

$$ Galway City   AMERICAN

Don't be scared off by the fact that this is a bar — it's also a fantastic, informal restaurant with a separate dining room. And if you're hankering for a little good ol' American fare, this is it. You can get burgers, chicken fingers, pizza, pasta, and vegetarian dishes, and at decent prices. The servings are sure to fill you, but the appetizer list is too enticing to pass up. Of course there's a full bar, but the wine list is pretty great too, with good choices from South Africa and Chile. If you do opt to sit somewhere in the vast pub area, you'll be in a lively atmosphere with a beautiful dark wooden decor.

Eyre Sq., Galway City. ☎ 091-56-3173. To get there: On the west side of the square. Main courses: £4.95–13 ($6.80–$19.25). MC, V. Open: Daily 11:00 a.m.–10:30 p.m.

Maxwell McNamaras

$$ Galway City IRISH-SEAFOOD-PASTA

Serving the good people of Galway since 1016, McNamara's is an institution. Waiting for dinner was never so interesting — with so much history to this comfortable and tasteful place, you're bound to get caught up reading the back of the menu. We're not sure if it's true that Columbus brought a McNamara burger with him when he set sail for the New World, but it makes for good conversation! But who knows, maybe he did — after all, the food is quite good. There are plenty of traditional dishes on the menu, but the Mixed Grill stands out as even more decadent than usual: lamb cutlet, sausage, bacon, burger, black-and-white pudding, tomato, and mushrooms. Irish dishes, seafood, and creative pasta dishes round out the menu, and the children's menu will make even the pickiest eater happy. The drink list is vast, with liqueurs, coffee drinks, draft beer, and an extensive wine list.

Williamsgate St., Galway City. ☎ 091-56-5727. To get there: Off Eyre Sq., on the corner of Williamsgate and Eglinton streets. Main courses: £5.25–11.25 ($7.75–$16.65). AE, DC, MC, V. Open: Daily 9:00 a.m.–10:00 p.m.

McDonagh's Seafood House

$$ Galway City   SEAFOOD

Fish doesn't get fresher or better than at this popular place. The McDonaghs, who've been at it for four generations, have had plenty of practice in the trade. The day's catch is personally inspected and chosen before it comes in the door. You choose exactly how you'd like your fish cooked, whether it's salmon, trout, or sole. Shrimp and lobsters come the way the sea made them: in the shell. If you're in the market for a light meal but don't want to pass up the chance for this great seafood, there's a fish-and-chips shop in the front of the house for take-out.

22 Quay St., Galway City. ☎ 091-56-5809. To get there: Located beside Jury's Inn, near the Spanish Arch. Main courses: £4.50–12 ($6.65–$17.75). AE, DC, MC, V. Open: Daily 12:00 p.m.–10:00 p.m.

O'Grady's

$$–$$$ Clifden   IRISH

This restaurant has thrived in Clifden for decades, thanks to fine food and cozy surroundings. Once you settle into one of the dimly lit nooks and scan the menu, you'll know why visitors and locals alike return to this little converted shop. Here you'll get simple foods done well, which might remind you of a home-cooked meal. But, of course, local lobster and lamb isn't often what you get at home! Desserts here are a wonderful end to a delicious meal.

Lower Market St., Clifden. ☎ *095-21-450. To get there: Take the N59 northwest from Galway or southwest from Westport. Main courses: £7.50–20 ($11.10–$29.60). AE, MC, V. Open: Mon–Sat 12:30 p.m.–2:30 p.m. and 6:00 p.m.–10:00 p.m.*

Mitchell's Restaurant

$$ Clifden   IRISH-ECLECTIC

Hearty, traditional fare is the staple of this restaurant, and thick stews, steaks, and fish dishes stand out. Noteworthy lighter meals — like seafood pastas, quiche, and salads — are served during the day. The decor is warm and rustic, with stone and brick walls, a big open fireplace, and local memorabilia throughout. There's also a children's menu.

Market St., Clifden, in the center of town. ☎ *095-21-867. To get there: Take the N59 northwest from Galway or southwest from Westport. Main courses: £6.50–10.95 ($9.60–$16.20). MC, V. Open: Mid-Mar–mid-Nov 12:00 p.m.–11:00 p.m.*

Aran Fisherman Restaurant

$$ Kilronan, Inishmore, Aran Islands   SEAFOOD-IRISH

Having a seafood meal on an island where the main livelihood is fishing is kind of like having a cheese steak in Philly — heavenly. That's exactly what eating at the Aran Fisherman is like. Just a stone's throw from where the seafood comes out of the sea, this restaurant offers shark, lobster, fish, and crab along with meat and vegetarian dishes. Meals come with organic vegetable salads from the island. Sitting on the outside patio completes the meal.

Kilronan, Inishmore, Aran Islands. ☎ *099-61-363. To get there: Three minutes walk west from the harbor, on the only road. Main courses: £5–12.50 ($7.40–$18.50). MC, V. Open: Daily 12:00 p.m.–10:00 p.m.*

Exploring County Galway

Ever wondered about the intricate patterns in an Aran knit sweater? Or where the verb "to lynch" comes from? Or where the smallest church in the world is? Read on for the answers.

Galway's top attractions

The Aran Islands

If you've held out long enough, now's your chance to buy an authentic, often-copied-but-never-reproduced hand-knit fisherman's sweater from the Aran Islands. And what a shopping excursion you're in for! The islands — Inishmore, Inishmaan, and Inisheer — are famous for being havens of traditional Irish culture. From the Gaelic language that islanders speak to their methods of livelihood (mainly fishing and tourism), this truly is the place to witness a way of life that the fast-paced world barely touches. People live in stone cottages and get around in horse-drawn carts, but conditions are a bit more advanced for tourists. You won't be able to bring your car there and will have to rely on carts or bikes to get around, but there are a number of fine accommodations, restaurants, and amazing little pubs. The main place to stay is Kilronan, on Inishmore, where the ferries drop off visitors and where you'll find the most amenities. There you'll also be in among sandy beaches and one of the Arans' most notable sites: prehistoric stone forts. Also, Inishmore has the smallest church in the world, taking up a measly 7 feet by 11 feet. Maybe they thought just a little prayer is better than nothing?

Located out in the middle of the Atlantic Ocean. To get there: See "Getting to and around the Aran Islands" earlier in this chapter. Time: Several hours at least.

Aran Islands

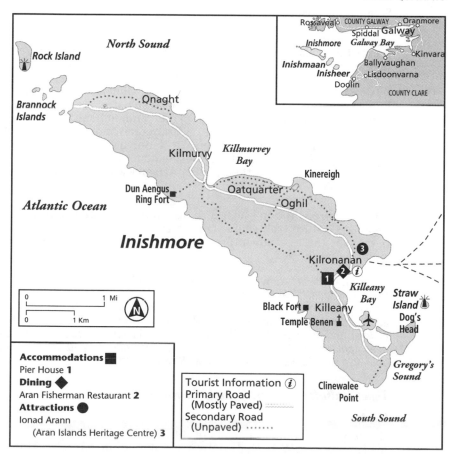

Accommodations ▰
Pier House **1**
Dining ◆
Aran Fisherman Restaurant **2**
Attractions ●
Ionad Arann
    (Aran Islands Heritage Centre) **3**

Tourist Information ⓘ
Primary Road
    (Mostly Paved) ‒‒‒‒‒
Secondary Road
    (Unpaved) ·······

Ionad Arann (Aran Islands Heritage Centre)

Kilronan, Inishmore, Aran Islands

You can get the skinny on all the islands' best attractions at the heritage centre in Kilronan. There you'll learn the history and culture of the islands and more about the interesting composition of the land, which is similar to the Burren in County Clare.

Kilronan, Inishmore, Aran Islands. ☎ 099-61-355. To get there: See "Getting to and around the Aran Islands" section earlier in this chapter. Admission: £2.50 ($3.70) adults, £2 ($2.95) seniors and students, £1.50 ($2.20) children, £6 ($8.90) family. Open: April–Oct daily 10:00 a.m.–7:00 p.m. Time: A half-hour.

Connemara National Park and Visitors Centre

Letterfrack

Some of the absolute best scenery in this part of Ireland is contained in this 5,000-acre park. Mountains, bogs, valleys, and forests make up the region, but most people come to catch sight of the famous Connemara ponies that make the park home. Four of the mountains that make up the impressive Twelve Bens range are in the park, including Benbaun, the highest of the twelve. It reaches 2,400 feet — pretty high for a country this size. If you keep a careful watch, you'll glimpse some of the park's hidden wonders. There are 4,000-year-old prehistoric structures, flowers that only grow here, and rare plants and animals. For instance, Connemara ponies were once the only purebred horses native to Ireland. As for the ones roaming Connemara National Park today, a fantastic legend says they are the direct descendants of the Arab horses that struggled ashore when the Spanish Armada was wrecked against the coast in 1588.

To make sure you don't miss a thing, the Visitors Centre (on the N59) organizes nature trail walks. Loners can take one of the two marked paths. For the less adventurous, the centre also has exhibitions and audio-visual shows.

Letterfrack, County Galway. ☎ 095-41-054 or 095-41-006. To get there: Clifden-Westport Road (N59). Bus Eireann (☎ 091-56-2000) takes a day tour of the Connemara from Galway Bus Station for £9 ($13.35) adult, £5 ($7.40) child between June and Sept. Park admission: £2 ($2.95) adults, £1.50 ($2.20) seniors, £1 ($1.50) children and students, £5 ($7.40) family. Open: Park open year-round. Visitor Centre open April, May, and Sept daily 10:00 a.m.–5:30 p.m.; June daily 10:00 a.m.–6:30 p.m.; July–Aug daily 9:30 a.m.–6:30 p.m. Time: Several hours.

Thoor Ballylee (W. B. Yeats's Summer Home)

Gort

One look from the battlements of this stone tower and you'll see what the famous poet W. B. Yeats drew inspiration from, and why. This tower was the poet's summer home and where he wrote most of his work. The view includes Galway's lush fields and forests. There's an audio-visual tour and museum dedicated to Yeats's life and work. Everything about the place has been restored to look just like it did when the poet lived there in the 1920s. Fans can buy his writings in the bookshop, and there are gardens and a picnic area that make for a gorgeous lunch stop when the weather's nice.

Gort, County Galway. ☎ 091-64-1436. To get there: Off Limerick–Galway Road (N18) or the Gort–Loughrea Road. Look for the sign. Admission: £3 ($4.45) adults, £2.50 ($3.70) seniors and students, 75p ($1.10) children. Open: Apr–Sept daily 10:00 a.m.–6:00 p.m. Time: An hour and a half.

Kylemore Benedictine Abbey

Kylemore

Sitting at the base of the mountains and on the shores of the lake, this abbey looks like a storybook castle — and it is, in a way. An English tycoon ordered the gorgeous Gothic building constructed for his adored wife, but when she died suddenly, he abandoned it. Later, a group of nuns escaping the horrors of World War I in Belgium took up residence and began the lengthy process of restoring the old place. They're still at it, but now they also run a world-renowned girls boarding school here. You can visit the striking reception rooms, where you'll see a video about the history of the estate; walk along the lake to the restored Gothic church; and visit the magnificent walled Victorian garden. The Abbey is known for its pottery, which you can watch being made (and can purchase in the craft shop). There's also a restaurant on the grounds.

Kylemore, Connemara. ☎ 095-41-145. To get there: On the Clifden-Westport Road. (N59), east of Letterfrack. Admission: £1.50 ($2.20) adults, £1 ($1.50) seniors and students, 50p (75 cents) children. Open: Apr–Oct daily 9:30 a.m.–6:00 p.m. Time: About an hour.

The top Galway City landmarks

Spanish Arch

During Medieval times, Galway Harbor was outside the thick city walls, leaving it exposed to any trouble. In the late 1500s, Spanish ships often sailed into the harbor with valuable cargos — wine, brandy, and produce. To protect against any trouble from the foreigners, a stone archway was constructed, and the Spanish would pass their goods through without coming into town. At night, the Spaniards would stroll outside the arch, leading to the name "Spanish Parade."

Located between Wolfe Tone Bridge and The Long Walk, at the mouth of the river.

Browne Doorway

Looking pretty odd at the head of Eyre Square, the Browne Doorway is a huge stone archway that's connected to nothing. For more than 75 years it's stood there, and although the park is accessible from any point (there are no walls), you'll be amazed to see how many people take the trouble to walk through the towering doorway. Dating from 1627, it comes from an old mansion on Lower Abbeygate Street, and has the coat of arms of the families Browne and Lynch.

Located on the northwest side of the square.

Breaker, breaker!: Bogland firsts

In 1907, from the middle of Derrygimlagh Bog, near Clifden, the first radio messages reached America care of Guglielmo Marconi's wireless station. You can see the ruins of the station still. Also in that famous bog, the first transatlantic flight touched down. In 1919, John Alcock and William Brown successfully completed the first hopping of the big pond, coming from Nova Scotia.

Lynch's Castle (now AIB Bank)

You expect lots of money to go into a castle, but this one's for the books! This fourteenth-century home of the legendary Lynch family was restored and now houses a bank, though you can still marvel at the coats of arms and stonework on the exterior.

Located on Abbeygate St. Upper between Shop and Market streets.

John F. Kennedy Plaque

In 1963, just months before he was assassinated, JFK spoke in Eyre Square on his historic trip to Ireland — the first time a sitting U.S. president had visited the country. From the park in the center of the square, which is named after him, Kennedy spoke to the people and received the "freedom of the city" (like the key to a city). There's a bronze plaque in the park showing the slain president's profile.

Located in Eyre Sq.

Lynch Memorial Window

James Lynch Fitzstephen, unyielding magistrate and mayor of Galway, earned his place in the dictionaries when he condemned and executed his own son (convicted for murder) in 1493 as a demonstration that the law does not bend even under family ties. That's where we get the word "lynch." The Lynch Memorial Window commemorates this event. It's set into a wall just above an ornate Gothic doorway on Market Street.

Located on Market St., one block northwest of Eyre Sq.

Other fun stuff to do

✔ **Salthill:** This fun little resort town is Ireland's closest thing to Coney Island. It makes for a fun day with the family. Walk along the boardwalk, eat fast food, play arcade games, and visit the Leisureland amusement park (☎ **091-52-1455**) to ride the Ferris wheel (possibly the only one in the country) and other amusement rides.

Location: To get there, take the R336 west from Galway.

✔ **Coole Park:** Once home to Lady Gregory — writer, friend of many an Irish luminary, and cofounder of Dublin's Abbey Theatre — the park's now home to red deer, red squirrels, and badgers, among others, and boasts beautiful nature trails, a lake, bountiful gardens, and a farmlike atmosphere, though the estate manor is gone. One of the most interesting parts of the park is the "Autograph Tree," which bears the carved initials of such famous people as George Bernard Shaw, Oliver St. John Gogarty, Sean O'Casey, and W. B. Yeats, Lady Gregory's friend and partner in the Abbey. In the restored courtyard there's a visitors centre, a place to buy light snacks, and picnic tables. It's here that the nature walks begin.

Location: Gort, County Galway. ☎ **091-63-1804.** To get there: North of Gort on the N18. Admission: £2 ($2.95) adults, £1.50 ($2.20) seniors, £1 ($1.50) children and students, £5 ($7.40) family. Open: Mid-April to mid-June Tuesday to Sunday 10:00 a.m. to 5:00 p.m.; mid-June to August daily 9:30 a.m. to 6:30 p.m.; September daily 10:00 a.m. to 5:00 p.m. Time: One or two hours.

✔ **Dunguaire Castle:** How better to tell the story of a castle's rich history than to show it? Each floor of Dunguaire Castle reflects a different and very colorful time in its history. It's been perfectly restored, and the interior is one of the finest in its class, with furnishings that interestingly mirror the time. According to legend, the castle was built on the site of the Palace of Guaire, sixth-century king of Connaught, and that's where the name comes from. Later it was owned by Oliver St. John Gogarty, poet, surgeon, and satirical model for Buck Mulligan, one the characters of James Joyce's _Ulysses._ Although born in Dublin, Gogarty lived mostly in Connemara.

Location: Kinvarra, County Galway. ☎ **091-637-108.** To get there: From the Gort-Kilcolgan Road (N18), take the N67. Admission: £2.50 ($3.70) adults, £2 ($2.95) seniors, £1.50 ($2.20) children and students. Open: April to September daily 9:30 a.m. to 5:30 p.m. Time: An hour and a half.

Organized Tours

Western Heritage Walking tour

This city walk of Galway, run by local guides, is an excellent rundown of the city's history.

Leaves at 2:30 p.m. from the Galway Tourist Office, Victoria Place, off Eyre Sq., daily June–Aug. Information: ☎ _**091-52-1699.** Price: £3.50 ($5.20) adults, £3 ($4.45) students. Time: Ninety minutes._

O'Neachtain bus tours

Connemara and Kylemore Abbey are the highlights of this scenic tour that includes other picture-taking highlights like Connemara ponies, the Quiet Man Cottage in County Mayo (see Chapter 19), turf-cutting bogs, Clifden, and the coast.

Departs Salthill Tourist Office daily at 9:55 a.m. and Galway Tourist Office (O'Neachtain Bus Stop, Kinlay House) daily at 9:45 a.m., both year-round. Returns 4:45 p.m. Information: ☎ 091-56-5056. Price: £10 ($14.80) adults, £8 ($11.85) students, £5 ($7.40) children.

Bus Eireann Connemara bus tour

This day tour of Connemara takes you through Clifden with a stop at Kylemore Abbey, but the focus of the tour is the beautiful mountain scenery. There are also some designated picture-taking stops.

Leaves Salthill at 9:45 a.m. and Galway Railway Station at 10:00 a.m. Runs Sun–Fri in July and Aug and Sun, Tues, and Thur in June and Sept. Returns at 5:00 p.m. Information: ☎ 091-56-3081. Price: £9 ($13.40) adults, £7.50 ($11.10) students and seniors, £5 ($8.15) for children, £22 ($32.55) for a family of two adults and three children.

Corrib Cruises cruise tour

Aboard the *Corrib Queen* (either of them — there are two boats with the same name) you'll tour the unspoiled shoreline of the lovely Lough Corrib, monastic ruins, and the village of Cong. The tour provides the best opportunity to photograph Ashford Castle.

Departs from Oughterard and Cong daily at 11:00 a.m., 2:45 p.m., and 5:00 p.m., May–Sept. Information: ☎ 092-46-029. Price: £6 ($8.90) per person.

Shopping

We know what you want: You want one of those thick Aran sweaters that'll make you look like one of the Clancy Brothers. In the following section we'll tell you where to find them.

Aran sweaters might be one of Ireland's biggest exports today, but they came from humble beginnings. Originally, the almost-waterproof wool sweaters were knit by the women of the islands to ensure fishermen stayed warm. The wives and mothers of the fishermen created a different pattern for each family. Sadly, this was to identify their men, should they drown off the dangerous coast.

Another great Galway item is Claddagh rings — you know, the ones with two hands clasping a heart below a crown. The hands symbolize friendship, the crown symbolizes loyalty, and the heart represents love. According to tradition, the wearer wears his or her ring with the crown pointing toward the fingertips to show he or she is in love or married. If, on the other hand, the heart is pointing toward the fingertips the wearer is said to be unattached. Traditionally the ring is worn on one's ring finger and serves as an engagement ring. The name comes from Claddagh, the oldest fishing village in Ireland, located on the west bank of the Corrib Estuary in Galway. In Gaelic *An Cladach* means "flat, stony shore."

There are a few shopping areas in Galway, but the best is the **Eyre Square Shopping Centre** (☎ 091-56-8302). It has more than 50 shops and an antique market under one glassed roof, and is lined by old stone walls. It's also home to the Vidiwall, a giant screen displaying music, tourism info, and animated shows. On Saturdays year-round there's also a traditional **Galway Saturday Market** next to the Collegiate Church of St. Nicholas.

Here are some specific shops to check out in Galway City and around the county.

Galway Woolen Market

The market specializes in Aran hand-knits, knitwear, linen, lace, sheep-skin, and gifts.

21–22 High St., Galway City. ☎ *091-56-2491.*

Kennys Bookshop and Art Gallery

This shop houses an excellent collection of contemporary Irish literature (including second-hand and antiquarian books), art prints, and maps. They locate the difficult-to-find stuff.

High St., Galway City. ☎ *091-56-2739.*

Roundstone Music

Famous for making a large and high-quality selection of bodhráns (Irish drums), this music shop features all kinds of other well-crafted instruments as well. Owner Malachy Kearns is something of a celebrity: He made the drums for the *Riverdance* ensemble, and is even featured on an Irish postage stamp.

Roundstone, Connemara. ☎ *095-35-808. Internet:* www.bodhran.com.

Thomas Dillon's

Thomas Dillon's is Galway's original maker of Claddagh rings, creating the famous rings since 1750. Also home of the Claddagh Ring Museum, which has on display the oldest rings in existence. There's no charge for checking out their tiny museum.

1 Quay St., Galway. ☎ *091-56-6365.*

Treasure Chest

Every local gift item you could want under one roof. Waterford Crystal, Royal Tara china, Belleek china, Claddagh rings, Aran knitwear, Irish linen, souvenirs, and more.

31–33 William St., Galway City. ☎ *091-56-7237.*

Nightlife in Galway City

Galway's not just a thriving city, it's a college town, and with that comes a pretty healthy nightlife. We've listed a number of great pubs and a couple good after-hours clubs, too.

Pub life

The Kings Head Pub

The Middle Ages live on in The Kings Head, if just for the original medieval fireplaces and windows. But it's all or nothing here, and every bit of the place looks the part of a pub from the 1500s. There's history galore associated with this place, and a chat with the barkeep will reveal some of its rich stories. This isn't a cramped, elbow-room pub, either: It's spread over three floors, though it's likely you'll stay downstairs with the music. There's Sunday brunchtime jazz sessions, too. And you can take your picture sitting on the throne, next to the downstairs fireplace!

15 High St., Galway City. ☎ *091-56-6630.*

The Quays Bar

No trip to Galway is complete without a stop in to this lively pub, a city institution since its opening in the 1600s, and today a place known for its live music. The whole thing is set in an old stone mansion: The front of the house has an authentic bar and is small with an Old World feel, and the back — while retaining the same traditional look — is vast, with plenty of room to move around. The pub grub is especially good, as locals will attest to.

Quay St. and Chapel Ln., Galway City. ☎ *091-56-8347.*

Skeff Bar

Every corner of this sprawling pub is distinct and impressive, making it an unquestioned "must-see." Some parts look like an upper-crust drawing room, with elegant couches, coffee tables, and Persian rugs, while other parts are distinctly Irish publike, with low stools or tall booths. Fireplaces, intricate ceiling work, and stained glass give the pub a posh feel. Staircases throughout lead to more bars upstairs. The food is Americanish and tasty, and there's music on weekends. Expect this popular pub to fill up almost any night of the week.

Eyre Sq., Galway City. ☎ *091-56-3173.*

The Snug

A gigantic, ceiling-high fireplace from the sixteenth century dominates this traditional pub, and smack inside the hearth are the best seats in the house! This is one of Galway's oldest buildings, and part of the fun is meandering around with a pint and reading all the articles on the walls that describe the place. It might be called The Snug, but it's got to have one of the most open interiors in the city. There's traditional music sessions every weekend, beginning on Thursday night.

William St., Galway City. ☎ *091-56-2831.*

E. J. Kings

Almost anyone who's been to Clifden is familiar with E. J. Kings, because once you go, you can't forget it. Always humming, Kings has many floors, and in the high season music fills the air. Seafood is the feature of the fantastic pub-food menu, but there's also good traditional fare. When it's cold, a welcoming fire warms the pub, and in nice weather the outdoor patio is the hottest spot. The atmosphere in Kings is relaxed and you're sure to get a warm welcome from the young, chatty staff.

The Square, Clifden. ☎ *095-21-330.*

Club life

Admission at these places ranges from £3 ($4.45) to £6 ($8.90).

Central Park

This is Galway's most popular club, and it's no surprise. It's fun and funky and always full of trendy young people. It doesn't open until 11:00 p.m., but don't wait much longer than that to go — it gets busy.

34 Upper Abbeygate St., Galway City. ☎ *091-56-5976.*

GPO Nightclub

Different DJs every night make for a varied and unexpected music selection, but you can expect it'll always be danceable.

21 Eglinton St., Galway City. ☎ *091-56-3073.*

Fast Facts: County Galway

AREA CODE(S)

091 and 099.

EMERGENCIES-HOSPITAL

Dial ☎ **999** for all emergencies. **University College Hospital** is on Newcastle Rd., Galway. ☎ **091-58-0580**. Need a late-night pharmacy? Try **Matt O'Flaherty Chemist**, 39 Eyre Sq., Galway (☎ **091-56-3526**).

INFORMATION

For visitor information and reservation services go to **Aras Fa'ilte**, Victoria Place, Eyre Sq. (☎ **091- 56-3081**), open year-round. They can also provide reservation services. For telephone directory assistance, dial ☎ **1190**.

GENEALOGY RESOURCES

Contact **Shoemakers Tower**, Medieval St., Eyre Square Centre, Galway (☎ 091-56-9649), or **Galway Family History Society West**, Venture Centre, Liosbaun Estate, Taum (☎ 091-75-6737).

INTERNET

The NetAccess Internet Cafe, Olde Malte Arcade, Hight St. (☎ 091-56-9772), has Internet access for Hotmail and AOL, plus printing capabilities.

POST OFFICE

Galway Post Office is on Eglinton St., Galway City (☎ 091-56-2051).

Chapter 19

Counties Mayo and Sligo

*N*orth of County Galway, Counties Mayo and Sligo boast some of the most beautiful scenery you can imagine, so beautiful that Mayo became the setting of *The Quiet Man,* a movie with John Wayne and Maureen O'Hara, probably the quintessential Irish-American Hollywood romance. And in Sligo poet W.B. Yeats found the inspiration for some of his greatest work.

What's Where? Mayo and Sligo's Major Attractions

Many of **County Mayo's** attractions relate to its proximity to water, with most of the area touching either the Atlantic or calm and striking **Clew Bay.** Beaches, of course, are a big part of life in this region. Mountains tower over the county, providing the best views, while bogs and cliffs add to the stunning, unspoiled scenery. The N5 (and a few smaller roads) take you to the towns of Westport, Castlebar, and Mayo's largest, Ballina. Venturing out for a drive west on the N59 takes you along twisty roads that lead to some of the most isolated and sparsely populated regions in the country. Around the county, the top attractions include

✔ **Westport House and Children's Zoo:** For history-minded adults, this grand eighteenth-century limestone house features an extraordinary interior, with an Italian marble staircase and a dining room full of antiques and Waterford Crystal. Kids can enjoy a zoo with ostriches, llamas, camels, and more.

✔ **Clare Island:** Sandy beaches and walking trails share space on this island with the ruins of **Clare Castle** and **Abbey,** huts from the Iron Age, and wildlife that includes seals and dolphins.

✔ **Ceide Fields:** This is the world's most extensive Stone Age monument, dating back 5,000 years.

✔ **Croagh Patrick:** This mountain is said to have been where St. Patrick fasted and prayed for 40 days, finally achieving divine inspiration.

✔ **The Quiet Man Heritage Cottage:** In the movie *The Quiet Man*, American John Wayne comes back to his birthplace in Ireland, falls in love with Maureen O'Hara, and eventually gets into a knock-down, drag-out brawl with her brother, played by Victor McLaglen. Romance! Excitement! And one of the best Irish-American films ever. Today, you can visit The Quiet Man Heritage Cottage, which isn't the real thing but is close enough to make you feel like you're there with the Duke in person.

Maybe the best compliment given to **County Sligo** comes from the many Irish writers who have fallen in love with the area over the years. Much of the county is known as "Yeats Country," because of the fondness the great poet W.B. Yeats had for the place — his last wish was to be buried here. The relatively small county has tributes to the poet in every corner, but its history goes back much further. You can find a heavy concentration of megalithic sites here, and in the towns of Carrowmore, Carrowkeel, and Knocknarea you can see ancient cemeteries and graves. **Sligo Town** is a walkable little metropolis where you can have a nice meal or find a place to stay before setting out to drive around the region. South of Sligo Town, **Strandhill** offers sandy beaches for relaxation. Major sights in County Sligo include

✔ **Sligo Abbey:** This medieval building, constructed in the mid-thirteenth century for Dominican monks, contains carvings, tomb sculptures, and a superbly carved high altar from the fifteenth century.

✔ **Sligo County Museum & Art Gallery:** This museum and gallery features memorabilia of the great poet William Butler Yeats (including his Nobel prize) and paintings by his brother Jack and father John.

✔ **Lissadell House:** Owned by a family that was friendly with W.B. Yeats, this Georgian mansion has an impressive interior and contains a collection of family memorabilia.

Because Mayo and Sligo are typically visited together, usually either en route from Galway north to Donegal or Northern Ireland or as a round-trip visit from Galway City, we discuss them together in this chapter.

Counties Mayo and Sligo

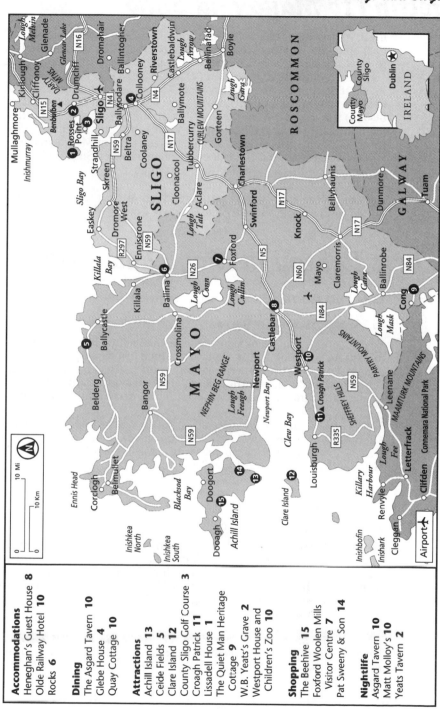

Accommodations
Heneghan's Guest House **8**
Olde Railway Hotel **10**
Rocks **6**

Dining
The Asgard Tavern **10**
Glebe House **4**
Quay Cottage **10**

Attractions
Achill Island **13**
Ceide Fields **5**
Clare Island **12**
County Sligo Golf Course **3**
Croagh Patrick **11**
Lissadell House **1**
The Quiet Man Heritage
Cottage **9**
W.B. Yeats's Grave **2**
Westport House and
Children's Zoo **10**

Shopping
The Beehive **15**
Foxford Woolen Mills
Visitor Centre **7**
Pat Sweeny & Son **14**

Nightlife
Asgard Tavern **10**
Matt Molloy's **10**
Yeats Tavern **2**

Getting to Mayo and Sligo

If you're driving from Dublin, take the N4 to Sligo City or the N5 to Castlebar and Westport in County Mayo. From Galway, take the N17 to meet the N5 in County Mayo or straight to Sligo. From Donegal, go south on N15 to Sligo. **Irish Rail (☎ 071-69-888)** services Sligo at Plunkett Station by the Ignatius Rice Bridge, and also services Westport, Foxford, Ballina, and Castlebar in County Mayo. **Bus Eireann (☎ 071-60-066)** travels year-round to Sligo, Strandhill, Drumcliff, and other major towns in County Sligo, and to Westport, Cong, Ballina, and other towns in County Mayo. In Sligo City, buses arrive at McDiarmada Station. Bus Eireann also has local service between Sligo and Strandhill and Rosses Point in July and August.

Aer Lingus has daily flights into both Sligo Airport (Strandhill, ☎ 071-68-280) and Knock Airport (Charlestown, County Mayo, ☎ 094-67-222).

Where to Stay in Mayo and Sligo

Olde Railway Hotel

$$ Westport, County Mayo

You're sure to have a relaxing time at this eighteenth-century coaching inn, where your comfort is obviously a high priority. Open fires blaze and a glass conservatory overlooks a garden patio. Antique period furniture fills the place, and they also serve excellent food. Expect lobster, Connemara lamb, and a vast wine list. This inn is in the heart of Westport.

The Mall (in the town centre, overlooking the Carrowbeg River), Westport, County Mayo. ☎ **098-25-166**. *Fax: 098-25-090. Internet:* www.anu.ie/railwayhotel. *E-mail:* railway@anu.ie. *To get there: In the center of town. Rates: £60–110 ($88.80–$162.80) double. AE, DC, MC, V.*

Heneghan's Guest House

$ Castlebar, County Mayo

From the library inside to the courtyard garden outside, this townhouse in the center of Castlebar is nothing if not homey. It's been in the same family since 1932, and has been tastefully restored and refurbished. Still, many old-fashioned accents remain. The owners provide many extras, including arrangements for fishing and walking, information about tracing your family roots, and packed lunches.

Newtown St., Castlebar, County Mayo. ☎ **094-21-883**. *Fax: 094-26-476. E-mail:* heneghans@eircom.net. *Internet:* http://castlebar.mayo/ireland.ie/heneghan.htm. *To get there: In the center of town. Rates: £40–44 ($59.20–$65.10) double. MC, V.*

Rocks

$ Ballina, County Mayo

This gorgeous home was designed and built by the owners, and it provides you with a perfect place to settle and explore the Northwest of the country. You have excellent fishing and swimming nearby and you can arrange pony-riding excursions. Kids will love the playground in back and the spacious lawns, and the home has a barbecue for grilling your own catch of the day.

Foxford Rd., Ballina, County Mayo. ☎ *098-22-140. To get there: Take Foxford Rd. from the town centre. Rates: £36–40 ($53.30–$59.20) double. No credit cards.*

Sligo Park Hotel

$$–$$$ Sligo Town, County Sligo

This is one of those hotels that just makes you feel like you're spoiling yourself — especially after you put your travel-weary body back together in the leisure centre, featuring a pool, steam room, and workout equipment. The hotel sits on well-groomed gardens and features scenic countryside all around. The rooms have large windows overlooking the landscaped gardens. You can't help but feel comfortable here, in Sligo's most modern accommodation.

Pearse Rd., Sligo Town. ☎ *071-60-291. Fax: 071-69-556. E-mail:* sligopk@leehotels. ie. *To get there: N4 becomes Pearse in town. Rates: £80–120 ($118.40–$177.60) double. AE, DC, MC, V.*

Tower Hotel

$$–$$$ Sligo Town, County Sligo

If you want to stay in the heart of Sligo Town, this place is for you: You can walk out the door and see the town, and the countryside is only a short way off. It's a luxury hotel, but small enough to pamper you with personal service. The rooms have every amenity you may want, including a pants press and tea and coffee facilities. Off from the lobby is the Links bar, proving the emphasis on golf in these parts.

Quay St., Sligo Town. ☎ *071-44-000. Fax: 071-46-888. E-mail:* towersl@iol.ie. *To get there: In the center of town, next to the City Hall. Rates: £70–120 ($103.60–$177.60) double. AE, DC, MC, V.*

Lisadorn

$ Sligo Town, County Sligo

This stately home is at the end of a flower-lined drive; a perfect welcome to Sligo's only three-star guesthouse. The place offers amazing hospitality and comfort for the cost, and all rooms provide the best conveniences. Only five minutes from town and ten minutes from the beautiful Rosses Point, Lisadorn is a great location.

Donegal Rd., Sligo Town. ☎ *071-43-417. Fax: 071-46-418. To get there: From the center of town, take the N15 north. Rates: £35–39 ($51.80–$57.70) double. MC, V.*

Sligo Town

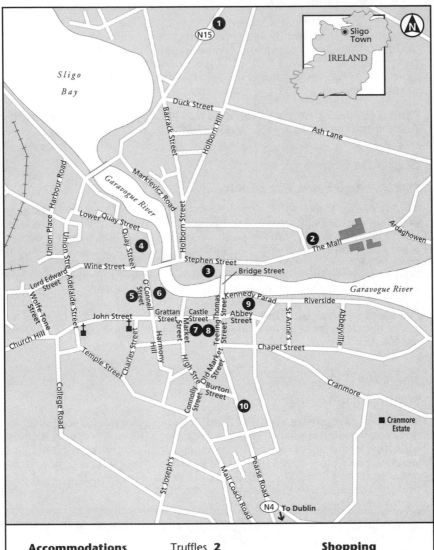

Accommodations
Lisadorn **1**
Sligo Park Hotel **10**
Tower Hotel **4**
Dining
The Cottage **8**

Truffles **2**
Attractions
Sligo Abbey **9**
Sligo County Museum
& Art Gallery **3**
Yeats Statue **3**

Shopping
Cat and Moon **8**
Kate's Kitchen **7**
Nightlife
Beezie's **5**
Hargadon **6**

Where to Dine in Mayo and Sligo

Quay Cottage

$$$ **Westport, County Mayo   SEAFOOD**

This little restaurant overlooks the harbor and is appropriately decked out with nautical treasures. Freshly prepared seafood is the focus of the menu, as well as daily specials and a surprisingly large vegetarian selection. Best of all, the prices are extremely reasonable for such quality food.

The Harbour, Westport, County Mayo. ☎ *098-26-412. To get there: On Westport Harbour at the entrance to Westport House. Main courses: £7.90–16.50 ($11.60–$24.40). AE, MC, V. Open: Mon–Sat 6:00 p.m.–10:00 p.m., Sun 1:00 p.m.–9:30 p.m.*

The Asgard Tavern

$$–$$$ **Westport, County Mayo   IRISH-STEAKS-SEAFOOD**

This nautical-themed restaurant is right on the water and serves award-winning food. Its filling and hearty lunches, such as stews and creamy pasta dishes, are served all day downstairs in the relaxing atmosphere of the pub. Dinner is served upstairs, in the tasteful, candlelit dining room. There, the menu is varied, including steaks and seafood creatively prepared. The Asgard Tavern pub serves exceptional pub food from 12:00 p.m. to 3:00 p.m. and 6:00 p.m. to 10:00 p.m. There's also music in the pub most nights.

The Quay, Westport, County Mayo. ☎ *098-25-319. To get there: Drive through Westport, take Coast Rd. one mile. Main courses: £7.40–14 ($10.95–$20.85). AE, DC, MC, V. Open: Sept–June Mon–Sat 6:30 p.m.–9:30 p.m.; July and Aug daily 6:30 p.m.– 9:30 p.m.*

Glebe House

$$$ **Collooney, County Sligo   IRISH**

An elegant Georgian house set amid gardens makes for a classy restaurant. The menu, which changes daily, prides itself on the use of organically grown vegetables from the house gardens. You can always expect a fish dish — the catch of the day — and you can expect beef and chicken meals creatively and tastefully prepared. Fresh herbs underscore the delicious food.

Collooney, County Sligo. ☎ *071-67-787. To get there: From the Collooney-Ballysadare Rd., turn left toward Collooney Railway Station. Main courses: £9.50–17 ($14.05–$25.15). AE, MC, V. Open: May–Oct daily 6:00 p.m.–9:00 p.m.; Nov–Apr Thurs–Sat 6:30 p.m.–9:30 p.m.*

Truffles

$$ **Sligo Town, County Sligo   PIZZA**

Chances are you didn't expect appetizing gourmet pizza in Ireland, but here it is! This little restaurant creates some absolutely delicious pizza, featuring fresh local herbs and vegetables and trademark Irish cheeses. The owner takes a hands-on approach to her work, and you can see her kneading dough or chopping up veggies to prepare her unique fare. The Irish cheese pizza stands out, and the sausage is like none you can have at home!

11 The Mall, Sligo Town. County Sligo. ☎ *071-44-226. To get there: On the north side of the Garavogue River, same street as Stephen St. (Stephen St. turns into The Mall.) Main courses: £5.95–11.95 ($8.80–$17.70). No credit cards. Open: Tues–Sat 5:00 p.m.–10:30 p.m., Sun 5:00 p.m.–10:00 p.m.*

The Cottage

$ Sligo Town, County Sligo   VEGETARIAN

Looking for a quick, wholesome vegetarian lunch without much fuss? Then this little cafe is what you want. You certainly don't have to be vegetarian to enjoy the food here, and given the choices you probably won't miss the lack of beefiness. The fare is tasty and you get plenty of it, so you'll be set until dinner. The Cottage features chili, pizza, and stuffed baked potatoes. Soups, salads, and melted cheesy sandwiches are also common fare. You can get table service or grab something to take out.

4 Castle St., Sligo Town. ☎ *071-45-319. To get there: Located in the center of town, near the post office. Main courses: £1.95–5 ($2.90–$7.40). No credit cards. Open: Mon–Fri 8:30 a.m.–9:00 p.m., Sat 8:30 a.m.–6:00 p.m.*

Exploring Mayo and Sligo

You may find tearing yourself away from all the gorgeous scenery in Mayo and Sligo hard, but there are several historic and cultural sites that you should see while you're there. We list some of the best in this section.

The top attractions

Westport House & Children's Zoo

Westport, County Mayo

The limestone house, sitting at the head of Clew Bay, is a gorgeous place with an extraordinary interior. Famous designers headed the building of it in the late eighteenth century, and the House features a marble staircase and dining room full of antiques and Waterford Crystal. Kids will go nuts at the children's zoo, where they can see ostriches, llamas, camels, and more. You can also enjoy boating, a miniature railroad, and dungeons, too.

Westport, County Mayo. ☎ *098-25-430. To get there: City centre in Westport. Admission: £6 ($8.90) adult, £3 ($4.45) children. Open: mid-May–June and Sept daily 2:00 p.m.–6:00 p.m.; July and Aug Mon–Sat 10:30 a.m.–6:00 p.m., Sun 2:00 p.m.–6:00 p.m. Time: Two hours or more.*

Clare Island

Clew Bay, County Mayo

This island is a sanctuary of gorgeous sandy beaches and walking trails. Knockmore Mountain is the heart of the island, and the ruins of Clare Castle and Abbey are nearby. The island is a historian's delight, with huts from the Iron Age and cooking implements from the Bronze Age (and the island is the resting place of the pirate queen Grace O'Malley as well). You can see seals and dolphins off the coast, and if you feel like sticking around for a while, there's a hotel on the island (contact through *Pirate Queen* ferry number later in this section).

Clew Bay, County Mayo. ☎ *01-872-4154. To get there: The Pirate Queen ferry (☎ 098-26-307) runs daily (weather permitting) and costs £10 ($14.80). It leaves from Roonagh Quay, Louisburgh, at 11:00 a.m., 2:25 p.m., and 6:00 p.m., and leaves from Clare Island at 10:00 a.m., 1:15 p.m., and 5:00 p.m. To get to Roonagh Quay: Follow signs from Louisburgh off the R335. Admission: Just ferry cost. Time: Varies, depending on length of stay.*

Ceide Fields

Ballycastle, County Mayo

Here lies the world's most extensive Stone Age monument, with a dwelling area, grazing grounds, and megalithic tombs from 5,000 years ago. Tools and pottery have recently been uncovered. Although a bog now covers most of the fields, portions have been cut out to show where the fields were partitioned by stone walls for growing food and grazing animals. The wild plants and flowers are world renowned, and the fields back up to some of the most captivating cliffs and rock formations in the country. You can also check out an interpretive centre that explains the area's past.

Ballycastle, County Mayo. ☎ *096-43-325. To get there: Take the R314 coastal road north from Ballina, five miles west of Ballycastle. Admission: £2.50 ($3.70) adult, £1.75 ($2.60) seniors, £1 ($1.50) children and students; £6 ($8.90) family. Open: Mid-Mar–May Tues–Sun 10:00 a.m.–5:00 p.m.; June–Sept daily 9:30 a.m.–6:30 p.m.; Oct daily 10:00 a.m.–5:00 p.m. Time: One hour.*

Croagh Patrick

Murrisk, County Mayo

According to legend, St. Patrick achieved divine inspiration on this mountain after praying and fasting for 40 days — although we don't suggest staying up there that long, no matter how beautiful the view. On the last Sunday of July, devout Irish Catholics climb the 2,500-foot mountain (many barefooted!) in memory of their patron saint. This famous mount is more than a religious site, though. Mayo and Clew Bay provide the absolutely gorgeous view from the mountain top. The climb takes about two hours and is tough work, but not impossible. And you can wear your shoes.

Murrisk, County Mayo. To get there: Between Louisburgh and Westport off the R395. Admission: Free. Open: Daylight hours. Time: Generally a few hours.

Sligo Abbey

Sligo Town, County Sligo

This is the city's only surviving medieval building, constructed in the mid-thirteenth century for Dominican monks. Inside are carvings and tomb sculptures, but the highlight is the superbly carved high altar from the fifteenth century; the altar is the only one of its kind in a monastic church in Ireland. The abbey was burned down in 1414 by a single lit candle and then was damaged again in the 1641 Rebellion. According to legend, worshippers saved the Abbey's silver bell from thieves by putting it in Lough Gill; it was retrieved later and is back in the Abbey. Legend also says that only those free from sin can hear its toll. We didn't hear it. We don't think anyone has heard it for a long time.

Abbey St., Sligo Town. ☎ 071-46-406. To get there: One block south from Kennedy Parade in the center of Sligo Town. Admission: £1.50 ($2.20) adult, £1 ($1.50) seniors, 60p (90 cents) children and students; £4 ($5.90) family. Open: Mid-June–Sept 9:30 a.m.–6:30 p.m. Time: Forty-five minutes.

Sligo County Museum & Art Gallery

Sligo Town, County Sligo

The Yeats family legacy is the cornerstone of this museum and gallery, which features memorabilia of the great poet William Butler and paintings by his brother Jack and father John. The special W.B. Yeats section includes his Nobel prize for literature (1923) and first editions of his complete works. Also inside is a small collection of objects from Sligo and all over Ireland, from prehistoric times to the Irish war for independence.

Stephen St., Sligo Town. ☎ 071-42-212. To get there: North side of the Garavogue River. Admission: Free. Museum Open: Tues–Sat 10:30 a.m.–12:30 p.m. and 2:30 p.m.– 4:30 p.m. Gallery Open: Tues, Thurs, and Sat 10:00 a.m.–12:00 p.m. and 2:00 p.m.– 5:00 p.m. Time: About an hour.

Lissadell House

Drumcliffe, County Sligo

W.B. Yeats called Lissadell House "that old Georgian mansion," which just doesn't do the place justice. It's a huge, squared stone house full of grandeur. Most notably, Lissadell House is owned by the Gore-Booth family, friends of Yeats. One of the daughters was Countess Markievicz (she married a Polish count), famous for her part in the Easter Rising and her trailblazing in British and Irish politics. Her sister, Eva, was a poet. During the Famine, Sir Robert mortgaged the house to help feed the starving. The interior of the house is impressive and contains a collection of family memorabilia.

Drumcliffe, County Sligo. ☎ 074-63-150. To get there: Off the N15 between Sligo and Donegal. Admission: £2.50 ($3.70) adult, 50p (75 cents) children. Open: June to mid-Sept Mon–Sat 10:30 a.m.–12:15 p.m., 2:00 p.m.–4:00 p.m. Time: Two hours.

The Quiet Man Heritage Cottage

Cong, County Mayo

Have you ever see the movie *The Quiet Man?* It's the one where American John Wayne comes back to his birthplace in Ireland and falls in love with Maureen O'Hara. In the movie, Wayne's character tells a local that he'd been born in the thatched-roof cottage, just like the seven generations of his family before him, and the local makes a wisecrack about Wayne buying the place to turn it into a tourist attraction. Ironically, you can now visit a replica of the original house — and yes, they do charge a small fee to the tourists. Unfortunately, no movie memorabilia remains, so all there is to see is the house.

Circular Rd., Cong, County Mayo (☎ 092-46-089). Admission: £2.75 ($4.10) adult, £1 ($1.50) children. Time: A half-hour.

Other fun things to do

- ✔ **Visiting W.B. Yeats's grave:** Yeats died in France but in 1948 his remains were brought to rest in Sligo — the place he always considered home. His grave in the Drumcliff churchyard is near a beautiful Celtic High cross. On the grave itself is an epitaph Yeats wrote: "Cast a cold eye on life, on death. Horseman pass by."

  Location: Five miles north of Sligo on the main Donegal road (N15).

- ✔ **Reading the Yeats statue:** One of the more interesting statues you'll find in Ireland is a cartoonish likeness of Sligo's famous poet near the banks of the Garavogue River, in town. Scrawled over his entire figure are the words of his own verse.

  Location: On Stephen Street, just across Hyde Bridge.

- ✔ **Taking the Yeats Water Bus Tour:** This boat tour takes you out on Lough Gill, from which you can view W.B. Yeats's Isle of Innisfree, and stops at Parkes Castle and Church Island. As you go, Yeats's poems are recited to coincide with visited areas.

  Location: Between Doorley Park in Sligo and Parkes Castle, seven miles west from Sligo on the Dromahair road (R287). Daily between March and October. The first trip leaves at 12:30 p.m. from the castle and the last leaves from Sligo at 5:30 p.m. The length of the trip is 50 minutes. Information: ☎ 071-64-266 or 087-259-8869. Price: £5 ($7.40) adults, £2 ($2.96) children, free under 12.

- ✔ **Golfing at the County Sligo Golf Course:** This is a difficult course that challenges top players, but dabblers can have fun playing it, too. The course is set between striking Atlantic beaches and the hill of Benbulben.

  Location: Rosses Point, County Sligo. ☎ 071-77-186. E-mail: cosligo@iol.ie. Par: 71. Fees: £27 ($39.95) midweek, £35 ($51.80) weekends.

Shopping in Mayo and Sligo

The Beehive

High-quality local crafts and traditional home baking from around Achill Island. Location overlooks the scenic Minaun Cliffs. Open Easter through November.

Keel, Achill Island, County Mayo (follow signs from Louisberg off the R335).
☎ *098-43-018.*

Foxford Woolen Mills Visitor Centre

The locally famous Foxford wool tweeds, rugs, blankets, and much more are all here. The mill, which you can tour, was started by a nun in 1892 and used to help the poor during the Famine.

Foxford, County Mayo (from Westport N5 northeast to N58 north). ☎ *094-56-756.*

Pat Sweeny & Son

A fascinating example of a local trading store, dating back to 1870. It has "everything from a needle to an anchor" and all the gifts, clothing, fishing gear, food, and petrol in between.

Achill Sound, Achill Island, County Mayo (follow signs from Louisburgh off the R335).
☎ *098-45-211.*

Cat and Moon

One-of-a-kind store for Irish handcrafted jewelry, contemporary art, Celtic-inspired home furnishings, jewelry, and more.

4 Castle St., Sligo Town. ☎ *071-43-686.*

Kate's Kitchen

A great stop for picnic food: meats, cheeses, salads, pâté, homemade baked bread, Irish chocolates, and preserves. The store also has soaps and potpourri.

24 Market St., Sligo Town. ☎ *071-43-022.*

Pub Life in Mayo and Sligo

Matt Molloy's

If you like traditional Irish music, this pub is worth visiting. It was started by the flutist from the famous band The Chieftains, who are often credited with the revival in Irish folk music. Inside, the pub is traditionally decorated and pretty roomy, and the back room features music nearly every night.

Bridge St., Westport, County Mayo. ☎ *098-26-655.*

Hargadon

This is the kind of pub that's so interesting to look at you may not pay attention to the pint in front of you! Beginning with the superb decor, the walls are dark wood, the floors are stone, and there's colored glass all over. You have plenty of little snugs to settle into, and you can look at various prints of the city in its early days throughout. The pub used to also be a grocery, and the walls still bear shelves with old goods.

4 O'Connell St., Sligo Town. ☎ *071-70-933.*

Yeats Tavern

Just a short walk from the grave of famous poet W.B. Yeats, this pub is a popular watering hole for locals and tourists alike. Inside you can find plenty of Yeats memorabilia. This pub features good pub grub at even better prices, and traditional music during the summer. In winter, there's music on weekends.

Drumcliff Bridge. Five miles out of Sligo Town on the main Donegal road. ☎ *071-63-117.*

Beezie's

The interior of this pub is beautiful — although from the bland exterior you may not guess it. There's stained glass and fireplaces throughout, and you can settle in easily. The name pays homage to a woman who would row from her home on Cottage Island to the pub until her death in the 1950s. Mondays and Thursdays the pub has live music, and on those nights the joint is hopping.

45 O'Connell St., Sligo Town. ☎ *071-43-031.*

Fast Facts: Counties Mayo and Sligo

AREA CODE(S)

071 and 074 for County Sligo; 092, 094, 096, 097, and 098 for County Mayo.

EMERGENCIES-HOSPITAL

Dial ☎ 999 for all emergencies. **Sligo General Hospital** is on Malloway Hill (☎ 071-42-212).

GENEALOGY RESOURCES

Contact the **Sligo Heritage and Genealogy Centre,** Temple St., Sligo (☎ 071-43-728); the

Mayo North Family History Research Centre, Castlehill, Ballina (☎ 096-31-809; Fax: 096-31-885); or the **South Mayo Family History Research Centre,** Main St., Ballinrobe (☎ 092-41-214; Internet: www.mayo-ireland.ie-roots.html).

INFORMATION

Tourist offices are located at Aras Reddan, Temple St., Sligo (☎ 071-61-201); and James St., Westport, County Mayo (☎ 098-25-739;

Internet: www.visitmayo.com), both open year-round. They can also provide reservation services. For telephone directory assistance, dial ☎ **1190.**

INTERNET

Futurenet Internet Cafe, Pearse House, Pearse Rd., Sligo (☎ **071-50-345**), has World Wide Web access for Hotmail and America Online, plus printing capabilities.

POST OFFICE

Sligo **General Post Office,** Wine St. (☎ **071-42-646**).

Chapter 20

County Donegal

Donegal's not the tourist hub of Ireland — not yet, anyway — but its people are proud of their county, and rightfully so. This northernmost corner of the country has plenty to boast about: brilliant coastline scenery, mountains, little seaside villages, museums, crafts, and exceptionally fresh seafood. About a third of the county is Irish-speaking. Natives love to think that these perks, along with the county's various other charms, make Donegal a particularly nice place to visit. (We agree.) The people you meet in the pub here may not be quite as willing to start up a chat as, say, folks in Kerry, but given the chance you'll find they're as warm and friendly as anyone in the country.

What's Where? County Donegal's Major Attractions

The heart of the county, **Donegal Town,** is a pretty tiny hamlet that nevertheless has plenty to offer in terms of places to eat, sleep, and drink — but don't expect to be wowed by attractions. The main draw is the town itself — a delightful, walkable village along the **River Eske.** To get a taste for the region you have to wander out and explore.

On your way to **Donegal Town,** from Sligo on the N15, you ramble into the resort town of **Bundoran.** This town is a popular vacation spot for Irish people from all over the island. In the summertime, you may notice the carnival-like atmosphere the place takes on. Farther up the road you hit **Ballyshannon,** a town right on the water and one of the oldest towns in Ireland. Keeping along the main road you get to the town of **Ballybofey,** which is a great starting point for touring the far reaches of the county. If you have the time and the inclination, steer your touring mobile onto the N56 and head to the coast. You can start in Donegal Town and round the coast clockwise, or head north and focus on the gorgeous **Inishowen Peninsula.** Either way, you'll creep along craggy cliffs that frame the wild ocean.

County Donegal

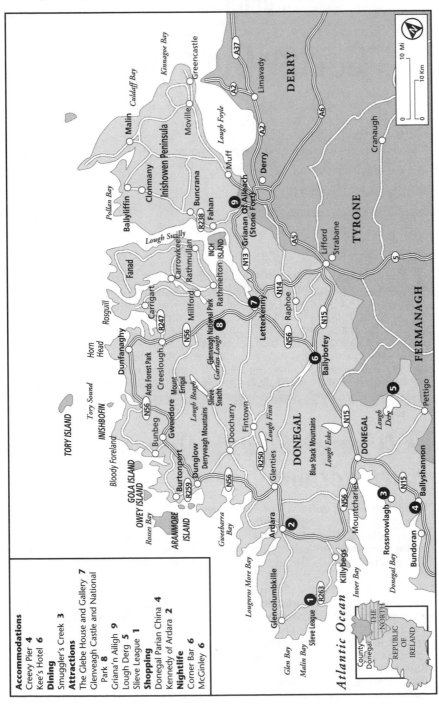

Accommodations
Creevy Pier **4**
Kee's Hotel **6**
Dining
Smuggler's Creek **3**
Attractions
The Glebe House and Gallery **7**
Glenveagh Castle and National
 Park **8**
Griana'n Ailigh **9**
Lough Derg **5**
Slieve League **1**
Shopping
Donegal Parian China **4**
Kennedy of Ardara **2**
Nightlife
Corner Bar **6**
McGinley **6**

Some great County Donegal attractions include

- **Glenveagh Castle and National Park:** Take a tour through this gorgeous castle, built in 1870 and filled with imposing rooms and incredible furnishings. The castle's gardens are beautiful, and the surrounding **National Park** features lakes, glens, woods, and red deer, and backs up to the **Derryveigh Mountains.**

- **Griana'n Ailigh:** This ring fort dates back to 1700 B.C., and looking out from it you can see **Lough Swilly** and **Lough Foyle.** A refurbished old stone church houses an interpretive centre, which also has a restaurant and craft shop.

- **Lough Derg:** Legend says that St. Patrick spent a Lenten season fasting on one of this lake's tiny islands, and at the interpretive centre you can get a real feel for the area's religious and historical import.

- **Donegal Castle:** Sitting beside the River Eske, this impressive fifteenth-century castle is filled with lovely furnishings, including Persian rugs and French tapestries. A half-hour guided tour is available.

- **The Glebe House and Gallery:** The late art collector Derek Hill's 1828 mansion is now open for visitors, who can see works by Picasso and Renoir, Jack Yeats, and many other Irish and Italian artists. The decor of the house is an exhibit in itself, with Islamic ceramics, Japanese art, and priceless wallpaper and textiles.

- **Slieve League:** Feeling fearless? Then stop off here to see the highest sea cliffs in Europe.

Getting to and around County Donegal

Local flights come into Donegal Airport, Carrickfinn, Kincasslagh (☎ 075-48-232), located 40 miles from Donegal Town. If you come by car, take the N15 north from Sligo or south from Strabane to Donegal Town. **Bus Eireann** (☎ 074-21-309) travels year-round to Donegal, Killybegs, Ballyshannon, and other towns in County Donegal. Bus pickup in Donegal is at the **Abbey Hotel,** on **The Diamond** in the town centre.

There's no local bus service, but you can easily walk through and around Donegal Town if you don't have a car.

Where to Stay in County Donegal

All the accommodations we've listed in this section have surprisingly great restaurants and pub grub on the premises, so you can get a warm bed and a good meal in one swipe!

Donegal Town

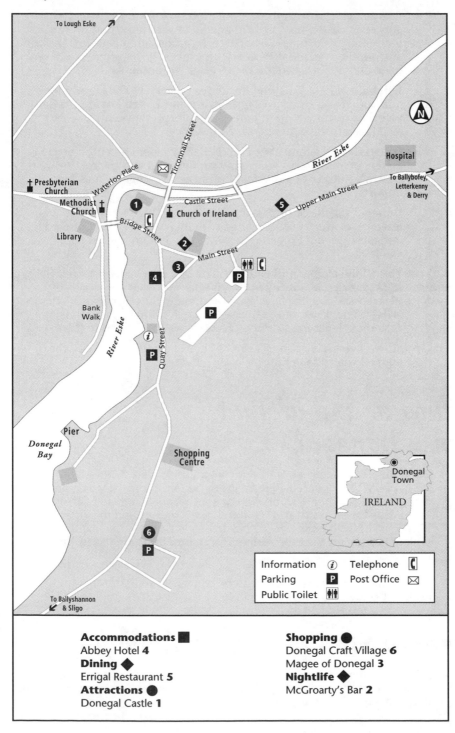

To Lough Eske

Tirconnaill Street

River Eske

Hospital

To Ballybofey, Letterkenny & Derry

Waterloo Place

Presbyterian Church

Methodist Church

Castle Street

Upper Main Street

Bridge Street

Church of Ireland

Library

Main Street

Bank Walk

River Eske

Quay Street

Pier

Donegal Bay

Shopping Centre

Donegal Town

IRELAND

To Ballyshannon & Sligo

Information	*i*	Telephone	C
Parking	P	Post Office	✉
Public Toilet	🚹🚺		

Accommodations ■
Abbey Hotel **4**
Dining ◆
Errigal Restaurant **5**
Attractions ●
Donegal Castle **1**

Shopping ●
Donegal Craft Village **6**
Magee of Donegal **3**
Nightlife ◆
McGroarty's Bar **2**

Kee's Hotel

$$ Stranorlar

This lovely hotel is a historic coaching inn, situated in a village that's perfect for touring Donegal. More than that, Kee's is a superb hotel. Friendliness abounds, the rooms are big and nice, and guests can enjoy a pool, open fireplaces, and a gym. The restaurant serves excellent food, and you can rent bikes from the hotel for seeing the village.

Stranorlar, Ballybofey, right where the N13 meets the N15. ☎ **_074-31-018._** _Fax: 074-31-917. To get there: On the N15 northeast from Donegal Town. Rates: £72–94 ($106.55–$139.10) double. AE, DC, MC, V._

Abbey Hotel

$$ Donegal Town

This comfortable hotel has tasteful and spacious rooms — some over-looking Donegal Bay, so be sure to ask about them. The hotel is in the heart of town, and beaches, boating, and horseback riding are all nearby. The Abbey restaurant is a real treat — not only is the food great, but the decor looks just like a traditional Irish kitchen. You'll feel comfortable and at home. There's also a modern-looking bar, the Eas Dun, that serves hot pub grub all day.

The Diamond, Donegal Town. ☎ **_073-21-014._** _Fax: 073-23-660. To get there: In the town centre. Rates: £70–80 ($103.60–$118.40) double. AE, DC, MC, V._

Creevy Pier

$ Ballyshannon

This family home offers a spectacular view of Donegal Bay, and swim-ming, fishing, and windsurfing happen at the doorstep. Staying here puts you in a great spot for touring the western part of the county. All rooms are comfortable and nice, and the restaurant specializes in international seafood dishes. The Captain's Cabin pub is a draw — sitting in front of the big stone fireplace with a drink is particularly relaxing.

Creevy Pier, Ballyshannon. ☎ **_072-51-236._** _Fax: 072-51-236. To get there: On the N15 south from Donegal Town or north from Sligo. Rates: £39–50 ($57.70–$74) double. MC, V._

Where to Dine in County Donegal

Smuggler's Creek

$$$ Rossnowlagh SEAFOOD

The view itself is enough to make Smuggler's Creek a memorable meal. From the conservatory dining room sitting atop a cliff you can look out at Donegal Bay, and if your timing's good, you may catch a fantastic sunset. Inside, the stone building is comfortable and aptly decorated with wooden stools, lobster pots, and porthole windows. Not surprisingly, seafood is a specialty here and, considering the low prices, is surprisingly gourmet. You can nosh on wild salmon hollandaise or the rich Smuggler's sea casserole — scallops, salmon, and prawns in a cream sauce. You can also sample steaks with trademark Irish whiskey sauce and pasta dishes. Even the bar menu is a notch above, with fresh paté and garlic mussels amid your usual soup and sandwiches.

Rossnowlagh. ☎ 072-52-366. To get there: A quarter mile off the R231, off the main Sligo-Donegal road (N15). Take the little no-name side road from the R231 to get closer to the water. Signs won't let you miss the turnoff. Main courses: £8–13.50 ($11.85–$20). AE, DC, MC, V. Open: Daily 12:00 p.m.–12:00 a.m.

Errigal Restaurant

$$ Donegal Town   FISH AND CHIPS (AND MORE)

Fish and chips is the house specialty at this local favorite. Errigal is a family-run restaurant and the menu's varied enough to appeal to any taste. It features fish dishes, steaks, chicken curry (an Irish favorite), sandwiches, and burgers. No light eating here; you'll leave full and satisfied. And with the cost, you won't go off your budget.

Upper Main St., Donegal. ☎ 073-21-428. To get there: In the town centre. Main courses: £4.50–7.50 ($6.65–$11.10). No credit cards. Open: Mon–Sat 9:00 a.m.–3:00 p.m. and 5:30 p.m.–11:00 p.m., Sun 3:30 p.m.–11:00 p.m.

Exploring County Donegal: The Top Attractions

Glenveagh Castle and National Park

Churchill

This gorgeous castle was built in 1870 and modeled after the royal Balmoral Castle in Scotland. Tours take you through the imposing rooms, each filled with incredible furnishings. A terrible story surrounds the castle: Before it was built, the infamous landowner John George Adair evicted 244 tenants during the harsh winter of 1861 to clear the land for construction. The surrounding National Park is a natural beauty. It backs up to the Derryveigh Mountains and includes the highest mountain in Donegal, Mount Errigal. The huge valley contains lakes, glens, woods, and alpine gardens. A herd of red deer has made the valley its home. Closer to the castle are fantastic gardens, some of the finest in the country. A visitor centre has an audiovisual show that explains the park interior.

Churchill, Letterkenny. ☎ 074-37-088. To get there: Northwest from Letterkenny on the main road to Kilmacrennan (N56). Admission: For Park or Castle, each £2 ($2.95) adult, £1.50 ($2.20) seniors, £1 ($1.50) children and students, £5 ($7.40) family. Open: Mid-Apr–Sept daily 10:00 a.m.–6:30 p.m.; Oct Sat–Thur 10:00 a.m.–6:30 p.m. Time: Two to three hours.

Griana'n Ailigh

Burt

You'll be amazed by the view from the battlements of this ring fort, which dates back to 1700 B.C. From them, you can perfectly see Lough Swilly and Lough Foyle. A refurbished old stone church houses an interpretive centre, which also has a restaurant and craft shop. You can visit the ancient woods next to the fort and a wetland habitat that's home to Hooper swans.

Burt, Inishowen. ☎ 077-68-000. To get there: Off the N13 northeast from Letterkenny or west from Derry. Admission: £2 ($2.95) per person, £5 ($7.40) family. Open: Summer daily 10:00 a.m.–6:00 p.m., winter daily 12:00 p.m.–6:00 p.m. Time: Forty-five minutes.

Lough Derg

Pettigo

We certainly won't ask you to participate in the three-day religious retreat on the island of St. Patrick's Purgatory each summer, but going to the visitor's centre to learn about the history-rich area is a good idea. Legend has it St. Patrick spent a Lenten season fasting on one of the lake's tiny islands, and since then devout Catholics have gone there for penance. The island is covered with a religious complex, and pilgrims must stay awake for three days, eating only one meal a day of dry bread and black tea. Visitors are welcome to visit the island, but we recommend investing the time in the centre to get a real feel for the area's religious and historical import.

Pettigo. To get there: From the Sligo-Donegal Road (N15) take R232 to Pettigo, and then R233 for five miles. The R233 ends at the water's edge, where you'll find a ferry (more like a rowboat, actually) to get to the island. Admission: Free, but you have to contact the visitor centre in Pettigo (☎ 072-61-546) before visiting the island. Open: Apr–Sept. Time (at the visitor's centre): A half-hour.

Donegal Castle

Donegal Town

Built in the fifteenth century by the O'Donnell chieftain, this castle is impressive and sits beside the River Eske. Inside, the lovely furnishings include Persian rugs and French tapestries — seventeenth-century supplements by the last owner, Sir Basil Brooke. He also added gables and many more windows. You can read handy information signs throughout that detail the history of the castle, and you can also take a half-hour guided tour.

For the "how to annoy insurance adjusters" file: Hugh Roe O'Donnell, descendant of the O'Donnell clan and sixteenth-century owner of Donegal Castle, burned down his own family home! Why? To ensure the English, who mounted a great campaign to seize Irish land and great homes, never got their hands on it. It was later rebuilt.

Donegal Town. ☎ 073-22-405. To get there: In Donegal City centre. Admission: £2 ($2.95) adult, £1.50 ($2.20) seniors, £1 ($1.50) children and students, £5 ($7.40) family. Open: June–Sept daily 9:30 a.m.–6:30 p.m. Time: An hour.

The Glebe House and Gallery

Churchill

This house was the pride of art collector Derek Hill and now the mansion allows visitors to see the grand collection. Hill's taste was diverse, and inside the gallery are works by Picasso and Renoir, as well as Jack Yeats and many other Irish and Italian artists. The decor of the house is an exhibit in itself, with Islamic ceramics, Japanese art, and priceless wall-paper and textiles. The 1828 building is set amid gardens and woods.

Churchill, Letterkenny. ☎ 074-37-071. To get there: From Donegal Town take the N15 north to Ballybofey and then the N13 north into Letterkenny. Admission: £2 ($2.95) adult, £1.50 ($2.20) seniors, £1 ($1.50) children and students, £5 (7.40) family. Open: Mid-May to Sept Sat–Thurs 11:00 a.m.–6:30 p.m. Time: One and a half hours.

Slieve League

Southwest County Donegal

The true fearless traveler shouldn't miss this attraction — an amazing view from the highest sea cliffs in Europe. At Carrick, turn off for the viewing point. There, you can decide whether to take the challenge and walk the ridge or just take in the view from the car.

Southwest County Donegal. To get there: From town, follow the main road, N56. Admission: Free. Time: Including walk, a half-hour.

Shopping in County Donegal

Donegal Craft Village

A collection of professionals working their crafts — pottery, jewelry, uillean pipes (Irish bagpipes), ceramics, batik, and more.

On the Ballyshannon-Sligo Road, Donegal Town. ☎ 073-23-312.

Donegal Parian China

You can find this distinctive brand of pottery within a huge visitor centre that gives you the opportunity to see craftspeople at work and have the process explained.

On the main Bundoran Road (N15), 500 yards from Ballyshannon. ☎ 072-51-826. Open weekdays, plus Sat and Sun from June until Sept.

Kennedy of Ardara

The Aran sweater shop that also features tweed suits, Irish table linen, cashmere sweaters, and lambswool knitwear.

Ardara (take the N56 northwest from Donegal). ☎ *075-41-106.*

Magee of Donegal

This is the largest fashion store in the county and the best source for the famous Donegal tweed. Take home superior handwoven clothing and accessories or a piece of souvenir woven cloth.

On The Diamond in Donegal Town centre. ☎ *073-22-660.*

Pub Life in County Donegal

McGroarty's Bar

This wonderful stone building houses a warm and cozy pub that's chock full of atmosphere. You won't find anything dreary about this brightly decorated pub, and the food is fantastic and varied. The music ranges from traditional Irish to folksy ballads on weekends, beginning on Thursday. An extra-pleasant aspect is the nonsmoking room — a rare thing in Ireland!

The Diamond, Donegal Town. ☎ *073-21-049.*

McGinley

This pub was recently renovated but great care was taken to ensure its traditional decor and atmosphere. The bar is huge, making plenty of places to pull up a stool. But if you'd rather, the lounge is spacious and comfortable. You can hear music four nights a week — traditional, as well as an Irish favorite: American Country-Western. Pub grub is served all day.

Glenfinn St., Ballybofey. ☎ *074-31-150.*

Corner Bar

If you're hankering for a pint and some conversation, go to the Corner. This is a no-nonsense Irish pub, where you can find plenty of locals engaged in lively chats who are eager to let you in. Friendliness is a staple of this pub, and the brick interior and smiling faces make it warm and comfortable.

Glenfinn St., Ballybofey. ☎ *074-31-361.*

Fast Facts: County Donegal

AREA CODE(S)

072, 073, 074, 075, and 077.

EMERGENCIES-HOSPITAL

Dial ☎ **999** for all emergencies. **Donegal District Hospital** is on Upper Main St. (☎ **073-21-105**).

GENEALOGY RESOURCES

Contact Donegal Ancestry, Old Meeting House, Back Ln., Ramelton, Letterkenny (☎ **074-51-266;** E-mail: donances@ indigo.ie; Internet: http:// indigo.ie-~donances).

INFORMATION

For visitor information go to the **Donegal Tourist Office,** Quay St., Donegal (☎ **073-21-148;** Internet: www.donegal. ie). Open year-round. For telephone directory assistance, dial ☎ **1190.**

POST OFFICE

Donegal Post Office, Tirconnail St. (☎ **073-21-001**).

Part VI
Northern Ireland

In this part . . .

Welcome to the North! Whether you immediately notice much difference or not, you've entered another country — one that's gotten a bit of a bad reputation after years of political violence. But don't be scared away. As we write this, the peace process in Northern Ireland is chugging along, and despite a few skirmishes during the June 2000 "marching season," Ulster has enjoyed a season of peace not seen in decades. If you choose to visit, we think you'll experience enough history, culture, stunning scenery, and warm hospitality to make the trip well worth your time.

We start this section with Derry City, Northern Ireland's second-largest city and one of the best examples of a walled city in Europe. We cover Derry City as well as County Derry and Counties Fermanagh and Tyrone in Chapter 21.

Next we take you to Belfast and the surrounding County Antrim. As Northern Ireland's largest city, Belfast has all the hotels and restaurants you'd expect, along with streets crammed with people pub-crawling and club-hopping into all hours of the night. It also makes a perfect home base for exploring County Antrim's great attractions. All this and more is covered in Chapter 22.

We end our tour of Northern Ireland with Counties Down and Armagh, where St. Patrick first started the spread of Irish Christianity. You can visit his grave here, but there are lots of other things to see, including an impressive eighteenth-century mansion surrounded by gardens, a unique aquarium, and some spectacular scenery courtesy of the Mountains of Mourne. For details, turn to Chapter 23.

Chapter 21

Counties Derry, Fermanagh, and Tyrone

● ●

In This Chapter

▶ Exploring inside and outside Derry's impressive walled city

▶ Finding your roots in the Ulster-American Folk Park

▶ Touring underground caves and rivers

▶ Finding famous Belleek china

● ●

A sure-fire way to detect when someone has definite opinions about Britain's presence in Northern Ireland is whether they refer to the main city of County Derry as "Derry" or "Londonderry." Nationalists — people who think Northern Ireland should be part of the Republic — say "Derry," the name of the area before Britain entered the picture in the seventeenth century. Loyalists — people who are loyal to England's crown — say "Londonderry." In general, most people, intending no political overtone, simply call the town "Derry" because it has half the syllables. However, those in the public eye, like newscasters, often take the middle ground and say "Derry-Londonderry" to avoid any problems.

What's Where? Derry, Fermanagh, and Tyrone's Major Attractions

Northern Ireland's second-largest city after Belfast, **Derry City**, is framed by huge seventeenth-century city walls that are about 30 feet thick and a mile in circumference. The walls are in such pristine shape that Derry ranks as one of the best examples of a walled city in Europe. There are also plenty of examples of Georgian architecture in Derry, which surrounds a square called the Diamond. Some other city highlights include

▶ **St. Columb's Cathedral and Chapter House Museum:** This 1613 Gothic cathedral towers above Derry's city walls.

▶ **Tower Museum:** This museum, housed in a replica sixteenth-century fort, covers Derry's history from prehistoric times to the present day.

✔ **Earhart Center:** Amelia Earhart landed in Derry in 1932, becoming the first woman to fly solo across the Atlantic, and this center in Ballyarnet will tell you the story.

Further south on the A5 is the town of Omagh, in **County Tyrone,** and past that the quaint **County Fermanagh,** which attracts vacationers for its resortlike qualities. **Lough Erne,** a long, pretty lake, runs the length of the County Fermanagh and is dotted with 154 little islands. The highlights of the county includes **Enniskillen,** a small town set on an island that connects the upper and lower parts of Lough Erne. Some of the best attractions in Tyrone and Fermanagh are

✔ **Ulster-American Folk Park:** A stop not to be missed! This outdoor folk park traces the roots of Irish emigration to America during the eighteenth and nineteenth centuries, with re-creations of Irish villages and town streets.

✔ **Marble Arch Caves:** Tour the caves on boats that glide through an underground river while the great cave guides point out rivers, waterfalls, winding passages, and echoing chambers.

✔ **Enniskillen Castle:** The vaults of this fifteenth-century castle, located in the west end of Enniskillen, hold fifteenth- and seventeenth-century models and figurines of old-time castle life.

✔ **Belleek Pottery Factory:** Belleek is Ireland's oldest and most famous pottery, and on these tours you can watch the Belleek craftspeople create the famous fine bone china.

✔ **Castle Coole:** This eighteenth-century Neoclassical-style house is one of the finest of its kind in the country.

Getting to and around Derry, Fermanagh, and Tyrone

The **City of Derry (Eglinton) Airport** (☎ **028-7181-0784**) is several miles from the city and serviced by **British Airways Express** (☎ **01496-30-2022**). To get to Derry from the airport, take a cab. The fare is around £6 ($9.90) to the city centre.

To get to Derry by car from Donegal, take the N15 to Strabane and then take the A5 north. To get to Enniskillen from Sligo, take the N16 (which becomes the A4 in Northern Ireland) east. To get to Omagh from Derry or Strabane, go south on the A5; from Enniskillen go north on the A32. If you are driving from the Republic into Northern Ireland make sure you notify your rental car company; extra insurance may be required.

Northern Ireland Railways (☎ **028-7134-2228**) services Derry year-round, and **Ulsterbus** (☎ **028-7126-2261**) travels year-round to Derry, Omagh, Enniskillen, and other major towns in Counties Derry, Tyrone, and Fermanagh.

Counties Derry, Fermanagh, and Tyrone

Accommodations	Dining	Earhart Center **1**	The Butter Market **8**
Beech Hill Country House Hotel **3**	Mulligan's Bar & Restaurant **8**	Enniskillen Castle **8**	Erneside Shopping Centre **8**
Killyhevlin Hotel **7**	Saddlers **8**	Marble Arch Caves **9**	Fermanagh Cottage
Silverbirch Hotel **6**	**Attractions**	Ulster-American Folk Park **5**	Industries **8**
White Horse Hotel **2**	Belleek Pottery **10**	**Shopping**	**Nightlife**
	Castle Coole **8**	Belleek China **10**	The Faerie Thorn **4**

Where to Stay in Derry, Fermanagh, and Tyrone

The Beech Hill Country House Hotel
$$ Derry City, County Derry

Whether you're strolling the gorgeous grounds of this elegant country house or curling up before the fire with a cup of tea, you'll know this is pampering at its best. Every detail of this hotel exudes style, from the canopy beds to the conservatory dining area. Every room is separately decorated and furnished to the hilt, and the Ardmore Restaurant serves locally caught seafood and home-grown seasonal vegetables. It's just outside of Derry City and within easy driving distance of the region's biggest attractions.

32 Ardmore Rd., Derry City, County Derry. ☎ *028-7134-9279. Fax: 028-7134-5366. E-mail:* beechhill@nisecrets.com. *Internet:* www.nisecrets.com/ beechhill. *To get there: Take the A6 south out of the city, toward Belfast, and follow signs. Rates: £75–80 ($123.80–$132) double. AE, MC, V.*

The Trinity Hotel
$$ Derry City, County Derry

This ultra-elegant hotel almost seems out of place in Derry, contrasting with the medieval look of the city. You'll find it simple, yet, despite the reasonable cost, posh. The architecture and materials are modern, but traditional Celtic designs give it a characteristically Irish feel. While the rooms aren't the most spacious around, the beds are super-comfortable and the furnishings are simple and sleek. Before you head into Derry City, be sure to check out one of the hotel's three bars, especially the stunning Conservatory Lounge.

22 Strand Rd., Derry City, County Derry. ☎ *028-7127-1271. Fax: 028-7127-1277. To get there: Strand Rd. is just north of the city centre and south of Foyle Bridge. Rates: £80–100 ($132–$165) double. AE, MC, V.*

The White Horse Hotel
$$ Derry City, County Derry

On the main road to the Giants Causeway in County Antrim (see Chapter 22) and only a few minutes from the airport, this hotel is great for venturing out to see the North. Although the dining and pub life is pretty run-of-the-mill, the rooms are fabulous. They've got canopy beds and porches that lead out to the groomed lawn, and tasteful wallpaper and pine furniture gives each room a country feel. There's fishing and golfing nearby.

68 Clooney Rd., Derry City, County Derry (five miles outside the city). ☎ *028-7186-0606. Fax: 028-7186-0371. To get there: From Derry take the A2 toward Limavady. Rates: £50–60 ($82.50–$99) double. AE, MC, V, DC.*

Derry City

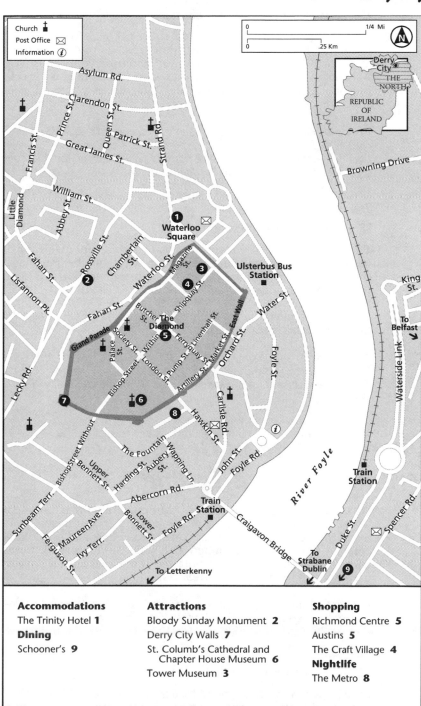

Church ✝
Post Office ⊠
Information ⓘ

0   1/4 Mi
0   .25 Km

Derry City
THE NORTH
REPUBLIC OF IRELAND

Asylum Rd.
Clarendon St.
Prince St.
Queen St.
Patrick St.
Strand Rd.
Francis St.
Great James St.
Browning Drive
William St.
Little Diamond
Abbey St.
Rossville St.
Chamberlain St.
Waterloo St.
Magazine St.
Shipquay St.

1 Waterloo Square

Ulsterbus Bus Station

King St.

Fahan St.
Lisfannon Pk.
Fahan St.
Butcher St.
The Diamond
Within
Fountain St.
Ferryquay St.
Linenhall St.
Water St.
Foyle St.
To Belfast
Waterside Link

2
3
4
5

Grand Parade
Society St.
Palace St.
Bishop Street
London St.
Pump St.
Artillery St.
Market St.
Orchard St.
Lecky Rd.

6
7
8

Cartisle Rd.
Hawkin St.

Bishop Street Without
The Fountain
Upper Bennett St.
Harding St.
Aubery St.
Wapping Ln.
John St.
Foyle Rd.
Train Station
River Foyle
Train Station

Sunbeam Terr.
MaureenAve.
Lower Bennett St.
Abercorn Rd.
Train Station
Craigavon Bridge
Duke St.
Spencer Rd.

Ferguson St.
Ivy Terr.
Foyle Rd.
To Strabane Dublin

9

To Letterkenny

Accommodations	**Attractions**	**Shopping**
The Trinity Hotel **1**	Bloody Sunday Monument **2**	Richmond Centre **5**
Dining	Derry City Walls **7**	Austins **5**
Schooner's **9**	St. Columb's Cathedral and	The Craft Village **4**
	Chapter House Museum **6**	**Nightlife**
	Tower Museum **3**	The Metro **8**

The Killyhevlin Hotel

$$ Killyhevlin, County Fermanagh

Located on the serene and beautiful shore of Lough Erne, The Killyhevlin Hotel provides views of the best this area has to offer, both from the lounge and the exceptional restaurant and from your room. Or you can walk just a few steps out of the door and take in the lake up close and personal. Rooms here make you feel immediately welcome, as does the staff. You can get bar snacks all day, and there's a lunchtime buffet.

Dublin Rd., Killyhevlin, Enniskillen, County Fermanagh. ☎ ***028-6632-3481.*** *Fax: 028-6632-4726. E-mail:* rodney@easynet.co.uk. *Internet:* www.killyhevlin.com. *To get there: Less than a mile north of Enniskillen, off the A32. Look for the sign. Rates: £80–95 ($132–$156.75) double. AE, MC, V DC.*

The Silverbirch Hotel

$$ Omagh, County Tyrone

This hotel, recently renovated and featuring a beautiful atrium, is by far one of the finest in the mid-Ulster region. Although the hotel has become quite modern, it's fantastically hidden on the outskirts of Gortin Glen National Park, giving it a timeless, rustic feel. The Buttery Grill is known throughout the area for its top-notch cuisine. The hotel staff, friendly and efficient, might be the highlight of your stay; someone's always on hand with a smile to help out.

5 Gortin Rd., Omagh, County Tyrone. ☎ ***028-8224-2520.*** *Fax: 028-8224-3360. E-mail:* info@silverbirchhotel.com. *Internet:* www.silverbirchhotel.com. *To get there: Just north of Omagh, on the B48. Rates: £35–82 ($57.77–$135.35) double. AE, MC, V DC.*

Where to Dine in Derry, Fermanagh, and Tyrone

What's the difference between a traditional Irish breakfast and an Ulster Fry? Well, along with your fried egg, sausage, bacon, black pudding, fried tomatoes, and toast you get *soda farls* and *potato cakes.* Soda farls are soft bread, fluffed with soda and buttermilk; potato cakes are made with mashed potatoes, flour, and butter. They're both fried up with the rest of the breakfast and are incredibly good.

But that's only one meal of the day, and you've got three to take care of. Here are some picks that'll make your stomach happy.

Schooner's

$$$ Derry City, County Derry SEAFOOD

Even if the food weren't great, the decor of Schooner's would be enough to make the place popular. (After all, how many restaurants can you name that have a 30-foot schooner incorporated into the furnishings?)

But the food *is* great! Seafood dishes like baked fillet of trout with hazelnut butter or plaice filled with smoked salmon and prawns fill the menu, but nonseafood lovers will love the rest. There's the mushroom stroganoff, for instance, plus various steaks and the Schooner's Specialty, a chicken breast stuffed with broccoli and cheese and wrapped in a puff pastry. The price is right, especially for food of this quality.

59 Victoria Rd., Derry City, County Derry. ☎ *028-7131-1500. To get there: Located on the east bank of the River Foyle. Main courses: £9.95–13.50 ($16.40–$22.30). AE, MC, V. Open: Daily 8:30 a.m.–10:00 p.m.*

Saddlers
$$ Enniskillen, County Fermanagh EUROPEAN

Horse lovers will delight at the equestrian atmosphere at Saddlers, where equipment and trappings cover the walls. The food is hearty and varied, from salads to steaks, plus barbecued pork ribs, pizzas, and mixed grills. The restaurant sits above the Horse Show bar, a great place for an after-dinner drink.

66 Belmore St., Enniskillen, County Fermanagh. ☎ *028-6632-6223. To get there: Dublin Rd. (A4) into town becomes Belmore St. Main courses: £5.95–10.95 ($9.80–$18.05). MC, V. Open: Daily 12:00 p.m.–2:30 p.m. and 4:00 p.m.–10:45 p.m.*

Mulligan's Bar & Restaurant
$$ Enniskillen, County Fermanagh IRISH-INTERNATIONAL

This family-run restaurant serves a wide selection that emphasizes local ingredients. The variety of dishes strikes a balance between local favorites and international cuisine. Everything that reaches the table is homemade, and it shows. For starters, there are savory patés and soups, which make way for tasty seafood dishes like local mussels or salmon, or Ulster meat dishes. The atmosphere is inviting and rustic, and there's live music to set the tone for a relaxing meal. Top pick: the Irish stew, which is made with a generous amount of Bushmills whiskey — it may be the best stew you'll ever eat.

33 Darling St., Enniskillen, County Fermanagh. ☎ *028-6632-2059. To get there: Main St. in city centre. Main courses: £8–12 ($13.20–$19.80). MC, V. Open: Daily 12:00 p.m.–3:00 p.m. and 4:00 p.m.–10:00 p.m.*

Exploring Counties Derry, Fermanagh, and Tyrone: The Top Attractions

St. Columb's Cathedral and Chapter House Museum
Derry City, County Derry

This cathedral — named for Saint Columb, founder of Derry — towers above the city walls. There's stained glass inside this Gothic cathedral that depicts the grim tale of one of the city's many sieges, this one involving the Protestants and Jacobites. James I ordered the construction of the cathedral in 1613, and a year later Londoners sent over a bell for the steeple with "Fear God. Honour the King." engraved in it. The Chapter House Museum displays the original keys of the city gates and an audiovisual presentation of the history of Derry City.

London St., Derry City, County Derry. ☎ *028-7126-7284 or 028-7126-7313. To get there: Inside the city walls south of The Diamond. Admission: £1 ($1.65) per person. Open: Mar–Oct daily 9:00 a.m.–1:00 p.m. and 2:00 p.m.–5:00 p.m.; Nov–Feb daily 9:00 a.m.–1:00 p.m. and 2:00 p.m.–4:00 p.m. Time: Forty-five minutes.*

Tower Museum
Derry City, County Derry

This museum really gets at the heart of Derry, covering its history from prehistoric times to the present day. It's housed in the O'Doherty Tower, a replica of the sixteenth-century medieval fort that stood in that spot. Upstairs are mementos from the wrecks of the Spanish Armada, and multimedia displays examine the city history, even delving into Northern Ireland's political "Troubles."

Union Hall Pl., Derry City, County Derry. ☎ *028-7137-2411. To get there: Inside the city walls, north of The Diamond. Admission: £3.50 ($5.75) per person, £7 ($11.55) family. Open: Oct–June Tues–Sat 10:00 a.m.–5:00 p.m.; July–Sept Mon–Sat 10:00 a.m.– 5:00 p.m., Sun 9:00 a.m.–5:30 p.m. Time: An hour.*

Earhart Center
Ballyarnet, County Derry

Amelia Earhart landed in Derry in 1932, becoming the first woman to fly solo across the Atlantic. To find out more about her historic flight, you can visit the Earhart Center in Ballyarnet.

Ballyarnet, County Derry. ☎ *02871-35-4040. To get there: Three miles north of Derry City on the A2. Admission: Free.*

Marble Arch Caves
Florencecourt, County Fermanagh

Exploring the Marble Arch Caves is a thrill. Visitors tour on boats that glide through an underground river while guides point out rivers, waterfalls, winding passages, and echoing chambers. The guides are great, giving detailed information about stalagmites and stalactites and the minerals that coat the walls. The tour includes walking sections, but nothing's dangerous or exhausting.

The Marble Arch Caves are hugely popular, so it's wise to book ahead. Also, it gets pretty chilly "down under," so bring a sweater. If there's been heavy rain, the caves occasionally close for safety reasons, so call if there's been bad weather.

Marlbank Scenic Loop, Florencecourt, County Fermanagh. ☎ *028-6634-8855. To get there: Off the A35, 12 miles south of Enniskillen. Once you're in the village of Florencecourt, near the border, there is a loop road that takes you out to the caves, with plenty of signs to point the way. Admission: £5 ($9.05) adults, £3 ($4.95) students and seniors, £2 ($3.30) children. Open: Mid-Mar to Sept daily 10:00 a.m.–4:30 p.m. Time: About two and a half hours.*

Enniskillen Castle

Enniskillen, County Fermanagh

This fifteenth-century castle, once the stronghold of powerful Irish chieftains, sits majestically in the west end of town, overlooking the River Erne. The castle contains a county museum with exhibits on the area's history, wildlife, and landscape, as well as the museum of the Royal Inniskilling Fusiliers. There are also models and figurines depicting old-time castle life.

Castle Barracks, Enniskillen, County Fermanagh. ☎ *028-6632-5000. To get there: West end of town across Castle Bridge from the A4. Admission: £2 ($3.30) adults, £1.50 ($2.50) seniors and students, £1 ($1.65) children, £5 ($8.25) family of two adults and two children. Open: May, June, and Sept Mon and Sat 2:00 p.m.–5:00 p.m., Tues–Fri 10:00 a.m.–5:00 p.m.; July and Aug Sat–Mon 2:00 p.m.–5:00 p.m., Tues–Fri 10:00 a.m.–5:00 p.m.; Oct–Apr Mon 2:00 p.m.–5:00 p.m., Tues–Fri 10:00 a.m.–5:00 p.m. Time: An hour and a half.*

Belleek Pottery Tours

Belleek, County Fermanagh

Belleek is Ireland's oldest and most famous pottery works, and on these tours you can watch the highly trained craftspeople create the famous fine bone china and then pick up some of the delicate ivory pottery to take home. There are guided tours, a museum, and a theater that shows a video about china making. The showroom tours (an overview of what the company makes and sells) run only on weekdays and last a half-hour.

Main St., Belleek, County Fermanagh. ☎ *028-6865-8501. To get there: Take the A46 northeast from Enniskillen. Admission: Free. Tours £1 ($1.65). Open: Mar–Sept Mon–Fri 9:00 a.m.–6:00 p.m., Sat, Tues–Fri 10:00 a.m.–5:00 p.m.; July and Aug Sat–Mon 2:00 p.m.–5:00 p.m., Tues–Fri 10:00 a.m.–5:00 p.m.; Oct–Apr Mon 2:00 p.m.– 5:00 p.m., Tues–Fri 10:00 a.m.–5:00 p.m. Time: An hour (including tour).*

Castle Coole

Enniskillen, County Fermanagh

This eighteenth-century Neoclassical-style house was completely refurbished by the state, resulting in its becoming one of the finest of its kind in the country. Most of the stone fittings and fixtures are from England and, extraordinarily, almost all of the original furniture is in place. The opulent State Bedroom has a bed that was specially made for King George IV to use during his 1821 visit to Ireland. There's also a Chinese-style sitting room and gorgeous woodwork and fireplaces throughout.

Off the Belfast-Enniskillen Rd. (A4), Enniskillen, County Fermanagh. ☎ *028-6632-2690. To get there: About a mile out of Enniskillen, just off the Belfast-Enniskillen Road (A4). Admission: £2.60 ($4.30) adults, £1.30 ($2.15) children, £6.50 ($10.75) family. Open: Apr Mon–Fri 1:00 p.m.–6:00 p.m., Sat and Sun 5:00 p.m.–9:00 p.m.; Sept Mon–Fri 1:00 p.m.–6:00 p.m.; May–Aug Fri–Wed 1:00 p.m.–6:00 p.m. Time: An hour.*

Ulster-American Folk Park
Castletown, County Tyrone

This immensely interesting folk park traces the roots of Irish emigration to America during the eighteenth and nineteenth centuries. It's outdoors, and visitors walk through re-creations of Irish villages and town streets, and of an emigrant ship. The park also exhibits re-creations of the places Irish emigrants went to as well, like an American street and a log cabin. The park sits on land where Thomas Mellon, who founded the Pittsburgh banking dynasty, lived as a boy.

The Ulster-American Folk Park has an excellent lineup of events to appeal to American visitors young and old alike. These include Independence Day celebrations in July, an Appalachian and Bluegrass music festival in September, and a Halloween Festival in October.

Mellon Rd., Castletown, Camphill, Omagh, County Tyrone. ☎ *028-8224-3292. To get there: Off the A5, three miles north of Omagh. Look for the signs. Admission: £3.50 ($5.75) adults, £1.70 ($2.80) students and children, £10 ($16.50) family. Open: Oct–Mar Mon–Fri 10:30 a.m.–5:00 p.m.; Apr–Sept Mon–Sat 11:00 a.m.–6:30 p.m., Sun 11:30 a.m.–7:00 p.m. Time: Two hours.*

More Fun Things to Do: The Top Derry Landmarks

Check out the following landmarks while touring Derry:

- ✔ **Derry City Walls:** At 26 feet high, about 30 feet thick, and encircling the city, the walls are an impressive sight, and make Derry one of Europe's only completely walled-in cities. They were built in 1618 and succeeded in keeping Derry safe from many attacks. In fact, the walls have never been breached, and are so impenetrable that they earned Derry the nickname "The Maiden City."

- ✔ **Bloody Sunday Monument:** Outside Butcher's Gate in the old city walls is an area known as the Bogside. This is where the Bloody Sunday massacre occurred in 1972, in which British soldiers shot 13 demonstrators dead. There's a moving monument on Rossville Street that honors the dead. The event inspired Brit Paul McCartney's song "Give Ireland back to the Irish," which has become an unofficial anthem of the Irish struggle for independence, as well as the song "Sunday, Bloody Sunday" by U2. Nearby is the "Free Derry Corner," an area of detailed and artistic wall murals. The most famous is the "You Are Now Entering Free Derry" mural.

Organized Tours

Guinness Essential Walking Tour of Historic Derry

This award-winning walking tour covers the city, pointing out major historical sites. It's run by the North's only member of the Association of Approved Tour Guides of Ireland.

Tours depart from the Tourist Information Centre at 10:30 a.m. and 2:30 p.m. daily between May and Oct. Information: Tourist Information Centre, 44 Foyle St., Derry, County Derry. ☎ 028-7126-7284. Price: £3 ($4.95) adults, children free. Price includes refreshments.

Lough Erne Boat Tour

You can take a boat tour of Upper Lough Erne River aboard the 63-seater *Kestrel.*

Trips last just under two hours and depart daily in July and Aug at 10:30 a.m., 2:15 p.m., and 4:15 p.m.; in May and June on Sun 2:30 p.m.; and in Sept on Tue, Sat, and Sun at 2:30 p.m. Information: Erne Tours Ltd., Round O Jetty, Brook Park, Enniskillen, County Fermanagh. ☎ 028-6632-2882. Price: £3 ($4.95) adults, £1.50 ($2.50) children under 14.

Charabanc Horse-Drawn Carriage Tours

This is the way to see the city! Get a tour of Derry while riding in a horse-drawn charabanc carriage.

Call ☎ 028-7127-1886 to be picked up anywhere in the city centre. First tour begins at 10:00 a.m., and then every hour thereafter until sunset. Runs daily from May 1–Oct 1. Information: Contact Martin McGowan, ☎ 028-7127-1886. Price: Varies depending on the phase of the moon (or Martin's whim). Ask when you call.

The Kingfisher Trail Holiday Guide

Anyone interested in cycling around Northern Ireland should pick up this guide, which allows you to custom-pick the route you'd like to make, no matter what level of cycling skill you have. With the guide, you can book accommodations along the trail and choose activities to do along the way. The trail loops around lakes, goes through forests, and winds into villages. Your tour can last anywhere from half a day to eight days. You can also create a multiactivity vacation by adding canoeing, jet-skiing, mountain biking, or archery into your cycling tour.

You can get the guide from the Tourist Information Centre, Wellington Rd., Enniskillen, County Fermanagh (☎ 028-6632-0121).

Shopping

In Derry, the best shopping is found in the inner city, in the **Richmond Centre,** a modern mall facing The Diamond and featuring more than 30 shops and boutiques. Enniskillen's large shopping complex, **Erneside Shopping Centre,** is a bilevel modern mall off Wellington Road. And don't forget you can pick up some Belleek china at the factory's showroom. (For details, see "Exploring Counties Derry, Fermanagh, and Tyrone: The Top Attractions," earlier in this chapter.)

Austins

This Victorian-style department store is a city landmark. It specializes in clothes, perfume, china, crystal, and linens. The coffee shop on the third floor has a great view of Derry City.

The Diamond, Derry City, County Derry. ☎ *028-7126-1817.*

The Butter Market

This historic market has studio workshops that make and sell all sorts of local crafts, including ceramic jewelry, screen prints, Celtic-inspired statuary, and leather goods. The cobble courtyard is nice just for browsing.

Enniskillen, County Fermanagh. ☎ *028-6632-4499.*

The Craft Village

Painstakingly restored to give an Old-World feel, this little "village" has loads of craft shops specializing in a variety of handmade Irish products. There's also a restaurant and coffee shop.

City centre, Derry City, County Derry. ☎ *028-7126-0329.*

Fermanagh Cottage Industries

Here's where you'll find traditional handmade Irish crafts, like blackthorn *shillelaghs* (walking sticks), Celtic jewelry, and hand-cut glass.

14 East Bridge St., Enniskillen, County Fermanagh. ☎ *028-6632-2260.*

Pub Life

Want to hear traditional Irish music in Derry? Head to **Waterloo Street,** just outside the city walls in front of Butcher and Castle Gates. Some of the best pubs for informal sessions lie along this route, including **Dungloe Bar** (☎ 028-7126-7761), **Bound for Boston** (☎ 028-7126-6351), **Castle Bar** (☎ 028-7126-3118), and **Peadar O'Donnell's** (☎ 028-7137-2318).

The Faerie Thorn

Two gorgeous gardens are the highlight of this traditional pub, which dates back to the 1600s and sits at the feet of the Sperrin Mountains. It used to be a grocery and pawn shop. The gardens have spectacular views of the countryside. Sit with a pint and take it all in. As for the food, you'll be ruined by the steak-and-Guinness pie.

14 Main St., Tobermore, County Derry. ☎ *028-7964-4385.*

The Metro

Plenty of little alcoves and mementos from across the globe make the Metro an interesting stop. The pub sits in the shadow of Derry's old city walls and serves a mean beef Guinness stew.

3–4 Bank Pl., Derry City, County Derry. ☎ *028-7126-7401.*

Fast Facts: Counties Derry, Fermanagh, and Tyrone

AREA CODE

028.

EMERGENCIES

Dial ☎ **999** for all emergencies.

GENEALOGY RESOURCES

Contact **The Genealogy Centre**, 4–22 Butcher St., Derry, County Derry (☎ **028-7137-3177**; Fax: 01504-3-3177), which has a computerized database with records as far back as the early seventeenth century, or **Heritage World**, 26 Market Sq., Dungannon, County Tyrone (☎ **01868-72-4187**; E-mail: irishwld@gpo.iol.ie; Internet: www.iol.ie.irishworld).

INFORMATION

For visitor information in Derry, go to the **tourist office** at 44 Foyle St., Derry (☎ **028-7137-7577**), open year-round. It can also provide reservation services. In County Tyrone, contact the **Omagh Tourist Information Centre** at 1 Market St., Omagh, County Tyrone (☎ **028-8225-0033**; Fax: 028-8225-1744; E-mail: tourism@omagh.gov.uk; Internet: www.omagh.gov.uk-tourism.htm). The **Fermanagh Tourist Information Centre** is located on Wellington Rd., Enniskillen (☎ **028-7032-3110**). For telephone directory assistance, dial ☎ **192.**

Chapter 22

Belfast and County Antrim

. . . .

In This Chapter

▶ Staying in luxury hotels that won't bankrupt you

▶ Getting a room with a view along the coast

▶ Finding the best places to eat or just have a pint

▶ Bringing out your inner adventurer

▶ Taking a *Titanic* (or other) tour of the city

▶ Shopping around

▶ Exploring the night life

. . . .

*W*hat do you think of when you first hear the name Belfast? A fantastic city surrounded by gorgeous and striking scenic drives, charming little towns, and amazing natural sights?

Right.

No, you probably think of news stories about sectarian violence, and while it's true that the region has seen its share of troubles for many years, it's also true that things aren't what they were five or ten years ago. Belfast isn't the militarized city it once was, though tension still lies not too deeply under the surface. The peace accords signed in 1998 prove that there is a real desire for stability in the region, but old wounds take a long time to heal.

Beyond politics and religion, though, beyond intolerance and nationalism, there's one undeniable fact about Ulster (the old Gaelic region in which all of Northern Ireland — plus Counties Cavan, Donegal, and Monaghan — lies): It's one of the most beautiful areas in all of Ireland.

What's Where? Belfast and County Antrim's Major Attractions

Belfast, the second-largest Irish city after Dublin, sits at the southern end of County Antrim, on the border with County Down. It's an architectural delight, with grand Victorian buildings among the stretches of shops and department stores. Much like Dublin, the city is having a renaissance of sorts, and is reclaiming the splendor of days past. It's a cosmopolitan place, with pubs and restaurants crammed with people until the wee hours. Belfast is one of those rare cities that's sure to provide a good time, no matter if you're looking for some *craic* (good times), culture, or fine cuisine. Hightlights of the city include

- ✔ **The Belfast Zoo:** This zoo has a children's farm, an island of spider monkeys, a Polar Bear Canyon, and much more.

- ✔ **Ulster Museum:** Northern Ireland's national museum has a collection that ranges from local history to ancient artifacts, plus works of art by Francis Bacon and Henry Moore.

- ✔ **Bailey's Belfast Pub Tour:** Bailey's Irish Cream hosts a good pub tour that visits six of Ireland's finest pubs.

To travel north out of the city toward the finest attractions around **County Antrim,** we suggest driving along the **Antrim coast** on the A2. The route takes you to **Carrickfergus,** just a few miles from Belfast. There you can visit **Carrickfergus castle,** the best example of a Norman fortified castle in Ireland.

Continuing up the A2, a day's drive will take you past gorgeous scenery — both the coastline on the right and the green landscape to the left. Eventually you'll be on the **Causeway Coast,** meaning it's time to pull over and end the spectacular drive. There's still a lot to see and do after you get to the coast though, such as the **Giant's Causeway,** sometimes called the eighth wonder of the world; the **Bushmills Distillery,** the oldest in the world; and for the adventurous, the **Carrick-A-Rede Rope Bridge.**

If you didn't get enough on the way up, head back along the coast as well; or, if you want to discover some of Northern Ireland's quaint villages, take the A29 south toward **Armagh.**

Getting to Belfast and County Antrim

Belfast International Airport (☎ 028-9448-4848) is about 19 miles from the city. British Airways, British Midland, and Aer Lingus all fly into the airport daily. There is also a **Belfast City Airport** (☎ 028-9045-7745) for flights within the country. To get to Belfast from Belfast International Airport, take the Airbus into city centre. The fare is £4.10 ($6.75). From Belfast City Airport, take a cab. The fare is around £4 ($6.60).

Another option if you're coming from Britain or Scotland is the ferry. **The Norse Irish Ferries** (☎ 0151-944-1010) travel between Belfast and London year-round; the fare includes accommodation, four-course meal, and a full breakfast. It's a lovely trip, but it takes a whopping 11 hours!

County Antrim

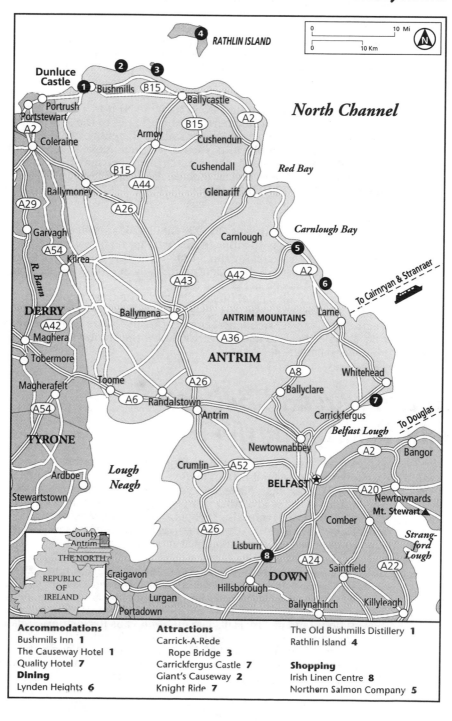

0   10 Mi
0   10 Km

RATHLIN ISLAND 4

Dunluce Castle
Bushmills B15
Portrush
Portstewart
A2
Coleraine
Ballycastle
B15
Armoy
Cushendun
A2

North Channel

Cushendall
Red Bay
Glenariff
Ballymoney
A44
B15
A29
A26
Garvagh

DERRY
A54
A42
Maghera
Tobermore
Magherafelt
A54
Kilrea
R. Bann

Carnlough
Carnlough Bay
5
A43
A42
A2
6
Ballymena
ANTRIM MOUNTAINS
A36
ANTRIM
Larne
To Cairnryan & Stranraer

Toome
A26
A6
Randalstown
Antrim
A8
Ballyclare
Whitehead
7
Carrickfergus
To Douglas

TYRONE
Ardboe
Stewartstown

Lough Neagh
Crumlin
A52
Newtownabbey
Belfast Lough
A2
Bangor
BELFAST
A20
Newtownards
Mt. Stewart ▲
Comber
Strang-ford Lough

County Antrim
THE NORTH
REPUBLIC OF IRELAND
Craigavon
Lurgan
Portadown
Lisburn
8
A24
DOWN
Saintfield
A22
Hillsborough
Ballynahinch
Killyleagh

Accommodations
Bushmills Inn **1**
The Causeway Hotel **1**
Quality Hotel **7**
Dining
Lynden Heights **6**

Attractions
Carrick-A-Rede
   Rope Bridge **3**
Carrickfergus Castle **7**
Giant's Causeway **2**
Knight Ride **7**

The Old Bushmills Distillery **1**
Rathlin Island **4**

Shopping
Irish Linen Centre **8**
Northern Salmon Company **5**

You'd be better off traveling by land to the northern U.K. and taking the ferry between Campbeltown and Ballycastle, County Antrim. The **Argyll & Antrim Steam Packet** (☎ 0870-552-3523) makes the trip in under three hours. Call for bookings. Other ferry services include **SeaCat** (☎ 01208-81-2508), which travels between Stranraer, Scotland, and Belfast, and **P&O European Ferries** (☎ 0990-98-0980), which travels between Cairnryan, England, and Larne, County Antrim. All ferries can carry vehicles.

If you're coming by car from Dublin take the N1 north to Belfast (N1 becomes the A1 in Northern Ireland). To get to the Antrim Coast from Belfast, take the A2, which runs along the entire coast. If you're driving from the Republic into Northern Ireland make sure you notify your rental car company because extra insurance may be required. Rental cars available in Belfast include **Avis** (☎ 028-9024-0404), **Budget** (☎ 028-9023-0700), **Hertz** (☎ 028-9073-2451), and **National** (☎ 028-9032-5520).

Northern Ireland Railways (☎ 028-9066-8258) services County Antrim extensively, with stops in Belfast, Portrush, Coleraine, Ballymoney, Ballymena, Antrim, Larne Harbour, Larne, Carrickfergus, Bangor, and Lisburn. Belfast Central Railway Station is located on East Bridge Street. **Ulsterbus** (☎ 028-9033-7004) travels year-round to Belfast, Larne, Ballycastle, Bushmills, and other major towns in County Antrim. The main bus stations in Belfast are Europa Bus Centre on Glengall Street and Langanside Bus Centre near the rail station. Double check to make sure you know the station from which you're departing.

Getting around Belfast and County Antrim

Unlike most towns in Ireland, Belfast is rather accessible by car. Parking is widely available and meters are used for pay parking. If you're walking Belfast, make sure you have a comfortable pair of shoes, and consider investing in an all-day bus ticket. **Belfast Citybus** (☎ 028-9024-6485) operates throughout the city. Most buses depart from Donegall Square in the city centre. Exact change is required. Multijourney tickets are available at most newsagents.

You can also get around by bike. **Recycle,** 1-5 Albert Square (☎ 028-9031-3113) rents bikes and provides safety helmets, security locks, and delivery to your accommodation. If pedaling is too much effort, call a cab. Taxi ranks in Belfast are located at Central Station, both bus stations, and at City Hall. The metered cabs in Northern Ireland are standardized London-style black taxis with yellow disks on the windshield. We recommend you take those. There are nonmeter cabs available as well, but always ask for the rate before you get into one because your foreign accent may cost you extra.

Where to Stay in Belfast and around County Antrim

Some Belfast hotels have lower rates for the weekends than during midweek. While business people are at home on weekends, you can benefit from cheap rooms at great hotels in the heart of the city.

Europa Hotel
$$$ Belfast

The rooms in this world-class hotel are decked to the nines — huge beds and sofas and beautiful oak furnishings. Despite this, you'll probably spend most of your time in the palatial Gallery Lounge or the cozy, traditional Lobby Bar, which features nightly music sessions. This hotel is a veritable landmark and is just a short walk to the heart of Belfast. President Bill Clinton stayed here on his historic trip to the country. You can stay in the Clinton suite, too — for a cool £350!

Great Victoria St., Belfast. ☎ **028-9032-7000.** *Fax: 028-9032-7800. E-mail:* res.eur@ hastingshotels.com. *Internet:* www.hastingshotel.com. *To get there: From the Westlink (M1) take Grosvenor Rd. toward City Hall, go right on Great Victoria St. Rates: £158 ($260.70) Mon–Thur, £80 ($132) Fri–Sun, double. AE, MC, V, DC. Weekend price doesn't include breakfast.*

Benedicts of Belfast
$$ Belfast

Brand-spanking new and in one of the fastest growing areas of the city, Benedicts has been hailed by the *Irish Times* as one of the best recent additions to Belfast. Rooms are big and airy and decorated in minimalist style, but the real attraction is the Gothic-looking bar and restaurant. Oak and pine paneling and plenty of intricate woodwork combine with chandeliers and stained glass to give this place a one-of-a-kind feel. Also, it's just minutes' walk to Queens University, The Ulster Museum, and Belfast's extreme shopping district.

7-21 Bradbury Pl., Shaftsbury Sq., Belfast. ☎ **028-9059-1999.** *Fax: 028-9059-1990. E-mail:* info@benedictshotel.co.uk. *To get there: From the Westlink (M1) take Grosvenor Rd. toward City Hall, go right on Great Victoria St. Rates: £70 ($115.50) Mon–Thur, £50 ($82.50) Fri–Sun, double. AE, MC, V.*

Madison's Hotel
$$ Belfast

This terminally stylish hotel sits on a tree-lined street in Belfast's university district, so there's plenty of restaurants and shops right there. Nothing is taken for granted in Madison's, where the lobby is as nicely decorated as the rooms. The restaurant is multileveled with hardwood and steel railings for an artsy look, and the food's been acclaimed by just about every critic. This place really epitomizes the hipness of Belfast, where European style meets casual Irish taste. Rooms have all the best amenities, like satellite TV and safe-deposit boxes.

59–63 Botanic Ave., Belfast. ☎ *028-9033-0040. Fax: 028-9032-8007. E-mail:* madisons@unite.co.uk. *Internet:* www.madisonshotel.com. *To get there: From the Westlink (M1) take Grovesnor Rd. toward City Hall, go right on Great Victoria St. From the square, pick up Botanic Ave. Rates: £75 ($123.75) Mon–Thur, £60 ($99) Fri–Sun, double. AE, MC, V.*

Ash-Rowan Guest House

$$ Belfast

This beautiful Victorian row home is tucked into a quiet, tree-lined avenue and offers a comfortable, serene place to stay. All four stories are decorated with country-style furniture, antiques, and fresh flowers from the garden in back. You have a choice of eight different breakfasts here, including the traditional (and filling) Ulster fry.

12 Windsor Ave., Belfast. ☎ *028-9066-1758. Fax: 028-9066-3227. To get there: From city centre, follow Bedford St. south past Queen's University and make a right on Windsor. Rates: £60 ($99) double. MC, V.*

Quality Hotel

$$$ Carrickfergus

Outfitted with Mediterranean stylings, this luxury hotel has a lot of the grandeur of its American counterparts. All rooms are deluxe, with king-sized beds and plenty of space, and there are incredible suites with jacuzzis. The hotel is practically on Carrickfergus Marina, and some rooms have views of the water — on a clear day you can see Scotland. Mac's Pub is traditional-looking and cozy, and the Boardwalk Restaurant is sleek and modern — the chef prepares your meal at an island in the center of the dining room. The hotel is only 20 minutes from Belfast.

75 Belfast Rd., Carrickfergus, County Antrim. ☎ *028-9336-4556. Fax: 028-9335-1620. To get there: Downtown, near Carrickfergus Castle. Rates: £120–170 ($198–$280.50) double. AE, MC, V, DC.*

The Bushmills Inn

$$ Bushmills

The warm glow from a turf fire greets you when you enter this fantastic inn, then comes the grand staircase, cozy oil lamps, and curious antiques that line the halls. The quaint individually decorated rooms in the Coaching Inn are complimented by the much larger cottage-style rooms in the Mill House on the banks of the River Bush. It's the kind of place that you want to spend the day in, exploring its many alcoves and hidden rooms. From the round library to the oak-beamed loft, you'll never want to leave. Don't pass up excellent Irish coffees (made, of course, with premium Bushmills whiskey) by the fire or a superb meal in the dining room. All around, an incredible place.

Belfast

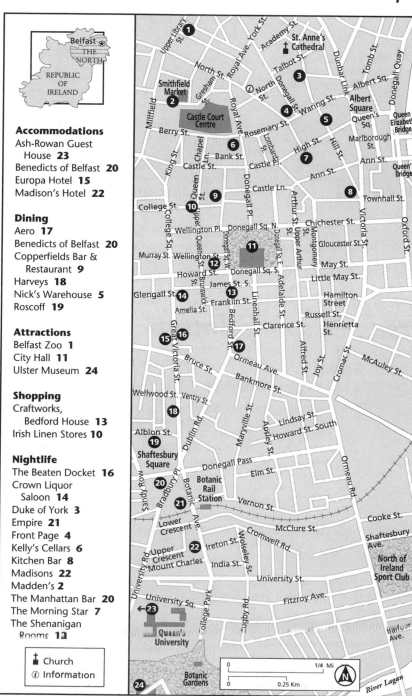

Accommodations
Ash-Rowan Guest
  House **23**
Benedicts of Belfast **20**
Europa Hotel **15**
Madison's Hotel **22**

Dining
Aero **17**
Benedicts of Belfast **20**
Copperfields Bar &
  Restaurant **9**
Harveys **18**
Nick's Warehouse **5**
Roscoff **19**

Attractions
Belfast Zoo **1**
City Hall **11**
Ulster Museum **24**

Shopping
Craftworks,
  Bedford House **13**
Irish Linen Stores **10**

Nightlife
The Beaten Docket **16**
Crown Liquor
  Saloon **14**
Duke of York **3**
Empire **21**
Front Page **4**
Kelly's Cellars **6**
Kitchen Bar **8**
Madisons **22**
Madden's **2**
The Manhattan Bar **20**
The Morning Star **7**
The Shenanigan
  Rooms **12**

✝ Church
ⓘ Information

9 Dunluce Rd. (A2), Bushmills, County Antrim. ☎ *028-2073-2339. Fax: 028-2073-2048. E-mail:* mail@bushmillsinn.com. *Internet:* www.bushmillsinn.com. *To get there: On the North Antrim Coast. Bushmills Inn is located on the A2 (called Main St. in Bushmills) on the banks of the Bush River. Rates: £68–128 ($102–$192) double. AE, MC, V.*

The Causeway Hotel
$$ Bushmills

Located right next to the famed Giant's Causeway, this hotel's view of the spectacular coast cannot be beaten. The rooms are large, but the furnishings aren't remarkable. That won't matter, though, because you'll be on the tip of the Antrim Coast and spending all your time looking at the amazing scenery! This old, family-run hotel dates back to 1836, and while it's been restored and has modern conveniences, it hasn't lost its feel of the old days.

40 Causeway Rd., Bushmills, County Antrim. ☎ *028-2073-1226. To get there: Off the A2, follow signs to the Giant's Causeway. Rates: £65 ($107.25) double. MC, V.*

Where to Dine in Belfast and around County Antrim

Roscoff
$$$$ Belfast   SEAFOOD

The decor is simple at this sleek restaurant, with frosted glass, black-and-white furnishings, and white walls covered with modern art. But the food's not so simple. Much of it is seeped in citrusey tastes, reminiscent of the Mediterranean. Try the steamed seafood platter of salmon, mako, monkfish, sole, prawns, and lobster, or the filet of salmon with asparagus and *chervil* (an herb).

7 Lesley House, Shaftsbury Sq., Belfast. ☎ *028-9023-0356. To get there: From the Westlink (M1) take Grovesnor Rd. toward City Hall, go right on Great Victoria St. Main courses: £29.95 ($49.40) set menu. AE, DC, MC, V. Open: Mon–Fri 12:30 p.m.– 2:15 p.m. and Mon–Sat 6:30 p.m.–10:15 p.m.*

Benedicts of Belfast
$$$ Belfast   EUROPEAN

Plenty of intricate woodwork, brick, and stone give one of Belfast's newest restaurants an Old-World feel. The interior is beautiful, but the food is to die for. Delicacies like seared loin of wild boar on white crab mash with a tarragon and prawn cream and red pepper oil are for the adventurous eaters, but there are also the old standbys (like honey and mustard-marinated pork cutlets) done in a new and creative way. It'll be difficult, but you must save room for dessert. Mouthwatering white chocolate and caramel cheesecake can put any diet on hold.

7–21 Bradbury Place, Shaftsbury Sq., Belfast. ☎ *028-9059-1999. To get there: From the Westlink (M1) take Grovesnor Rd. toward City Hall, go right on Great Victoria St. Main courses: £9.95–13.50 ($16.40–$22.30). AE, MC, V. Open: Mon–Sat 12:00 p.m.–2:30 p.m. and 5:00 p.m.–10:30 p.m., Sun 12:00 p.m.–4:00 p.m. and 5:00 p.m.–9:30 p.m.*

Aero

$$$ Belfast   INTERNATIONAL

Stylish, modern decor gives Aero a crisp feel, and its big windows look out over Belfast's busy streets. The menu is difficult to classify — the dishes hail from all over the globe, and are uniquely and creatively prepared. Excellent starters include the char sui chicken spring rolls with black bean and ginger dressing or crostini of Italian Coppa ham with moon-dried tomatoes. Like us, you'll wish you could try them all, but don't miss the spinach, brie, and sun-dried tomato *samosas* (a small pastry turnover filled with a meat or vegetable mixture) served with mixed leaves and chili oil.

44 Bedford St., Belfast. ☎ *028-9024-4844. To get there: From the Westlink (M1) take Grovesnor Rd. to Bedford St. Main courses: £9.25–11.25 ($15.25–$18.55). AE, MC, V. Open: Daily 5:00 p.m.–10:30 p.m.*

Nick's Warehouse

$$–$$$ Belfast   INTERNATIONAL

Set in an old warehouse, this place exudes charm, and despite the size of the place, it is quite intimate. The service is wonderful (we recommend you let them choose something for you if you can't decide). The menu changes frequently but you won't be disappointed with the options.

35 Hill St., Belfast. ☎ *028-9043-9690. To get there: From the Westlink (M1) take Divis St. and a left on Skipper St. Main courses: £5.95–18.50 ($9.80–$30.55). AE, DC, MC, V. Open: Mon–Fri 12:00 p.m.–3:00 p.m., Tues–Sat 6:00 p.m.–9:00 p.m.*

Copperfields Bar & Restaurant

$$ Belfast   IRISH

You can't beat the location or the prices at this great restaurant. The food, interestingly crafted by chef Arthur Corry, is varied to suit every taste, but focuses mainly on traditional Irish dishes — with fantastic flair. Specials change daily and are always creative, and all ingredients are fresh and local. What makes this place so popular, in addition to the food, are the comfy sofas and cozy booths.

9 Fountain St., Belfast. ☎ *028-9024-7367. To get there: From the Westlink (M1) take Divis St. and a right on Fountain St. Main courses: £4–10 ($6.60–$16.50). AE, DC, MC, V. Open: Sun–Wed 11:30 a.m.–8:00 p.m., Thur–Sat 11:30 a.m.–9:00 p.m.*

Harveys
$$ Belfast AMERICAN

Feeling homesick? One foot into Harveys and you'll be transported back to the ol' U.S. of A. American flags adorn the walls and the menu is chock-full of favorites from home. For a break from stews and sausages, you can have burgers, pizza, tacos, and steaks, and the house speciality is the "Frisco Bay," a mixture of shrimp, crab claws, lobster, and mussels in a scampi sauce.

95 Great Victoria St., Belfast. ☎ *028-9023-3433. To get there: From the Westlink (M1) take Grovesnor Rd. toward City Hall, go right on Great Victoria St. Main courses: £4.95–8.50 ($8.15–$14.05). MC, V. Open: Mon–Thur and Sun 5:00 p.m.–11:30 p.m., Fri and Sat 5:00 p.m.–12:00 a.m.*

Lynden Heights
$$$ Ballygarry IRISH

Situated on the southern end of the Glens of Antrim, this restaurant probably has the best view of any restaurant on the Northern Coast. The staff is really friendly and chatty, and the wine list is as good as it is long. Regional dishes like duck, pheasant, and salmon round out the menu, and everything's enhanced by fresh local produce. This really is a wonderful stop for anyone driving the coast road, both for a delicious meal and a chance to see the view at leisure.

97 Drumnagreagh Rd., Ballygally, County Antrim. ☎ *028-2858-3560. To get there: On the Antrim Coast Rd., off the A2 on the B148. Main courses: £10–18 ($16.50–$29.70). AE, MC, V. Open: Wed–Sat 5:00 p.m.–9:15 p.m. Sun 12:30 p.m.–8:00 p.m.*

Exploring Belfast and County Antrim

While most of the attractions in this section are around County Antrim rather than in Belfast itself, Belfast is a great city to walk around and explore, and also makes an ideal base for visiting the other attractions in the County.

The top attractions

City Hall
Belfast

Modeled on St. Paul's Cathedral in London, Belfast's City Hall was built in 1888 after Queen Victoria conferred city status on Belfast. The building is made of smooth Portland stone with a central copper dome that rises 173 feet into the sky and is visible for miles. In front, there's a statue of the queen and a memorial to the victims of the *Titanic*, which was built in a Belfast shipyard.

Donegall Sq., Belfast. ☎ *028-9032-0202, ext. 2618. Admission: Free tours of the interior available. Tour times: June–Sept Mon–Fri 10:30 a.m., 11:30 a.m., 2:30 p.m.;*

Sat 2:30 p.m. Oct–May Mon–Sat 2:30 p.m. Otherwise by arrangement. Reservations required. Time: Forty-five minutes.

Belfast Zoo

Belfast

This zoo is much more than a place to look at animals. There's a Children's Farm, an island of spider monkeys, an enclosure for primates and other African animals, a Polar Bear Canyon, and pools for penguins and sea lions, to name a few. The zoo houses many endangered animals, and it faces a fantastic view of Belfast Lough. You can even have lunch in the Ark Restaurant!

Antrim Rd., Belfast. ☎ 028-9077-6277. To get there: Take Donegall St. from the city centre north and go right on Antrim Rd. Bus: 45, 46, 47, 48, 49, 50, 51. Admission: £ 4.40 ($7.25) adult, £ 2.20 ($3.65) child. Open: Apr–Sept daily 10:00 a.m.–5:00 p.m.; Oct–Mar 10:00 a.m.–3:30 p.m. Time: Two hours.

Giant's Causeway

Bushmills

It's likely you'll never see another site as strange and awesome as the Giant's Causeway, a three-mile stretch of roughly 40,000 tightly packed, mostly hexagonal basalt rock columns — some up to 40 feet tall — that jut up from the foot of a cliff and eventually disappear under the sea. The experts will tell you the Causeway was formed by an ancient volcanic eruption, but according to legend Finn MacCool built the causeway as a path across the sea to a rival giant in Scotland, where there are similar formations. There's a cluster of rocks that form a seat, called The Wishing Chair. Legend says this is where MacCool sat as a boy and made wishes that came true. (An aside: In 1842, the writer William Thackeray noted in his *Irish Scetch Book*, "Mon Dieu! And I have traveled a hundred and fifty miles to see that?" Just goes to show, even the eighth wonder of the world can't please everybody!) A bus takes you down to the shore (the hale and hearty among you can walk), where you can walk around and explore.

44 Causeway Rd., Bushmills, County Antrim. ☎ 028-2073-1855. To get there: Off the A2 along the North Antrim Coast. Bus Eireann (☎ 071-60-066) takes a day tour of Giant's Causeway from Donegal Bus Station for £9 ($13.30) adult, £7 ($10.35) child July and Aug. Admission: Free. Open: Mid-Mar to May daily 11:00 a.m.–5:00 p.m.; June daily 11:00 a.m.–5:30 p.m.; July–Aug daily 10:00 a.m.–7:00 p.m.; Sept–Oct Mon–Fri 11:00 a.m.–5:00 p.m., Sat–Sun 10:30 a.m.–5:30 p.m. Time: Forty-five minutes to an hour.

The Old Bushmills Distillery

Bushmills

A thorough and well-guided tour of the world's oldest distillery awaits you at Bushmills, where you get to see the nitty-gritty of the distillery process. You'll even enter a room that's so heady with whiskey fumes the workers have to get a ride home at the end of the day because they've inhaled so much alcohol! (No fear; a couple minutes won't affect you.) The water used is from the local River Bush and all the ingredients are grown around Ireland. The shop has every Bushmills product you can imagine, from fudge to golf towels, and of course every kind of whiskey they make. The tour ends, appropriately enough, with a taste test.

Main St., Bushmills, County Antrim. ☎ *028-2073-1521. To get there: On the A2 along the North Antrim Coast. Admission: £2.50 ($4.15) adults, £2 ($3.30) seniors and students, £1 ($1.65) children. Open: Jan–May and Sept–Dec Mon–Thurs 9:00 a.m.–12:00 p.m. and 1:30 p.m.–3:30 p.m., Fri 9:00 a.m.–12:00 p.m.; June–Aug Mon–Thurs 9:00 a.m.–4:00 p.m. Time: Two and a half hours.*

Carrick-A-Rede Rope Bridge

Larrybane

Here's one for the Indiana Jones in all of us! This heart-stopping rope bridge, spanning a chasm 60 feet wide, is not for the fainthearted: It wiggles and shakes underfoot while the sea crashes 80 feet below, and no matter how brave you are, you're in for a scare (though later you can tell yourself it was a thrilling adventure). The bridge is the only access to a salmon fishery on the small island at its far end.

Larrybane, County Antrim. ☎ *028-2073-2143. To get there: On the A2 along the North Antrim Coast. Admission: Free. Open: Apr to mid-Sept during daylight hours. Time: A half-hour.*

Carrickfergus Castle

Carrickfergus

During this impressive, well-preserved castle's 800-year history, it grew from a small castle to an unequaled Norman fortress. Historic, life-sized figures make an eerie presence throughout the grounds, and a fascinating audiovisual presentation really brings the castle's exciting history to life. You'll have fun walking along the parapets and looking out to sea. The Castle's keep doubles as a unique period "game room," where you can try on costumes or engage in some oversized medieval games, like chess or "Dragons and Ladders."

Marine Highway, Carrickfergus, County Antrim. ☎ *028-9335-1273. To get there: Take the A2 north of Belfast. Admission: £2.70 ($4.45) adults, £1.35 ($2.25) child and senior citizen, £7.30 ($12.05) family. Combined tickets are available for Carrickfergus Castle and Knight Ride at £4.85 ($8) adults, £2.40 ($3.95) child and senior citizen, £13.50 ($22.30) family. You can purchase the tickets at either venue. Open: Apr–Oct Mon–Sat 10:00 a.m.–6:00 p.m.; Apr–May Sept–Oct Sun 2:00 p.m.–6:00 p.m.; Jun–Aug Sun 11:00 a.m.–8:00 p.m.; Nov–Mar Mon–Sat 10:00 a.m.–4:00 p.m., Sun 2:00 p.m.– 4:00 p.m. Time: Two hours.*

Knight Ride

Carrickfergus

This is the fun way to learn! Kids travel throughout the interactive history tour while sitting in a giant helmet that weaves through Carrickfergus's lively past. Sounds, smells, and sights of the battles and a nineteenth-century market highlight this exciting ride. There's even a spooky haunted house in the "Dark Ride." Afterward, a fantastic walk-through exhibit incorporates the information, with a scale model of the town and audiovisual presentations.

Heritage Plaza, Carrickfergus. ☎ *028-9336-6455. To get there: Take the A2 north of Belfast. Admission: £2.70 ($4.45) adults, £1.35 ($2.25) child and senior citizen, £7.30 ($12.05) family. Combined tickets are available for Carrickfergus Castle and Knight Ride at £4.85 ($8) adults, £2.40 ($3.95) child and senior citizen, £13.50 ($22.30) family. You can purchase the tickets at either venue. Open: Apr–Sept Mon–Sat 10:00 a.m.–6:00 p.m., Sun 12:00 p.m.–6:00 p.m.; Oct–Mar Mon–Sat 10:00 a.m.–5:00 p.m., Sun 12:00 p.m.–5:00 p.m. Time: An hour and a half.*

More fun stuff to do in Belfast and around County Antrim

✔ **Taking Bailey's Belfast Pub Tour:** Belfast has some of Ireland's finest pubs, many authentically Victorian. The famed Bailey's Irish Cream hosts a good pub tour of the city that covers some of the best of them. You get the inside scoop on six pubs, most with traditional music. And because the tour's always of different pubs, you could take it more than once and not really be doing it twice!

Location: Great Victoria Street, Belfast. Tour departs from the Crown Bar, upstairs from Flannigan's Pub. ☎ **094-9068-3665.** To get there: From Donegall Square go about three blocks east to Victoria Street. Admission: £5 ($8.25) adult. Open: April through September Tuesday 7:00 p.m., Saturday 4:00 p.m. Time: About four hours.

✔ **Visiting the Ulster Museum:** This is Northern Ireland's national museum with a diverse collection that ranges from local history to ancient artifacts, including treasures from sunken ships of the Spanish Armada. The fourth floor houses an impressive art gallery with works by greats like Francis Bacon and Henry Moore. For the rough crowd, check out the huge, bird-eating spider and Giant Irish Deer. There's also a collection of twentieth-century fashion in the Costume Gallery.

Location: Stranmillis Road, Belfast. ☎ **028-90381-2251.** To get there: From city centre, take Great Victoria Street south to University Road, and veer left onto Stranmillis Road. Bus: 69, 70, 71. Admission: Free. Open: Monday through Friday 10:00 a.m. to 5:00 p.m., Saturday 1:00 p.m. to 5:00 p.m., and Sunday 2:00 p.m. to 5:00 p.m. Time: An hour.

✔ **Touring the Antrim Coast:** This spectacular drive takes you along sea-splashed cliffs and into small coastal towns with picturesque harbors. Major attractions along the road include the Giant's Causeway and Carrick-A-Rede Rope Bridge (see earlier in the chapter) plus Dunluce and Kinbane Castle ruins — both of which offer beautiful views of the sea and cliffs. You could also venture off the coastal road into the Glens of Antrim, famed for both its story-tellers and traditional culture.

Location: Start off from Belfast on the A2 north, which stretches as far as Derry. Time: Anywhere from several hours to two days, depending on how many stops you make.

✔ **Exploring Rathlin Island:** Rathlin's strategic position between Ireland and Scotland has made it the site of many battles and massacres over time. One of the bloodiest occurred on the Hill of Screaming, where a force of Campbells slaughtered MacDonnells in 1642. Today the tiny, boomerang-shaped island is a peaceful place and the home of thousands of seabirds, including puffins, and only about 100 people. Storytelling, song, and music flourish here, and islanders are always happy to welcome visitors. A small minibus takes tourists around Rathlin, the ancestral home of local patriot Christian Anderson; there's a guesthouse, pub, and restaurant there, and visitors can explore the White Cliffs and caves. On the eastern end of the island is Bruce's Cave, where the Scottish King Robert the Bruce hid after being defeated by the English. He watched a spider meticulously trying to reach the top of the cave by its thread. The spider's perseverance motivated the king to return to his country and win back his kingdom.

Location: Off the coast of Ballycastle. To get there: Take the ferry from Ballycastle (call ☎ **028-2076-9299** for info). Admission: Cost of boat ride. Round trip £7.60 ($12.55) adults, £5.60 ($9.25) seniors, £3.80 ($6.25) children. Runs daily at 10:30 a.m. and 5:00 p.m. from Ballycastle and at 9:00 a.m. and 4:00 p.m. from Rathlin during the spring and summer. During the winter, 10:30 a.m. and 4:00 p.m. from Ballycastle and 9:00 a.m. and 3:00 p.m. from Rathlin. Time: You're locked into the boat schedule, so your trip will be from 10:30 a.m. until 3:00 p.m. or 4:00 p.m., depending on the season.

✔ **Golfing at Royal Portrush.** These are three excellent 18-hole courses, all of which offer amazing sea-side views of the northern Antrim Coast.

Located: Dunluce Rd., Portrush, County Antrim. ☎ **028-7082-2311**. To get there: From Belfast, take the M2 north to Ballymena and then the A26 to Ballymoney. At the roundabout, follow the sign to Portrush (about ten miles down the road). Par: 72. Fees: £55 ($90.75) midweek, £65 ($107.30) weekends. Open: 6:30 a.m. until sundown.

Utilizing Organized Tours

In addition to the tours in this section, see "Taking Bailey's Belfast Pub Tour" under " More fun stuff to do in Belfast and around County Antrium," earlier in this chapter.

Citybus bus tours

A three-hour tour covering all the high points of Belfast. The commentary is very interesting, and this is probably the fastest way to see and hear it all.

Tours operate June–Sept and depart from Castle Place, two blocks north of Donegall Square. Information: City Bus, Donegall Square West Ticket kiosk. ☎ *028-9045-8484. Price: £8 ($13.20) adults, £7 ($11.55) students, £5.50 ($9.07) seniors and children, £18 ($29.70) family.*

Titanic — a (bus) tour to remember

Offered by Citybus, this tour goes out to the Harland and Wolff ship-yards, where the *Titanic* was built; stops in the office of the designer, Thomas Andrews; and visits the *Titanic* memorial at City Hall (with a stop for tea at Waterfront Hall), the *Titanic* exhibition at Cultura's Folk and Transport Museum, and the little town of Comber, home to Mr. Andrews and the statue they erected in his honor. It lasts three and a half hours and the fare includes entry to the transport museum.

See the previous Citybus listing for all information.

The Old Town of Belfast walking tour

A 90-minute tour of the original city ramparts. Local experts lead the tours and trace the city back to its origins. They can answer even the most difficult of questions.

Runs year-round on Saturdays, departing at 2:00 p.m. from the Tourist Information Centre on North St. Information: Tourist Information Centre, ☎ *028-9023-1221.*

Shopping in Belfast and County Antrim

Belfast's City Hall is a perfect landmark for the shopping district, which is just across the street. There you'll find posh (and expensive) British department stores, Irish shops, and American stores like the Gap, the Disney Store, and Levi's.

Craftworks

A wide range of quality crafts fill this shop, and all products are beauti-fully on display. You'll find ceramics, jewelry, handpainted silk scarves, musical instruments, and more.

Bedford House, 16 Bedford St., Belfast. ☎ *028-9224-4465.*

Halls

This shop was established in 1850, and its years of experience show. Halls specializes in Celtic jewelry, but also has Donegal tweed rugs, Aran sweaters, and figurines made from compressed peat.

Queen's Arcade, Belfast. ☎ *028-9032-0446.*

Irish Linen Centre

Much more than just a shop, this center gives the history of the famous Ulster linen and conducts handweaving demonstrations — and of course sells plenty of Irish linen, from coats to clothes.

Market Sq., Lisburn. ☎ *028-9066-3377.*

Irish Linen Stores

A variety of Irish linen fills this shop, with tea towels the specialty. Most of the linen carries the trademark green shamrock design.

Fountain Centre, College St., Belfast. ☎ *028-9032-2727.*

Northern Salmon Company

Chemical-free fresh and smoked salmon is yours to take home from this respected company. You can watch the entire process, from salmon harvesting to packaging. There's even a mail-order service, so you can order it from home.

New Rd., Glenarm, Ballymena. ☎ *028-2884-1691.*

Enjoying Nightlife in Belfast and County Antrim

Belfast is a bustling city, so you may want to broaden your scope beyond the pubs to include a few clubs. But true to form, we include the best of both in the following sections.

Club life

The Manhattan Bar

This flashy neon dance club is where all the clubbers go. It's an exciting late-night venue with a carnival atmosphere. Warning: The popularity of Manhattan means less-than-friendly doormen.

23 Bradbury Place, Belfast. ☎ *028-9023-3131.*

The Beaten Docket

This modern and popular bar turns into a great nightclub on Friday and Saturday nights, and is open into the wee hours of the morning. The best part about the club is that the miminum age is set at 30, which tends to filter out the young'uns. You'll have a blast and wonder where the time went.

48 Great Victoria St. (opposite the Europa hotel), Belfast. ☎ *01232-24-2986.*

Pub life

Though all of the exceptional watering holes that follow are located in Belfast, we also want to make a plug for the local pubs we had the pleasure to find in small towns around Antrim. While none were remarkably decked out or steeped in history, some of our fondest evenings were spent in these anonymous coastal pubs, chatting with the friendly locals. Belfast may have the most atmospheric pubs in the county, but the best ones are what you make them.

Crown Liquor Saloon

Unquestionably the most famous pub in Belfast and an attraction in itself, the Crown holds the unique distinction of being the only pub owned by the state. (By The National Trust, to be exact, which is a charity founded to protect the best of Britain's heritage.) Inside you'll be taken aback by the wonderful traditional design that includes hand-painted tiles, glass works, carved wood, brass fittings, and gas lamps. Truly a perfect Irish watering hole. You've got to try the local Strangford Lough oysters — they're excellent. You may want to find your *snug* (small partioned areas in pubs) early — the Crown tends to fill up with friendly faces most evenings.

44 Great Victoria St., Belfast. ☎ *028-9024-9476.*

The Shenanigan Rooms

It's all about ambiance here. Huge old beer barrels make perfect places around which to pull up a stool and rest a pint. Then there's the long, medieval feasting tables for the more sociable, where people can gather around. Everything's wooden, and different levels and tiny secluded areas give the place a unique look. It's always jumping here, which we guess has as much to do with the great atmosphere as it does the incredible pub grub!

21 Howard St., Belfast. ☎ *028-9023-0603.*

Madisons

One of the city's newest and most stunning bars, Madisons is named for the modern hotel it's housed in, though it's a far cry from the standard hotel bar. Using an Art Nouveau theme and sporting a striking copper and ceramic bar top, it's a sophisticated and hip gathering place of young professionals and students from the nearby Queens University. There's an over-25 club downstairs that's great for dancing.

59-63 Botanic Ave., Belfast. ☎ *028-9033-0040.*

Kelly's Cellars

Not only is this the oldest continuously used licensed pub in Belfast, but Kelly's was the popular meeting place for the United Irishmen (one member of which was Wolfe Tone), who organized the 1798 Rebellion. The name is misleading; Kelly's is a two-storied building with a stone-floored bar downstairs and restaurant upstairs. If you get hungry, try the Black Velvet Steak Pie — it's incredible.

30 Bank St., Belfast. ☎ *028-9032-4835.*

The Morning Star

You have to go down an alley between High and Ann streets to find this historic pub, but you can't miss its striking green-and-red facade, and anyway, it's worth the hunt. The Star serves up the best pint of Caffrey's (Belfast's hometown brew) in town. That's reason enough to go, but the comfortable interior and unique horseshoe bar are attractions as well.

17–19 Pottingers Entry, Belfast. ☎ *028-9032-3976.*

Fast Facts: Belfast and County Antrim

AREA CODE

028.

EMERGENCIES-HOSPITAL

Dial ☎ 999 for all emergencies. The **Belfast City Hospital** is on Lisburn Rd. (☎ 028-9032-9241).

GENEALOGY RESOURCES

Contact the **Irish Heritage Association,** Queens Rd., Belfast, BT39DT (☎ 028-9045-5325), or the **Ulster Historical Foundation,** Balmoral Buildings, 12 College Square East, Belfast BT1 6DD (☎ 01232-33-2288; Fax: 01232-23-9885; E-mail enquiry@uhf.org.uk; Internet: www.uhf.org.uk).

INFORMATION

For visitor information go to the **tourist office** at St. Anne's Court, 59 North St. (☎ 028-9023-1221) open year-round. They can also provide reservation services (☎ 0800-40-4050). For telephone directory assistance, dial ☎ 192.

Best pubs for traditional music

Some of the best pubs in Belfast to get those toes atappin' include **Madden's,** 74 Smithfield (☎ 028-9024-4114); the **Duke of York,** 11 Commercial Court, off Lower Donegall Street (☎ 028-9024-1062); the **Empire,** 42 Botanic Avenue (☎ 028-9032-8110); **Front Page,** 106-110 Donegall Street (☎ 028-9032-4924); and **Kitchen Bar,** 16 Victoria Square (☎ 028-9032-4901).

Chapter 23

Counties Down and Armagh

· ·

In This Chapter

▶ Finding St. Patrick's grave

▶ Touring the Mourne Mountains

▶ Discovering the history of transportation

· ·

South of Belfast, with the Irish Sea on the east and the border of the Republic (and Counties Louth and Monaghan) just below, Counties Down and Armagh boast several important religious sites. You can visit them either as day trips from Belfast or en route from Belfast back toward Dublin (or the other way 'round if you're traveling counterclockwise around the country).

This is the land of St. Patrick, the patron saint of the country, who planted the first roots of Irish Christianity here in the fifth century. Born in Britain somewhere around 389 A.D. and brought to Ireland as a slave, Patrick spent four years as a shepherd for a Druid. During that time his spirituality flourished, and after escaping slavery, Patrick trained for the priesthood, probably in France. He returned to Ireland as a missionary, sure that God was directing him to spread Christianity in the pagan land, and began the difficult task of converting the Irish and establishing churches.

Over the years, people around the world have gotten to know Patrick as the inspiration for annual drunken revelries every March 17, but believe it or not, St. Patrick's Day is a holy day in Ireland. People attend Mass, businesses and schools are closed, and until recently, pubs were closed, too. Some cities and towns in Ireland hold parades on March 17, but doing so is really an American practice, and all the drunkenness such parades inspire is not necessarily held in high regard in the auld country.

What's Where? Counties Down and Armagh and Their Major Attractions

The little town of Downpatrick, in **County Down,** is filled with fine Georgian architecture, and is where you can find the grave of St. Patrick. It is located in a staid graveyard behind a pretty church on a hill.

Counties Down and Armagh

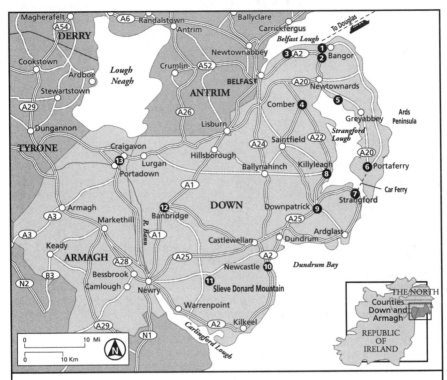

Accommodations
Burrendale Hotel **10**
Culloden Hotel **3**
Dufferin Arms Coaching
  Inn **8**
Dining
El Porto Cafe **13**
The Lobster Pot **7**
The Olde Priory Inn Bar & Restaurant **3**
Attractions
Exploris **6**
Mountains of Mourne **11**

Mountains of Mourne
  Information Centre **10**
Mount Stewart House and Gardens **5**
St. Patrick's Grave **9**
Ulster Folk & Transport Museum **1**
Shopping
Ferguson Linen Centre **12**
Nightlife
Grace Neill's Inn **2**
Harry's Bar **12**
Siglu **8**
Tourist Trophy Lounge **4**

But first things first. You're probably coming from Belfast (assuming you're making a clockwise circular path around the country, beginning in Dublin), so here are some of the attractions you can see along the way:

- ✔ **Ulster Folk and Transport Museum:** Only about five miles from Belfast on the A2, this outdoor museum is devoted to presenting rural life as it was in the 1800s.

- ✔ **Mount Stewart House and Gardens:** Located in **Newtownards,** about ten miles east of Belfast, this impressive eighteenth-century mansion is surrounded by spectacular gardens.

- ✔ **Exploris:** Underwater tunnels give you a fish-eye view of life in the Irish Sea. It's the closest you can come to being underwater without getting wet.

- ✔ **The Mountains of Mourne:** These enthralling mountains (along the A2 coastal road) contain the highest peaks in Northern Ireland.

Moving farther south and a little west, you reach **County Armagh. Armagh City** is one of Ireland's oldest towns — going as far back as St. Patrick. Christianity took hold here and eventually spread out across the country, and two **St. Patrick's Cathedrals** are here — one Catholic and one Protestant. The cathedrals sit opposite each other on hills that rise above the town, but the Protestant one provides the greater draw for visitors: It boasts the remains of Brian Boru, the great High King.

Getting to Counties Down and Armagh

The nearest airports are in Belfast, which is also the destination for ferries from England and Scotland. See Chapter 22 for information.

If you're coming by car from Dublin, take the N1 north to Newry (N1 becomes the A1 in Northern Ireland). From Newry take the A28 to Armagh. To get to the coast, from Newry take the A2 southeast (the A2 runs along the entire coast). If you're driving from Ireland into Northern Ireland make sure you notify your rental car company because extra insurance may be required.

Northern Ireland Railways (☎ 028-9127-0141) services Newry, Portadown, Lurgan, Lisburn, and Bangor year-round. **Ulsterbus** (☎ 028-9033-3000) travels year-round to Newry, Portadown, Armagh City, and other major towns in Counties Armagh and Down.

Where to Stay in Counties Down and Armagh

Culloden Hotel

$$$ Holywood, County Down

This is the only five-star hotel in Northern Ireland, and it wears that distinction well. Set in a former Gothic mansion on 12 acres of beautiful, secluded gardens and surrounded by the picturesque Holywood Hills, the Culloden will blow you away. Even from the outside the hotel is gorgeous, and the posh rooms and antique-studded lobby drive the point home. Tony Blair and John Major have recently stayed here.

Bangor Rd., Holywood, County Down. ☎ ***028-9042-5223.** Fax: 028-9042-6777. E-mail:* res.cull@hastingshotels.com. *Internet:* www.hastingshotels.com. *To get there: On the A2, northeast of Belfast. Rates: £88–186 ($145.20–$306.90) double. MC ,V, AE, DC.*

Burrendale Hotel

$$–$$$ Newcastle, County Down

This hotel really has it all. Between the beauty salon, bistro, and bar, there are enough reasons to stay in for the day, but with the Mourne Mountains, a sandy beach on the Irish Sea, and two large parks at the hotel's doorstep, we bet you'll hardly be in your room at all. The Vine Restaurant and the Cottage Kitchen Restaurant are highlights of the place, which locals and visitors alike rave about. And they have varied menus so everybody's happy. Golfers can go crazy: There are 15 courses nearby — including one of the best on the island, Royal County Down.

51 Castlewellan Rd., Newcastle, County Down. ☎ ***028-4372-2599.** Fax: 028-4372-2328. To get there: Off the A2 toward Downpatrick. Rates: £90–110 ($148.50–$181.50) double. AE, DC, MC, V.*

Dufferin Arms Coaching Inn

$ Killyleagh, County Down

Sitting in the shadow of Killyleagh Castle, this charming inn is nestled in the little town of Killyleagh, on the road between Downpatrick and Belfast. It has some of the finest and most comfortable rooms you can find, all decorated in country colors and with beautiful wooden furniture — some rooms even have four-poster beds. The whole place is much larger than it looks from the outside, with a pub, library, guest lounge, and a downstairs dining area that's so cozy you may think you're in someone's warm kitchen. The inn has been operating since 1803, and you won't find an unfriendly face.

35 High St., Killyleagh, County Down. ☎ *028-4482-8229. Fax: 028-4482-8755. E-mail:* `dufferin@dial.pipex.com`. *To get there: On the A22, south of Belfast. Rates: £65 ($107.30) double. MC, V.*

Where to Dine in Counties Down and Armagh

The Lobster Pot

$$$ Strangford, County Down   SEAFOOD-IRISH-EUROPEAN

Lobster is, not surprisingly, the house specialty here. Plenty of really great Irish and classically European dishes are served, but the seafood is the highlight of the fare. The house has recently been refurbished, but none of the old-fashioned stylings have been lost. The decor is comfortable and homey, and the service is quick and quick to please. For when the weather's nice, there's a lovely beer garden, so you can drink your dessert.

9–11 The Square, Strangford, County Down. ☎ *028-4488-1288. To get there: Take the A25 east from Downpatrick. Main courses: £9.95–15.50 ($16.40–$25.60). AE, MC, V. Open: Mon–Sat 11:30 a.m.–9:30 p.m., Sun 12:30 p.m.–8:30 p.m.*

The Olde Priory Inn Bar & Restaurant

$$ Holywood, County Down   IRISH

This is the most popular place to eat and meet in Holywood, and the eclectic decor and super-friendly staff make it a gem. The head chef, well known in these parts, utilizes the best produce of the area and creates a unique and ever-changing daily specials board. The menu features many kid-friendly meals, but the best draw in the place is the Sunday brunch, which is a four-course feast. There's an in-house baby-sitting service on Sundays as well, so parents can enjoy the four-course meal without the kinder!

13 High St., Holywood, County Down. ☎ *028-9042-8164. To get there: On the A2, northeast of Belfast. Main courses: £5–10.50 ($8.25–$17.35). AE, DC, MC, V. Open: Daily 11:30 a.m.–10:30 p.m.*

El Porto Cafe

$–$$ Portadown, County Armagh   EUROPEAN

This popular place is really two restaurants in one. Downstairs is a busy European-style cafe, serving mostly sandwiches (such as the house's special hot roast beef on a baguette) and homemade soups. The atmosphere is friendly and good music is always playing in the background. Upstairs, a classy Old World restaurant offers a gourmet but well-priced menu in comfortable surroundings.

10 Market St., Portadown, County Armagh. ☎ 028-3839-4343. To get there: On the A3 west from Belfast or the A27 north from Newry. Main courses: £3.50-7.50 ($5.75–$12.40). MC, V. Open: Mon–Sat 9:00 a.m.–5:15 p.m.

Exploring Counties Down and Armagh: The Top Attractions

St. Patrick's Grave
Downpatrick, County Down

Sitting atop the Hill of Down is Down Cathedral, a small yet austere church, but what's next to the church makes it famous. The little church-yard reputedly has the remains of Ireland's patron saint, St. Patrick. A rock slab with the word "Patric" across it marks the spot, which sits in the shadow of a tenth-century cross.

Down Cathedral, 33 Cathedral St., Downpatrick, County Down. ☎ 028-4461-4922. To get there: On the A7 south from Belfast. Admission: Free. Open: Daylight hours. Time: Fifteen minutes.

Ulster Folk & Transport Museum
Holywood, County Down

Original nineteenth-century buildings that once stood across Northern Ireland now make up this outdoor museum devoted to presenting rural life in the 1800s. You can walk among farmhouses, churches, and houses, and past schools, a bank, and a print shop, just to name a few. You can even see people demonstrating how to thatch a roof and cook over an open fire, and others practicing traditional Ulster crafts like lacemaking, spinning, and printing. Across the road is an exhibit on Irish railways, considered among the finest of its kind in Europe. Also, an exhibit called "Car in Society" shows a fine collection of automobiles. You can also find out about a couple of Belfast-built creations-cum-disasters: the *Titanic* and the DeLorean automobile.

153 Bangor Rd., Holywood, County Down. ☎ 028-9242-8428. To get there: Off the A2, seven miles east of Belfast. Admission: £3 ($4.95) adults, £2 ($3.30) children. Open: July–Aug Mon–Sat 10:30 a.m.– 6:00 p.m., Sun 12:00 p.m.–5:00 p.m.; Apr–June and Sept Mon–Fri 9:30 a.m.–5:00 p.m., Sat 10:30 a.m.–6:00 p.m., Sun 12:00 p.m.– 6:00 p.m.; Oct–Mar Mon–Fri 9:30 a.m.–4:00 p.m., Sat and Sun 12:30 p.m.–4:30 p.m. Time: An hour and a half.

Mount Stewart House and Gardens
Newtownards, County Down

Though its interior is just grand, with a fabulous entrance hall and the famous George Stubbs painting *Hambletonian*, this impressive eigh-teenth-century mansion almost pales in comparison to the spectacular gardens surrounding it. There's a fabulous Shamrock Garden, which has an Irish harp-shaped topiary and a flowerbed shaped like a red hand (the emblem of Ulster) enclosed in a hedge shaped like a shamrock. Spanish and Italian gardens are in the back, and a colorful sunken garden sits in the east yard.

Newtownards, County Down. ☎ 028-4278-8387. To get there: On the A2 three miles southeast of Newtownards, along the Ards Peninsula. Admission: House, garden, and temple £3 ($4.95) adults, £1.50 ($2.50) children. Garden and temple £2.70 ($4.45) adults, £1.35 ($2.30) children. Open: House Apr and Oct Sat and Sun 1:00 p.m.–6:00 p.m.; May–Sept Mon and Wed–Sun 1:00 p.m.–6:00 p.m. Garden Apr–Sept daily 10:30 a.m.–6:00 p.m.; Oct Sat and Sun 10:30 a.m.–6:00 p.m. Time: One hour.

Exploris
Portaferry, County Down

Exploris is Northern Ireland's only public aquarium, giving a fish-eye view of life in the Irish Sea via dark, underwater tunnels of stone with windows letting onto the illuminated green waters. It's the closest you can come to being underwater, short of strapping on a wetsuit. You can get an up-close view and find out about all marine life, from tiny plankton to deadly sharks, and see unique species like camouflage octopi and wolf fish, and you may also have an opportunity to feel starfish, sea urchins, and stingrays in the Touch Tank. Exploris is an undersea adventure you won't soon forget.

The Rope Walk, Portaferry, County Down. ☎ 028-4272-8062. To get there: On the A2, on the tip of the Ards Peninsula. Admission: £3.85 ($6.35) adults, £2.70 ($4.45) children, seniors, and students, £12 ($19.80) family of three adults and four children. Open: Mar–Aug Mon–Fri 10:00 a.m.–6:00 p.m., Sat 11:00 a.m.–6:00 p.m., Sun 1:00 p.m.–6:00 pm; Sept–Feb Mon–Fri 10:00 a.m.–5:00 p.m., Sat 11:00 a.m.–5:00 p.m., Sun 1:00 p.m.–5:00 p.m. Time: Two hours.

The Mountains of Mourne
County Down

You can drive the circular route around these enthralling mountains or take a bus tour, but either way you pass 15 striking summits, all rising more than 2,000 feet. Every few miles present a different, exciting vista, and lakes, streams, beaches, and heather-covered valleys fill out the landscape. One of the highlights of the area is the Annalong Cornmill, an old, working mill with a water wheel and an exhibition on water-powered technology.

The Information Centre is located at 10 Central Promenade, Newcastle, County Down. ☎ 028-4372-2222. To get there: Take the coastal road (A2). Bus Eireann gives a day tour of Mountains of Mourne from Dublin for £20 ($33) (including lunch) in July and Aug. Call ☎ 01-836-6111 for information. Time: Several hours.

More Fun Things to Do in Counties Down and Armagh

Ferguson Linen Centre

This is the world's only manufacturer of double damask linen — the store even supplies the White House. You can get a guided tour of the factory or simply pick up some linen sheets, tablecloths, handkerchiefs, or napkins.

54 Scarva Rd., Banbridge, County Down. ☎ *028-4062-3491.*

Royal County Down Golf Course

There are all kinds of historical and cultural experiences you can have in Down and Armagh, but if you want to sneak away for a game of golf, we won't tattle on you. The par-72 Royal County Down is the top course in the area, attracting the top players in Europe with stunning views and challenging holes.

Newcastle, County Down (☎ *028-4272-3314; E-mail:* royal.co.down@virgin. net*). Greens fees £50 ($82.50) mid-week, £60 ($99) weekends.*

Pub Life

In addition to the places that we list in this section, there's another so weird that we just can't leave it out. About a mile from Killyleagh Town, in Delamont Country Park, is Siglu (☎ **028-4482-8333**), a clear structure that looks like an igloo. Originally designed as a place for skiers to slide in for a schnapps or a warm drink, it's now a popular spot for merry-makers. From afar, Siglu looks like a glowing dome, and inside (it's much larger than it looks from the outside) it has a center bar and plenty of room to relax with a drink. Check it out; it's an experience you won't forget!

Grace Neill's Inn

Many pubs claim to be the oldest in Ireland, but this one really is. Don't believe us? The *Guinness Book of World Records* says so, and those people know their pubs. The old part of the tavern practically defines what an Irish pub should look like, and even though it's been extended to include a lounge and conservatory, the whole place keeps the Old World style. The pub grub is great, too.

33 High St., Donaghadee, County Down. ☎ *028-9188-2553.*

Harry's Bar

The best thing about Harry's is what it serves: 14 draft beers! You won't be left wanting, that's for sure. The pub is traditionally decorated, and the pub grub is fantastic. Try the boiled ham with Irish whiskey sauce.

7 Dromore St., Banbridge, County Down. ☎ *028-4066-2794.*

Tourist Trophy Lounge

You may think this pub is about you. Actually, the TT is on the route of the famous Tourist Trophy car races of the 1920s. The lounge is full of photos and mementos of those crazy racy days, so there's always entertainment. Downstairs is the traditional North Down House pub, a favorite of locals. The combination makes for a great "pit stop" in this small town just southeast of Belfast, on the A21.

1–3 Railway St., Comber, County Down. ☎ *028-9187-4554.*

Fast Facts: Counties Down and Armagh

AREA CODE

028.

EMERGENCIES

Dial ☎ **999** for all emergencies.

INFORMATION

For visitor information go to the **tourist offices** at 74 Market St., Downpatrick, County Down (☎ **028-4461-2233**), or **Town Hall,** Newry, County Down (☎ **028-3026-8877**). For telephone directory assistance, dial ☎ **192.**

Part VII
The Part of Tens

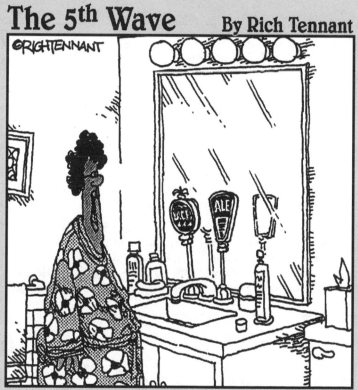

The 5th Wave   By Rich Tennant

©RICHTENNANT

"Douglas, I'd like to talk to you about the souvenirs you brought back from our trip to Ireland."

In this part . . .

In this part we give you a couple fun "extras." You can skip this part completely and still have a great trip, or read on for some bonus information.

In Chapter 24, we tell you about what we consider to be the top ten, absolute best highlights of our travels through Ireland and Northern Ireland. If you're still undecided about what to see in Ireland after reading the previous chapters, maybe this will help you out.

If you're a serious shopper, check out Chapter 25. There we give you the scoop on the best and most popular Irish products and where to find them. We also give you ten shopping tips — from how to find the best bargains to the best ways to get all your treasures home in one piece.

Chapter 24

The Top Ten Highlights of Ireland and Northern Ireland

*T*hese attractions and experiences rank as some of the biggest and best in the Republic and the North (refer to the chapters noted in parentheses for more information).

Driving the Ring of Kerry

The Ring, a southeast peninsula jutting out into the Atlantic Ocean, runs you past stunning coastline, craggy mountains, and colorful fishing villages. (See Chapter 16.)

Standing atop the Majestic Purple Cliffs of Moher

You can look down 760 feet to the crashing waves of the Atlantic, and possibly see the Aran Islands in the distance. (See Chapter 17.)

Bending Over Backward to Kiss the Blarney Stone

You have to lean backward with your head upside down to kiss the smooth stone, but it's worth the effort: At worst, you can say you did it; at best, you walk away with the gift of gab — the legendary reward for your kiss. (See Chapter 15.)

Pub-crawling in Temple Bar

You'll feel like a Dubliner for sure winding down the cobbled streets of Dublin's trendy Temple Bar neighborhood on an authentic pub-crawl, sipping creamy pints of Guinness and tapping your feet to traditional Irish music. (See Chapter 11.)

Watching Glass Blowers at the Waterford Crystal Factory

Watch as Waterford Crystal pieces are blown before your very eyes. Afterward, you can tour the factory and buy a flawless piece from the gallery/shop. (See Chapter 14.)

Taking a Ferry out to the Stark Aran Islands

Once there, you can tour them by horse-pulled cart and have a fresh-fish dinner before leaving with a signature wool fisherman's sweater. (See Chapter 18.)

Driving Around Killarney's Mountains and Lakes

Make your way through the mountains that surround the still and awesome lakes of Killarney, while hunting down waterfalls and slowing to avoid the goats that sleep in the road. (See Chapter 16.)

Walking Out on the Giant's Causeway

This mysterious stretch of pillarlike stones reaches out into the sea and was, legends say, mythical giant Finn MacCool's walkway to Scotland. (See Chapter 22.)

Strolling amid the Stately and Magnificent Powerscourt Gardens

Ponds and statues accent the vast spread of flowers, plants, and shrubs that make these gardens among the finest in Europe. (See Chapter 13.)

Discovering the Ancient Secrets of Newgrange and the Hill of Tara

In County Meath, just north of Dublin, prehistoric tombs and the meeting place of Ireland's High Kings help explain the county's early history. (See Chapter 12.)

Chapter 25

Shopping! Great Irish Buys and Ten Tips on Buying Them

In This Chapter
- ▶ Deciding what to purchase
- ▶ Getting the best prices
- ▶ Figuring out what to lug home

Sure, there are a handful of travelers who come back from their trip with nothing more than a few blisters, maybe a tan, and a notebook full of observations and sketches, but most of us are a little bit more acquisitive than that. In this section we run through the best buys in Ireland, and offer a few tips on, say, buying an Irish sweater without losing your shirt.

Finding Ireland's Best Buys

Shopping on the Emerald Isle means much more than buying cheesy leprechauns and mini thatched-roof cottages as souvenirs, and in fact, there are certain products Ireland is known for that people travel from around the world to buy. For instance, wool fisherman's sweaters from the Aran Islands have come to signify Ireland like almost nothing else, and people return home wearing them as if they're the Irish flag itself. Waterford Crystal is also treasured worldwide, and the selection and quality found in Ireland is unmatched. These items, and others, are uniquely Irish and will remind you of your trip and Ireland's charm long after you return home. And who knows, some of them might even end up as family heirlooms.

China

Fine bone china is made in Belleek, a tiny town in Northern Ireland, but you can purchase it all over the country. The operation there is reportedly Ireland's oldest pottery, in operation since 1857, and the china is characterized by its ivory color flecked with pink.

Crystal

One of Ireland's finest exports, Waterford Crystal, is a perfect example of classic craftsmanship. Even today, a whopping 45 percent of the pieces produced by the factory — from bud vases to mantle clocks — are thrown out for slight imperfections! You can find Waterford Crystal throughout the Republic, but the best selection is at the source: Waterford City, County Waterford.

Lace

In the 1860s, Poor Clare nuns in Kenmare began teaching local girls to make lace in hopes of helping the struggling economy. The beautiful needlepoint lace is now famous worldwide. A great place to see examples of (and purchase) the lace is at the courthouse next to the tourist office in Kenmare.

Linen

Irish linen is characterized by its delicate weavings and how it gracefully adorns any table. Although you'll find linen-making stores throughout the Republic, Belfast is known as the linen capital of the world, and it sells some of the finest and best linen selections.

Pottery

Irish pottery is a treasure, made daily by local artisans and often bearing Celtic and country designs. County Clare is Ireland's pottery haven, where you'll find unique and traditional styles.

Tweed

There's an idealized look of the Irish that invariably includes a bit of tweed, whether it's a cap, a cape, a jacket, trousers, or a skirt. The best place to find handmade clothing is in the northwest, in County Donegal. (There are loads of handweaving shops throughout the rest of the county as well.)

Wool

Everyone's familiar with those dense, off-white cable pullovers called "fisherman's sweaters." They're warm, handwoven, and made with pure wool. The finest you'll find are from the Aran Islands, off the west coast. You can find them all over Ireland, but be sure to check the tag — it will mention the Aran Islands if it's authentic.

Irish clothing size comparison charts

The United States and Ireland have different systems for measurements (except for men's shirt and suit sizes, which are the same in both countries). Use the following charts only as guides to steer you toward a near fit. Be warned, however, that clothing size is often much more subjective than it should be, and sizes vary among manufacturers and from store to store.

Women's Coats and Dresses

United States	4	6	8	10	12	14	16	18
Ireland	6	8	10	12	14	16	18	20

Women's Shoes

United States	5	6	7	8	9	10
Ireland	4	5	6	7	8	9

Men's Shoes

United States	7	8	9	10	11	12
Ireland	6	7	8	9	10	11

Ten Tips for Shopping Wisely in Ireland

Keep the following smart-shopper guidelines in mind as you tour Ireland:

1. **Shop around.** Prices vary dramatically from shop to shop and market stall to market stall. They usually go down as you get farther away from touristy places, and you may find the same item for less in a shop on a lower-rent street. Let the store owners know you're comparing prices, and the asking rate may go down on the spot. Also, be sure to check prices for items available at home so you know if you're getting a bargain by buying them abroad.

2. **Peruse street markets.** This is a fun way to do business, especially if it comes to haggling, which is likely. Irish street vendors are real characters and you'll have an experience that's hard to come by at home. The quality of the merchandise is iffier than in established shops, but you can get great deals on everything from designer knockoffs to identical items from shops that are overstocked.

3. **Forget designer clothing.** Unless you're looking for particularly Irish clothes, you probably won't find any bargains on European designer clothes. Just because you're in Europe doesn't mean you'll get great deals on French or Italian clothes hot off the runway.

4. **Shop selectively.** Don't buy every trinket you see. Go for the items that truly capture the spirit and culture of Ireland and will hold the best memories. Before you buy it, make sure that leprechaun doll or Guinness keychain is something you really want. Also, take into consideration that whatever you buy should be able to fit in your luggage (unless you're planning to mail some things home).

5. **Don't let yourself be led by the nose.** On most escorted tours, the guide will take or direct you to shops that offer "special prices" to people on your tour. Ninety percent of the time this means the tour guide is getting a kickback for bringing in revenue. Usually, the store passes the burden along to you by jacking up the prices. Although some guides do give honest recommendations, and some of those kickback arrangements don't adversely affect you via markups, knowing when a recommendation is on the level is impossible. Be cynical and comparison shop. If it seems too expensive, it probably is.

6. **Act like an old shopping hand.** Scrutinize labels, kick the proverbial tires, and otherwise show that you know what you're doing (even if you don't, really). Shopkeepers who see a savvy customer are less likely to try to pull the wool over your eyes — even when you're trying on sweaters.

7. **Dress respectably, but not too well.** You want merchants to know you're a potential paying customer and not riffraff, but you don't want to give them the idea you're loaded. Especially in markets, prices can go up on the spot if you look willing to pay anything.

8. **Count your change, and make sure the receipt is complete and accurate.** Don't be rude about it, but make sure you aren't dealing with a rotten shopkeeper who's trying to scam or shortchange you. (And even if there's no malice aforethought, cashiers have been known to make mistakes.) The receipt is important because you will need it for any VAT refund (see the Appendix for more on this).

9. **Ship breakables home.** It may cost a bit more, but the longer you lug your purchases around with you, bouncing down the road of your trip, the greater the chances that your Waterford Crystal will end up Waterford shards.

Some antique shops have the resources to ship large items to you back home. If you're in the market for furniture, be sure to ask about shipping before you fall in love with the Victorian dining room table that won't quite fit in your suitcase. Also, you can save yourself time and hassle should something go wrong with a purchase being shipped home if you snap a photo of it before it's wrapped up. This photo makes excellent proof of purchase when it comes to insurance claims.

10. **Evaluate your carrying capacity.** If you find that you're running out of room in your luggage, ship fragile items home first, and then mail home any unneeded personal stuff (like dirty laundry) rather than entrusting all your purchases to the postal system.

Appendix

Quick Concierge

●●●

Ireland Facts at Your Fingertips

American Express

The only American Express offices in Ireland are in Dublin (41 Nassau St.; ☎ 01-617-5597) and Galway (International Hotel, East Avenue Road; ☎ 64-35722). In an emergency, you can dial collect ☎ 1-44-1-273-571-600 to report lost or stolen travelers checks.

ATMs

ATMs (called *service tills* in Ireland) are located all over the country. The major networks are Plus and Cirrus.

Business Hours

Banks are open Monday through Wednesday and Friday from 10:00 a.m. to 12:30 p.m. and from 1:30 to 3:00 p.m.; on Thursday from 10:00 a.m. to 12:30 p.m. and from 1:30 p.m. to 5:00 p.m. Some banks are beginning to stay open through the lunch hour. Most business offices are open from 9:00 a.m. to 5:00 p.m., Monday through Friday. Stores and shops are open from 9:00 a.m. to 5:30 p.m. Monday through Wednesday and Friday to Saturday, and from 9:00 a.m. to 8:00 p.m. on Thursday. Some stores offer Sunday hours, especially during tourist season.

Credit Cards

Visa, MasterCard, American Express, and Diners Club are widely used in Ireland, but Discover is not accepted.

Currency

The Republic of Ireland uses the Irish punt (often called a pound), while Northern

Ireland uses the British pound. The best sources for current currency exchange information are on the Internet, at www.cnn.com/TRAVEL/CURRENCY and www.xe.net/ict. You can exchange money anywhere you see the Bureau de Change sign, but generally, you get the best rates at banks.

Customs

You can't bring firearms, ammunition, explosives, narcotics, poultry, plants and their immediate byproducts, domestic animals, or snakes into Ireland. Also, you may bring in no more than 200 cigarettes, one liter of liquor, and two liters of wine.

If you're flying out of or back to the United States, you can find information about what goods you can bring in and out on the U.S. State Department's Web site at http://travel.state.gov.

Dentists and Doctors

If you need to see a dentist or physician, your best bet is to ask the concierge or host at your hotel or guesthouse for a recommendation. Otherwise, consult the Golden Pages of the Irish telephone book or the Yellow Pages of the Northern Ireland telephone book, or contact your local consulate for a recommendation. Many emergency rooms have walk-in clinics if you can't find a doctor who can help you right away. Expect to pay for treatment up front and be reimbursed after the fact by your insurance company.

Driving Rules

You must have a valid driver's license from your home country to drive in Ireland. The speed limit is 60 mph (96 km/h) unless otherwise posted. Speed limit signs have a red circle with the limit written inside in black. The Irish drive on the left side of the road.

Drugstores

Drugstores are usually called *chemist shops* or *pharmacies.* Look under "Chemists — Pharmaceutical" in the Golden Pages of the Irish telephone book or "Chemists — Dispensing" in the Yellow Pages of the Northern Ireland telephone book.

Pack prescription medications (in their original-label vials) in your carry-on luggage. Bring along copies of your prescriptions, in generic form rather than under a brand name, in case you lose your pills or run out.

Electricity

The standard electrical current is 220 volts in the Republic of Ireland, 240 volts in Northern Ireland. You need both a transformer and a plug adapter (available at many hardware stores and sometimes airports) for appliances such as hair dryers. Computers and sensitive electronic equipment may require more than the standard over-the-counter voltage converter.

Embassies and Consulates

The American Embassy is at 42 Elgin Rd., Ballsbridge, Dublin 4 (☎ 01-668-8777); the Canadian Embassy resides at 65/68 St. Stephen's Green, Dublin 2 (☎ 01-678-1988); the British Embassy is at 33 Merrion Rd., Dublin 4 (☎ 01-205-3700); and you can find the Australian Embassy at Fitzwilton House, Wilton Terrace, Dublin 2 (☎ 01-676-1517). In addition, there is an American Consulate at 14 Queen St., Belfast BT1 6EQ (☎ 028-9032-8239).

Emergencies

For the Garda (police), fire, or other emergencies, dial ☎ 999.

Internet Access and Cyber Cafes

You can find public access terminals in shopping malls, hotels, and hostels, especially in the larger towns and more tourist-centered areas. Additionally, there are an increasing number of Internet cafes sprouting up across the island. We list some in the "Fast Facts" section at the end of each chapter. You can also find out the addresses and phone numbers of cafes online from www.iica.net.

Liquor Laws

You must be age 18 or over to be served alcoholic beverages in Ireland. Likewise, you can purchase alcoholic beverages by the bottle at liquor stores, pubs displaying *off-license* signs, and at most supermarkets. Ireland has very severe laws and penalties regarding driving while intoxicated, so don't even think about it.

Mail

Post offices in the Republic are called *An Post* and are bright green. In Northern Ireland, they're called *post offices* and are red. The Republic's main postal branch is on O'Connell St., Dublin 1 (☎ 01-872-6666). Major branches in the Republic and Northern Ireland are open 9:00 a.m. to 6:00 p.m., Monday through Saturday.

If you need mail sent to you while on your trip, have the sender address the mail with your name, care of the General Post Office, Restante Office, and the town name. Your mail will be held there for you to pick up. Only the larger post office branches (those that we list in the "Fast Facts" sections of this book) provide this service.

Police

In Ireland, a law enforcement officer is called a *garda;* in the plural, it's *gardai* (pronounced *gar*-dee) or simply "the Guards." Dial ☎ 999 to reach the *gardai* in an emergency in both the Republic of Ireland and Northern Ireland.

Restrooms

Public restrooms are usually simply called toilets, or are marked with international symbols. In the Republic of Ireland, some older toilets carry the Gaelic words *Fir* (Men) and *Mna* (Women). You can find restrooms at shopping complexes and multistory car parks. Some cost 10p (15 cents) to enter. Free rest rooms are available to customers of sightseeing attractions, museums, hotels, restaurants, pubs, shops, theaters, and department stores. Gas stations normally do not have public toilets.

Safety

The Republic of Ireland has enjoyed a traditionally low crime rate, particularly when it comes to violent crime. However, you should take normal precautions to protect youself and your belongings. Don't carry large amounts of money or important documents like your passport or airline tickets when strolling around. Don't leave cars unlocked or cameras, binoculars, or other expensive equipment unattended. Be alert and aware of your surroundings, and don't wander in lonely areas alone at night. Ask at your hotel about which areas are safe and which are not.

In the north of Ireland, safety is a somewhat greater concern because of the political unrest that has prevailed there for the past 30 years. Before traveling to Northern Ireland, contact the U.S. State Department and the Northern Ireland Tourist Board to obtain the latest safety recommendations. The U.S. Department of State 24-hour hotline (☎ 202-647-5225) provides travel warnings and security recommendations, as well as emergency assistance.

Smoking

Recent legislation makes it illegal to smoke in public areas (such as public offices, schools, and banks). Smoking is banned on public transportation and in taxis. Some B&Bs do not allow smoking; check before making a reservation.

Taxes

Sales tax is called *value-added tax* (VAT) and is often already included in the price quoted to you or shown on price tags. In the Republic, VAT rates vary — for hotels, restaurants, and car rentals, it's 12.5 percent; for souvenirs and gifts, it's 17.36 percent. In Northern Ireland, the VAT is 17.5 percent across the board. You can obtain a VAT refund on products such as souvenirs. The easiest way to make a VAT-free purchase is to arrange for a store to ship the goods directly abroad to your home; such a shipment is not subject to VAT.

If you want to take your goods with you, you must pay the full amount for each item, including all VAT charges. To have the tax refunded to you, get a full receipt that shows the store's name and address, as well as VAT paid. (Customs does not accept cash register tally slips.) When you depart Ireland; go to the Customs Office at the airport to have your receipts stamped. Send the stamped receipts to the store where you made the purchase, which will then issue a VAT refund check to you by mail.

Telephone

Phone numbers in Ireland are currently in flux, because digits are being added to accommodate expanded service. Every effort has been made to ensure that the numbers and information in this guide are accurate at the time of writing. The Irish toll-free number for directory assistance is ☎ 1190. From the United States, the (toll) number to call for directory assistance is ☎ 00353-91-770220.

Coin phones in the Republic and Northern Ireland cost either 20p or 30p, and the amount of time you get to talk depends on how far you're calling. The most efficient way to make calls from public phones is to use a *Callcard* (in the Republic) or *Phonecard* (in the North). Both are prepaid cards that you can purchase at phone company offices, post offices, and many retail outlets (such as newsstands).

Throughout this guide, phone numbers are preceded by their city codes (Dublin numbers are preceded by the city code 01, for example), but you can drop the city codes if you call within the same city.

If you think that you'll want to call home regularly while in Ireland, you may want to open an account with Swiftcall (toll-free in Ireland ☎ 0800-794-381; Internet: www.swiftcall.com). Its rates offer you considerable savings, not only from Ireland to the United States but also vice versa. Premiere WORLDLINK (☎ 800- 432-6169) offers an array of additional services for overseas travelers — such as toll-free voice-mail boxes, fax, mail, and news services.

Time

Ireland is five time zones earlier than the eastern United States (when it's noon in New York, it's 5:00 p.m. in Ireland).

Tipping

Most hotels and guesthouses add a service charge to the bill, usually 12.5 percent to 15 percent. Always check to see what amount, if any, has been added to your bill. Giving additional cash gratuities is appropriate if you've received exceptional service or if the hotel has charged less than 12.5 percent. For porters or bellhops, tip 50p (75 cents) to £1 ($1.50) per piece of luggage. For taxi drivers, hairdressers, and other providers of service, tip as you would at home, an average of 10 to 15 percent.

A 10 to 15 percent tip is appropriate at restaurants, but make sure it hasn't already been added to your check before leaving anything.

Weather Updates

The best site on the Web for Ireland's weather forecasts is http://cnn.com/WEATHER/cities/world.html.

Toll-Free Numbers and Web Sites

Airlines

Air Canada
☎ 800-361-5373
www.aircanada.ca

Aer Lingus
☎ 800-223-6537
www.aerlingus.ie

American Airlines
☎ 800-433-7300
www.americanair.com

British Airways
☎ 800-AIRWAYS
www.britishairways.com

Continental Airlines
☎ 800-231-0856
www.continental.com

Delta Air Lines
☎ 800-241-4141
www.delta-air.com

Northwest Airlines
☎ 800-225-2525
www.nwa.com

Trans World Airlines (TWA)
☎ 800-221-2000
www.twa.com

United Airlines
☎ 800-241-6522
www.ual.com

US Airways
☎ 800-428-4322
www.usairways.com

Virgin Atlantic
☎ 800-862-8621
www.virgin.com

British Midland
☎ 800-788-0555
www.britishmidland.co.uk

Car rental agencies

Alamo
☎ 800-327-9633
www.goalamo.com

Argus
☎ 01-490-9999
www.argus-rentacar.com

Avis
☎ 800-331-1212 in continental United
States; 800-TRY-AVIS in Canada
www.avis.com

Budget
☎ 800-527-0700
www.budgetrentacar.com

Hertz
☎ 800-654-3131
www.hertz.com

Murrays Europcar/AutoEurope
☎ 800-223-5555
www.europecar.ie

National
☎ 800-CAR-RENT
www.nationalcar.com

Where to Get More Information

Contacting Irish tourist boards

To get your planning under way, contact the following offices of the Irish Tourist Board and the Northern Ireland Tourist Board. They're eager to answer your questions, and have bags of genuinely helpful information, which is mostly free of charge.

In the United States
Irish Tourist Board, 345 Park Ave., New York, NY 10154; ☎ 800-223-6470 (within the United States), or 212-418-0800; Fax: 212-371-9052.

Northern Ireland Tourist Board, 551 Fifth Ave., Suite 701, New York, NY 10176; ☎ 800-326-0036 (within the

United States), or 212-922-0101; Fax: 212-922-0099.

In Canada
Irish Tourist Board, 160 Bloor St. E., Suite 1150, Toronto, ON, M4W 1B9; ☎ 416-929-2777; Fax: 416-929-6783.

Northern Ireland Tourist Board, 2 Bloor St. W., Suite 1501, Toronto, ON, M4W 3E2; ☎ 800-576-8174 (within Canada) or 416-925-6368; Fax: 416- 925-6033.

In the United Kingdom
Irish Tourist Board/Bord Fáilte, 150 New Bond St., London W1Y 0AQ; ☎ 020-7493-3201; Fax: 020-7493-9065.

Northern Ireland Tourist Board, 11 Berkeley St., London W1X 5AD; ☎ 020-7766-9920; Fax: 020-7766-9929.

In Australia

Irish Tourist Board, 36 Carrington St., 5th Level, Sydney, NSW 2000; ☎ 02-9299-6177; Fax: 02-9299-6323.

Surfing the Net

The following sites provide a variety of cultural and visitor information:

D-Tour: A Visitor's Guide to Ireland for People with Disabilities (http://ireland.iol.ie/infograf/dtour). This site offers various resources for disabled travelers in Ireland, including extensive listings of wheelchair-accessible accommodations.

Go Ireland (www.goireland.com). A well-organized guide to lodging, dining, pubs, getting around, entertainment, sightseeing, and car rentals.

Heritage of Ireland (www.heritageireland.ie). A lovely tour of Ireland's historic attractions.

Ireland for Visitors (http://goireland.about.com). This compendium of Web sites from About.com includes dozens of categories, from Dining to Package Tours to Travelogues.

Irish Tourist Board (www.ireland.travel.ie). The most comprehensive online guide to travel in the Republic of Ireland, the official site of the Irish Tourist Board (Bord Failte) provides information for most tourism facilities as well as access to Gulliver, an online accommodations booking service.

Northern Ireland Tourist Board (www.ni-tourism.com). This site offers abundant pages packed with all the information you need to get started planning your travels in Northern Ireland.

Making Dollars and Sense of It

Expense	Amount
Airfare	
Car Rental	
Lodging	
Parking	
Breakfast	
Lunch	
Dinner	
Babysitting	
Attractions	
Transportation	
Souvenirs	
Tips	
Grand Total	

Notes

Fare Game: Choosing an Airline

Travel Agency: _____ Phone: _____

Agent's Name: _____ Quoted Fare: _____

Departure Schedule & Flight Information

Airline: _____ Airport: _____

Flight #: _____ Date: _____ Time: _____ a.m./p.m.

Arrives in: _____ Time: _____ a.m./p.m.

Connecting Flight (if any)

Amount of time between flights: _____ hours/mins

Airline: _____ Airport: _____

Flight #: _____ Date: _____ Time: _____ a.m./p.m.

Arrives in: _____ Time: _____ a.m./p.m.

Return Trip Schedule & Flight Information

Airline: _____ Airport: _____

Flight #: _____ Date: _____ Time: _____ a.m./p.m.

Arrives in: _____ Time: _____ a.m./p.m.

Connecting Flight (if any)

Amount of time between flights: _____ hours/mins

Airline: _____ Airport: _____

Flight #: _____ Date: _____ Time: _____ a.m./p.m.

Arrives in: _____ Time: _____ a.m./p.m.

Notes

Sweet Dreams: Choosing Your Hotel

Enter the hotels where you'd prefer to stay based on location and price. Then use the worksheet below to plan your itinerary.

Hotel	Location	Price per night

Menus & Venues

Enter the restaurants where you'd most like to dine. Then use the worksheet below to plan your itinerary.

Name	Address/Phone	Cuisine/Price

Places to Go, People to See, Things to Do

Enter the attractions you would most like to see. Then use the worksheet below to plan your itinerary.

Attractions	Amount of time you expect to spend there	Best day and time to go

Going "My" Way

Itinerary #1

☐ _____
☐ _____
☐ _____
☐ _____

Itinerary #2

☐ _____
☐ _____
☐ _____
☐ _____

Itinerary #3

☐ _____
☐ _____
☐ _____
☐ _____

Itinerary #4

☐ _____
☐ _____
☐ _____
☐ _____

Itinerary #5

☐ _____
☐ _____
☐ _____
☐ _____

Itinerary #6

☐ _____
☐ _____
☐ _____
☐ _____

Itinerary #7

☐ _____
☐ _____
☐ _____
☐ _____

Itinerary #8

☐ _____
☐ _____
☐ _____
☐ _____

Itinerary #9

☐ _____
☐ _____
☐ _____
☐ _____

Itinerary #10

☐ _____
☐ _____
☐ _____
☐ _____

Notes

_____

_____

_____

_____

_____

_____

_____

_____

_____

_____

_____

_____

_____

_____

_____

_____

_____

_____

Index

• *L* •

IDG BOOKS WORLDWIDE
BOOK REGISTRATION

Register
This Book
and Win!

We want to hear from you!

Visit **http://my2cents.dummies.com** to register this book and tell us how you liked it!

- ✔ Get entered in our monthly prize giveaway.

- ✔ Give us feedback about this book — tell us what you like best, what you like least, or maybe what you'd like to ask the author and us to change!

- ✔ Let us know any other *For Dummies*® topics that interest you.

Your feedback helps us determine what books to publish, tells us what coverage to add as we revise our books, and lets us know whether we're meeting your needs as a *For Dummies* reader. You're our most valuable resource, and what you have to say is important to us!

Not on the Web yet? It's easy to get started with *Dummies 101*®: *The Internet For Windows*® *98* or *The Internet For Dummies*®[3] at local retailers everywhere.

Or let us know what you think by sending us a letter at the following address:

For Dummies Book Registration
Dummies Press
10475 Crosspoint Blvd.
Indianapolis, IN 46256

™

**BESTSELLING
BOOK SERIES**